LIBRARY OF HEBREW BIBLE/
OLD TESTAMENT STUDIES

713

Formerly Journal for the Study of the Old Testament Supplement Series

Editors
Claudia V. Camp, Texas Christian University, USA
Andrew Mein, Durham University, UK

Founding Editors
David J. A. Clines, Philip R. Davies and David M. Gunn

Editorial Board
Alan Cooper, Susan Gillingham, John Goldingay,
Norman K. Gottwald, James E. Harding, John Jarick, Carol Meyers,
Daniel L. Smith-Christopher, Francesca Stavrakopoulou,
James W. Watts

THE END OF HISTORY AND THE LAST KING

Achaemenid Ideology and Community Identity in Ezra–Nehemiah

David Janzen

t&tclark
LONDON • NEW YORK • OXFORD • NEW DELHI • SYDNEY

T&T CLARK

Bloomsbury Publishing Plc

50 Bedford Square, London, WC1B 3DP, UK

1385 Broadway, New York, NY 10018, USA

29 Earlsfort Terrace, Dublin 2, Ireland

BLOOMSBURY, T&T CLARK and the T&T Clark logo are trademarks of Bloomsbury Publishing Plc

First published in Great Britain 2021

This paperback edition published in 2022

Copyright © David Janzen, 2021

David Janzen has asserted his right under the Copyright, Designs and Patents Act, 1988, to be identified as Author of this work.

Cover design: Charlotte James

All rights reserved. No part of this publication may be reproduced or transmitted in any form or by any means, electronic or mechanical, including photocopying, recording, or any information storage or retrieval system, without prior permission in writing from the publishers.

Bloomsbury Publishing Plc does not have any control over, or responsibility for, any third-party websites referred to or in this book. All internet addresses given in this book were correct at the time of going to press. The author and publisher regret any inconvenience caused if addresses have changed or sites have ceased to exist, but can accept no responsibility for any such changes.

A catalogue record for this book is available from the British Library.

Library of Congress Control Number: 2020949137.

ISBN:	HB:	978-0-5676-9801-8
	PB:	978-0-5676-9800-1
	ePDF:	978-0-5676-9802-5

Series: Library of Hebrew Bible/Old Testament Studies, ISSN 2513-8758, volume 713

Typeset by: Trans.form.ed SAS

To find out more about our authors and books visit www.bloomsbury.com and sign up for our newsletters.

*For Patricia and for my parents,
without whose support this would not have been possible*

Contents

List of Abbreviations	ix
Chapter 1	
INTRODUCTION:	
COMMUNITY IDENTITY, ACHAEMENID IDEOLOGY,	
AND THE COMPOSITION OF EZRA–NEHEMIAH	1
1. The Approach and Outline of the Argument	1
2. The Composition and Authorship of Ezra–Nehemiah	12
3. The Persian-Period Date of Ezra–Nehemiah	27
Chapter 2	
COMMUNITY IDENTITY IN EZRA–NEHEMIAH	40
1. Ezra 1–6: The Ideal Generation	40
2. Ezra 7–10: The Epigone, Part 1	54
3. Nehemiah 1:1–13:3: The Epigone, Part 2	62
4. Nehemiah 13:4-34: The Epigone, Conclusion	74
Chapter 3	
THE BENEFICENT KING IN ACHAEMENID IDEOLOGY	
AND IN EZRA–NEHEMIAH	79
1. Introduction: The Background of Achaemenid Ideology	79
2. Achaemenid Ideology, Part 1: The Beneficent King	89
3. Community and Beneficent King in Ezra–Nehemiah	109
4. Conclusion: From Colonizers to Colonized	128
Chapter 4	
THE KING, GOD, AND TORTURE	131
1. Achaemenid Ideology, Part 2: The Necessity of Torture	131
2. The Community and Imperial and Divine Violence in Ezra–Nehemiah	140
3. The End of History and the Last King, Part 1	155

Chapter 5
EMPIRE AND IDEOLOGY IN
PERSIAN-PERIOD JUDAH   165
 1. Ezra–Nehemiah within the Temple Community's Factions 165
 2. Empire and Community Identity in the Persian-Period
   Temple Community   185
 3. Post-exilic Prophetic Critiques of Empire   205
 4. Conclusion: The End of History and the Last King, Part 2   212

Chapter 6
CONCLUSION:
THE STRUGGLE OVER COMMUNITY IDENTITY IN THE PERSIAN PERIOD   216

Bibliography   223
Index of References   254
Index of Authors   268

ABBREVIATIONS

A¹Pa	Artaxerxes I, Persepolis a
A²Ha	Artaxerxes II, Hamadan a
A²Hc	Artaxerxes II, Hamadan c
A²Sa	Artaxerxes II, Susa a
A²Sd	Artaxerxes II, Susa d
A³Pa	Artaxerxes III, Persepolis a
AASOR	Annual of the American Schools of Oriental Research
AB	Anchor Bible Commentary
ABC	*Assyrian and Babylonian Chronicles*, ed. Grayson Albert Kirk, TCS 5 (Locust Valley, NY: J. J. Augustin, 1975)
ABD	*Anchor Bible Dictionary*, 6 vols, ed. David Noel Freedman (New York: Doubleday, 1992)
ABRL	Anchor Bible Research Library
AchHist	Achaemenid History
ACSS	Ancient Civilizations from Scythia to Siberia
ActIr	Acta Iranica
ADPV	Abhandlungen des Deutschens Palästina-Vereins
AfO	*Archiv für Orientforschung*
Alc.	*Alcibiades*
Alex.	*Alexander*
Anab.	*Anabasis*
ANEM	Ancient Near Eastern Monographs
Ant.	*Jewish Antiquities*
AOAT	Alter Orient und Altes Testament
AOAT 256 K2	Cyrus Cylinder
AoF	*Altorientalische Forschungen*
AOS	American Oriental Series
ArsOr	*Ars Orientalis*
Art.	*Artaxerxes*
ATANT	Abhandlungen zur Theologie des Alten und Neuen Testaments
ATM	Altes Testament und Moderne
AWCH	Ancient World—Comparative Histories
AWN	*Ardā Wīrāz Nāmag*
BAI	Bulletin of the Asia Institute
BASOR	Bulletin of the American Schools of Oriental Research
BCSMS	Bulletin of the Canadian Society of Mesopotamian Studies

BEATAJ	Beiträge zur Erforschung des Alten Testament und des antiken Judentum
BerO	Berit Olam
Bib	*Biblica*
BibInt	*Biblical Interpretation*
BibIr	Bibliotheca Iranica
BJSUCSD	Biblical and Judaic Studies from the University of California, San Diego
BKAT	Biblischer Kommentar, Altes Testament
BlTh	*Black Theology*
B. Qam.	Baba Qamma
BT	The Bible Translator
BTS	Biblisch-theologische Studien
BW	BibleWorld
BWANT	Beiträge zur Wissenschaft vom Alten und Neuen Testament
BZ	*Biblische Zeitschrift*
BZABR	Beihefte zur Zeitschrift für altorientalische und biblische Rechtsgeschichte
BZAW	Beihefte zur Zeitschrift für die alttestamentliche Wissenschaft
BzI	Beiträge zur Iranistik
CAD	*Chicago Assyrian Dictionary*, 21 vols, ed. Erica Reiner et al. (Chicago: University of Chicago Press, 1956–2011)
CBET	Contributions to Biblical Exegesis and Theology
CBQ	*Catholic Biblical Quarterly*
CeO	Classica et Orientalia
CII	Corpus inscriptionum iranicarum
CII 1/2/1	Darius, Bisitun (Akkadian version)
CIS	*Corpus inscriptionum semiticarum*
ClE	Classical Essays
CMa	Cyrus, Murghab a
CMb	Cyrus, Murghab b
CMc	Cyrus, Murghab c
Cyr.	*Cyropaedia*
DB	Darius, Bisitun (Old Persian version)
DCLY	Deuterocanonical and Cognate Literature Yearbook
DD	*Dādestān ī Dēnīg*
DDAH	Debates and Documents in Ancient History
Dk	*Dēnkard*
DNa	Darius, Naqš-i-Rustam a
DNb	Darius, Naqš-i-Rustam b
DNc	Darius, Naqš-i-Rustam c
DNd	Darius, Naqš-i-Rustam d
DPd	Darius, Persepolis d
DPe	Darius, Persepolis e
DSa	Darius, Susa a
DSab	Darius, Susa ab
DSe	Darius, Susa e

DSf	Darius, Susa f
DSi	Darius, Susa i
DSj	Darius, Susa j
DSm	Darius, Susa m
DSo	Darius, Susa o
DSp	Darius, Susa p
DSs	Darius, Susa s
DSt	Darius, Susa t
DZc	Darius, Suez c
EI	*Eretz Israel*
EIr	*Encyclopedia Iranica* (www.iranicaonline.org)
ELS	Edinburgh Leventis Studies
FAT	Forschungen zum Alten Testament
FMPS	Financial and Monetary Policy Studies
FOTL	Forms of Old Testament Literature
FRLANT	Forschungen zur Religion und Literatur des Alten und Neuen Testaments
FzB	Forschung zur Bibel
GBd	*Greater Bundahišn*
Ger.	*Mount Gerizim Excavations I: The Aramaic, Hebrew and Samaritan Inscriptions*, ed. Yitzhak Magen, Haggai Misgav, and Levana Tsfania, JSP 2 (Jerusalem: Israel Antiquities Authority, 2004)
Giṭ.	*Giṭṭin*
HANEM	History of the Ancient Near East Monographs
HAT	Handbuch zum Alten Testament
HBM	Hebrew Bible Monographs
HBS	Herders biblische Studien
HCOT	Historical Commentary on the Old Testament
HCS	Hellenistic Culture and Society
Hell.	*Hellenica*
Herm	Hermeneia
Hist.	Historia
HN	*Hādōxt Nask*
HOS	Handbook of Oriental Studies
IBd	*Indian Bundahišn*
IBHS	Bruce K. Waltke and M. O'Connor, *An Introduction to Biblical Hebrew Syntax* (Winona Lake, IN: Eisenbrauns, 1990)
ICC	International Critical Commentary
IEJ	*Israel Exploration Journal*
IIJ	*Indo-Iranian Journal*
INJ	*Israel Numismatic Journal*
INR	*Israel Numismatic Research*
Int	*Interpretation*
IrAnt	*Iranica antiqua*
IrAntSup	Suppléments à Iranica antiqua
IrSt	*Iranian Studies*

ISFCJ	International Studies in Formative Christianity and Judaism
JA	*Journal asiatique*
JAJSup	Journal of Ancient Judaism Supplement Series
JANEH	*Journal of Ancient Near Eastern History*
JBL	*Journal of Biblical Literature*
JCS	*Journal of Cuneiform Studies*
JHS	*Journal of Hebrew Scripture*
JJS	*Journal of Jewish Studies*
JNES	*Journal of Near Eastern Studies*
JPersSt	*Journal of Persianate Studies*
JSJ	*Journal for the Study of Judaism*
JSOT	*Journal for the Study of the Old Testament*
JSOTSup	Journal for the Study of the Old Testament: Supplement Series
JSP	Judea and Samaria Publications
JSS	*Journal of Semitic Studies*
JTS	*Journal of Theological Studies*
KAT	Kommentar zum Alten Testament
LAI	Library of Ancient Israel
LHBOTS	Library of Hebrew Bible/Old Testament Studies
LSTS	Library of Second Temple Studies
LXX	Septuagint
LXX^A	Codex Alexandrinus
LXX^B	Codex Vaticanus
LXX^L	Lucianic Recension
LXX^S	Codex Sinaiticus
m.	Mishnaic tractate
MDIA	Monographs of the Danish Institute at Athens
Mid.	*Middot*
MT	Masoretic Text
MX	*Dādestān ī Mēnōg ī Xrad*
Nat. hist.	*Natural History*
NCBC	New Century Bible Commentary
NEA	*Near Eastern Archaeology*
NICOT	New International Commentary on the Old Testament
OBO	Orbis biblicus et orientalis
Oec.	*Economist*
OeO	Oriens et Occidens
OG	Old Greek
Oik	Oikumene
OIS	Oriental Institute Seminars
OLA	Orientalia Lovaniensia analecta
Or	*Orientalia*
OTL	Old Testament Library
OTM	Oxford Theological Monographs
OTRM	Oxford Theology and Religion Monographs
OTS	Old Testament Studies
PapVin	Papyrologica Vindobonensia

PEQ	*Palestine Exploration Quarterly*
Pers	Persika
PF	Persepolis Fortification Text
PFS	Persepolis Fortification Seal
PHSC	Perspectives on Hebrew Scripture and its Contexts
PLO	Porta linguarum orientalium
RB	*Revue biblique*
RBS	Resources for Biblical Study
RE	Rulers and Elites
RevQ	*Revue de Qumran*
RTRPA	*Recueil de travaux relatifs à la philologie et à l'archéologie*
RV	*Rigveda*
SAA	State Archives of Assyria
SAOC	Studies in Ancient Oriental Civilization
SBLAB	Society of Biblical Literature Academia Biblica
SBLAIL	Society of Biblical Literature Ancient Israelite Literature
SBLBE	Society of Biblical Literature Biblische Enzyklopädie
SBLDS	Society of Biblical Literature Dissertation Series
SBLEJL	Society of Biblical Literature Early Judaism and its Literature
SBLIVBS	Society of Biblical Literature International Voices in Biblical Studies
SBLMS	Society of Biblical Literature Monograph Series
SBLSymS	Society of Biblical Literature Symposium Series
SCO	*Studia Classici e Orientali*
SEÅ	*Svensk exegetisk årsbok*
SEFJ	Suomen Eksegeettisen Seuran julkaisuja
SEG	Supplementum Epigraphicum Graecum
SemeiaSt	Semeia Studies
SFSHJ	South Florida Studies in the History of Judaism
SHBC	Smyth & Helwys Bible Commentary
SJOT	*Scandinavian Journal of the Old Testament*
SLC	Studies in Latino/a Catholicism
SPOT	Studies on Personalities of the Old Testament
SR	*Studies in Religion*
SSN	Studia Semitica Neerlandica
STAR	Studies in Theology and Religion
StHel	Studia Hellenistica
StIr	*Studia Iranica*
StJud	Studia Judaica
StSam	Studia Samaritana
TAD	*Textbook of Aramaic Documents from Ancient Egypt*, 4 vols, ed. Bezalel Porten and Ada Yardeni (Winona Lake, IN: Eisenbrauns, 1986–99)
TAD C2.1	Darius, Bisitun (Aramaic version)
TCS	Texts from Cuneiform Studies
Tg.	*Targum*
Tg. Neof.	*Targum Neofiti*

Tg. Onq.	*Targum Onqelos*
Them.	*Themistocles*
TIEIUP	Travaux de l'Institut d'études iranienne de l'Université de Paris
TLSM	Trends in Linguistics. Studies and Monographs
Transeu	*Transeuphratène*
TSAJ	Texts and Studies in Ancient Judaism
TSSI	*Textbook of Syrian Semitic Inscriptions*, 3 vols, ed. John C. L. Gibson (Oxford: Clarendon Press, 1971–82)
TTCSGOT	T&T Clark's Study Guides to the Old Testament
TTS	Trierer theologische Studien
TynBul	*Tyndale Bulletin*
UCOIP	University of Chicago Oriental Institute Publications
UNHAII	Uitgaven van het Nederlands Historisch-Archaeologisch Instituut te Istanbul
Var. hist.	*Various Histories*
Vd	*Vīdēvdād*
VT	*Vetus Testamentum*
VTSup	Vetus Testamentum Supplements
WANEM	Worlds of the Ancient Near East and Mediterranean
WBC	Word Biblical Commentary
WMANT	Wissenschaftliche Monographien zum Alten und Neuen Testament
WUNT	Wissenschaftliche Untersuchungen zum Neuen Testament
XE	Xerxes, Elvend
XPa	Xerxes, Persepolis a
XPb	Xerxes, Persepolis b
XPc	Xerxes, Persepolis c
XPd	Xerxes, Persepolis d
XPf	Xerxes, Persepolis f
XPh	Xerxes, Persepolis h
XPl	Xerxes, Persepolis l
Y.	*Yasna*
Yt	*Yašt*
ZA	*Zeitschrift für Assyriologie*
ZAW	*Zeitschrift für die alttestamentliche Wissenschaft*
ZBKAT	Zürich Bibelkommentare. AT

Chapter 1

INTRODUCTION:
COMMUNITY IDENTITY, ACHAEMENID IDEOLOGY,
AND THE COMPOSITION OF EZRA–NEHEMIAH

1. *The Approach and Outline of the Argument*

In Ezra 2, near the beginning of Ezra–Nehemiah, readers encounter a list of names that claims the temple community in Judah is descended from migrants from Babylonia. The genealogical distinction this list creates between the community and the peoples who live nearby is so important to the book's message that the author felt compelled to repeat it in Nehemiah 7, and to emphasize at numerous points throughout the book that there must be no marriage outside of this group, and that those who have entered into such unions must break up their families, since outsiders have no place in this community. Establishing group identity and using it to distinguish the temple community from other peoples is such an important focus of the work that one reader describes Ezra–Nehemiah as "fundamentally concerned with issues of identity and boundaries."[1] This is a common assessment of the book as a whole,[2] and certainly of

1. H. Zlotnick-Sivan, "The Silent Women of Yehud: Notes on Ezra 9–10," *JJS* 51 (2000): 3–18 (3).
2. E.g., Philip F. Esler, "Ezra–Nehemiah as a Narrative of (Re-Invented) Identity," *BibInt* 11 (2003): 413–26; Ralf Rothenbusch, *"...Abgesondert zur Tora Gottes hin": Ethnisch-religiöse Identitäten im Esra/Nehemiabuch*, HBS 70 (Freiburg: Koch Neff & Volkmar, 2012), 247–428; Raik Heckl, *Neuanfang und Kontinuität in Jerusalem: Studien zu den hermeneutischen Strategien im Esra-Nehemia-Buch*, FAT 104 (Tübingen: Mohr Siebeck 2016), 410–11; Donna Laird, *Negotiating Power in Ezra–Nehemiah*, SBLAIL 26 (Atlanta: SBL Press, 2016), 2; Lena-Sofia Tiemeyer, *Ezra–Nehemiah: Israel's Quest for Identity*, TTCSGOT (London: Bloomsbury T&T Clark, 2017), 1.

individual sections such as Ezra 9–10, in which the community agrees it cannot tolerate marriages between group members and outsider women,[3] or such as the Nehemiah Memoir, in which Nehemiah constructs a wall that physically isolates Jerusalem, and in which he also demands that the community avoid marriages with outsiders,[4] or, of course, such as the list of Ezra 2 and Nehemiah 7.[5] One could certainly argue that the author of Ezra–Nehemiah—and the next section of the chapter will discuss the concept of the authorship of the book—intended to do other things besides create a distinct identity for his or her community. Some see the book as a story about a period in the group's past that demonstrated the fidelity of their God,[6] for example, or see it as emphasizing the role of the Persian kings in the execution of the divine will.[7] Authors certainly can focus on more than one issue in the same writing, but in her close reading of

---

3. E.g., Tamara Cohn Eskenazi and Eleanore P. Judd, "Marriage to a Stranger in Ezra 9–10," in *Second Temple Studies 2: Temple Community in the Persian Period*, ed. Tamara C. Eskenazi and Kent H. Richards, JSOTSup 175 (Sheffield: JSOT, 1994), 266–85; Harold C. Washington, "Israel's Holy Seed and the Foreign Women of Ezra–Nehemiah: A Kristevan Reading," *BibInt* 11 (2003): 427–37 (427–9); Willa M. Johnson, *The Holy Seed Has Been Defiled: The Interethnic Marriage Dilemma in Ezra 9–10*, HBM 33 (Sheffield: Sheffield Phoenix Press, 2011), 80–92; Donald P. Moffat, *Ezra's Social Drama: Identity Formation, Marriage and Social Conflict in Ezra 9 and 10*, LHBOTS 579 (New York: Bloomsbury, 2013); Benedikt Hensel, "Ethnic Fiction and Identity-Formation: A New Explanation for the Background of the Question of Intermarriage in Ezra–Nehemiah," in *The Bible, Qumran, and the Samaritans*, ed. Magnar Kartveit and Gary N. Knoppers, StJud 104, StSam 10 (Berlin: W. de Gruyter, 2018), 133–48.

4. E.g., Christian Frevel and Benedikt J. Conczorowski, "Deepening the Water: First Steps to a Diachronic Approach to Intermarriage in the Hebrew Bible," in *Mixed Marriages: Intermarriage and Group Identity in the Second Temple Period*, ed. Christian Frevel, LHBOTS 547 (New York: Bloomsbury T&T Clark, 2011), 15–45 (23–5).

5. E.g., Jonathan E. Dyck, "Ezra 2 in Ideological Critical Perspective," in *Rethinking Contexts, Rereading Texts: Contributions from the Social Sciences to Biblical Interpretation*, ed. M. Daniel Carroll R., JSOTSup 299 (Sheffield: Sheffield Academic Press, 2000), 129–45. Some argue that Ezra 2 portrays the group as descended not only from Judean migrants from Mesopotamia, but also from Judeans whose ancestors never lived there. As Chapter 2 discusses, however, regardless as to how this list might have been read before it was incorporated into Ezra–Nehemiah, in its current context it links the community to the Babylonian migrants alone.

6. So, e.g., Lisbeth S. Fried, *Ezra: A Commentary* (Sheffield: Sheffield Phoenix Press, 2015), 1.

7. So, e.g., H. G. M. Williamson, *Ezra, Nehemiah*, WBC 16 (Waco, TX: Word Books, 1985), l.

Ezra–Nehemiah, Tamara Eskenazi refers to the community as "the central focus of the book."[8] It seems difficult to come away from even a cursory reading of the work without seeing it as emphasizing to at least some degree the identity of the community at the center of its story.

This monograph focuses on the community identity that Ezra–Nehemiah creates and that the author sees as differentiating his or group from others in Palestine, and its specific interest is in the way the author shapes this identity in response to Achaemenid ideology. The ruling dynasty of Persia at the time Ezra–Nehemiah was written justified its imperial control by explaining to its subjects how its kings made their lives better than they could ever be without them. The ideology those kings broadcast describes the peoples they have colonized as unable to live in peace, happiness, or prosperity without their rule, and so this identity of the colonized is a central aspect of the Achaemenid worldview, since the empire based its legitimacy in important part on humanity's need for its rule. Ezra–Nehemiah is a document composed by a member of one of those colonized groups, and so the book's adoption of Achaemenid ideology is particularly evident in its portrayal of the identity it constructs for the author's community. The Judean temple assembly Ezra–Nehemiah depicts is the equivalent of the colonized peoples the Achaemenids describe, a group that should strive to be loyal to its Persian rulers, something that in Ezra–Nehemiah amounts to loyalty to the people's God, as well. Things besides Achaemenid ideology shaped the author's view of the world and the identity and place of his or her community in it, and we also see in Ezra–Nehemiah traditional Yahwistic references to Israel's God as creator and the one who controls history, who demands fidelity from this community, and who punishes them if they fail to conform to the law as revealed to Moses. The Yahwism of Ezra–Nehemiah, however, is a variety that is entirely compatible with Achaemenid ideology. Given that the Achaemenids consistently refer to Auramazda as creator and "the great god," it might not seem as if Yahwism could easily fit with the dynasty's worldview, but, as Chapter 3 discusses, the Achaemenids were willing to adapt their claims to local worldviews so that they could be accepted by the colonized. In Ezra–Nehemiah, Yhwh takes Auramazda's place, authorizing and directing Persian rule in a manner corresponding to the ways in which the Achaemenids referred to their relationship with the divine, and in the book the kings make life better for the community as they all work together to fulfill the divine will.

---

8. Tamara Cohn Eskenazi, *In an Age of Prose: A Literary Approach to Ezra–Nehemiah*, SBLMS 36 (Atlanta: Scholars Press, 1988), 48.

Achaemenid ideology and some traditional aspects of Yahwism help to explain why the author depicted the identity of his or her community in the way he or she did, but, as other readers have pointed out, economic and political factors played a role in shaping the way the post-exilic community understood itself. To take one example of an aspect of communal identity Ezra–Nehemiah emphasizes, if the author is adamant that the group's members are all descended from Judean migrants from Babylonia and that, as a result, they cannot allow marriages to individuals outside of this group, perhaps this exclusive understanding of community really reflects an economic fear that these marriages would cause their land to pass to other groups when the children of such unions inherited from their parents.[9] Perhaps, on the other hand, this aspect of community identity we see in Ezra–Nehemiah was motivated by a desire to protect the economic interests of the wealthy,[10] or was an attempt to limit the power of the elite in Judah,[11] or to protect the political rights of a group claiming a close relationship to the Achaemenids.[12] Or, to take another example, if Ezra–Nehemiah insists that the community is defined in important part

---

9. E.g., Jon L. Berquist, *Judaism in Persia's Shadow: A Social and Historical Approach* (Minneapolis: Fortress Press, 1995), 117; Tamara Cohn Eskenazi, "The Missions of Ezra and Nehemiah," in *Judah and the Judeans in the Persian Period*, ed. Oded Lipschits and Manfred Oeming (Winona Lake, IN: Eisenbrauns, 2006), 509–29 (517–24); Herbert R. Marbury, "Reading Persian Dominion in Nehemiah: Multivalent Language, Co-option, Resistance, and Cultural Survival," in *Focusing Biblical Studies: The Crucial Nature of the Persian and Hellenistic Periods*, ed. Jon L. Berquist and Alice Hunt, LHBOTS 544 (New York: T&T Clark International, 2012), 158–76 (167–70).

10. E.g., Cheryl B. Anderson, "Reflections in an Interethnic/Racial Era on Interethnic/Racial Marriages in Ezra," in *They Were All Together in One Place? Toward Minority Biblical Criticism*, ed. Randall C. Bailey, Tat-siong Benny Liew, and Fernando F. Segovia, SemeiaSt 57 (Atlanta: Society of Biblical Literature, 2009), 47–64 (53–5).

11. E.g., Lisbeth S. Fried, "The Concept of 'Impure Birth' in 5th Century Athens and Judea," in *In the Wake of Tikva Frymer-Kensky*, ed. Steven Holloway, Jo Ann Scurlock, and Richard Beal, GPP 4 (Piscataway, NJ: Gorgias Press, 2009), 121–41 (137); Wolfgang Oswald, "Foreign Marriages and Citizenship in Persian-Period Judah," *JHS* 12 (2012): art. 6 (13–15).

12. E.g., Kenneth G. Hoglund, *Achaemenid Imperial Administration in Syria-Palestine and the Missions of Ezra and Nehemiah*, SBLDS 125 (Atlanta: Scholars Press, 1992), 236–40; I. Fröhlich, "*Mamzēr* in Qumran Texts—the Problem of Mixed Marriages from Ezra's Time: Law, Literature, and Practice," *Transeu* 29 (2005): 103–15; John Kessler, "Persia's Loyal Yahwists: Power, Identity and Ethnicity in Achaemenid Judah," in Lipschits and Oeming, eds, *Judah and the Judeans in the Persian Period*, 91–121 (111).

by the necessity to keep the law, perhaps that is because Pentateuchal law received official recognition by the Persians as imperial law, just as Artaxerxes' letter in Ezra 7:12-26 states when the king commands Ezra to bring "the law of your God and the law of the king" to the community.[13] On the other hand, perhaps that letter is fictitious,[14] and the Persians had no general policy of codifying the law codes of their colonized peoples,[15] and the centrality of the law in defining community is the result not of an imperial decree but of a broader cultural movement in the fifth-century BCE Eastern Mediterranean to create law codes.[16] Or, to take one more example, perhaps the wall that Nehemiah builds to separate the community (or Jerusalem, at least) from the surrounding peoples was really authorized by Artaxerxes because the Persians wanted to strengthen defenses close to Egypt, which had recently rebelled,[17] or simply because Jerusalem had become wealthy enough that it needed and could afford a wall.[18]

13. E.g., Thomas Willi, *Juda—Jehud—Israel: Studien zum Selbstverständnis des Judentums in persischer Zeit*, FAT 12 (Tübingen: J. C. B. Mohr, 1995), 91–117; Peter Frei, "Persian Imperial Authorization: A Summary," in *Persia and Torah: The Theory of Imperial Authorization of the Pentateuch*, ed. James W. Watts, SBLSymS 17 (Atlanta: Society of Biblical Literature, 2001), 5–40; David Carr, "The Rise of Torah," in *The Pentateuch as Torah: New Models for Understanding its Promulgation and Acceptance*, ed. Gary N. Knoppers and Bernard M. Levinson (Winona Lake, IN: Eisenbrauns, 2007), 39–56 (53–5).

14. E.g., David Janzen, "The 'Mission' of Ezra and the Persian-Period Temple Community," *JBL* 119 (2000): 619–43; Sebastian Grätz, *Das Edikt des Artaxerxes: Eine Untersuchung zum religionspolitischen und historischen Umfeld von Esra 7,12-26*, BZAW 337 (Berlin: W. de Gruyter, 2004), 147–91; Bob Becking, *Ezra, Nehemiah, and the Construction of Early Jewish Identity*, FAT 80 (Tübingen: Mohr Siebeck, 2011), 50.

15. E.g., Gary N. Knoppers, "An Achaemenid Imperial Authorization of Torah in Yehud?," in Watts, ed., *Persia and Torah*, 115–34; Reinhard G. Kratz, "Temple and Torah: Reflections on the Legal Status of the Pentateuch between Elephantine and Qumran," in Knoppers and Levinson, eds, *The Pentateuch as Torah*, 77–103 (79–81); Kyong-Jin Lee, *The Authority and Authorization of Torah in the Persian Period*, CBET (Leuven: Peeters, 2011).

16. Gary N. Knoppers and Paul B. Harvey, Jr., "The Pentateuch in Ancient Mediterranean Context: The Publication of Local Lawcodes," in Knoppers and Levinson, eds, *The Pentateuch as Torah*, 105–41.

17. E.g., D. Bodi, "La clémence des Perses envers Néhémie et ses compatriotes: Faveur ou opportunisme politique?," *Transeu* 21 (2001): 69–86.

18. Oded Lipschits, *The Fall and Rise of Jerusalem: Judah under Babylonian Rule* (Winona Lake, IN: Eisenbrauns, 2005), 168–73.

There is intuitive sense in concluding that economic and geopolitical factors can shape a group's actions and attitudes, and thus its sense of self, but as the final main chapter of the monograph argues, we have little evidence that the specific community identity we see in Ezra–Nehemiah was widely accepted in post-exilic Judah. This suggests that if such factors affected Ezra–Nehemiah's portrayals of empire and community, their effect was felt by only a smaller group within the Judean temple assembly, and did not impact the assembly as a whole. That final main chapter also argues that Ezra–Nehemiah derived from a faction or group at the top of the assembly's socio-economic ladder, and that this faction found it financially and politically expedient to embrace the Achaemenids' portrayal of the empire and adopt the dynasty's depiction of the colonized as they thought about their own community in Judah. They experienced concrete benefits in looking at the world in the same way the empire did, and in trying to convince others within the community to accept this worldview. Other Persian-period biblical writings, however, largely reject the imperial portrayals of empire and community Ezra–Nehemiah accepts because these benefits did not extend far beyond its author's privileged faction. As a result, this monograph does not focus on economic and geopolitical factors that affected the entire post-exilic community, but argues that Ezra–Nehemiah's depiction of community identity can be best explained as something that reflects Achaemenid ideology, which only a very elite group within the temple assembly was willing to accept.

As the following chapters demonstrate how imperial thought shaped the worldview readers encounter in Ezra–Nehemiah, the investigation will take certain claims in the book at face value even when it is not clear that they are actually true, since the book's claims, true or false, are what broadcast the author's beliefs. So, for example, although there is no consensus in the field as to whether the Aramaic correspondence of Ezra 4–6 and 7 was truly composed by Achaemenid kings and imperial bureaucrats,[19] for our purposes this point is moot, since our interest is in

---

19. For the question of the historical validity of Artaxerxes' letter of Ezra 7, see above. For arguments that generally conclude the material of Ezra 4–6 does not reflect actual imperial correspondence, see, e.g., Dirk Schwiderski, *Handbuch des nordwestsemitischen Briefformulars: Ein Beitrag zur Echtheitsfrage der aramäischen Briefe des Esrabuches*, BZAW 295 (Berlin: W. de Gruyter, 2000), 343–80; Diana Edelman, *The Origins of the "Second" Temple: Persian Imperial Policy and the Rebuilding of Jerusalem*, BW (London: Equinox, 2005), 182–99; Lester L. Grabbe, "The 'Persian Documents' in the Book of Ezra: Are They Authentic?" in Lipschits and Oeming, eds, *Judah and the Judeans in the Persian Period*, 531–70. For some defenses of this correspondence as consisting of genuine documents produced by the Achaemenids

trying to understand the author's worldview, what he or she believed, and the presence of this correspondence in the work gives us every indication that the author believed it to be authentic. And, to take another example, we will not ask whether or not the Persians actually did give some sort of official authorization to Jewish law, since in the story of Ezra 7 Artaxerxes obviously does so. And we will not, to take just one more example, dispute the presentation in Ezra 2 and Nehemiah 7 of the movement of over forty-two thousand migrants from Babylonia to Judah just after Cyrus's capture of Babylon in 539 BCE, even though Bob Becking rightly refers to this mass movement of Judeans as a "myth,"[20] since there is no archaeological evidence for a major change in Judah's population at this time,[21] and it never reached this level at any point in the Persian period.[22] The author believed there was such a massive movement of Judeans immediately after the exile, however, and since our main goal is to understand his or her worldview and portrayal of the community about whom he or she writes, the question as to the historical veracity of this mass migration does not concern us.

The next two sections of this chapter do address some historical questions in regard to the composition and date of Ezra–Nehemiah, but after establishing it as a work of the early or mid-fourth century BCE, the following chapters will move to a more literary focus, reading Ezra–Nehemiah in dialogue with Achaemenid inscriptions and other imperial media. Chapter 2 opens the core of the investigation with an examination of the community identity with which Ezra–Nehemiah presents readers. The work portrays two different generations of the post-exilic community, one in Ezra 1–6, the first returnees from Babylonia, and one

and their administrative apparatus, see, e.g., Richard C. Steiner, "Bishlam's Archival Search Report in Nehemiah's Archive: Multiple Introductions and Reverse Chronological Order as Clues to the Origin of the Aramaic Letters in Ezra 4–6," *JBL* 125 (2006): 641–85; H. G. M. Williamson, "The Aramaic Documents in Ezra Revisited," *JTS* 59 (2008): 41–62.

20. Bob Becking, "'We All Returned as One!' Critical Notes on the Myth of a Mass Return," in Lipschits and Oeming, eds, *Judah and the Judeans in the Persian Period*, 3–18 (6–7).

21. Oded Lipschits, "Between Archaeology and Text: A Reevaluation of the Development Process of Jerusalem in the Persian Period," in *Congress Volume Helsinki 2010*, ed. Martti Nissinen, VTSup 148 (Leiden: Brill, 2012), 145–65 (149–51).

22. So, e.g., Charles E. Carter, *The Emergence of Yehud in the Persian Period: A Social and Demographic Study*, JSOTSup 294 (Sheffield: Sheffield Academic Press, 1999), 199–204; Lipschits, *The Fall and Rise of Jerusalem*, 267–71.

in Ezra 7–Nehemiah 13, the time of Ezra and Nehemiah during the reign of Artaxerxes I, a narrative that begins some generations after the end of the preceding section.[23] One could also structure the book by shifts in the prominent leaders who dominate its different sections—Sheshbazzar, Zerubbabel, and Jeshua in Ezra 1–6, Ezra in Ezra 7–10, and Nehemiah in Nehemiah 1–13[24]—or by the main challenges faced in its different parts—the temple construction in Ezra 1–6, the foreign marriage crisis of Ezra 7–10, and the wall construction of Nehemiah 1–7, followed by a celebration of the totality of the work in Nehemiah 8–13, when all of the challenges have been overcome.[25] However, examining the differences in the ways Ezra–Nehemiah portrays the two generations of Ezra 1–6 and Ezra 7–Nehemiah 13 proves most helpful when trying to get a sense of the book's presentation of group identity, because the two generations are fairly different: Ezra 1–6 depicts an ideal group, the sort of community fourth-century readers should strive to be as far as the author is concerned, but Ezra 7–Nehemiah 13 shows readers the group they have become after generations in the land, and this identity is far from ideal.[26] In Ezra 1–6, migrants from Babylonia, part of the good center of the world in Achaemenid thought, act in loyalty to the king who acts in loyalty to Yhwh, and they build the temple under royal orders. The genealogy of Ezra 2 carefully distinguishes them as Judeans from Mesopotamia, different than the colonized peoples already present in Palestine when they arrive, and the loyal community of Ezra 1–6 seems like a group of colonizers sent out by the king from the empire's center to its margins, fulfilling the divine will as mediated by the king to make the world a better place. This generation is defined principally by its loyalty to the king, who has chosen them alone to construct Yhwh's temple, and so

23. For others who adopt this as the basic structure of the work, see, e.g., Michael W. Duggan, *The Covenant Renewal in Ezra–Nehemiah (Neh 7:72B–10:40): An Exegetical, Literary, and Theological Study*, SBLDS 164 (Atlanta: Society of Biblical Literature, 2001), 60–7; Sara Japhet, *From the Rivers of Babylon to the Highlands of Judah: Collected Studies on the Restoration Period* (Winona Lake, IN: Eisenbrauns, 2006), 260–1.

24. So, e.g., Reinhard G. Kratz, *The Composition of the Narrative Books of the Old Testament*, trans. John Bowden (London: T&T Clark International, 2005), 50.

25. This follows Tamara Eskenazi's structuring of the book; for her explanation and rationales, see *In an Age of Prose*, 37–126.

26. As Diana Edelman notes, the ideal beginning of Ezra 1–6, like other ideal beginnings in biblical literature such as Eden and the exodus, is followed by disobedience ("Ezra 1–6 as Idealized Past," in *A Palimpsest: Rhetoric, Ideology, Stylistics, and Language Relating to Persian Israel*, ed. Ehud Ben Zvi, Diana V. Edelman, and Frank Polak, PHSC 5 [Piscataway, NJ: Gorgias Press, 2009], 47–59 [56]).

by preserving genealogical boundaries and excluding Palestinian natives from their building project, they manifest such loyalty and maintain the core of their identity. They are Yahwists, but this is not a defining characteristic of the community, since the other Yahwists in Palestine, who were not sent by the king to build, are outside of the genealogical boundaries of Ezra 2, and act in disloyalty to royal orders as they try to prevent the community from following the king's command to construct the temple.

But this story of a loyal generation is followed by one of an epigone, a later and lesser generation, in Ezra 7–Nehemiah 13. After some generations in the land, the distinction between the group and the peoples around them has blurred. They have intermarried with those peoples and so have violated not only the genealogical boundary of Ezra 2 but the law of their God, which Artaxerxes has adopted as royal law, adherence to which is supposed to be a defining aspect of their identity. Once again, loyalty to the king lies at the center of group identity, as adherence to divine law is also adherence to royal law, but the longer the community remains at the margins of the empire, the more disloyal and the less like its ideal self it becomes, and since the same holds true for its leadership, they now depend upon figures whom the king sends from the center of the world—Ezra and Nehemiah, specifically—to save them. The community's tendency to disloyalty to their God and king could result in their annihilation, Ezra–Nehemiah warns, and the epigone proves incapable of keeping the law and so of being like the loyal generation of Ezra 1–6, and thus needs Achaemenid rule if they hope to survive. They depend on the king to send officials like Ezra and Nehemiah to enforce the boundaries of law and genealogy that manifest the community's loyalty and their separation from the disloyal peoples around them, something in which even Nehemiah's wall, a physical and protective barrier, plays a role.

This sort of community identity grounded in the need to be loyal subjects of the king, Chapters 3 and 4 argue, is one that reflects the Achaemenids' self-presentation and their understanding of what their colonized peoples are like, and why that identity means those peoples need Achaemenid rule. The dynasty, as Chapter 3 discusses, explained that the world was in such dreadful shape that Auramazda appointed them to rule and so to return it to the paradisiacal state that this god created and intended for humanity. Yhwh takes Auramazda's place in Ezra–Nehemiah—Chapter 3 points out that the Achaemenids allowed for that sort of regional variation in broadcasting their ideology—and in the book the kings are largely who they claim to be on their inscriptions, faithful servants of the divine who make the world a better place for their loyal subjects. The community of Ezra 1–6 comes from the good center of the world, and their loyalty to the king, who speaks for God, allows them to work with the generous kings of Persia, who make their temple-building possible. It is the Achaemenid who authorizes and enforces Torah, adopting it into the empire's judicial system, and who sends Ezra to save the community from the destruction its anomism merits; following divine guidance, the king also sends Nehemiah to rebuild Jerusalem and its wall, and Nehemiah, like Ezra, acts to enforce the law and so to save the community from itself. Over time, the temple assembly in Judah has become one of the colonized peoples whom the Achaemenids describe in their inscriptions, a group that depends upon the king to make their lives better and enforce divine law so they do not destroy themselves. The Achaemenids in Ezra–Nehemiah are as beneficent as their inscriptions say they are, and without them there would be no temple or cult, no Jerusalem, and no community in Judah at all.

Yet the Achaemenids also loom in the background of Ezra–Nehemiah's narrative as a potentially dangerous and destructive force, since any future exile or annihilation of the community would be carried out at the Achaemenids' hands, as far as Ezra–Nehemiah's author is concerned. In this narrative world, such destruction would be the result of a divine order to punish the epigone that relentlessly insists on failing to acknowledge the social boundaries that should distinguish it from the peoples around them. Torah demands the community must separate itself from the peoples, says Ezra–Nehemiah, and since the book has placed Torah within the empire's system of justice, fidelity to God's law through such separation is a way for the community to manifest its loyalty to the king. This view of Persia as a danger as well as a God-given necessity reflects Achaemenid ideology as well, however, for as Chapter 4 discusses, the Achaemenids claimed the right to torture their disloyal subjects, and they massacred and exiled populations who rebelled and refused to allow them to impose their divinely willed leadership that makes the world a better place. The author of Ezra–Nehemiah did not invent the notion that Yhwh can use a foreign king to punish the people, but no other writing in the Hebrew Bible claims that a foreign empire adopts Yahwistic law into its judicial system, something that reflects the Achaemenid understanding that their royal law has a divine origin. The result, then, is that any violent acts of the Persians in Judah, even the annihilation of the community, will always be justified as far as the author of the book is concerned, since divine and royal law, like divine and royal will, are aligned, and a loyal subject of the king is a faithful servant of Yhwh. In Ezra–Nehemiah, just as in Achaemenid ideology, fear of imperial violence is good because it forces the people to be loyal to the divine/royal law, and this is so because Ezra–Nehemiah depicts the epigone just as Achaemenid ideology portrays the colonized, as people who cannot remain faithful to divine/royal will without such fear as motivation. And while even the threat of massive imperial violence does not cause Ezra–Nehemiah to criticize Achaemenid rule, Chapter 4 also argues that the book does criticize the empire, insofar as it is suspicious of local imperial officials in regions around Judah. Like the members of Ezra–Nehemiah's community, such officials who remain too long away from the good lands at the center of the empire can become corrupt and act against the divine and royal will, and this sort of corruption is simply part of the original character of the local leadership of the peoples who live near Judah. Ezra–Nehemiah is always pro-Achaemenid, but is not always pro-empire.

Despite the book's willingness to condemn the imperial apparatus in Palestine, however, there is no good future for the Judean temple assembly in Ezra–Nehemiah outside of the imperfect empire ruled by the perfect king. The story of the epigone shows readers a community that has lived for too long away from the good center of the empire to be loyal to God and king without the leadership the Achaemenid sends from that center. Life under Persian rule is as good as things can get for the community, as far as Ezra–Nehemiah is concerned, since the alternative is destruction that God will order the kings to carry out. In a sense, history has reached a sort of conclusion for the author, and, as Chapter 4 also argues, this too reflects Achaemenid ideology. The dynasty's own media portray Darius, the first Achaemenid, as putting the world in its place, making it better according to divine will, while all later kings merely preserve what he has done. Even in their self-description, as Chapter 4 explains, the later Achaemenids did little to distinguish themselves from the other kings who followed Darius; in a sense, they were all the last king, since history had reached its divinely intended end in Darius's work, and all his successors had to do was to maintain that order, their identical reigns benefitting all of the world under their rule. This picture of an end of history ruled by its last dynasty is one that Ezra–Nehemiah adopts, as it presents a people who can only be who God intends them to be when the Achaemenids rule over them.

This sort of alignment of imperial rule and violence with divine will can seem alarming to modern readers, and, as Chapter 5 discusses, others within the community to which Ezra–Nehemiah was addressed would have had similar qualms about such a wholesale appropriation of imperial ideology, which is why other biblical writings of the Persian period provide a very different picture of who the community is in relation to the empire than Ezra–Nehemiah does, marginalizing the Achaemenids in their worldviews and even ignoring them entirely. Chapter 5 turns to a study of the Persian-period temple assembly and its various factions, arguing that we cannot see Ezra–Nehemiah's depiction of community identity as something that was broadly accepted in Judah. Ezra–Nehemiah represents the views of an elite that was closely associated with the governor's office, which is why it privileges imperial ideology. Other writings that are commonly dated to the Persian period or shortly thereafter—specifically, Haggai, First Zechariah, Third Isaiah, Malachi, Chronicles, and Second Zechariah—alert us to the existence of other groups in the assembly from different social locations whose portrayals of empire and community identity have little in common with Ezra–Nehemiah's. As far as we can tell, there would have been few in the Persian-period temple assembly who would have been willing to define the community as the abject colonized people utterly dependent on the Achaemenids that Ezra–Nehemiah portrays. As Chapter 6 concludes, because Ezra–Nehemiah is the only history-like writing from the Persian period that focuses on events during that time, it can be tempting to see its picture of the community, a picture formed through Achaemenid ideology, as one that was widely accepted. Chapter 5's study of different assembly factions and the writings they produced tells us, however, that Ezra–Nehemiah's understanding of empire and identity would have appealed only to the very elite.

2. *The Composition and Authorship of Ezra–Nehemiah*

The previous section of the chapter refers to the author of Ezra–Nehemiah, but given the fact that so much of the material in the book seems to come from individual sources, such as its many lists of names, its two Aramaic sections, and the first-person narratives of Ezra and Nehemiah, it might seem to make more sense to refer to a compiler rather than an author. Given as well that many argue that the work, as well as individual sections of it that originally existed as separate documents, were put together over a period of centuries,[27] it might also seem more appropriate to refer to a series of compilers and redactors. The number and variety of accounts scholars have produced about the prehistory of

---

27. E.g., Juha Pakkala, *Ezra the Scribe: The Development of Ezra 7–10 and Nehemia 8*, BZAW 347 (Berlin: W. de Gruyter, 2004); Jacob L. Wright, *Rebuilding Identity: The Nehemiah-Memoir and its Earliest Readers*, BZAW 348 (Berlin: W. de Gruyter, 2004); Joseph Blenkinsopp, *Judaism: The First Phase. The Place of Ezra and Nehemiah in the Origins of Judaism* (Grand Rapids, MI: Eerdmans, 2009), 86–90; Sean Burt, *The Courtier and the Governor: Transformations of Genre in the Nehemiah Memoir*, JAJSup 17 (Göttingen: Vandenhoeck & Ruprecht, 2014), 70.

sources such as the Nehemiah Memoir and the material associated with Ezra means that, without a lengthy monograph devoted to the topic, we cannot hope to resolve with any sort of thoroughness issues of the composition of the various sources the author of Ezra–Nehemiah included, and so we will have to content ourselves with a comparatively brief argument that shows there is not enough evidence to say much with any confidence about the redactional history of the documents that eventually became part of Ezra–Nehemiah. Shifts from Hebrew to Aramaic, from first-person narration to third-person, and from narrative to lists of names tell us that originally independent material has been included in the work, but many other attempts to posit redaction in the book based on evidence beyond such obvious shifts are established on unreliable foundations, and there is often little good evidence that allows us to determine with any certainty the process of composition and the extent of the sources the author found and appropriated. The wide disagreement in scholarship about issues surrounding the redaction and extent of documents that found their way into Ezra–Nehemiah is simply a result of the fact that earlier material has been edited and shaped so that it is well integrated into a final writing that broadcasts particular messages, a process that most likely occurred, as the final section of the chapter argues, in the early or mid-fourth century BCE, not long before the end of the Persian period. The individual responsible for incorporating a diverse set of traditions into the writing as we know it had to choose to include some of the material at his or her disposal, and had to edit and combine the information he or she did select in such a way that it created a single and coherent document. Perhaps under this set of circumstances there is no clear way to distinguish a compiler from an author, but it is hardly unreasonable to see someone who chooses, organizes, edits, and shapes pre-existing sources into an entirely new writing that he or she is creating, one that conveys his or her own messages, as an author.[28]

Since the notion that the Chronicler was responsible for Ezra–Nehemiah has, for good reasons, largely been abandoned by biblical scholars,[29] the question as to whether or not we can refer to the work as a single writing with one author should begin with the matter as to whether Ezra 1–10

---

28. Jeffrey Tigay makes precisely this point when referring to the author of the Akkadian version of the Epic of Gilgamesh, a figure who also had to integrate and weave together older materials to create a unified story; see Tigay's *The Evolution of the Gilgamesh Epic* (Philadelphia: The University of Pennsylvania Press, 1982), 42.

29. See the arguments in H. G. M. Williamson, *Israel in the Books of Chronicles* (Cambridge: Cambridge University Press, 1977), 37–59; Eskenazi, *In an Age of Prose*, 14–36; Japhet, *From the Rivers of Babylon*, 1–37, 169–82.

and Nehemiah 1–13 were originally two separate compositions. This is a minority view in the field,[30] since even by the time of the Septuagint translation Ezra–Nehemiah existed as a single unit, and the Masoretic tradition always treats it as such. Quite a bit of evidence in the text itself points in the same direction: Ezra 4:8-23 refers to local opposition to the construction of Jerusalem's wall, a matter that is never otherwise discussed in Ezra 1–10 but that is resolved in Nehemiah 1–6; there are narratives about Ezra in the third person in Ezra 7 and 10 as well as Nehemiah 8; in Ezra 7, Artaxerxes orders Ezra to teach the law, something we do not see him do until Nehemiah 8;[31] the importance of avoiding marriages outside of the community is emphasized in Ezra 9–10 as well as in Nehemiah 10 and 13; both Ezra 9 and Nehemiah 9 contain prayers focused on the consequences of the people's failure to keep the law; and, as we will discuss in the following chapters, both Ezra 1–10 and Nehemiah 1–13 present the Persian kings as faithful intermediaries between God and the people, and emphasize the need for the community to remain loyal to Persia and the divine law. Ezra 1–10 as a block of material seems well integrated with Nehemiah 1–13 and both sections, as Chapter 2 demonstrates, reflect the same views of empire and identity.

To turn to more contentious issues in regard to the composition of the book, this section of the chapter argues that attempts to locate redactional seams—signs in the wording and content of the text that purportedly function as evidence of redaction—often overlook other ways of making sense of the text, for these sorts of studies can portray material as illogical that really is not, and sometimes rely on the dubious assumption that modern scholars better understand biblical Hebrew than the people who wrote in and spoke it as a native language. To explain these ideas, we can begin with a relatively uncomplicated hypothesis about redaction in Ezra–Nehemiah, that of Yonina Dor's analysis of the pre-history of Ezra 9–10. Dor argues that inconsistencies and repetitions in these chapters provide evidence of redactional seams, and concludes that the story is based on

---

30. Although see James VanderKam, "Ezra–Nehemiah or Ezra and Nehemiah?," in *Priests, Prophets and Scribes: Essays on the Formation and Heritage of Second Temple Judaism in Honour of Joseph Blenkinsopp*, ed. Eugene Ulrich et al., JSOTSup 149 (Sheffield: Sheffield Academic Press, 1992), 55–75; David Kraemer, "On the Relationship of the Books of Ezra and Nehemiah," *JSOT* 59 (1993): 73–92; Becking, *Ezra, Nehemiah*, 27–8.

31. See on this point Christiane Karrer-Grube, "Scrutinizing the Conceptual Unity of Ezra and Nehemiah," in *Unity and Disunity in Ezra–Nehemiah: Redaction, Rhetoric, and Reader*, ed. Mark J. Boda and Paul L. Redditt, HBM 17 (Sheffield: Sheffield Phoenix Press, 2008), 136–59 (139–42).

three originally independent sections—9:6-15; 10:2-6; and 10:7-44—with 9:1-5 and 10:1 added by the redactor who put Ezra 9–10 together in the form we now find it. One obvious sign we are working with material originally composed by different authors is that all of Ezra 9 is narrated by Ezra in the first person, just as 7:27–8:36 is,[32] and all of Ezra 10 is in the third person. Ezra 9 sets forth a problem that the community will have to solve, stating that some of its members have intermarried with foreign women, something that might result in the group's annihilation, while Ezra 10 provides the solution of having the community members who entered into such relationships send those women away.[33] But in 10:2-6 and 7-44 we see two originally separate sources, Dor argues, because they provide scenes of two different assemblies that work to resolve the same problem, although Dor notes that the two sections are structured quite similarly.[34] These two blocks of material were combined first, Dor concludes, and then someone else combined 10:2-44 with 9:6-15 and composed 9:1-5 and 10:1, the framing verses.[35]

Dor identifies three sorts of redactional seams: one based on a change from first- to third-person narration; one based on the repetition of assembly scenes; and one necessitated by the belief that there were originally three separate documents that we now find combined, a process that demands linking material. The first of these three does seem to indicate that the author of Ezra–Nehemiah has different sources at his or her disposal, but the second redactional seam Dor identifies appears to be much less obvious and, in fact, the claim that there is such a seam misses the logic of the story, something that is a common problem in many arguments for redaction in the book. There is no lack of logic or unity in Ezra 10 as it currently exists that demands the sort of hypothetical redaction Dor proposes, for in 10:1-5 the assembly agrees as to what needs to be done, but they specifically ask Ezra to do it (10:4), and this suggests this story is not complete until Ezra acts, which he does not do until later in the chapter. In 10:6-8, preparations are made for a formal assembly, and when

---

32. One could argue that 8:35-36 really is not part of Ezra's first-person narration (for example, Joseph Blenkinsopp, *Ezra–Nehemiah: A Commentary*, OTL [London: SCM, 1989], 171; Pakkala, *Ezra the Scribe*, 65–6), but we could also see it as Ezra's own summary of the journey he undertook in the first part of Ezra 8 (e.g., Philip Y. Yoo, *Ezra and the Second Wilderness*, OTRM [Oxford: Oxford University Press, 2017], 87).

33. Yonina Dor, "The Composition of the Episode of the Foreign Women in Ezra ix–x," *VT* 53 (2003): 26–47 (28–9).

34. Dor, "The Composition of the Episode," 34–6.

35. Dor, "The Composition of the Episode," 43–7.

it convenes in 10:9-15 it is Ezra who leads the deliberations, doing what the community asked in 10:1-5. The assembly of 10:1-5 (or 10:2-6, as Dor sees it) is simply preparation for the action that takes place in the formal assembly of 10:9-44 (or 10:7-44, according to Dor), which concludes the action begun earlier, and so it makes more sense to see 10:1-44 as a single story.[36]

This sort of failure to see that the text makes logical sense as it stands and needs no hypothetical act of redaction to explain it means that arguments for redaction like this are based on questionable evidence, and we will refer to other such dubious arguments for redaction below. Yet, since there clearly is a break between the end of the first-person narration in Ezra 9 and the third-person narration that starts at the beginning of Ezra 10, then it appears very likely that someone has placed two originally separate writings (or parts of two separate writings) together, and we would then expect that there is material in these chapters composed by the writer who attached them to each other. Finding that linking material in this case, however, is not easy. Is 9:1-5 framing material composed by a redactor, as Dor argues? Since these verses continue the first-person narration of 7:27–8:36, it seems simpler to conclude that Ezra 9 was originally part of that source, which was assumedly written by Ezra. It is possible that Ezra's prayer of 9:6-15 had some origin outside of the story Ezra is presented as narrating, but if so it has been well integrated into it, since it begins by continuing the first-person narration of the earlier section and is specifically addressing the problem of intermarriage raised in 9:1-5. So even if we could somehow determine that the prayer of 9:6-15 has been added to the pre-existing first-person narrative of 7:27–9:5, we could not know with certainty whether this was done by the author of Ezra–Nehemiah or at an earlier stage. All of the material that follows Ezra 9 in which Ezra plays a pivotal role—that is, Ezra 10 and Nehemiah 8—is narrated in the third person, just as the introduction to Ezra's work in 7:1-11 is, and this suggests the author was drawing on an originally independent source or sources about Ezra distinct from the first-person

---

36. So while there are others who offer more complicated models of redaction in Ezra 10, these are generally not based on the idea that the chapter is founded on two originally distinct stories of assemblies, although Dor is not the only one to make this argument (see, e.g., Blenkinsopp, *Ezra–Nehemiah*, 187). Both Pakkala (*Ezra the Scribe*, 83–111) and Rothenbusch (*"...Abgesondert zur Tora Gottes hin"*, 127–42), for example, describe multi-stage processes of redaction in the chapter, but both see parts of 10:2-6 and 10:7-44—the two assemblies that Dor argues were originally from different sources—as belonging to the original stratum of Ezra 10.

material, or was composing this third-person material him or herself based on oral traditions and/or other records, or came across the first- and third-person material after it had already been combined.

It is not clear why the text should shift from the first-person narration of 7:27–9:15 at a point where the community must deal with the issue of intermarriage that Ezra 9 raises. Perhaps the author encountered a text in which Ezra 9 and 10 were already linked, or perhaps the document in the first person that the author was working with had no resolution to the intermarriage issue, or perhaps he or she had access to a different document in the third person with a resolution that he or she preferred, or perhaps the author simply invented a solution or relied on oral traditions in Ezra 10. There may be a shift from first- to third-person narrative voice that alerts us to the fact that pre-existing material has been combined by someone, but the story continues logically. So it is possible that 10:1 is linking or framing material, as Dor claims, but it is also possible that 10:1 is merely the continuation of an earlier source about Ezra written in the third person, and that the author of Ezra–Nehemiah did not use the first part of that material. We would expect that at least the list of names in 10:18b-43 of the men who had married outsiders came from some written source that pre-existed the final form of Ezra–Nehemiah, but we cannot know if that source included all or part of Ezra 10:1-18a or whether it was from a different document altogether.

The case is, then, that there are so many possible ways to make sense of the origins and composition of Ezra 9–10 that it is very difficult to determine just how much of it pre-existed in written form the work of the author of Ezra–Nehemiah, and we begin with this as an example to make the larger point that there is often little we can know with certainty about the composition of the book. The fact that, as Dor notes, there is a repetition of key words and phrases in Ezra 9 and 10[37] suggests the material in both chapters has been shaped in relation to each other, but it is difficult to say if this was done by the author of Ezra–Nehemiah or if he or she found the first- and third-person material already linked in this manner. Working with a variety of material, not all of which was necessarily in written form, the author must have composed some sort of linkages between the sources that he or she used, and may well have edited the first-person narrative he or she came across in order to fit it together with the other information we see in Ezra 10, so as to have both chapters broadcast the messages that he or she wanted them to broadcast now that they were part of the same book. On the other hand, the author

---

37. Dor, "The Composition of the Episode," 27.

could have come across a document in which Ezra 10 had already been carefully linked to the preceding material. There sometimes are obvious seams in Ezra–Nehemiah, such as the shifts from first- to third-person narration and from narrative to list that we see here, but there is no clear way to determine the process through which this material was formed into the shape in which we now find it. Moreover, arguments that identify redactional seams beyond very obvious ones such as this shift in narrative voice are much less persuasive, and can often invent redactional work and redactors when none is needed to explain the current shape of the text.

The idea that it is very difficult to determine the precise extent of most of the pre-existing material the author has integrated into Ezra–Nehemiah, and that it is equally difficult to determine the history of editing of this material and how it was incorporated into the work, is not a commonly accepted one, however, and many arguments for redaction appeal to putative flaws in the writing style as evidence. So in studies of the opening of the story of Ezra, for example, one often encounters the claim that Ezra 7:1b-5, the genealogy that links Ezra to Aaron, is a later redactional insertion into the Ezra material,[38] since, some scholars argue, it appears to interrupt what they understand to be the original introduction to Ezra in 7:1a and 6. Ezra's profession as a scribe in 7:6 "is introduced rather awkwardly," as Juha Pakkala puts it,[39] since we would expect this information at the very beginning of his introduction, and since the first verb of which Ezra is the subject does not appear until 7:6, even though his name first appears in 7:1, at the beginning of the genealogy.[40] Or, to take another example from the introduction to Ezra, Philip Yoo and Pakkala refer to the "awkward repetition" of the word ספר in 7:11—a translation of the MT here refers to the letter that Artaxerxes gave to "Ezra the priest, the scribe (הספר), the scribe (ספר) of the words of the commandments of Yhwh"— and see this awkwardness as evidence that the second half of the verse is a later addition.[41] We could identify a multitude of other arguments in the scholarly literature on Ezra–Nehemiah that rely on locating an awkward writing style as evidence that points to redactional insertions, but we can begin with these hypotheses that explain the opening of Ezra 7 as examples. One obvious problem with approaches like them is that

---

38. E.g., Williamson, *Ezra, Nehemiah*, 89; Blenkinsopp, *Ezra–Nehemiah*, 136; Christiane Karrer, *Ringen um die Verfassung Judas: Eine Studie zu den theologisch-politischen Vorstellungen im Esra-Nehemiah-Buch*, BZAW 308 (Berlin: W. de Gruyter, 2001), 234; Pakkala, *Ezra the Scribe*, 24–6.
39. Pakkala, *Ezra the Scribe*, 26.
40. For his larger argument about 7:1b-5, see Pakkala, *Ezra the Scribe*, 23–6.
41. Pakkala, *Ezra the Scribe*, 32; Yoo, *Ezra and the Second Wilderness*, 84–5.

they assume that modern scholars, who do not speak biblical Hebrew as a native language, can identify problems in the text where the ancient writers, who actually spoke the language and were part of ancient Judah's literary culture, could not, and given that this is unlikely, we should search for ways of making sense of the writing style and its logic before we turn to redaction in order to explain it. Even if the original versions of Ezra 7:1-6 and 7:11 did undergo expansion through redaction, we would expect that redactors would want to add or alter material as seamlessly as possible.

So if it seems "awkward" to non-native speakers of biblical Hebrew that Ezra's priestly genealogy of 7:1b-5 comes before his introduction as a scribe in 7:6, it is unlikely it seemed this way to the individual who put 7:1-6 into its final form since we would assume the writers tried to make their compositions as unawkward as possible. In the context of Ezra–Nehemiah as a whole, it makes perfect sense that the author would want the first thing readers encounter about Ezra to be a genealogy that proves his status as a priest. The most important thing Ezra does in Ezra 7–10 is to lead the community in its separation from foreign women, and he does so in his office as priest (10:10, 16). Chapter 2 argues that an important emphasis of Ezra–Nehemiah is its claims in regard to the failures of the community's leadership, something that includes the priesthood, and that the community is dependent upon the Achaemenid to send them good leaders from the center of the empire, like Ezra, who teaches them the law when the priests of Judah have not done so; indeed, as Gary Knoppers points out, Ezra indicts the priestly leadership he finds in Judah, since some among them, even descendants of Jeshua, the first post-exilic high priest, have married outsider women.[42] So 7:1b-5 establishes Ezra's impeccable genealogical credentials for doing the most important work the book ascribes to him, as he acts when the existing priestly leadership, mired in sin, does not, and readers need not worry that he is like those priests of Ezra 2:62-63 who were unable to prove their right to serve in the priestly office because of a lack of genealogical evidence. Moreover, in this section of the book Artaxerxes entrusts Ezra with conveying the generous gifts from the king to the temple and with using the money to supply the cult (Ezra 7:15-22), assumedly in his role as priest. All of this is to say that to see Ezra's priestly genealogy in 7:1b-5 as "awkward" and

---

42. Gary N. Knoppers, "Ethnicity, Genealogy, Geography, and Change: The Judean Communities of Babylon and Jerusalem in the Story of Ezra," in *Community Identity in Judea's Historiography: Biblical and Comparative Perspectives*, ed. Gary N. Knoppers and Kenneth A. Ristau (Winona Lake, IN: Eisenbrauns, 2009), 147–71 (153–6).

as a sign of redaction is to miss the point that the author may have found Ezra's descent from Aaron to be the first important thing readers should know about him. Pakkala's belief that the placement of the verb in 7:6, far removed from the first appearance of Ezra's name in 7:1, is itself a sign of redaction is belied by the fact that we see precisely the same sort of construction elsewhere in biblical Hebrew.[43]

And if we see an "awkward repetition" of the word ספר in Ezra 7:11— the MT here reads עזרא הכהן הספר ספר דברי מצות יהוה "Ezra the priest, the scribe, the scribe of the words of the commandments of Yhwh"—it is unlikely that this putative awkwardness is the result of redaction, since we would imagine that a hypothetical redactor who wanted to specify that Ezra was "the scribe of the words of the commandments of Yhwh," and who inserted material to an existing text that read עזרא הכהן הספר in order to make that point, would have had no need to repeat the word ספר, and could simply have inserted דברי מצות יהוה after the word הספר that was already present in the text he or she was altering, needing only to remove its definite article. It is possible, first of all, that we simply see a copying error in 7:11. The LXX reflects a Hebrew text that reads the same words, but without the definite article on the first appearance of ספר. The Hebrew the OG translator received for this verse is עזרא הכהן ספר ספר דברי מצות יהוה "Ezra the priest, the scribe of the book of the words of the commandments of Yhwh," and the translator read the first occurrence of ספר as the noun "scribe" (סֹפֵר in Masoretic pointing) and the second as the noun "book" (סֵפֶר). Given the Hebrew text the LXX reflects, it is likely that the repetition of ספר is due to dittography, and that the original text read עזרא הכהן ספר דברי מצות יהוה "Ezra the priest, the scribe of the words of the commandments of Yhwh." After the word ספר was accidentally doubled, the tradents behind the MT and LXX dealt with that differently, the former inserting the definite article on the first occurrence of the word and the latter deciding to read the two occurrences as referring to different things. And even in the less likely case that the MT does reflect the original text, then we simply see an author foreshadowing Ezra's two major acts in the book, his leadership in ending the foreign marriages, where he acts in his role as priest, and his leadership in teaching the law in Nehemiah 8, where he is primarily characterized as a scribe (8:1, 4, 5, 9, 13).[44]

---

43. For an explanation and examples, see Heckl, *Neuanfang und Kontinuität*, 224–6.

44. So Ezra 9–10 never refers to Ezra as a scribe, and there he appears as the one true priest who has avoided marrying foreign women. Nehemiah 8:2, 9 do also refer to Ezra as a priest, but the emphasis in that chapter is on his position as scribe, the

To raise these sorts of objections against attempts to identify incidences of redaction is not to deny that redaction occurred in ancient Judean literature; as Joel Baden points out, the very fact that we have contradictory stories in the Pentateuch tells us that body of work underwent redaction,[45] and if there is no equivalent to this in Ezra–Nehemiah there are still obvious signs of redaction, such as shifts from Hebrew to Aramaic and in voice of narration. In Ezra–Nehemiah, we can see that lists in Nehemiah 11 and 12 in the MT were expanded beyond their original forms, since we cannot appeal to parablepsis to explain the differences between the longer MT versions of these lists of names and the shorter versions inherited by the OG, as Deirdre Fulton has shown.[46] But without being able to compare the MT and OG here, we would have no way of knowing that the former contains insertions in Nehemiah 11 and 12, for no faults in writing style or logic alert us to these additions, and many attempts to identify redactional seams in the book without such obvious evidence simply appear to miss the points that a single author is trying to emphasize, and so these claims for redaction are often a result of a failure to see the logic of the text. To take just one more example of this in an argument about redaction in the Ezra material, we can look at Pakkala's claim that Ezra 8:15b-20 is a later expansion. The verses come after Ezra's list of those who made the journey from Babylonia to Judah with him (8:1-14) and after his statement that the group encamped by a river in Babylonia for three days (8:15a). Ezra goes on to say in 8:21 that they prepared for the long journey at that spot, but in 8:15b-20 Ezra says he discovered that no Levites had planned on making the trip with the group and so he embarked upon a successful search for Levites in Babylonia willing to accompany them. It would not be possible for that to happen in a three-day period, Pakkala argues, and so he sees this section of the story as one example of the writing of a pro-Levitical redactor, whom he sees at work throughout the Ezra material, one who has not, at this point, created an entirely logical final text.[47] What we see in

---

office that Ezra 7:6 associates with his knowledge of the law. By also referring to him as priest, Neh. 8 again contrasts Ezra with the priests born in Judah who have failed to teach the law as he does.

45. Joel S. Baden, "Why Is the Pentateuch Unreadable? Or, Why Are We Doing This Anyway?," in *The Formation of the Pentateuch: Bridging the Academic Cultures of Europe, Israel, and North America*, ed. Jan C. Gertz et al., FAT 111 (Tübingen: Mohr Siebeck, 2016), 243–51.

46. Deirdre N. Fulton, *Remembering Nehemiah's Judah: The Case of MT and LXX Nehemiah 11–12*, FAT 2/80 (Tübingen: Mohr Siebeck, 2015).

47. Pakkala, *Ezra the Scribe*, 79–81. He argues here as well that parts of 8:15b-20 were added even later. For a summary of the material he sees as pro-Levitical additions, see *Ezra the Scribe*, 301.

Ezra 8, however, is not the work of an incompetent and illogical redactor, but the work of a single author—Ezra, assumedly, since this is part of the first-person narration in the Ezra material—that tells a logical story. In 8:15-20 as a whole we discover that (1) the group encamped for three days, at which point Ezra realized there were no Levites, and (2) that Ezra set out to find some and was successful. But the story does not say that event (2) happened during the three-day period during which event (1) took place, and it is perfectly possible to read the narrative as saying that event (2) took place after the three days of event (1). Only after the Levites joined them did the group prepare in 8:21 for the journey.[48]

Arguments about redaction in the Nehemiah Memoir are often made on precisely the same sort of questionable evidence. Jacob Wright, for example, argues that Neh. 1:1b-11a, virtually all of Nehemiah 1, was not part of Nehemiah's original work.[49] For one thing, he writes, the date formula in 1:1b—"the twentieth year"—makes no sense because it does not name the king to whose reign the date refers. The opening of the Memoir in 1:1a, he concludes, was originally followed by 1:11b, which introduces Nehemiah as cupbearer to the king, and by 2:1a, which refers to "the twentieth year of Artaxerxes." There is also a redactional seam between 1:4 and 5, Wright argues, telling us that 1:1b-11a was added in stages. The conclusion of 1:4 has a periphrastic construction, combining the verb היה with participles; ואהי צם ומתפלל "I was fasting and praying," Nehemiah says there. But 1:5 opens with a *wāw*-consecutive form, ואמר "and I said," the introduction to Nehemiah's prayer of 1:5-11. This transition "is extremely rough," says Wright, and if the two verses had been composed by the same person, he or she would have continued the string of participles at the end of 1:4 into 1:5.[50] The redactional seam Wright identifies here is not based on some putative fault of logic in the text but on the writing style and grammar of the Hebrew, yet given that a writer who actually spoke ancient Hebrew as a native language followed the periphrastic construction with a verb in the *wāw*-consecutive, it is unlikely that either this writer or his or her readers found the transition to be "rough." The participles of 1:4 refer to a single unit of action—Nehemiah is fasting and praying at the same time—while the *wyqtl* form that opens 1:5 signals to readers that we come across a new and later action, the specific prayer of 1:5-11, that follows upon what Nehemiah has just done in 1:4 (see *IBHS* §32.2.1). This is not to claim that someone

---

48. For 8:15b-20 as an original part of the Ezra Memoir, see also, e.g., Blenkinsopp, *Ezra–Nehemiah*, 164, and Yoo, *Ezra and the Second Wilderness*, 86.
49. Wright, *Rebuilding Identity*, 7–23.
50. Wright, *Rebuilding Identity*, 11.

such as the author of Ezra–Nehemiah could not have inserted a prayer from a different source that he or she puts into the mouth of Nehemiah at this point, but it is to assert that there is no obvious redactional seam based on the writing style that functions as evidence for this putative insertion. We would expect that any redactor would try to make the transition from pre-existing material to insertion as seamless as possible, and we will have to acknowledge that the ancient Judean writers would have been better judges of what an ancient Judean literary culture would have considered to be seamless or awkward and rough than we are. Wright certainly does seem correct when he argues that it is odd that the Nehemiah Memoir would open with a regnal year that does not name the king who is reigning, but the Nehemiah Memoir as we encounter it has been incorporated into Ezra–Nehemiah, and readers already know that Artaxerxes is king because Ezra 7 has told them that. We cannot be certain that Nehemiah 1 originally opened the Memoir,[51] but if it did then we would imagine that the author of Ezra–Nehemiah has removed the reference to the regnal year in what is now Neh. 1:1 to communicate a sense of continuity in the transition from Ezra's story to Nehemiah's.

Arguing that a particular transition in the text is "awkward" or "rough," that verbs appear in the wrong position or form, is to assume that we know more about how ancient Judeans wrote, read, and heard sentences and paragraphs written in biblical Hebrew than they did. To identify what we consider to be problems with the logic or writing style as signs of redaction is to assume the redactors were awkward, rough, and illogical writers—bad writers, to put it bluntly—despite the fact that we do not live in their culture and are not native speakers of their language, and so are in a poor position to make these sorts of judgments. It is one thing

---

51. Because it is difficult to determine the genre of the Memoir, it is possible that the author of Ezra–Nehemiah has used only a fraction of it, and that Neh. 1 was not originally its opening. The Memoir does have similarities with ancient Near Eastern royal inscriptions—see Sigmund Mowinckel, "Die vorderasiatischen Königs- und Fürsteninschriften," in *Eucharistérion: Studien zur Religion und Literatur des Alten und Neuen Testaments. Hermann Gunkel zum 60. Geburtstage, dem 23. Mai 1922*, ed. Hans Schmidt, FRLANT 36 (Göttingen: Vandenhoeck & Ruprecht, 1923), 278–322, and Burt, *The Courtier and the Governor*, 95–113—and with Udjahorresnet's inscription from the Persian period—see Joseph Blenkinsopp, "The Mission of Udjahorresnet and Those of Ezra and Nehemiah," *JBL* 106 (1987): 409–21—but Sean Burt has also pointed out that it reflects aspects of the Court Tales that we see in Ahiqar, Esther, and Dan. 1–6 (*The Courtier and the Governor*, 113–24). If we cannot be entirely sure what model or combination of them Nehemiah was following in the Memoir, then we cannot be entirely sure of the extent of the original work.

to see the sort of contradiction, repetition, and distinct writing styles that we do in the Pentateuch, but those particular and obvious signs of different sources that have been redacted into a single work are absent in Ezra–Nehemiah. The book has its own obvious signs of the inclusion of pre-existing material—changes from Hebrew to Aramaic, from third- to first-person narration, and from narration to lists—but we simply will not always know which parts of the work were in pre-existing documents that the author included, nor how extensive the author's reworking of this material might have been, nor how much of the book is the author's own writing based on thorough reworkings of oral traditions or documents that we do not directly see in the text.

It is because the author has done such a good job of composition and of integration of earlier materials that, beyond the obvious signs of his or her inclusion of earlier texts mentioned above, there is little agreement as to the extent and composition history of the sources the author drew upon. So, to take as an example a brief examination of the material in Nehemiah 1–13 that is not part of Nehemiah's first-person narration, there is no consensus as to the original relationship between Nehemiah 8, which focuses on Ezra's teaching of the law, Nehemiah 9, the Levites' prayer about Israel's habitual failure to keep it, and Nehemiah 10, the community's agreement that they will keep the law from that time forward. Some argue that Nehemiah 9–10 naturally follows upon Nehemiah 8, and so that all three chapters were part of the Ezra material before the author of Ezra–Nehemiah incorporated this block of text into the book,[52] while others see Nehemiah 9–10 as material attached to Nehemiah 8 at a later point.[53] But there is also no consensus as to whether Nehemiah 9 and 10 were originally part of the same document that was incorporated into the current form of the book,[54] or even as to whether or not the text of the community's agreement in Neh. 10:31-40 [30-39] was originally a single document or was compiled in stages.[55] The list of Babylonian

---

52. E.g., D. J. A. Clines, *Ezra, Nehemiah, Esther*, NCBC (Grand Rapids, MI: Eerdmans, 1984), 189–90; Blenkinsopp, *Ezra–Nehemiah*, 294–5.

53. E.g., Williamson, *Ezra, Nehemiah*, 308–9; Antonius H. J. Gunneweg, *Nehemia*, KAT 19/2 (Gütersloh: Gütersloher Verlagshaus, 1987), 118.

54. Contrast, e.g., Lester L. Grabbe, *Ezra–Nehemiah* (London: Routledge, 1998), 178, with Mark J. Boda, "Redaction in the Book of Nehemiah: A Fresh Proposal," in *Unity and Diversity in Ezra–Nehemiah: Redaction, Rhetoric, and Reader*, ed. Mark J. Boda and Paul L. Redditt, HBM 17 (Sheffield: Sheffield Phoenix Press, 2008), 25–54 (36–7).

55. Contrast, e.g., Titus Reinmuth, *Der Bericht Nehemias: Zur literarischen Eigenart, traditionsgeschichtlichen Prägung und innerbiblischen Rezeption des*

migrants in Neh. 7:6-73, which parallels Ezra 2:1–3:1, would appear to have been a list originally unconnected to the Nehemiah Memoir, which breaks off just before this, after Nehemiah has led the construction of Jerusalem's wall in Nehemiah 1–6 and has noted in 7:1-4 that the city has few inhabitants. There is no consensus, however, as to the point at which the Nehemiah Memoir resumes; for some it is at 11:1-2, which refers to the repopulation of Jerusalem,[56] while others see the series of lists in Nehemiah 11 as evidence the whole chapter is from a different source, and argue the Memoir does not pick up until 12:27, which opens the story of the dedication of the wall Nehemiah built.[57] It is also possible that the list of 7:6-73 was already attached to the Nehemiah Memoir by the time the author of Ezra–Nehemiah came across it.[58]

If in many cases scholars disagree as to where particular sources begin and end, and as to how and in what stages they might have been composed and attached to each other, it would be best to conclude that this is because the author of Ezra–Nehemiah has so tightly integrated pre-existing material into the work that redactional seams are rarely obvious. This would have involved a process of altering material in writings that the author adapted, changing them so they fit the larger work and broadcast the ideas the author wanted the book to communicate. And so when we see similar messages and structures in different parts of Ezra–Nehemiah, we need not argue that this is due to the author of one originally independent writing imitating the work of another originally independent section; it is virtually impossible to tell how the author of Ezra–Nehemiah might have altered any particular document at his or her disposal, but we would assume that he or she wanted all of this earlier work to fit together, with the result that part of his or her efforts as a writer would involve creating parallels in pre-existing material where none previously existed. So we need not assume that similarities between Ezra 9–10 and Neh. 13:23-29, both of which address the issue of marriages between community members and individuals outside of the group, are due to the fact that the former was written in imitation of the latter[59] or vice versa.[60] Given that both passages

---

Ich-Berichts Nehemias, OBO 183 (Göttingen: Vandenhoeck & Ruprecht, 2002), 211–13, and Rothenbusch, *"...Abgesondert zur Tora Gottes hin"*, 230, with Williamson, *Ezra, Nehemiah*, 230, and Yoo, *Ezra and the Second Wilderness*, 69–70.

56. E.g., Williamson, *Ezra, Nehemiah*, 268; Grabbe, *Ezra–Nehemiah*, 59–60.
57. E.g., Reinmuth, *Der Bericht Nehemias*, 209.
58. So Burt, *The Courtier and the Governor*, 56–61.
59. Frevel and Conczorowski, "Deepening the Water," 30–2.
60. Juha Pakkala, "Intermarriage and Group Identity in the Ezra Tradition (Ezra 7–10 and Nehemiah 8)," in Frevel, ed., *Mixed Marriages*, 78–88 (80).

discuss a common issue, we might expect to see some sort of overlap in vocabulary, but it is also possible that some of their shared aspects reflect the work of the author of Ezra–Nehemiah. Arguing that Nehemiah 7–8 has been shaped in imitation of Ezra 2–3, and that Nehemiah 9–10 follows the model of Ezra 9–10, Reinhard Kratz writes that even though these similarities in distinct sections of the book might make readers think one author has been responsible for all of the material in these chapters, "the unitary principle of imitation does not of itself prove literary unity."[61] The claim is true in principle, but it is easier to explain similarities of theme, style, vocabulary, and structure in different parts of the book on the assumption that a single author appropriated and altered older sources and wrote some of the material him- or herself than it is to hypothesize the existence of a number of different authors who came into contact with each other's work, each creating documents that would, with virtually no need for further alteration, fit the compositional goals of a final compiler of Ezra–Nehemiah.

The argument throughout this part of the chapter has been that there is far less evidence than often assumed for many of the redactional seams in Ezra–Nehemiah scholars have proposed, even though the author was clearly including earlier texts at some points. While James VanderKam, for example, claims that only sixty-seven verses in Ezra–Nehemiah do not come from pre-existing sources,[62] it is very doubtful that we could ever know precisely how many verses the author composed or, for that matter, altered in pre-existing documents that he or she adapted for the work. Since we can read the book as a coherent writing that consistently communicates a particular set of messages, including ones about community identity, it is perfectly appropriate to refer to Ezra–Nehemiah as having an author rather than a redactor or compiler, let alone a whole series of them. If we see a lack of consensus about so many issues of redaction in the book, that is because of the author's work of integration, and so there is no need to posit more than one author of the work in this sense, someone who gathered disparate materials and wove them into a single composition expressing his or her ideas. It is certainly possible that some of that earlier material was put together in stages by different writers, but there is almost nothing we can really know about that, since modern scholars do not have enough knowledge to trace those developments with any confidence, and once we realize that evidence for redaction is fairly

---

61. Kratz, *The Composition of the Narrative Books*, 82.
62. VanderKam, "Ezra–Nehemiah or Ezra and Nehemiah?," 63–4.

3. The Persian-Period Date of Ezra–Nehemiah

It may not have taken hundreds of years to put Ezra–Nehemiah together, but simply because its stories are set in the Persian period, with the last clearly datable event being Nehemiah's journey to Babylon in 433 BCE (Neh. 13:6), there is no guarantee that the author did not compose the work at a much later date. We do not have space here to deal with all of the attempts to date the final form of the book to the Hellenistic period, so it helps to know that there are no obvious signs of Hellenistic composition, no Greek loan words or references to distinct aspects of Hellenistic culture or to specific events that took place after the Persian period. This point is not, to be fair, the unanimous position in scholarship, but there is no consensus that any specific part of the book can be dated to the Hellenistic period. So Dirk Schwiderski, for example, argues that the correspondence in Ezra 4–6 reflects the letter writing style of the Hellenistic period,[63] but while he does show that those letters do not entirely fit the expected style of official Achaemenid composition, it is not clear that this is due to a Hellenistic epistolary culture rather than to editing intended to fit them into the larger narrative of which they are now a part.[64] Or, to take another example, Sebastian Grätz argues that since the Aramaic correspondence in those chapters portrays the "elders" of the temple community as its leaders, this reflects the political arrangement of Hellenistic Judea.[65] The elders of Ezra 5–6, however, are simply the equivalent of the heads of the ancestral houses, important community leaders in Ezra–Nehemiah and in the actual Persian-period temple community, as Chapter 5 discusses. The בית אבות "ancestral house" developed as the basic social grouping of the Judeans in Babylonian exile,[66] and their leadership was referred

---

63. Schwiderski, *Handbuch des nordwestsemitischen Breifformulars*, 343–80.

64. See, e.g., Blake W. Conklin, "[Review of] Dirk Schwiderski, *Handbuch des nordwestsemitischen Breifformulars*," *JSS* 48 (2003): 137–40.

65. Sebastian Grätz, "Die Aramäische Chronik des Esrabuches und die Rolle der Ältesten in Esr 5–6," *ZAW* 118 (2006): 405–22.

66. See Joel Weinberg, *The Citizen-Temple Community*, trans. D. L. Smith-Christopher, JSOTSup 151 (Sheffield: JSOT, 1992), 49–61; H. G. M. Williamson, "The Family in Persian Period Judah: Some Textual Reflections," in *Symbiosis, Symbolism, and the Power of the Past: Ancient Israel and their Neighbors from the*

to variously as "heads," "elders," and שרים "leaders,"[67] and so as early as Ezekiel we see references to "the elders of Judah/Israel" (8:1; 14:1; 20:1, 3) as the office of the community leadership in exile at the time the ancestral house was forming.

Others have argued that parts of Ezra–Nehemiah respond to aspects of Hellenistic culture or to events in the Hellenistic period, but this is a different matter than locating specific references in the book to cultural and political events and issues that can clearly be dated to that time. Raik Heckl, for example, claims that Ezra 9–10 responds to challenges of the Seleucid period,[68] but Ezra–Nehemiah never actually mentions the Seleucids; Hugh Williamson argues Ezra 1–6 reacts against the construction of the Samarian temple at Gerizim[69]—which, at the time he made the argument, was understood to have been built at the beginning of the Hellenistic period—but Ezra–Nehemiah never refers to Gerizim. The difficulty with dating a text to a particular period based on the argument that its ideas reflect the kinds of ideas that people at a particular point in time would have held is that the same themes and ideas, and so the same texts, can appeal to many different groups in many different periods.[70] Perhaps Ezra 1–6 was created as a response to Gerizim, but it can also be read in the way we will read it in the next chapter, as a text that defines a Persian-period community and emphasizes its loyalty to Persia. Neither reading, however, guarantees anything in regard to the date; even though we now know that Gerizim was constructed in the fifth century BCE,[71]

Late Bronze Age through Roman Palaestina, ed. William G. Dever and Seymour Gitin (Winona Lake, IN: Eisenbrauns, 2003), 469–85 (477–8); David Janzen, *Chronicles and the Politics of Davidic Restoration: A Quiet Revolution*, LHBOTS 655 (London: Bloomsbury T&T Clark, 2017), 39–47.

67. I. Eph'al, "The Western Minorities in Babylonia in the 6th–5th Centuries B.C.: Maintenance and Cohesion," *Or* 47 (1978): 74–90 (76–9); Williamson, "The Family in Persian Period Judah," 475; Janzen, *Chronicles and the Politics of Davidic Restoration*, 46–7.

68. Heckl, *Neuanfang und Kontinuität*, 296–7.

69. H. G. M. Williamson, *Studies in Persian Period History and Historiography*, FAT 28 (Tübingen: Mohr Siebeck, 2004), 244–70.

70. See Benjamin D. Sommer, "Dating Pentateuchal Texts and the Perils of Pseudo-Historicism," in *The Pentateuch: International Reflections on Current Research*, ed. Thomas B. Dozeman, Konrad Schmid, and Baruch J. Schwartz, FAT 78 (Tübingen: Mohr Siebeck, 2011), 85–108.

71. Yitzhak Magen, Haggai Misgav, and Levana Tsfania, *Mount Gerizim Excavations Volume I: The Aramaic, Hebrew and Samaritan Inscriptions*, JSP 2 (Jerusalem: Israel Antiquities Authority, 2004), 1.

there clearly could have been Judeans in the Hellenistic period who wanted to promote the Yahwistic sanctuary in Jerusalem over the one in Samaria,[72] just as there could have been Judeans of that era who wanted to contrast the beneficent kings of Persia portrayed in Ezra 1–6 with Seleucid rulers of whom they disapproved.[73]

Israel Finkelstein sees signs of Hellenistic-era work in Ezra–Nehemiah, and argues that lists in the book that include geographical names, such as the list of wall builders in Nehemiah 3 or that of Babylonian migrants in Ezra 2, could not have been composed in the Persian period, since quite a number of the sites named in such lists were not settled when the Achaemenids were in power but were inhabited in the Hellenistic period. He finds Nehemiah 3 especially suspicious, since he also argues there is no good archaeological evidence for the construction of a wall around Jerusalem in the Persian period,[74] although his arguments in this regard have not been widely followed, since archaeologists generally accept the existence of a Persian-period wall, albeit around a small version of the city.[75] In regard to Finkelstein's claims concerning the settlement of sites in Palestine in the Persian period, Ziony Zevit argues that the site surveys on which Finkelstein depends to determine settlement at particular locales during particular periods simply cannot provide evidence for the sorts of conclusions Finkelstein draws,[76] but even if we are to accept that they could, lists of settlements in Ezra–Nehemiah likely combine the reality of sites where people associated with the temple in Jerusalem actually lived with an ideal picture of Judah drawn from earlier texts like

---

72. See, e.g., Heckl, *Neuanfang und Kontinuität*, 381–7.
73. Heckl, *Neuanfang und Kontinuität*, 407–8.
74. For Finkelstein's discussion of the sites named in Neh. 3 and his argument against a Persian-period city wall, see his *Hasmonean Realities behind Ezra, Nehemiah, and Chronicles*, SBLAIL 34 (Atlanta: SBL Press, 2018), 3–27; for his discussion of the sites named in Ezra 2, see *Hasmonean Realities*, 29–50.
75. E.g., Oded Lipschits, "Persian Period Finds from Jerusalem: Facts and Interpretations," *JHS* 9 (2009): art. 20; Margaret Steiner, "The Persian Period City Wall of Jerusalem," in *The Fire Signals of Lachish: Studies in the Archaeology and History of Israel in the Late Bronze Age, Iron Age, and Persian Period in Honor of David Ussishkin*, ed. Israel Finkelstein and Nadav Na'aman (Winona Lake, IN: Eisenbrauns, 2011), 307–15; David Ussishkin, "On Nehemiah's City Wall and the Size of Jerusalem during the Persian Period: An Archaeologist's View," in *New Perspectives on Ezra–Nehemiah: History and Historiography, Text, Literature, and Interpretation*, ed. Isaac Kalimi (Winona Lake, IN: Eisenbrauns, 2012), 101–30.
76. Ziony Zevit, "Is There an Archaeological Case for Phantom Settlements in the Persian Period?," *PEQ* 141 (2009): 124–37.

Joshua 15.[77] If we want to see the place names in a text like Nehemiah 3 as a kind of map, it is one that creates a sense of identity for the people, just as other biblical lists like this do,[78] showing the community the true (if not actual) extent of their land and its continuity with that of the pre-exilic ancestors.

Some scholars have argued that Sanballat, Tobiah, and Geshem, Nehemiah's main opponents according to his Memoir, were actually figures from the Hellenistic period, or at least, in the case of Sanballat, from a time in the Persian period later than that of Nehemiah, which would mean that the Memoir underwent editing in the Hellenistic period. Sanballat is known from *TAD* A4.7, a letter sent in 407 BCE by the Judean community in Elephantine to Bagohi, the governor of Judah, that describes an attack on their Yahwistic sanctuary. In this letter they say they have also communicated this information to "Delaiah and Shelemaiah, the sons of Sanballat, the governor of Samaria" (A4.7.29), but this, Sebastian Grätz argues, puts Sanballat in the late fifth century, not in 445 BCE when Nehemiah says he built the wall in Jerusalem (Neh. 2:1; 6:15).[79] Nehemiah 2:19 and 3:35 [4:3] refer to Tobiah as an Ammonite, but Lester Grabbe argues this figure is actually the one known from the Zenon Papyri of the third century and the father of the central figure of the Tobiad Romance, found in Josephus's work (*Ant.* 12.154-236), which means that he was a well-known figure in the region during the Ptolemaic period.[80] As for Geshem/Gashmu the Arab (Neh. 2:19; 6:6), inscriptional evidence tells us there was a king of that name ruling as a client to the Achaemenids to the south

---

77. This argument has been made in one form or another since at least the time of Gerhard von Rad's analysis of the settlement list in Neh. 11:25-36 in *Das Geschichtsbild des Chronistischen Werkes*, BWANT 54 (Stuttgart: Kohlhammer, 1930), 21–5. It has been made more recently as well; see Williamson, *Ezra, Nehemiah*, 349–50; Eskenazi, *In an Age of Prose*, 115; Oded Lipschits, "Literary and Ideological Aspects of Nehemiah 11," *JBL* 121 (2002): 423–40 (439–40).

78. For this point in regard to geographical lists in Joshua, see Stephen C. Russell, "Enemies, Lands, and Borders in Biblical Crossing Traditions," *JANEH* 4 (2017): 163–76.

79. Sebastian Grätz, "The Adversaries in Ezra/Nehemiah—Fictitious or Real? A Case Study in Creating Identity in Late Persian and Hellenistic Times," in *Between Cooperation and Hostility: Multiple Identities in Ancient Judaism and the Interaction of Foreign Powers*, ed. Rainer Albertz and Jakob Wöhrle, JAJSup 11 (Göttingen: Vandenhoeck & Ruprecht, 2012), 73–88 (81).

80. Lester L. Grabbe, "Hyparchs, *Oikonomoi* and Mafiosi: The Governance of Judah in the Ptolemaic Period," in *Judah between East and West: The Transition from Persian to Greek Rule (ca. 400–200 BCE)*, ed. Lester L. Grabbe and Oded Lipschits, LSTS 75 (London: T&T Clark, 2011), 70–90 (73–4, 77–80).

of Judah in the fifth century (*TSSI* 2.25), but, Finkelstein points out, later kings in the region bore the same name.[81]

There is no reason, however, why the Sanballat of the Elephantine correspondence could not have acted as governor of Samaria during Nehemiah's time. The Elephantine community says they wrote to Sanballat's sons, not to Sanballat himself, and the reply they receive from Delaiah and Bagohi in *TAD* A4.9 does not mention him at all. If he was even alive by the time his son and Bagohi agreed to support the rebuilding of the Yahwistic temple in Elephantine, he was no longer an active ruler, and so it is perfectly possible that he was born in, say, the 470s, and was already governor when Nehemiah arrived in Palestine in 445.[82] The fact that we know of fifth-century rulers near Judah named Sanballat and Geshem makes it much more reasonable to assume that they were actually Nehemiah's opponents rather than figures a Hellenistic redactor was recalling from long ago and inserting into the narrative, and if we have no good reason to doubt that Nehemiah referred to them as his adversaries, then it is hard to see why he should not also have referred to Tobiah as such. The fact that there was a third-century figure called Tobiah from Ammon does not mean that someone of the same name, perhaps even from the same family,[83] could not have acted as a local ruler in Ammon during the Persian period. Since Nehemiah calls him "the Ammonite servant" (Neh. 2:19), Tobiah was probably the governor of Ammon, a province that likely existed as early as the Neo-Babylonian period,[84] and so, like Sanballat, he was an official in the local imperial apparatus, as Geshem was a client ruler who owed allegiance to the Achaemenids.

---

81. Finkelstein, *Hasmonean Realities*, 75.

82. See also, e.g., Oded Tammuz, "Will the Real Sanballat Please Stand up?," in *Samaritans: Past and Present*, ed. Menahem Mor and Friedrich V. Reiterer, StJud 53, StSam 5 (Berlin: W. de Gruyter, 2010), 51–8 (53).

83. H. G. M. Williamson, for example, argues that the fifth-century Tobiah was from the same family as the third-century figure by that name (*Studies in Persian Period History*, 18). Diana Edelman objects that this is unlikely, since the Tobiad estate at 'Iraq el-Emir shows no signs of occupation between the eleventh and third centuries BCE ("Seeing Double: Tobiah the Ammonite as an Encrypted Character," *RB* 113 [2006]: 570–84 [574–6]). Of course, the Tobiads could simply have moved their base of operations in the Ptolemaic period, or expanded them to 'Iraq el-Emir at that time.

84. See, e.g., Ephraim Stern, *Archaeology of the Land of the Bible, Volume II: The Assyrian, Babylonian, and Persian Periods 732–332 BCE*, ABRL (New York: Doubleday, 2001), 454–60; Oded Lipschits, "Ammon in Transition from Vassal Kingdom to Babylonian Province," *BASOR* 335 (2004): 37–52.

Beyond the fact that the events of Ezra–Nehemiah are all set in the Persian period, the lists of high priests in Neh. 12:10-11 and 22 suggest a date of composition for the work in that era as well, and more specifically in the early or mid-fourth century. The narratives of Ezra–Nehemiah refer to only two high priests, Jeshua, named as a member of the first Babylonian group to migrate to Judah (Ezra 2:2; 3:2, 8, etc.) and Eliashib, the high priest of the time of Ezra (Ezra 10:6) and Nehemiah (Neh. 3:1, 20; 13:4, etc.). The list of Neh. 12:10-11 says Eliashib is the grandson of Jeshua and the grandfather of יונתן "Jonathan," although 12:22 calls Eliashib's grandson יוחנן "Johanan."[85] Both lists end one generation after Jonathan/Johanan, with a high priest by the name of Jaddua, so assumedly Jaddua was in office when Ezra–Nehemiah was written, since the natural termination point of this list that extends beyond the events of the book's narrative would be the author's present. *TAD* A4.7, the letter written in 407 BCE to the governor of Judah, says that the community in Elephantine had written to יהוחנן כהנא רבא "Jehohanan the chief priest" and other cultic personnel in Jerusalem at the time their temple was attacked (A4.7.17-19) in 411 BCE, which suggests that this Jehohanan is identical with Johanan, named as Eliashib's grandson in Neh. 12:22.[86] Ezra–Nehemiah names Eliashib as high priest around the time of Ezra's journey to Judah in 458 (Ezra 10:6), and upon Nehemiah's return from Babylon in or soon after 433 (Neh. 13:4-6). If Eliashib was born soon after 500, he would have been old enough to be high priest by the time Ezra arrived, and old enough for his son Jehohanan—a different figure than his grandson of the same name, but someone who, Ezra 10:6 says, has a chamber in the temple—to also have been working as a priest by that time,[87] and he would have been

---

85. LXX^AB 12:22 actually make Johanan Eliashib's great-grandson, since after the name Ελιασιβ these textual traditions read Ιωαδα καὶ Ιωα καὶ Ιωαναν. We likely see parablepsis here on the part of a Greek copyist, as καὶ Ιωα repeats the first part of the following καὶ Ιωαναν.

86. The same individual's name could be spelled as both יוחנן and יהוחנן. The name of one of Josiah's sons, for example, appears as both יואחז (2 Chron. 36:2, 4) and יהואחז (2 Chron. 36:1); the name of the Judean king who succeeded Ahaziah is spelled יהואש (2 Kgs 12:2, 3 [1, 2]) and יואש (2 Kgs 11:2; 12:20 [19]); the name of the king who surrendered Jerusalem to Nebuchadnezzar in 598 appears as יהויכין (2 Kgs 24:6, 8) and יויכין (Ezek. 1:2); and the list could go on. In all of these cases the prefixes -יהו and -יו both represent the divine name, and a personal name with this prefix could use either spelling, even when referring to the same individual.

87. If Eliashib was born soon after 500, then his son named in 10:6 as working in the temple could already have been in his early twenties by the time Ezra arrived in 458. Ezra 3:8, like some passages in Chronicles, says that Levites began cultic

near the end of his career when Nehemiah left for Babylon. If we assume twenty years per generation, then Eliashib's grandson Johanan could have been born in the 450s, and in office when the Elephantine temple was destroyed, and we would then assume that Jaddua, perhaps born in the 430s, was high priest at least by the early fourth century.[88] Although Neh. 12:22 is often read as suggesting that its list of high priests was compiled during the reign of an Achaemenid king named Darius, an interpretation that would put Jaddua in office before Darius II died in 405 BCE or during the reign of Darius III (336–330 BCE), the verse says only that a list of priestly ancestral houses was recorded "during the reign of Darius the Persian,"[89] something unconnected to the earlier list of high priests

service at age twenty (1 Chron. 23:24, 27; 2 Chron. 31:17), but no biblical source provides a minimum age at which priests could enter their office. Josephus writes that Aristobulus, during the time of Herod the Great, became high priest when he was seventeen (*Ant.* 15.50).

88. Lisbeth Fried argues that the Johanan of 12:22 is the same high priest whose name appears on a fourth-century Judean coin and who is named by Josephus in *Ant.* 11.297 ("A Silver Coin of Yoḥanan Hakkôhēn," *Transeu* 26 [2003]: 65–85). This is a possibility, but given how common the name Johanan/Jehohanan is—there are thirteen or fourteen different figures in the Hebrew Bible with this name—it is also possible that the Johanan whose name appears on the coin is a high priest after the time of Jaddua (so, e.g., Ya'akov Meshorer, *A Treasury of Jewish Coins: From the Persian Period to Bar Kokhba* [Jerusalem: Yad Ben-Zvi Press, 2001], 14). Fried dates the coin to the first half of the fourth century, but Benjamin Scolnic suggests the priest named on the coin might be Onias (the name is a diminutive of Johanan), Jaddua's son (*Chronology and Papponymy: A List of the Judean High Priests of the Persian Period*, SFSHJ 206 [Atlanta: Scholars Press, 1999], 247–8). Josephus says that Onias was high priest at the time of Alexander's death (*Ant.* 11.347), but this claim is from the last section of *Ant.* 11 where Josephus also misdates the construction of Gerizim to the time of Alexander, so it is quite possible that Onias took office earlier in the fourth century. Nehemiah 12 provides readers with the names of six high priests from Jeshua to Jaddua, and it is likely that these take us from the beginning of the Persian period to the mid-fourth century. See also James C. VanderKam, *From Joshua to Caiaphas: High Priests after the Exile* (Minneapolis: Fortress, Press, 2004), 85–99

89. According to 12:22, "as for the Levites, in the days of Eliashib, Joiada, and Johanan, and Jaddua, their ancestral heads were recorded, and the priests during the reign of Darius the Persian." Commentators often acknowledge that the wording does not seem very clear; for attempts to rewrite it, see, e.g., Wilhelm Rudolph, *Esra und Nehemiah samt 3. Esra*, HAT 1/20 (Tübingen: Mohr, 1949), 194; Gunneweg, *Nehemia*, 151; Klaus-Dietrich Schunck, *Nehemia*, BKAT 23 (Neukirchen-Vluyn: Neukirchener Verlag, 2008), 337. As it stands, the verse says that the priestly names were recorded "during the reign of Darius the Persian," and the context suggests that

in the verse. Josephus tells a story about a high priest named Jaddua, a son of Johanan, whose brother left Jerusalem to found the temple at Gerizim in collaboration with Sanballat, the governor of Samaria, at the time of Alexander's conquest (*Ant.* 11.302-325), but since we now know Gerizim was built in the fifth and not the late fourth century, then the story Josephus relates has misdated important characters and events, and cannot help us establish at what time Jaddua took office.[90]

Despite the fact that Ezra–Nehemiah portrays Ezra's arrival in Judah as preceding Nehemiah's, and of the two as present in Judah at the same time (Neh. 8:9; 10:2; 12:26, 36), some interpret the statement that Ezra's journey to Palestine took place during the seventh year of Artaxerxes (Ezra 7:7) as occurring not during the seventh year of Artaxerxes I (458 BCE) but during the reign of Artaxerxes II (398), a matter that has been a point of contention in the field for more than a century. The later date of Ezra's arrival, however, is unlikely the correct one. If it were, then when the narrative says Ezra went to the chamber of "Jehohanan the son of Eliashib" (Ezra 10:6), the verse would indicate that this Jehohanan is not a literal son of Eliashib, but Eliashib's grandson who, we learn from *TAD* A4.7, was in office by the final decade of the fifth century. It is not impossible that the word בן in the phrase יהוחנן בן אלישיב refers to a grandson rather than a son,[91] but this is quite unlikely, since Eliashib is never treated as the founder of a priestly dynasty, and only in that case would we expect

---

this was a list of the heads of priestly ancestral houses, just as the first part of the verse refers to the creation of a list of the heads of Levitical ancestral houses during the time of the four high priests named in the verse.

90. For some of the problems associated with depending on Josephus's story for accurate historical construction at this point, see Lester L. Grabbe, "Josephus and the Reconstruction of the Judean Restoration," *JBL* 106 (1987): 231–46; Williamson, *Studies in Persian Period History*, 74–89; Peter Höffken, "Einige Beobachtungen zum Juda der Perserzeit in der Darstellung des Josephus, *Antiquitates* Buch 11," *JSJ* 39 (2008): 151–69; Rainer Albertz, "The Controversy about Judean versus Israelite Identity and the Persian Government: A New Interpretation of the Bagoses Story (*Jewish Antiquities* XI.297-301)," in *Judah and the Judeans in the Achaemenid Period: Negotiating Identity in an International Context*, ed. Oded Lipschits, Gary N. Knoppers, and Manfred Oeming (Winona Lake, IN: Eisenbrauns, 2011), 483–504; Gary N. Knoppers, "The Samaritan Schism or the Judaization of Samaria? Reassessing Josephus's Account of the Mount Gerizim Temple," in *Making a Difference: Essays on the Bible and Judaism in Honor of Tamara Cohn Eskenazi*, ed. David J. A. Clines, Kent Harold Richards, and Jacob L. Wright, HBM 99 (Sheffield: Sheffield Academic Press, 2012), 163–78.

91. E.g., Fried, *Ezra*, 395.

the word to refer to any of his descendants rather than a literal child. In Ezra 10:6, Jehohanan is more likely the name of one Eliashib's actual sons, who worked as a priest in the temple and whose brother Joiada would succeed their father as high priest, as Neh. 12:10-11 and 22 tell us.[92] The narrative of Ezra–Nehemiah certainly treats Ezra as if he arrived in Judah during the reign of the same Artaxerxes whom Nehemiah served, since he teaches the law in Nehemiah 8, after Nehemiah has completed the construction of the city wall, and Neh. 8:9 even mentions the presence of Nehemiah while Ezra teaches, although some see the reference to Nehemiah in that verse as the addition of the writer who combined the Ezra and Nehemiah materials.[93] Yet, supporters of the later date for Ezra's arrival point out, if we assume Ezra came to Judah in 458, then Nehemiah 8 has him teach the law after Nehemiah's construction of the wall, more than a decade after Ezra's arrival, and it seems odd that he would wait so long to do this. Moreover, they argue, Nehemiah's Memoir never refers to Ezra, indicating that Nehemiah did not know him, and Ezra's prayer of Ezra 9 refers to the existence of a גדר "wall" during his time (9:9), which suggests that Nehemiah's wall had already been constructed.[94]

None of this is terribly compelling evidence to contradict Ezra–Nehemiah's chronology for Ezra's arrival, as Williamson argues.[95] In regard to Ezra's mention of a גדר, for example, not only does the word

---

92. E.g., Williamson, *Ezra, Nehemiah*, 151–2.

93. E.g., Blenkinsopp, *Ezra–Nehemiah*, 288; Kyung-Jin Min, *The Levitical Authorship of Ezra–Nehemiah*, JSOTSup 409 (London: T&T Clark International, 2004), 106; Rothenbusch, *"...Abgesondert zur Tora Gottes hin"*, 53. Contra Pakkala (*Ezra the Scribe*, 149), however, the fact that 8:9 uses the singular verb form ויאמר and makes both Ezra and Nehemiah its subject is not evidence of a redactor later inserting Nehemiah's name, since the use of a singular verb form with a plural coordinate subject is quite common in biblical Hebrew (*IBHS* §16.3.2c).

94. A standard list of arguments for Ezra's arrival in 398 BCE can be found in André Lemaire, "Fifth- and Fourth-Century Issues: Governorship and Priesthood in Jerusalem," in *Ancient Israel's History: An Introduction to Issues and Sources*, ed. Bill T. Arnold and Richard S. Hess (Grand Rapids, MI: Baker Academic, 2014), 406–25 (417). See also Lester L. Grabbe, *Judaism from Cyrus to Hadrian*, 2 vols (Minneapolis: Fortress Press, 1992), 1:91–2. As Grabbe points out, earlier arguments that Ezra arrived in the thirty-seventh year of Artaxerxes I (428 BCE) have rightly been abandoned (*Judaism from Cyrus to Hadrian*, 1:90–1).

95. Williamson provides an even more extensive list of arguments for Ezra's arrival later than 458, as well as explanations as to why these are not strong enough to make any date other than 458 a more likely option for his journey to Palestine (*Ezra, Nehemiah*, xxxix–xliv).

almost always refer to small walls, such as ones around a vineyard (e.g., Num. 22:24; Ps. 80:13 [12]), but it is used for walls associated with the temple complex (Ezek. 42:7, 10), while חומה and קיר are the normal terms for city walls. גדר can be used metaphorically in the sense of something that provides protection (Ezek. 13:5; 22:30), which may well be its sense in Ezra 9:9, since in 9:8 Ezra uses the word יתד "stake" in a similar metaphorical sense.[96] And even if we assume that Nehemiah 8 is historically accurate, and Ezra and the Levites taught the law more or less as this story says they did, if we want to date this event to the early fourth century on the assumption that Ezra traveled to Judah in 398, then we must conclude the story is not entirely accurate, since 8:9 says Nehemiah[97] was present during the teaching. Yet, assuming this story has some historical basis, it is equally likely that Ezra went to Judah in 458, taught the law soon upon his arrival, and that Ezra–Nehemiah's author decided to date the story later, putting it in Nehemiah's time in order to construct the important conclusion of Nehemiah 8–13, in which, as the next chapter discusses, the people learn the law, resolve to keep it, but discover they cannot do so without the leadership of Nehemiah, the king's representative. As it is just as likely the events narrated in this passage took place—if indeed they took place at all—before the juncture where we now encounter it as it is that it took place later than Nehemiah's time, it is not useful for dating Ezra's arrival. The fact that the Nehemiah Memoir does not mention Ezra is of no more help in this regard, since we cannot know how much of that Memoir the author of Ezra–Nehemiah decided to include. Perhaps the Memoir originally did refer to Ezra, but the author of Ezra–Nehemiah excluded that passage since it did not fit his or her larger goals. Perhaps, on the other hand, Ezra died before Nehemiah arrived, and the author simply moved a story about him teaching the law to a later point in time. And while some argue for a fourth-century date for Ezra's journey based on theories as to how his orders from the king may have reflected a broader Persian attempt

---

96. Donald P. Moffat, "The Metaphor at Stake in Ezra 9:8," *VT* 63 (2013): 290–8.

97. MT 8:9 says נחמיה הוא התרשתא "Nehemiah, who was the governor" was present as Ezra and the Levites taught the law, but the Hebrew text behind the OG refers only to נחמיה, making no reference to his office. The OG likely reflects the original reading, since there is no clear reason why הוא התרשתא would have fallen out of the text, while one can see why a scribe working in the tradition behind the MT would have added the two other words to specify the figure involved. We see a similar discrepancy between the MT and OG in Neh. 10:2 [1].

to confront the Egyptian revolt that began in 404 BCE,[98] these theories run up against the problem that it is not entirely clear if Ezra had any mission from the king at all. As the first section of this chapter mentions, there is no consensus in scholarship as to whether Ezra 7:12-26, a letter purportedly written by Artaxerxes that orders Ezra to carry out particular tasks in the satrapy of Across-the-River, was actually composed by the king or reflects Achaemenid policy. Since the author was far closer to the events than we are, and since we lack good evidence to doubt his or her claim that Ezra traveled to Judah before Nehemiah did, it is much more likely that Ezra arrived in Judah in 458.

The author combined originally independent traditions about Ezra and Nehemiah to create a new narrative with a message that, as we will discuss in Chapter 5, was not widely accepted in his or her community. That lack of acceptance helps to explain why the writing was unable to displace those earlier traditions, which continued to circulate independently, with the result that Ben Sira refers to Nehemiah but not Ezra (49:13), while Josephus's stories of Ezra (*Ant.* 11.120-158) and Nehemiah (11.159-183) are not connected to each other as they are in Nehemiah 8–12. Even 1 Esdras, which is a reworking of Ezra–Nehemiah and the end of Chronicles,[99] refers to Ezra but not Nehemiah. The fact that such traditions

---

98. E.g., Alexander Fantalkin and Oren Tal, "Judah and its Neighbors in the Fourth Century BCE: A Time of Major Transformations," in *From Judah to Judaea: Socio-economic Structures and Processes in the Persian Period*, ed. Johannes Unsok Ro, HBM 43 (Sheffield: Sheffield Phoenix Press, 2012), 133–96 (169–80); Lemaire, "Fifth- and Fourth-Century Issues," 417–18.

99. As Juha Pakkala points out, 1 Esdras simplifies more difficult passages in Ezra–Nehemiah ("Why 1 Esdras is Probably Not an Early Version of the Ezra–Nehemiah Tradition," in *Was 1 Esdras First? An Investigation into the Priority and Nature of 1 Esdras*, ed. Lisbeth S. Fried, SBLAIL 7 [Atlanta: Society of Biblical Literature, 2011], 93–107 [95–100]), and provides Ezra with more prestige than Ezra–Nehemiah does, even claiming in 1 Esd. 9:39, 40, 49 that he was the high priest (pp. 104–5). The chronology of 1 Esdras is also clearer than in Ezra–Nehemiah, and in 1 Esdras the community begins to rebuild Jerusalem at the same time as they start their work on the temple (2:18; 6:8-9), and so the exchange of letters between the Persian officials and Artaxerxes in 1 Esd. 2:16-30 makes far more chronological sense in its context than the same correspondence in Ezra 4:6-24 does in its location. In 1 Esdras, Ezra teaches the law as soon as he arrives (9:37-55), just as the king orders (1 Esd. 8:23//Ezra 7:25), instead of waiting thirteen years as he does in Ezra–Nehemiah. All of this is evidence for the argument that the author of 1 Esdras knew not only of the book of Chronicles, but of Ezra–Nehemiah, as well.

continued to exist independently in Judah need not be taken as evidence for a late date for Ezra–Nehemiah,[100] however, but simply reflects the widespread rejection of the book's ideology by the fourth-century Judean temple community, something that marginalized the work, with the result that it lacked the authority within Second Temple Judaism of a decisive account of the first century of the post-exilic period that could close off alternative stories of these two figures.

Chapter 5 will explain why we would expect such a negative reaction to Ezra–Nehemiah in fourth-century Judah, part of a broader discussion of the temple community and the social location of the book's author within it. At this stage of the investigation it is enough to say in regard to that community that some members of it lived within the borders of the small province of Judah, and others likely lived outside of them[101] but saw a key aspect of their identities as defined by their membership in that group. As mentioned above, the community was divided into בית אבות "ancestral houses," the basic social grouping that developed among Judeans in exile, and the leadership of these houses had some role in local government, as did figures among the temple personnel.[102] The author of Ezra–Nehemiah

---

100. Contra, e.g., Christopher M. Jones, "Embedded Written Documents as Colonial Mimicry in Ezra–Nehemiah," *BibInt* 26 (2018): 158–81 (158–61).

101. So, e.g., David Janzen, "Politics, Settlement, and Temple Community in Persian-Period Yehud," *CBQ* 64 (2002): 490–510; N. Na'aman, "In Search of Reality behind the Account of the Philistine Assault on Ahaz in the Book of *Chronicles*," *Transeu* 26 (2003): 47–63 (60–1).

102. For discussions of this local level of government in Persian-period Judah see, e.g., Rainer Albertz, "More and Less than a Myth: Reality and Significance of Exile for the Political, Social, and Religious History of Judah," in *By the Irrigation Canals of Babylon: Approaches to the Study of Exile*, ed. John J. Ahn and Jill Middlemas, LHBOTS 526 (New York: T&T Clark International, 2012), 20–33; Janzen, *Chronicles and the Politics of Davidic Restoration*, 34–63. The argument that there was no local government in Judah aside from that directly appointed by Persia (so Lisbeth Fried, *The Priest and the Great King: Temple-Palace Relations in the Persian Empire*, BJSUCSD 10 [Winona Lake, IN: Eisenbrauns, 2004], 129–37, and Jeremiah W. Cataldo, *A Theocratic Yehud? Issues of Government in a Persian Period*, LHBOTS 498 [New York: T&T Clark International, 2009], 67–117) simply does not fit what we know of Achaemenid rule, which permitted a wide range of local forms of government alongside officials appointed by the Persians, including democracies, monarchies, and temple communities. See Anne Fitzpatrick-McKinley, *Empire, Power and Indigenous Elites: A Case Study of the Nehemiah Memoir*, JSJSup 169 (Leiden: Brill, 2015), 65–80; Janzen, *Chronicles and the Politics of Davidic Restoration*, 15–23; Pierre Briant, *Kings, Countries, Peoples: Selected Studies on the Achaemenid Empire*, trans. Amélie Kuhrt, OeO 26 (Stuttgart: Franz Steiner, 2017), 43–6.

argues that their identity as a colonized people is and should be as the Achaemenids defined it, and that a good life is not possible without Achaemenid leadership, just as the Persian kings proclaimed. This message to the temple community that they are who the Achaemenids say they are, a colonized group who depend upon the Persian kings to make them a good and moral people safe from destruction, does not appear to have been one that the majority of the temple community could accept. Before we can discuss the reluctance of the fourth-century temple community to widely embrace this message, however, we must explain how Ezra–Nehemiah reflects Achaemenid ideology, and we begin to do so in the next chapter as we investigate how the book constructs this group identity.

Chapter 2

COMMUNITY IDENTITY IN EZRA–NEHEMIAH

1. *Ezra 1–6: The Ideal Generation*

To understand the degree to which Achaemenid ideology influenced the worldview of Ezra–Nehemiah's author, specifically in regard to the identity of the community who appears in the book, we begin with a discussion of that identity as Ezra–Nehemiah presents it. As Chapter 1 mentions, for the purposes of this investigation it is best to divide the book into two parts: Ezra 1–6, where we see an ideal community sent by the king; and Ezra 7–Nehemiah 13, the story of an epigone, a later and lesser generation that struggles and often fails to be the ideal group we see in Ezra 1–6, and so that fails to embody the identity it should have. A community's identity is what defines it, but it also distinguishes it from other groups—if there were no such distinctions then we would not have distinct groups, after all—and so some aspects of group identity are like borders that define a community over against people it understands to be outsiders. Ezra 1–6, as we will see in this section of the chapter, puts particular emphasis on genealogy, cultic participation, and loyalty to Persia as distinguishing marks of community identity, but the key aspect of this generation's identity is its loyalty to the king. It is Cyrus who chooses the Judeans in Babylonia to go to Jerusalem and build the temple, and by refusing to allow others to join the group and its construction project the community adheres to royal orders. The narrative of Ezra 1–6 contrasts their loyalty with the disloyalty of the native population of Palestine, but as time goes on these boundaries that distinguish the community from the peoples around it prove permeable, and in the story of the later and sometimes corrupt generation of Ezra 7–Nehemiah 13 that the following sections of the chapter discuss, these borders have to be repaired and reinforced, and other types of boundaries are emphasized, specifically the community's dedication to divine law and the wall of Jerusalem that physically separates and protects the group, in attempts to return the community to its ideal nature. Here as well it is loyalty to the king, who authorizes the construction of the wall and the enforcement of divine law, making the latter part of his own judicial system, that is key to community identity. As the following two chapters discuss, both the picture of the ideal community and that of the epigone reflect a worldview shaped by Achaemenid thought, for the ideal community sent from the center of the empire in Ezra 1–6 is absolutely loyal to the king, working with him and so reaping the rewards of his generosity, an ideal colonized people from the Achaemenids' perspective. The community of Ezra 7–Nehemiah 13, however, has been absent from the imperial center for so long that they tend toward disloyalty to God and king, and without the Achaemenids to send them true leadership from the center of empire they would soon destroy themselves, and so they cannot continue without Achaemenid rule, which is exactly how imperial ideology presented things.

So important do community boundaries seem to the author of Ezra–Nehemiah that we might expect the book to open with Ezra 2, which begins by introducing the community as בני המדינה העלים משבי הגולה "the people of the province, the ones going up from the captivity of the exile" (2:1), and then lists the group migrating from Babylonia to Judah by ancestral house. Terms like גולה and שבי are used frequently in Ezra–Nehemiah to identify the community,[1] limiting it to those descended from Judean ancestral houses that were located in Babylonia, the result of the exile or captivity of Nebuchadnezzar, and whose members "returned," as 2:1 also puts it, to Judah. Ezra 2, that is, provides us with one way to define the community, since one is either descended from Judean ancestral houses in Babylonia or one is not (although, as we will see, Ezra 2 makes this genealogical identity of the community somewhat more complicated than it might at first seem). There are subdivisions within this group—"the people of Israel" in 2:2-35 and various groups of temple personnel in 2:36-58—but their totality is described as "all Israel" (2:70) and "all the assembly" (2:64), terms the book uses with some regularity to identify the community.[2] By naming the community "the exile" and "the captivity,"

---

1. The community is הגולה "the exile" in Ezra 1:11; 2:1; 4:1; 6:19, 20, 21; 8:35; 9:4; 10:6, 7, 8, 16; Neh. 7:6, and note also Aramaic גלותא in Ezra 6:16. They are the שבי "captivity" in Ezra 2:1; 3:8; 9:7; Neh. 1:2, 3; 7:6; 8:17.

2. For the identification of the community as "Israel," see, e.g., Ezra 4:3; 6:16, 17, 21; 9:1; 10:1, 2; Neh. 2:10; 9:1; 10:40 [39]; 11:3, 20; 12:47. For other places where the book refers to the group as the קהל "assembly," see Ezra 10:8, 14; Neh. 5:13; 8:2, 17.

the book links the group to the Babylonian Judeans, the group still literally in exile, from whom they descend,[3] and even as "the assembly" they are "the assembly of the exile" (Ezra 10:8; Neh. 8:17). The work does not open with Ezra 2, however, but with a story that tells readers how that community came to return to Judah in the first place, and Ezra 1 is another key to group identity, and assumedly a more important one, since the author structured the work so that readers encounter it first.

Throughout Ezra–Nehemiah it is clear that Israel holds a unique position among the peoples in their relationship to Yhwh, and if that is one of the things Ezra 1 foregrounds when it refers to the exiles in Babylonia as Yhwh's people (1:3), this opening of the work emphasizes even more strongly the role of Cyrus of Persia in initiating the community's return to Judah. It is "Yhwh the God of the heavens" who is responsible for Cyrus's rule and who has ordered him to build a temple in Jerusalem (1:2), but we receive no direct divine speech here or anywhere else in Ezra–Nehemiah. Yhwh apparently communicates through prophets, as far as the author is concerned—Ezra 5:1 and 6:14 say Haggai and Zechariah prophesied, for example—and 1:1 even opens with a reference to Jeremiah, but Ezra–Nehemiah never quotes prophets speaking on God's behalf.[4] Cyrus, on the other hand, reports the divine order to build the temple, and he decides on his own initiative, as far as the author makes readers aware, that those who belong to the people of this God should do the actual work (1:3). Notably, when the community will claim in 4:1-3 that they alone are responsible for the temple to the exclusion of other Yahwists in Palestine, they will base their claims not on a divine command but a royal one, and 3:7 also emphasizes that construction takes place according to Cyrus's (but not God's) רשיון "order."[5] Cyrus's decision as to the group

---

3. The term "Israel" refers only to Judeans in the diaspora in Ezra 7:7, 13, 28, and to Judeans in Palestine and the diaspora at places such as Ezra 2:59; Neh. 8:1, 14, 17.

4. We do encounter prophetic speech in Neh. 6:10, but these are the prophet's own words, not God's, and Nehemiah says in 6:12 that the prophet had been bribed to lie to him.

5. רשיון is a *hapax legomenon*, but it comes from a Semitic root that refers to having authority or control. The Aramaic רשו or רשותא from the same root refers to control or authorization (e.g., *Tg. Onq.* Exod. 21:8; *Tg. Neof.* Exod. 12:23), and the Aramaic verb רשי means "to permit, allow" (e.g., *Tg.* 2 Chron. 20:10), while *ršyn* in Syriac means "possession" (Peshitta 3 Ezra 1:7), which reflects the basic sense of one's control or authority over something or someone. Even in Eastern Semitic, the general sense of the Akkadian verb *rašû* is "to possess, come into possession" of something (*CAD* 14.193). Given the textual and linguistic context, then, biblical

who should build the temple is in accordance with divine desire, however, since after Cyrus makes the decision that Yhwh's people should go to Jerusalem and construct the temple, the narrative says that God "roused" some of the Judean exiles to return (1:5), just as God had "roused" Cyrus (1:2). And Cyrus, again on his own initiative, orders that those going up to Jerusalem be supported with silver, gold, and other supplies (1:4), and he himself brings out the vessels of the first temple so they can return with the community to Jerusalem (1:7-11). So if Yhwh has roused Cyrus to act, Cyrus makes a number of decisions on his own that shows him as moving beyond the basic divine order and acting to benefit the community returning to Judah. Temple construction may begin with a divine command, something to which Cyrus faithfully responds, but the king's generosity shows him to be more than a marionette controlled by God.[6]

By opening the work in the way he or she does, the author presents the community as like a colony sent by the Persians to Palestine,[7] and John Kessler has argued that the Judean community that migrated from Babylonia literally was such a colony sent by royal order, "Persia's loyal Yahwists," as he calls them.[8] Whether or not Kessler's historical argument is correct, Ezra–Nehemiah presents readers with a picture of the community very much like this, and the work that they must undertake for the king is good, not onerous, for he acts at Yhwh's command, and is exceedingly generous to the community.[9] He is God's loyal Persian,

---

Hebrew רשיון reflects the authority Cyrus exercises. In 2 Esdras, the word is translated as ἐπιχώρησις "permission," although the less literal 1 Esdras uses γραφέν "written order" (5:53).

6. Contra, e.g., Douglas J. E. Nykolaishen, "The Restoration of Israel by God's Word in Three Episodes from Ezra–Nehemiah," in Boda and Redditt, eds, *Unity and Diversity in Ezra–Nehemiah*, 176–99 (181–3).

7. So also Gary Knoppers, "Exile, Return and Diaspora: Expatriates and Repatriates in Late Biblical Literature," in *Texts, Contexts and Readings in Postexilic Literature: Explorations into Historiography and Identity Negotiation in Hebrew Bible and Related Texts*, ed. Louis Jonker, FAT 2/53 (Tübingen: Mohr Siebeck, 2011), 29–61 (47–9).

8. Kessler, "Persia's Loyal Yahwists," 91–121.

9. Lisbeth Fried argues that Ezra 1–6 is constructed around an original building inscription for the Jerusalem temple that emphasizes, as ancient Near Eastern building inscriptions tend to, the generous role of the king; see her *The Priest and the Great King*, 159–77. This may or may not be true, but her argument reflects the generosity of the kings that Ezra 1 and other chapters in this part of the work emphasize.

to rework Kessler's phrase, not only dedicated to Yhwh's command but interpreting it in ways that benefit the Judean community and the temple, and so in the book's first scene, an important part of the community's identity is its connection to the king: they follow his orders because he is loyal to Yhwh, and he works to their benefit. The Persian kings are not as peripheral to the construction of the temple in the narrative of Ezra 1–6 as some suggest,[10] for without the actions and great generosity of Cyrus—and, in a later chapter, of Darius—the temple would not exist at all, according to the narrative. It is important to the author that this relationship between God, king, and community be established in the text first, identifying the community as a group who seem like loyal colonists the king sends from the imperial center of Babylon—and Chapter 3 will discuss Babylon's place as part of the center of the world as the Achaemenids understand it—before defining its identity in a genealogical sense in Ezra 2.

We have already discussed how Ezra 2 goes on to identify the group, linking the concepts of "Israel" and "assembly" to the exilic Judean community in Babylonia, from which the temple assembly in Palestine descends. Not all scholars agree that the list in this chapter establishes genealogical boundaries that define the community in Judah solely by its relationship to its parent group in Mesopotamia, and that is because the names of the ancestral houses said here to have sent members from Babylonia are grouped together with geographical names from Palestine. So 2:3, for example, states that 2,172 members of בני פרעש "the descendants of Parosh" migrated to Judah, where Parosh is both the name of the ancestral house and the ancestor from whom its members understand themselves to be descended, and 2:4 refers to the number of "the descendants of Shephatiah" who made the journey from Babylonia, and so on. When we reach 2:21, however, we read of "the descendants of Bethlehem," and this proper noun seems to be a geographical rather than a personal name, as do all the names that follow through 2:35, with the result that 2:21-35 appears to list people grouped by Palestinian settlements rather than ancestral houses with members migrating from Babylonia. This shift from groups named by ancestral houses in 2:3-20 to groups named by settlements in 2:21-35 has led some scholars to conclude that Ezra 2 describes a community made up not only of people whose families descended from Judean exiles in Babylonia but also of people who

---

10. See, e.g., Jan Clauss, "Understanding the Mixed Marriages of Ezra–Nehemiah in the Light of Temple-Building and the Book's Concept of Jerusalem," in Frevel, ed., *Mixed Marriages*, 109–31 (114–18); Laird, *Negotiating Power in Ezra–Nehemiah*, 72–3.

were already living in the places named in 2:21-35 when the Babylonian Judeans arrived, reflecting a post-exilic group that was not exclusively made up of migrants.[11] Regardless as to how this list may originally have been used or formed, however, in its current context, with 2:1 introducing it as an enumeration of "the ones going up from the captivity of the exile," it creates a community that is descended from Babylonian Judeans alone. We certainly do see geographical names in 2:21-35, but the list treats those names as if they were family names, ancestors from whom the returnees are descended, for in all but four cases 2:21-35 refers to "the descendants of" those names. When we read about "the descendants of Bethlehem" (2:21) or "the descendants of Jericho" (2:34), Bethlehem and Jericho seem just like the ancestral names of 2:3-20; if readers would have understood the name of each of the ancestral houses in 2:3-20 to refer to the common ancestor of that house, they would have understood each of the names in 2:21-35 to refer to the ancestor of those who at one time lived in the settlement that bore his name. This conflation of a common ancestor with a geographical name is not uncommon in genealogies in the Hebrew Bible, and certainly names such as "Israel" and "Judah" function as both place names and as the ancestors of the peoples who lived in those places, and there are many examples of this in the genealogies of Chronicles where, for example, Canaan is both a place but also the ancestor of the Canaanites (1 Chron. 1:13-16), and Bethlehem is both a place but also the ancestor of the Bethlehemites (2:51, 54; 4:4). Given that 2:1 introduces the list as an enumeration of those who migrated from Babylon, readers would have understood a phrase such as "the descendants of Bethlehem" as referring to Judean migrants whose ancestors lived in Bethlehem before the exile, and so who were descended from an ancestor with that name.[12]

---

11. E.g., Grabbe, *Ezra–Nehemiah*, 14; Williamson, "The Family in Persian Period Judah," 479; Japhet, *From the Rivers of Babylon to the Highlands of Judah*, 96–116; Ralf Rothenbusch, "Die Auseinandersetzung um die Identität Israels im Esra- und Nehemiabuch," in *Die Identität Israels: Entwicklungen und Kontroversen in alttestamentlicher Zeit*, ed. Hubert Irsigler, HBS 56 (Freiburg: Herder, 2009), 111–44 (126–36).

12. It is not clear why five of the names in 2:21-35 are preceded by אנשי "people of" rather than by בני "descendants of" (2:22, 23, 27, 28; the final verse here refers to "the people of Bethel and Ai," while each of the other four refers to "the people of" only one settlement). The case may be that the original compiler of the list did not recognize those names as ancestors of the people who had lived in those places. In that case, "the people of Anathoth" (2:23), for example, would be understood in the current context of this list as people whose ancestors lived in that settlement before the exile, even if they were not descended from someone named Anathoth.

So one important part of the community's identity in Ezra–Nehemiah is that they are all descended from ancestral houses exiled to Babylonia. The community is an extension of "the exile" and the "captivity," it is the part of the group of Babylonian Judeans that returns to Judah, the people who, as Ezra 1 tells readers, is commissioned by Cyrus and roused by God. And while this boundary of descent might appear at first to be a stable border that distinguishes the community in Palestine from outsiders, things are a bit more complicated than that, for some of the migrants from Babylonia "were not able to make known their ancestral house and their seed, if they were from Israel" (2:59). The same is true for some priestly families who were unable to prove through written genealogical records (כתבם המתיחשים) that they actually were part of the priesthood, and so had to wait for divination to be performed through Urim and Thummim to resolve the matter (2:61-63). Yet the issue is dropped at this point—except, of course, when these verses repeat in Neh. 7:61, 63-65—and the apparent ambiguity in regard to the descent of some community members does not appear to bother the author, given that readers encounter no report that resolves the matter. What that seems to signal, then, is that being unable to prove one's descent from Israel—from the Judeans removed to Babylonia by Nebuchadnezzar, in other words—is not actually problematic for the author, and that what is genealogically decisive for community membership is the ability to prove that one's ancestors were associated in some fashion with the Judean community in Babylonia—for 2:59 is clear that those who could not prove their descent did come from Babylonia—even if one cannot prove that one had pre-exilic Judean ancestors.[13]

By Ezra 2, then, readers can identify the community as one with a specific royal commission and thus a specific relationship to the king, a group entirely from Babylonia and sent like colonizers from the center of the empire to its margins to do the divine will as mediated by Cyrus. And by the end of Ezra 2, the narrative begins to emphasize the community's association with the temple and its cult, another important aspect of its

---

13. As Joseph Blenkinsopp points out, the names of seventeen non-priestly ancestral houses in Ezra 2:3-19 keep repeating throughout the book, but most of their eponymous ancestors have names that do not appear in pre-exilic writings, and some (Zattu, Azzad, Ater, Bigvai) are foreign, which suggests that some of the Babylonian migrants were not descended from Judeans deported to Babylon (*Judaism: The First Phase*, 82–3). By including 2:59, 61-63, the author admits the possibility that not everyone in the community was descended from pre-exilic Judeans, which may have been a long-accepted fact in the group.

identity. Upon their arrival in Judah, the ancestral houses donate sixty-one thousand gold drachmas[14] to the construction of the temple (2:69), an astonishing sum of money. It amounts roughly to between seven and nine talents of gold, around or perhaps well over two hundred kilograms, depending on the specific weight of the drachma the author had in mind.[15] In a discussion of Persian taxation, Herodotus says the entire satrapy of Across-the-River paid three hundred and fifty talents of silver annually in tribute (3.91.1); he values gold at thirteen times the weight of silver (3.95.2), which means that the community's first round of donation to construct the temple was the equivalent of somewhere between ninety and one hundred and twenty talents of silver, or between one-quarter and one-third of the annual tribute Herodotus claimed the entire satrapy, of which Judah was just one small and impoverished part, paid the Persians

---

14. The word דרכמונים most likely refers to "drachmas" rather than to "darics," even though the daric was a gold coin and drachmas were issued in silver. No darics have ever been discovered from Persian-period Judah (Stern, *Archaeology of the Land of the Bible, Volume II*, 557–8), and some Judean coins of the period followed Athenian prototypes in their weights (such as that of the drachma) and imagery, since Judah's main trading partners adhered to such standards also (so, e.g., Stern, *Archaeology of the Land of the Bible, Volume II*, 565–9; Meshorer, *A Treasury of Jewish Coins*, 17; Izak Cornelius, "'A Tale of Two Cities': The Visual Imagery of Yehud and Samaria, and Identity/Self-Understanding in Persian-period Palestine," in Jonker, ed., *Texts, Contexts and Readings in Postexilic Literature*, 213–37 [220–7]). "Drachma" is also the translation of the word in the Septuagint; the ן– ending on the singular form of דרכמון suggests the word is an abstract substantive (*IBHS* §5.7b), and so it likely refers not to actual coins but to the weight of the drachma, a more abstract concept, since drachmas were never issued in gold.

15. The Athenian drachma weighed about 4.3 grams, but the average weight of the Philistian drachmas was 3.58g, very close to the weight of a recently identified Persian-period Judean drachma, although the few other known Judean drachmas of the period are slightly lighter (Haim Gitler, "The Earliest Coin of Judah," *INR* 6 [2011]: 21–33 [23–6]). Drachmas minted in different Greek and Phoenician regions had different weights (see Vadim S. Jigoulov, *The Social History of Achaemenid Phoenicia: Being a Phoenician, Negotiating Empires*, BW [London: Routledge, 2010], 73–85), but if we imagine that the word דרכמון refers to the accepted weight of the Athenian drachma, then the equivalent weight of 61,000 of them gives us over 260 kilograms of gold. A talent weighed between twenty-eight and thirty kilograms (Marvin A. Powell, "Weights and Measures," *ABD* 6.897–908 [905]), so this amount of gold amounted to somewhere between 7.8 and 9.4 talents. But if the author was envisioning drachmas around the weight of those produced more locally, then the amount of gold in question was between 7.3 and 7.8 talents.

over the course of a year.¹⁶ And the community from Babylonia does not only donate unstintingly, they immediately begin the construction of the altar so they can initiate the cult (3:2-6). Dedication to proper Yahwistic worship is one part of the community's ideal identity, and it is linked to their dedication to the law, for they build the altar in Ezra 3 so they can sacrifice "as it is written¹⁷ in the law of Moses, the man of God" (3:2), and they celebrate Sukkoth "as it is written," and all of the cultic festivals כמשפט "according to the regulation" (3:4).

By this point, then, Ezra–Nehemiah has drawn a series of mutually dependent borders that define the community: it derives from ancestral houses associated with the Judeans exiled to Babylon, the group that has been commissioned by the king for a cultic act that God has ordered Cyrus to complete; it is devoted to that work and so is loyal to the king who has sent them to complete it; and it acts in accordance with Torah. As they begin to build the temple in earnest in 3:7 according to the order of Cyrus, their first acts are to donate an incredibly generous sum to the project and devote themselves to the cult as the law demands. To truly show that these things are boundaries that identify the group, we need to show that, as far as Ezra–Nehemiah is concerned, they exclude as well as include, that they make the community different than the groups of people around them, and we get the first glimpse of outsiders in 3:3, a verse that says the community acts to establish the altar because they were in dread of עמי הארצות "the peoples of the lands." The narrative does not explain

---

16. It is not entirely clear that we can trust Herodotus's report about the taxation system he claims was established under Darius; Michael Jursa, for example, argues that there were no large flows of silver from Babylonia to Persia, and that it may not even have been possible for the Achaemenids to have calculated how much silver that satrapy sent to them every year ("Taxation and Service Obligations in Babylonia from Nebuchadnezzar to Darius and the Evidence for Darius' Tax Reform," in *Herodot und das Persische Weltreich/Herodotus and the Persian Empire*, ed. Robert Rollinger, Brigitte Truschnegg, and Reinhold Bichler, CeO 3 [Wiesbaden: Harrassowitz, 2011], 431–8). But given that the amount of annual tax that Herodotus depicts the Persians as gathering would have been understood by his readers to be a vast amount, thirty times the annual tribute the Athenian Empire received (Christopher Tuplin, "Managing the World: Herodotus on Achaemenid Imperial Organization," in Rollinger, Truschnegg, and Bichler, eds, *Herodot und das Persische Weltreich*, 39–63 [54]), what matters as far as we are concerned is that readers of Ezra–Nehemiah would have understood the donation to be a huge sum, the equivalent of about one-fifth or even one-quarter of the annual tribute that went to Athens.

17. The Hebrew text reflected in the OG here appears to be כתובים rather than the MT's כתוב.

in 3:3 who these peoples are, and the very term "people(s) of the land(s)" in Ezra–Nehemiah appears to be an intentionally vague phrase[18] that has the sense of "nearby but foreign groups." No explanation is given in 3:3 as to why the community should fear them, but that issue becomes the focus of Ezra 4. Here we read about "the people of the land" (4:4), who are described as צרי יהודה "the adversaries of Judah" (4:1). They are Yahwists (4:2), but they are not part of "the descendants of the exile" (4:1)—"King Esarhaddon of Assyria brought us here," they say—and so they are certainly not associated with the Babylonian Judeans, yet they wish to construct the temple with the immigrant Judean group. The community refuses the request, however, stating that they alone must build, since that was Cyrus's command (4:3).

The opening of this conflict with the peoples links the main identifying features of the community. If it is important to emphasize that they are descended from ancestral houses in Babylonia, and that they alone can renew the temple cult in Jerusalem, that is because Cyrus has chosen this specific group to perform this specific task. It is their loyalty to the king, in short, that grounds the genealogical and cultic boundaries that help to define the community. Yahwism is, of course, part of the community's identity; the book refers to Yhwh as "the God of Israel" (e.g., Ezra 1:3; 3:2; 4:1; 5:1; 7:6; 9:4), and Cyrus calls the Judeans in Babylonia Yhwh's people (1:3), but Ezra–Nehemiah does not use Yahwism to distinguish the temple community from the people of the land who appear in Ezra 4, since the people of the land in this chapter are Yahwists themselves. Unlike the story of 2 Kgs 17:24-41, which describes groups of foreigners exiled to Samaria by Assyria as practicing a kind of syncretistic Yahwism of which the author of that text disapproves, Ezra–Nehemiah nowhere condemns the version(s) of Yahwism practiced by the people of the land. They can have no part in the construction of the temple not because they do not properly worship Yhwh but because they are not part of the particular people Cyrus has chosen to engage in this particular project.

The community was right to be in fear of the people of the land, for they have the ability to interfere with their work, as the remainder of Ezra 4 demonstrates. The peoples make them afraid to build, and pay money to "counselors" who frustrate their building plans (4:4-5). These counselors, we discover in 4:8-10, are members of the Persian bureaucracy in the province of Samaria and the satrapy of Across-the-River. The

---

18. See the analysis of the phrase in John Tracy Thames, Jr., "A New Discussion of the Meaning of the Phrase *'am hā'āreṣ* in the Hebrew Bible," *JBL* 130 (2011): 109–25, especially 120–5.

chronological markers of 4:6-7 place us in the reign of Artaxerxes, not Cyrus, and the exchange of letters between "the people of Across-the-River" (4:11) and imperial officials with Artaxerxes in 4:11-22 concerns the construction of the wall of Jerusalem, not the temple.[19] Richard Steiner has argued that the Aramaic section of Ezra 4:8–6:18 is an archival search report, and that sometimes the documents in such reports were arranged in reverse chronological order, which would explain why the letters about the construction of the wall in 4:11-22 precede those that discuss the construction of the temple in Ezra 5–6.[20] Even if this is true, however, the author of Ezra–Nehemiah could simply have omitted 4:8-23, the Aramaic section that deals with the construction of Jerusalem's wall, or placed it in a more chronologically appropriate position. In the location where readers actually encounter this correspondence, they get the sense that the steps undertaken by "the people of Across-the-River" and Persian officials in the satrapy (4:8-9) to oppose the wall-building were just like those that the people of the land undertook to stop the construction of the temple.[21] So although the exchange of letters in 4:11-22 results in Artaxerxes' command of 4:23 that the construction of Jerusalem's wall be halted, 4:24 concludes the first sequence of the Aramaic correspondence by stating that "the work of the house of God in Jerusalem stopped, and it was stopped until the second year of the reign of Darius, the king of Persia."

Ezra 4 tells us, then, that not only are the people of the land outside the genealogical boundaries of the community, they are the anti-community, their lack of Babylonian descent and exclusion from the temple project distinguishing them from Ezra–Nehemiah's group. And because it was

19. So Thames argues that "the people of the land" named in 4:4 are not responsible for the letter of 4:11-16 ("A New Discussion of the Meaning," 118–19). Insofar as the chronology of the material in Ezra 4 is confusing, that may seem true, but it appears that the author has placed the letter of 4:11-16 in its current position as an example of the bribery for which the people of the land are said to be responsible in 4:4-5 (see below). Fried equates the officials named in 4:8-9 with the people of the land ("The *'am hā'āreṣ* in Ezra 4:4 and Persian Imperial Administration," in Lipschits and Oeming, eds, *Judah and the Judeans in the Persian Period*, 123–45 [129–30, 136–7]), but in the context of the narrative they are, or at least act just like, the "counselors" whom the people of the land pay to advance their agenda against the community.

20. Steiner, "Bishlam's Archival Search Report in Nehemiah's Archive," 661–5.

21. For explanations like this for the placement of 4:8-23, see Clines, *Ezra, Nehemiah, Esther*, 76; Antonius H. J. Gunneweg, *Esra*, KAT 19/1 (Gütersloh: Gerd Mohn, 1985), 90; Japhet, *From the Rivers of Babylon*, 162; Lisbeth S. Fried, "Ezra's Use of Documents in the Context of Hellenistic Rules of Rhetoric," in Kalimi, ed., *New Perspectives on Ezra–Nehemiah*, 11–26 (20–3).

the king who chose that community to build the temple, the people of the land are, unlike Ezra–Nehemiah's group, disloyal to the king as they oppose the project he has ordered the Babylonian Judeans to complete,[22] and so this is yet another way to define the community from Babylonia in distinction from the people of the land. The latter group's disloyal plan to stop the construction of the temple is unsuccessful, however, for in 5:1–6:18, the second part of this Aramaic section, Darius, prompted by the words of the community leaders as forwarded to him by his officials in Across-the-River (5:11-17), searches for and finds a written order by Cyrus to rebuild the temple (6:1-5). This discovery in the royal archives reveals Cyrus to have been even more generous than Ezra 1 claimed, since 6:4 says that Cyrus ordered the cost of the construction to be borne by Persia, and Darius adds to this royal generosity by saying the empire will pay for the temple's sacrifices (6:9).[23] The use of Aramaic documents in Ezra–Nehemiah portrays the community as aligning itself with the empire and its use of Aramaic correspondence to project and maintain power, argues Don Polaski,[24] and that is certainly the case with Ezra 5:1–6:18, where the community appeals to the king through the imperial bureaucratic mechanism of the Aramaic letter, with the result that the Achaemenid supports his loyal Yahwists against the peoples who oppose them and royal command. This portion of the Aramaic section portrays Darius and Cyrus as motivated by nothing except their own generosity; the text says nothing directly here about divine intervention, for while 5:1 and 6:14 mention the presence of Haggai and Zechariah, their words go unreported, as Jeremiah's words do in 1:1, unlike the words of the kings in Ezra 5–6, which ensure the community's success.[25] (Artaxerxes' words

---

22. So at least in regard to community identity as Ezra–Nehemiah portrays it, we need not decide whether it was defined on an ethnic or cultic basis; for a discussion of this debate, see Kristin Weingart, "What Makes an Israelite an Israelite? Judean Perspectives on the Samarians in the Persian Period," *JSOT* 42 (2017): 155–75. Ezra–Nehemiah uses both genealogical (or ethnic) and cultic boundaries to define the community, although these are not the only ones the book uses.

23. If the author makes no mention of this generosity earlier in the narrative, that is assumedly to allow the Judean community to demonstrate their own dedication to the temple through their vast donations to the project in 2:68-69.

24. Don Polaski, "Nehemiah: Subject of the Empire, Subject of Writing," in Kalimi, ed., *New Perspectives on Ezra–Nehemiah*, 37–59 (38).

25. Haggai and Zechariah obviously have some role in the rebuilding, but because the narrative's reference to their work is so vague, with the result that readers do not learn what they said, they are not catalysts of the project (contra Christopher R. Lortie, "These Are the Days of the Prophets: A Literary Analysis of Ezra 1–6," *TynBul* 64 [2013]: 161–9).

in the letter of 4:17-22 obviously have a different effect, which Chapter 4 discusses.)

In Ezra 1–6, the people of the land function as foils of the temple community, and their presence in the narrative allows the author to emphasize aspects of the community's identity that distinguish them from others. The people of the land lie outside of the genealogical identity established for the community in Ezra 2, and so they are not part of the group chosen by the king who act like loyal colonists from the empire's center, and thus have no place in the community's cultic work done in obedience to royal orders. It is loyalty to the king, not loyalty to Yhwh, that determines who may be in association with the cult; in opposing the construction of the temple, the people of the land put themselves in opposition to the king, and so show themselves to be disloyal. Thanks to Darius, however, the descendants of the exile are able to complete the temple by that king's sixth year (6:15),[26] and as the community celebrates Passover and Unleavened Bread (6:19-22), the story of this generation ends as בני ישראל השבים מהגולה וכל הנבדל מטמאת גוי הארץ אלהם "the descendants of Israel, the ones returning from the exile, that is, all who separated themselves from the impurity of the nations of the land to them," participate in the cult in the restored temple (6:21). As many scholars point out, the *wāw* in וכל could be read as the conjunction ("and") rather than as the *wāw explicativum* ("that is"),[27] and in that alternative interpretation, it is "the ones returning from the exile and all who separated themselves from the impurity of the nations of the land" who participate in the cult. Given the author's sustained focus on the migrant community up to this point in the narrative and the sustained distinction between the community and the people of the land in Ezra 3–4, however, an inclusivist reading of 6:21, in which non-migrants join "the descendants of the exile" to participate in the Yahwistic cult, does not appear as the more likely one. Christopher Jones argues that, since 2:59-63 acknowledges that not all of the migrants can prove their descent from Israel, those genealogical boundaries are

---

26. In 515 BCE, in other words. Since the story begins in the first year of Cyrus, or 538, Ezra 1–6 covers a period of twenty-four years, although the author may not have known how long the kings of Persia reigned, nor in what order, as the next section of the chapter discusses.

27. So, e.g., Peter H. W. Lau, "Gentile Incorporation into Israel in Ezra–Nehemiah?," *Bib* 90 (2009): 356–73; John Kessler, "Images of Exile: Representations of the 'Exile' and 'Empty Land' in the Sixth to Fourth Century BCE Yehudite Literature," in *The Concept of Exile in Ancient Israel and its Historical Contexts*, ed. Ehud Ben Zvi and Christoph Levin, BZAW 404 (Berlin: W. de Gruyter, 2010), 309–51 (333–4).

only temporary markers of identity, superseded by a devotion to the restored Yahwistic cult that would incorporate even the Yahwists whom 4:1-3 calls "the adversaries of Judah."[28] Nehemiah's reuse of Ezra 2's list of migrants in Nehemiah 7 as a basis for enrolling the community in genealogies much later in the narrative, however, means that, in the context of Ezra–Nehemiah as a whole, Ezra 2 is not a temporary way to determine communal boundaries, and so it does not seem that the author of Ezra–Nehemiah means to discard it as a marker of identity here in Ezra 6:21. Ethnicity and cult are two mutually reinforcing boundaries of identity for the book,[29] and the narrative of Ezra 9–10, which is also concerned with the "impurity" of the peoples of the lands and the separation of the community from them, will certainly continue to emphasize the first of those two aspects of community identity, since those chapters portray anyone outside of "the people of Israel" as impure. As Matthew Thiessen points out, if simple separation from the peoples was all that was needed to join the cult, then there would be no need for a list like Ezra 2 to define the community in the first place,[30] nor would there be any need to insist on the validity of those genealogical boundaries in Ezra 9–10 and again in Nehemiah 7; 10:31-32 [30-31]; and 13:1-3, 23-28, yet the appearance of the genealogical list not once but twice in the narrative tells us that this is a border continually meant to distinguish the temple community from others.

In Ezra–Nehemiah, it is the king who sets the agenda in regard to determining community identity, for he chooses one group of people in particular to fulfill a command given by God. The community of Ezra 1–6, then, is distinguished from the peoples especially through their loyalty to the king. The rest of Ezra–Nehemiah will continue to emphasize the need for separation between the peoples and the migrant community dedicated to the cult and linked to the king, but the borders of group identity the narrative has already constructed will need maintenance, and new boundaries will be created to reinforce and further define that identity. The community's "adversaries," the people of the land, receive little in the way of definition from the narrative in Ezra 1–6 or elsewhere in the book, because their role in the story is to be the group outside of "Israel" and "the exile"; they are the disloyal peoples who that community

---

28. Christopher M. Jones, "Seeking the Divine, Divining the Seekers: The Status of Outsiders Who Seek Yahweh in Ezra 6:21," *JHS* 15 (2015): art. 5.

29. So also Esler, "Ezra–Nehemiah as a Narrative of (Re-Invented) Israelite Identity," 419–20; Clauss, "Understanding the Mixed Marriages," 110–14.

30. Matthew Thiessen, "The Function of a Conjunction: Inclusivist or Exclusivist Strategies in Ezra 6.21 and Nehemiah 10.29-30?," *JSOT* 34 (2009): 63–79 (71–2).

should strive not to be.³¹ The longer the community remains in the land at the margins of the empire, however, the more like the peoples it tends to become, and as the narrative moves on we will see that it warns that there will be grave consequences for a failure to maintain clear boundaries of identity between the community and the peoples.

2. Ezra 7–10: The Epigone, Part 1

Ezra 1–6 provides us with a picture of the community being and acting as it should, but the events of Ezra 7–Nehemiah 13 take place much later. The story of the first generation of Ezra–Nehemiah ends in the sixth year of Darius (515 BCE), a quarter century after it began, and 7:7 moves us forward to the seventh year of Artaxerxes (458), about three generations after the completion of the temple. It is not impossible that the author had a clear sense of the order and length of the reigns of the kings named in Ezra–Nehemiah, but it is unlikely that most readers did. Fifth- and fourth-century Greek authors could confuse one Achaemenid king with another,³² and so we might suppose many readers of Ezra–Nehemiah among the elite in Judah, and perhaps even the author, did the same. Readers may well have been unsure as to how much time elapsed between the reigns of Darius and Artaxerxes, but the book does contain at least the chronological marker Chapter 1 discusses, the genealogy of high priests in Neh. 12:10-11 that makes Eliashib, the high priest of the time of Ezra and Nehemiah (e.g., Ezra 10:6; Neh. 13:4, 28), the grandson of Jeshua, the high priest associated with the first post-exilic generation (e.g., Ezra 2:2; 3:2, 8-9; 4:3), and this tells readers that something in the neighborhood of two generations separates Ezra 6 from Ezra 7. The precise dates of the events of Ezra 7–Nehemiah 13 hardly matter to the narrative's presentation of community identity, however, for what is significant is that the

---

31. See Dalit Rom-Shiloni, "From Ezekiel to Ezra–Nehemiah: Shifts of Group Identities within Babylonian Exilic Ideology," in Lipschits, Knoppers, and Oeming, eds, *Judah and the Judeans in the Achaemenid Period*, 127–51 (134–5); and, in the same volume, Katherine Southwood, "The Holy Seed: The Significance of Endogamous Boundaries and their Transgression in Ezra 9–10," 189–224 (201–2).

32. For example, Lysias claims that Xerxes, not Darius, fought at Marathon (*Funeral Oration* 30), Aeschines suggests that Xerxes fought Alexander the Great (*Against Ctesiphon* 132), and Isocrates equates Xerxes and Artaxerxes II (*Panathenaicus* 157-158). For a discussion of these passages, see Lloyd Llewellyn-Jones, "The Great Kings of the Fourth Century and the Greek Memory of the Persian Past," in *Greek Notions of the Past in the Archaic and Classical Eras: History without Historians*, ed. John Marincola, Lloyd Llewellyn-Jones, and Calum Maciver, ELS 6 (Edinburgh: Edinburgh University Press, 2012), 317–46.

generation associated with the events in these chapters is a later one and that it continually fails to live up to the ideal picture of the community in Ezra 1–6. This later generation struggles to maintain its unique identity that distinguishes it from the people of the land, and as its communal boundaries start to crumble, they must be reinforced, for Ezra 7–Nehemiah 13 is clear that the group's very existence will depend upon its ability to be the people it should.

Readers are given no inkling of the grave danger in which the community stands as the story of the new generation opens in Ezra 7–8. This material repeats the pattern of Ezra 1–2, in fact: a Persian king with divine prompting (7:6)[33] issues a decree to a group of Judeans in Babylonia to migrate to Judah and carry out an order on behalf of both him and God (7:12-26), an order that reflects particular royal generosity in regard to the temple (7:15-24), and so Judeans make the journey, listed once again by their ancestral houses (8:1-14, 18-19), and bear vessels for the temple in Jerusalem (8:25-27, 33). There is a second migration from the center of empire here, one which sounds just like the first one, and again we see a group loyally acting under royal orders, a new generation of colonists, as it were, just as was the case in the first section of the book. The list of Judean ancestral houses in 8:3-14 who sent members to Judah is virtually identical to that of 2:3-15, omitting only two of the family names from those verses, and upon arrival in Judah they are called "the ones coming from the captivity, the descendants of the exile" (8:35), a description that mimics the introduction to the first generation of migrants in 2:1. This later group seems, in short, no different than the first one that made the journey when Cyrus was king. And from this point on, it becomes increasingly important in Ezra–Nehemiah that there are Judeans who live at the center of the world whom the king can send to correct a wayward community in the colonies seemingly intent on its own destruction as it abandons the identity that distinguishes it from the peoples around. The longer the group remains in Judah at the imperial margins, the more it needs the Achaemenid to send leaders to help them live up to their true identity.[34]

---

33. According to 7:6, "the king gave to him [Ezra], according to the hand of Yhwh his God that was upon him, all that he asked him" (Chapter 4 discusses this verse in more detail). The third-person narrative of 7:1-10 does not mention what Ezra asked of Artaxerxes, but the king's largesse revealed in his letter of 7:12-26 assumedly responds to those requests. Unlike Ezra 1, it is Ezra rather than God who takes the initiative here, but God is still involved in motivating the king to act.

34. See David Janzen, "A Colonized People: Persian Hegemony, Hybridity, and Community Identity in Ezra–Nehemiah," *BibInt* 24 (2016): 27–47.

The bulk of Artaxerxes' letter in 7:12-26 that creates a royal mission for Ezra is devoted to the king's generosity in regard to the temple, thus explaining why 6:14 refers to him as one of the temple's benefactors, but its last two verses order Ezra to implement "the law of your God and the law of the king" by appointing judges and teaching this law throughout the satrapy of Across-the-River (7:25-26).[35] Ezra–Nehemiah never presents Ezra as acting on so expansive a stage—although this claim about the promulgation of the divine law throughout the satrapy provides fourth-century readers with one explanation as to why the Pentateuch was also read in Samaria—just as it never depicts the Persian kings as doing anything not directly concerned with the community's affairs, but the book does portray Ezra as drawing attention to the law in the province of Judah, and the first time we see this is in Ezra 9–10. Ezra 7 introduces him as "a scribe skilled in the law of Moses" (7:6) and as someone who "established his heart to seek the law[36] and to do and teach statute and regulation in Israel" (7:10). He gets a chance to display his legal expertise as soon as he arrives, when he is told that the members of the community, "the holy seed," have not נבדלו "separated themselves" from "the peoples of the lands" because they have intermarried with women from those peoples (9:1-2). This reverses the situation of the generation of Ezra 1–6, who celebrated the cult in the new temple as a people who "had separated themselves (נבדל) from the nations of the land" (6:21), and Ezra refers to the actions of his generation as מעל "rebellion" (9:4). Ezra adopts the

---

35. The case is not just that the law Ezra brings is for Yahwists in the satrapy (contra, e.g., Gary N. Knoppers, "Beyond Jerusalem and Judah: The Mission of Ezra in the Province of Transeuphrates," *EI* 29 [2009]: 78*–87*), because in 7:25 Artaxerxes empowers Ezra to establish judges throughout the satrapy "for all who know the law of your God" (reading דת as reflected by the Versions rather than the MT's דתי) and, Artaxerxes adds, "those who do not know you will teach." So it may seem ridiculous to believe that a Persian king would demand a whole satrapy to be subject to the laws of just one of its peoples (so, e.g., Williamson, *Studies in Persian Period History and Historiography*, 42–3; Lisbeth S. Fried, *Ezra and the Law in History and Tradition*, SPOT [Columbia, SC: University of South Carolina Press, 2014], 17–21), but that is the scenario 7:25-26 presents, and Chapter 4 discusses the author's rationale for this. We need not see this as a historical event, but that is how Ezra–Nehemiah presents it, and so 8:36 says that those who migrated to Palestine with Ezra gave דתי המלך "the laws of the king" to the satraps and governors of Across-the-River, suggesting that this group has been ordered to mediate between the king and his officials in regard to the law.

36. MT has תורת יהוה here in 7:10, and 1 Esd. 8:7, the parallel verse, reflects the same Hebrew text, but 2 Esd. 7:10 has only τὸν νόμον. It is likely that יהוה was added as an early insertion.

attitude of a mourner (9:3),[37] and in his prayer of 9:6-15 we learn why: this scholar of the law, charged by the king to enact it, believes God may destroy the community, since intermarriage violates an important divine commandment (9:10-15). The prayer uses the word פליטה "survivor" four times to describe the community (9:8, 13, 14, 15), since Ezra emphasizes that the community's עון "iniquity" and אשמה "guilt" have both been great since the time of the pre-exilic ancestors (9:6-7), and that resulted in being placed under the control of "the kings of the lands, through the sword, through captivity, and through plundering, and through shame, as it is this day" (9:7). The group that currently resides in Judah is all that survives. "We are slaves," says Ezra (9:9), but the current state of slavery and shame could be worse; God has shown favor to the community by leaving a "survivor" in "his holy place" (9:8), and "inclined to us steadfast love in regard to the kings of Persia, to give us life" (9:9).

Perhaps the most important thing readers learn about Ezra–Nehemiah's construction of group identity here is that the people and their ancestors have continually failed to be the sort of community they should be, one that is faithful to divine law. This failure to live up to their ideal identity is part of their actual identity in this part of Ezra–Nehemiah, and punishment for this failure explains why Ezra describes the community as slaves. As Chapter 3 discusses, the word עבדים that Ezra uses to refer to the community's slavery was likely the translation of an Old Persian term the Achaemenids used to refer to all of their subjects, regardless of their rank, but in this context the community's slavery cannot be read only as a reference to its place as a people colonized by Persia, for it is also the result of divine punishment. Ezra does not speak about this slavery in negative tones, and his prayer does not contradict the view of the Persians in Ezra 1–6 as the figures through whom God now works. The very fact that he can describe the community as a "survivor," Ezra says, is a result of God's תחנה, a word that normally refers to a plea for deliverance,[38] but that here has the sense of "grace, mercy," as it does in Josh. 11:20. As ideal as the first post-exilic generation of Ezra 1–6 was, Ezra's people has a long history of disobedience that culminated in the punishment of the exile. The current version of the community is merely a survivor left over from

---

37. For tearing one's garments and pulling out one's own hair as acts of mourning in ancient Judean culture, see Rüdiger Schmitt, "Rites of Family and Household Religion," in *Family and Household Religion in Ancient Israel and the Levant*, ed. Rainer Albertz and Rüdiger Schmitt (Winona Lake, IN: Eisenbrauns, 2012), 429–73 (434).

38. This is its sense in virtually all of its appearances; see, e.g., 1 Kgs 8:28, 30, 38, 45; Jer. 36:7; 37:20; Pss. 6:10; 55:2 [1]; 119:170; 2 Chron. 33:13.

the original nation, the remnant of the holy seed now returned to God's holy place, and the best way to act is as the generation of Ezra 1–6 did, in loyalty to their king and so in loyalty to God, who communicates through the king. Just as the first post-exilic generation excluded the people of the land from the work of temple construction as the king commanded (4:3) and separated themselves from the peoples' impurity (6:21), this generation must clearly distinguish themselves from the peoples and not intermarry with them, since that is what God's law demands. The law did not play an overly important part in defining community identity in Ezra 1–6, where it is mentioned only in notices that state the community acted in accordance with it (3:2, 4; 6:18), but the law must be emphasized now. In failing to maintain their distinct identity as defined by genealogy, Ezra says, the community has failed to maintain their distinct identity as those faithful to the law, and he invokes this legal boundary around the community to reinforce the genealogical one, which is disintegrating.

The community's long tendency to sin is part of their identity as well, readers realize now, although it is not an ideal part, something Ezra–Nehemiah has been signaling since the beginning of its story with its repetitive use of the words "exile" and "captivity" to identify the group as one whose sin has earned it a punishment that still continues. So what we see in Ezra 9–10 is clearly action undertaken to maintain community identity[39] as the author of Ezra–Nehemiah understands it, and if adherence to the law is introduced as a way to shore up the group's genealogical boundary, it is also introduced here as a necessary part of who the people should be. History has shown that obedience to the law is all that stands between the community's life and death, Ezra claims, and in Artaxerxes' letter to Ezra, the king says that he will punish those who fail to keep "the law of your God and the law of the king" (7:26). Artaxerxes may command Ezra to teach the law throughout the satrapy, but it has a special place in regard to the identity of the temple community since, as Ezra 9–10 says, it bans community members from marrying outsiders, and so it distinguishes them from all other peoples. Ezra's claim that the law forbids this kind of intermarriage may be a reference to passages in the Pentateuch such as Exod. 34:11-16 and Deut. 7:1-4—Ezra's prayer

---

39. This is a common scholarly description of Ezra 9–10; see, e.g., Eskenazi and Judd, "Marriage to a Stranger in Ezra 9–10"; Esler, "Ezra–Nehemiah as a Narrative," 420–1; Ralf Rothenbusch, "The Question of Mixed Marriages between the Poles of Diaspora and Homeland: Observations in Ezra–Nehemiah," in Frevel, ed., *Mixed Marriages*, 60–77 (64–5); Johnson, *The Holy Seed Has Been Defiled*, 80–92; Katherine E. Southwood, *Ethnicity and the Mixed Marriage Crisis in Ezra 9–10: An Anthropological Approach*, OTM (Oxford: Oxford University Press, 2012), 2–3.

"basically" quotes Deuteronomy 7, writes Bob Becking[40]—but Ezra also uses language of holiness and purity to distinguish between his group and the peoples of the land. The community is "the holy seed" whom God has graciously permitted to live in "his holy place," and Ezra contrasts this with נדת עמי הארצות "the uncleanness of the peoples of the lands," תועבתיהם "their abominations," and טמאתם "their impurity" (9:11), language that reflects Priestly and Holiness material from the Pentateuch, like Lev. 15:19-33; 18:24-30; 21:1-5; and 22:2-3.[41] The texts in the law that forbid intermarriage do not actually stipulate what to do if Israelites have taken illegitimate spouses, and so the community's eventual decision in Ezra 10 to force these women from the community (10:3, 19) reflects no explicit Pentateuchal command,[42] but the use of purity language means that any step besides the expulsion of the outsiders would be inadequate. In the Priestly and Holiness material in the Pentateuch, what is impure or unclean must not come into contact with the holy,[43] and so in the instructions in Leviticus 13 concerning those whose skin diseases make them טמא "impure," those so afflicted may not live within the community (13:45-46); only if the disease is healed can such a person undergo ritual cleansing and be permitted to return (14:1-9). By opening Ezra 9–10 with reference to the community as "the holy seed" and using the language of impurity to define the outsiders whom community members have married, the story points to only one correct resolution of the problem it identifies.

40. Becking, *Ezra, Nehemiah*, 53–4.
41. E.g., Jonathan Klawans, *Impurity and Sin in Ancient Judaism* (Oxford: Oxford University Press, 2000), 44–5; Christine E. Hayes, *Gentile Impurities and Jewish Identities: Intermarriage and Conversion from the Bible to the Talmud* (Oxford: Oxford University Press, 2002), 27–8; Saul M. Olyan, "Purity Ideology in Ezra–Nehemiah as a Tool to Reconstitute the Community," *JSJ* 35 (2004): 1–16 (5); Clauss, "Understanding the Mixed Marriages," 128–30; Southwood, *Ethnicity and the Mixed Marriage Crisis*, 136–40; Hannah K. Harrington, "The Use of Leviticus in Ezra–Nehemiah," *JHS* 13 (2012): art. 3.
42. Japhet, *From the Rivers of Babylon*, 141–51. Some also argue that this is not a strict application of Pentateuchal law, since Exod. 34:11-16 and Deut. 7:1-4 forbid marriages to both male and female Canaanites, not just marriages to foreign women (e.g., Becking, *Ezra, Nehemiah*, 52–3), but Ezra 9:2 says nothing about community members having married foreign men.
43. As Hannah Harrington puts it, impurity is the "antonym" of holiness in such texts, and there is a "holiness–impurity polarity" there, as purity protects the sanctuary and maintains the holiness of the people. See Hannah K. Harrington, *The Purity and Sanctuary of the Body in Second Temple Judaism*, JAJSup 33 (Göttingen: Vandenhoeck & Ruprecht, 2019), 24–5; quotes from p. 24.

So the legal boundary that 9:6-15 draws around the community is at the same time a purity boundary, one that demands an immediate physical separation between the holy community in God's holy place and the impure peoples. The idea that foreign peoples are inherently impure is not a Pentateuchal one,[44] but by linking the peoples of the lands to the Pentateuchal understanding of impurity, Ezra uses language that confronts the community with the binary choice of expelling the foreign women or facing destruction, even without explaining how these foreigners are impure.[45] The language of holiness and purity is of real benefit for those seeking clear social definitions and a lack of ambiguity; things or people either are pure or they are not, and if they are not they must have no contact with the holy, and complete separation is necessary.[46] Holiness is part of the community's identity in Ezra–Nehemiah, an aspect of the purity boundary Ezra invokes and something he links directly to the group's adherence to the law and their need to maintain a genealogical distinction from those outside of the group, and so the genealogical, legal, and holiness/purity boundaries in Ezra–Nehemiah really all function to create the same distinction of identity. In fact, since in Ezra 7 Artaxerxes orders Ezra to set up judges throughout the satrapy, and not just Judah, to enforce "the law of your God and the law of the king" (7:25-26), divine and royal law exist in a single legal system. Chapter 4 discusses this issue in more detail, but we can note here that, given this background for the story of Ezra 9–10, those who fail to maintain the genealogical and holiness boundaries that should distinguish the community are also disloyal subjects of the king who authorizes and enforces the law that demands such boundaries, something else that violates the community's true identity.

The community agrees with Ezra's analysis that these marriages are a grave threat to the integrity and survival of the community, and they join him in his mourning (10:1) and want to "turn aside the anger of our God from us in regard to this matter" (10:14). "We have rebelled (מעלנו) against our God" (10:2), they say, parroting Ezra's language from 9:4, which he repeats in 10:10, just as he repeats the point from 9:1 that they

---

44. See, e.g., Karrer, *Ringen um die Verfassung Judas*, 270–1; Hayes, *Gentile Impurities*, 26–9; Hannah K. Harrington, "Holiness and Purity in Ezra–Nehemiah," in Boda and Redditt, eds, *Unity and Diversity in Ezra–Nehemiah*, 98–116.

45. Harrington, *The Purity and Sanctuary of the Body*, 120–3.

46. A point well-articulated by Mary Douglas; for the application of the idea to Ezra 9–10, see David Janzen, *Witch-hunts, Purity and Social Boundaries: The Expulsion of the Foreign Women in Ezra 9–10*, JSOTSup 350 (Sheffield: Sheffield Academic Press, 2002), 47.

must be separated (בדל in the Niphal) from "the peoples of the land" (10:11), something the community has acknowledged is "according to the law" (10:3). Ezra 10 repetitively uses the verb ישב in the Hiphil to describe the illicit marriages (10:2, 10, 14, 17, 18), a verb that is used for marriage nowhere outside of Ezra–Nehemiah;[47] the community has "caused foreign women to dwell" in a holy place where the impure does not belong,[48] and by designating the outsiders as impure, the text describes a boundary that has failed. Encouraged by Ezra, "the descendants of the exile" (10:7) or "the assembly of the exile" (10:8) take action here and agree to expel the outsiders (10:3, 19), and so the account concludes with a list of the names of men, ordered by ancestral house, who had illegitimately caused foreign women to dwell within the group (10:18-44). It is a list that looks much like those of Ezra 2 and 8:1-14 that name the ancestral houses that sent migrants to Judah, and all of the ancestral houses of priests and laity named in Ezra 10 appear also in the list of Ezra 2:3-39.[49] Thanks to Ezra, sent by the king, and the law, which the king promulgated, incorporated into his own legal system, and promised to enforce, we see a purified and holy community at the end of this episode, one whose boundaries have been reinforced and whose ancestral houses are once again properly separated from outsiders. A legal boundary has been used here to shore up a failing genealogical one, and the observance of genealogical purity through adherence to the law once again reflects loyalty to the king, since he was the one who commanded the law be enforced by his judicial system, and who sent Ezra to teach the law throughout the satrapy. Loyalty to God through obedience to the law is also loyalty to the king, and in Ezra 10 this loyalty restores the community's ideal identity as holy, pure, and law abiding, at least for the moment. Readers will learn, however, that the legal boundary meant to distinguish them from the peoples of the lands is not nearly as impermeable as it ought to be, and that, sadly, the community's inability to live up to an ideal law-abiding identity and remain in loyalty to their royal and divine suzerains is a central aspect of who they are.

47. Southwood, *Ethnicity and the Mixed Marriage Crisis*, 166–7.
48. David Janzen, "The Cries of Jerusalem: Ethnic, Cultic, Legal, and Geographic Boundaries in Ezra–Nehemiah," in Boda and Redditt, eds, *Unity and Diversity in Ezra–Nehemiah*, 117–35 (128).
49. Some scholars want to amend the opening of 10:38, ובני ובנוי, which in the MT and Versions continues the list of the descendants of Bani (10:34-43), to מבני בנוי "from the descendants of Binnui," thereby introducing an ancestral house, the descendants of Binnui, not hitherto named in the book (e.g., Williamson, *Ezra, Nehemiah*, 144; Fried, *Ezra: A Commentary*, 406). This does reflect the reading of 1 Esd. 9:34, but the verse in 2 Esdras reads with the MT and other Versions.

3. *Nehemiah 1:1–13:3: The Epigone, Part 2*

The account of Ezra 9–10 is followed by the opening of the Nehemiah Memoir, where we find ourselves "in the twentieth year" (Neh. 1:1). Since the story of Ezra 7–10 takes place during the reign of Artaxerxes, readers know the date of 1:1 is a regnal year of the same king, something Nehemiah confirms in 2:1,[50] and so we stand thirteen years after Ezra's journey to Palestine, and find Nehemiah in Susa, at the very center of the Persian Empire. When he is visited there by kin from the Judean temple community, he asks them "about the Judeans,[51] the survivor (פליטה) that was left over from the captivity (השבי), and about Jerusalem" (1:2).[52] We are reminded that, despite this generation's successful (if belated) adherence to the law in Ezra 9–10, we are still reading about a group that God has permitted to survive the punishment for its sin, and that is still in "captivity," still undergoing some aspect of that punishment. His kin tell him that "the ones left over from the captivity" suffer "great evil" and

---

50. As Chapter 1 discusses, if this was the original opening of the Nehemiah Memoir, then the text most likely included Artaxerxes' name at this point, but the author of Ezra–Nehemiah removed it to create continuity with the preceding episode. But there is some sort of confusion with the dates we see in Neh. 1 and 2, since 1:1 opens Nehemiah's story as we find it here in the month of Chislev, while 2:1 goes on to say Nehemiah spoke with Artaxerxes in the month of Nisan in the same year. Chislev, however, is the ninth month in the standard Babylonian calendar that had been adopted by this point throughout the ancient Near East, including by the Persians, and Nisan is the first month (see Mark E. Cohen, *Cultic Calendars of the Ancient Near East* [Bethesda, MD: CDL Press, 1993], 297–305; Sacha Stern, *Calendars in Antiquity: Empires, States, and Societies* [Oxford: Oxford University Press, 2012], 71–2, 170–1). No satisfactory solution has been proposed to explain this error, although see Williamson, *Ezra, Nehemiah*, 169–70, for a summary. Positing this as a sign of redaction (e.g., Wright, *Rebuilding Identity*, 7–8) is not a necessary solution to the problem, since a redactor would want to write as logically as a single author and avoid an error like this.

51. Nehemiah's use of the term יהודים here and elsewhere in the Memoir may suggest he is thinking only of the community in Judah or also of everyone who could trace their ancestry back to the pre-exilic kingdom; see Karrer, *Ringen um die Verfassung Judas*, 147–52, for a discussion of the scholarly debate. In the context of Ezra–Nehemiah, however, the discussion in Neh. 1 focuses solely on the temple community in Judah.

52. The words פליטה and שבי, as we have seen, are used in Ezra 1–10 to describe the temple community, but, except for the appearance of שבי in Neh. 1:3, they appear nowhere else in the Nehemiah Memoir, and so it is possible that the author of Ezra–Nehemiah has inserted them into the Memoir at this point.

"shame," since Jerusalem is without wall and gates (1:3). Since we would assume Nehemiah would have been aware that the wall had never been restored after Nebuchadnezzar's destruction of it, his mourning, fasting, and prayer in 1:4 is a response to the evil and shame still experienced by the community, the result of their on-going punishment for their sin, as Nehemiah makes clear in his prayer of 1:5-11.[53] Nehemiah reacts to the issue of the community's sin as Ezra did in Ezra 9, where we also see mourning, fasting, and prayer, and Nehemiah's prayer here, like Ezra's, addresses the issue of the community's ongoing punishment for its sins (1:6-7).

Nehemiah's prayer, however, sounds much less dire than Ezra's, for Nehemiah emphasizes the effectiveness of repentance (1:8-10). Nehemiah, we learn in Nehemiah 2, intends to rebuild Jerusalem and its wall (2:3-5), reversing the community's evil and shame, and given his point about repentance, readers can have some hope that he will succeed, since Ezra has just led the community to repent of its marriages to outsiders in the preceding chapters, purifying itself according to the law and making itself more like the ideal people it should be. The very fact that Artaxerxes agrees to Nehemiah's request in Nehemiah 2 thus seems less surprising, even though he was the king who originally put a stop to the construction of Jerusalem's wall in Ezra 4. The author gives us no sense as to when during the king's reign he might have given that earlier order, but now, says Nehemiah, Artaxerxes gives him leave to build Jerusalem (2:5) and even grants Nehemiah's request to provide timber to construct the city wall (2:8). His success may have something to do with the fact that he is Artaxerxes' cupbearer (1:11), portrayed by the narrative as someone who interacts regularly with the king, and for whom the king demonstrates personal concern (2:2). However, Nehemiah says that Artaxerxes responded positively to his request "according to the good hand of my God that was upon me" (2:8), pointing to divine action rather than his close relationship with the king as the decisive factor in Artaxerxes' acquiescence to his petition.[54] The author of Ezra–Nehemiah had used a similar

---

53. Williamson argues that Nehemiah's strong reaction to his kin's news means he is not responding to the fact that the Babylonians destroyed the wall almost a century and a half earlier, but to a destruction of the wall that Williamson believes Ezra 4:23 refers to (*Ezra, Nehemiah*, 172). But 4:23 says nothing about a destruction of walls and a burning of gates, and so Nehemiah here is actually reacting to the state of the people, the "great evil" and "shame" they suffer, not that of the wall.

54. See also Manfred Oeming, "The Real History: The Theological Ideas behind Nehemiah's Wall," in Kalimi, ed., *New Perspectives on Ezra–Nehemiah*, 131–49 (138–43).

expression to refer to divine action to dispose Artaxerxes positively to Ezra's requests (Ezra 7:6), and if God did not intervene to shape the king's first response to the construction of the wall in Ezra 4, perhaps that was due to the community's failure in the sin of intermarriage that Ezra went on to correct. After the events of Ezra 9–10, however, the community is better, more law-abiding, and since God acts positively in response to Nehemiah's request to Artaxerxes, it would seem that the community truly deserves to have its shame in regard to the wall lifted.

At this point, then, the community appears like the ideal generation of Ezra 1–6, and, in fact, the story of Nehemiah's effort to construct the wall follows the same basic pattern as that of the temple construction in that earlier section of the book: the Judeans embark upon a building project based on an order from the king of Persia, who acts in accordance with the divine will, and although the community is opposed in their work by local groups, they succeed. Just as in Ezra 7–8, the author repeats a pattern from the earlier story of the ideal generation, and in this case the repetition serves to have readers draw connections between the current generation and that of Ezra 1–6, giving us the impression of a reformed group once again loyally working with the king to execute the divine will in regard to a building project. The king does not intervene in this story to support the construction as Darius did in Ezra 6, but Nehemiah, who is his personal envoy and the governor of Judah (5:14), is constantly on the scene to safeguard the royal will. The list of those who built the wall in Nehemiah 3 might remind us somewhat of the lists of the community in Ezra 2 (the ideal generation), Ezra 8 (yet another group coming from the center of empire), and Ezra 10 (the purified community), but here the figures named by their ancestral houses, some of which correspond to the family names from those earlier lists, are building together with the various פלכים "work groups" (3:9, 12, 14, 16, 18) that owe labor as a tax to the king.[55] Community and empire work together here but, as in Ezra 1–6, their building project meets with opposition. In Ezra 4, "the people of the land" bribed local imperial officials, while here Nehemiah says that the wall-building project was "a great evil" to Sanballat and Tobiah, who, as Chapter 1 discusses, are both local officials, and both of them are

---

55. For explanations of פלך as a work group under royal control, see D. Bodi, "*Néhémie* ch. 3 et la charte des bâtisseurs d'une tablette néo-babylonienne de l'époque perse," *Transeu* 35 (2008): 55–70; I. Milevski, "Palestine's Economic Formation and the Crisis of Judah (Yehud) during the Persian Period," *Transeu* 40 (2011): 135–66 (150); Ran Zadok, "Some Issues in Ezra–Nehemiah," in Kalimi, ed., *New Perspectives on Ezra–Nehemiah*, 151–81 (164).

Yahwists,[56] just like the opponents of Ezra 4:1-5. They are hostile to the very notion that "someone had come to seek the good of the Israelites" (Neh. 2:10), and so, just like the opponents of Ezra 4, they act in direct opposition to the will of the king, while the community under Nehemiah's leadership builds with him.

So as in Ezra 1–6, an important part of the community's identity here is that they are loyal subjects to the king who build at his orders, something emphasized in the actions of their opponents who act as foils, and just as in Ezra 7–10 this demonstration of loyalty is led by someone from the center of the empire whom the king has commissioned. The distinction between the loyal community and disloyal Palestinian Yahwists who are not members of it is highlighted when Sanballat and Tobiah, now joined by Geshem the Arab, ask if the community is rebelling (מרדים) against the king (2:19), repeating the language used by the corrupt officials in Ezra 4:15, who describe Jerusalem as קריא מרדא "a rebellious city." In making these sorts of accusations here it is really the three outsiders who are rebellious, since they use such slander to oppose the king's will. Sanballat repeats this accusation when he asks of the community, היעזבו להם "Will they free themselves?" (3:34 [4:2]),[57] and the danger he poses at this point is that he speaks these words in front of "the army of Samaria." An attack by "Sanballat, Tobiah, the Arabs, and the Ammonites" (4:1 [7]),[58] opponents who surround Judah to its north, east, and south, is a real possibility according to 4:1-17 [7-23], as they consider using their armed forces

---

56. Tobiah, of course, has a Yahwistic name, and we encounter him in the Yahwistic temple in Neh. 13. Sanballat, as Chapter 1 discusses, is the same figure whom *TAD* A4.7.29 identifies as "the governor of Samaria" and as having two sons with Yahwistic names. Sanballat depicts himself as a Yahwist in Neh. 6:6, argues Gary Knoppers, for he suggests there that he and Nehemiah are not part of "the nations" ("Nehemiah and Sanballat: The Enemy without or within?," in *Judah and the Judeans in the Fourth Century B.C.E.*, ed. Oded Lipschits, Gary N. Knoppers, and Rainer Albertz [Winona Lake, IN: Eisenbrauns, 2007], 305–31 [327–8]).

57. The translation of these words is disputed; see Williamson, *Ezra, Nehemiah*, 213–14; Schunck, *Nehemia*, 123. The verb עזב can have the sense of "to free," as it does in Exod. 23:5; Deut. 32:36; 1 Kgs 14:10; Job 10:1; etc., and this meaning, suggesting the community is trying to free itself from Persian rule, fits the key way in which Sanballat elsewhere justifies his reaction against the wall throughout this section of the book.

58. The MT adds "and the Ashdodites" to the end of this list, but this is missing in the OG. The word may have been added to the MT as a later interpolation on the basis of Neh. 13:24 and/or to create an enemy to the west of the province to make the community's situation appear more dire.

in support of their false claim that Judah is rebelling against Artaxerxes. They continue to propagate this lie as the wall nears completion, and they tell Nehemiah they will report to the king that "you and the Judeans are planning to rebel (למרוד)," and that Nehemiah intends to set himself up as a king, and will have prophets proclaim him as such (6:6-7). Nehemiah, however, enforces the king's will and steadfastly refuses to abandon the construction project, and recognizes as lies the words spoken by prophets whom Sanballat and Tobiah have bribed to frighten him (6:10-14).

As in Ezra 4, Yahwism is not something that distinguishes the community from those outside of it; Sanballat and Tobiah are Yahwists, as are Shemaiah and Noadiah, two of the prophets whom Nehemiah identifies by name as opposed to his work. In the narrative of the wall construction, it is loyally working with the king who enacts the divine will that distinguishes the community from outsiders, and the king is represented by Nehemiah, whom he has sent. The very fact that officials disloyal to the king could launch an attack on Jerusalem points to the necessity of the wall: the community will constantly be at the mercy of such people, subject to their evil whims that oppose the desire of the Achaemenid and God, until this wall can be built. The community needs a defense so it can remain loyal to the king and not be coerced into supporting whatever disloyal plans these corrupt local leaders might hatch.[59]

This physical barrier between the community—or Jerusalem, at any rate—and their adversaries does not solve all of their problems, however. No sooner does Nehemiah refer to the completion of the wall than he discusses the influence Tobiah wields within the community because both he and his son have married group members (6:17-19). Ezra 9–10 said nothing about the existence of marriages between community members and foreign men, but the law(s) to which Ezra referred in Ezra 9:10-15 banned all marriages with foreigners, and so in the years between that time and the completion of the wall at least some within the community

---

59. Paul Byun argues that the final form of Neh. 1–13 has been constructed in such a way that it plays down the effectiveness of the wall ("Diminishing the Effectiveness of the Wall in Nehemiah: A Narratological Analysis of the Nehemiah Memoir and Third-person Narration," *JHS* 18 [2018]: art. 5), but this argument ignores not just the large amount of space devoted to the wall construction in Neh. 3–4 and 6, but also the fact that Nehemiah has embarked upon a joint building project, in which the wall is built along with Jerusalem and is only one part of that project (Neh. 2:3-5). This is why the culmination of Nehemiah's story (before the denouement of Neh. 13) is a third-person narrative of the dedication of the wall and the repopulation of the city it protects (Neh. 11–12). Nehemiah's own first-person narrative in Neh. 4 demonstrates the real need for such protection.

have once again violated the genealogical, legal, and purity boundaries that are supposed to separate the group from those around it so they can maintain their true identity and remain loyal to God and the king who promulgates and enforces divine law. The physical barrier of the wall cannot overcome the community's own tendency to sin, which has allowed Tobiah to exercise insidious influence within the group. Nor can it stop the community from displacing its own members out among the peoples, once again illegitimately mixing the holy with the impure and violating the purity boundary meant to separate the group from outsiders. Community members have been forced to sell their children into slavery (5:5) because their land has been taken by "their Judean kin" (5:1) after they defaulted on the interest owed on funds they borrowed in order to survive a famine (5:2-3, 7). As Nehemiah convenes "a great assembly" to deal with the problem, he specifically notes that the community had been purchasing "our kin, the Judeans sold to the nations," even as some group members are now forcing others to sell their own children, "your kin," to the peoples once more in order to survive (5:7-9). Some in the community blame the financial crisis on מדת המלך, a tax owed to the crown for, among other things, use of royal land,[60] but, Nehemiah says, the problem is the community itself, since some of them have taken advantage of the failure of other Judeans to keep up with their loan payments and have seized their land, and he finds the solution not in trying to reduce an imperial tax but in demanding the community stop charging interest to its own members and to return land taken in pledge for the loans (5:10-11). Nehemiah does not use the verb ישב in the Hiphil to address the problem of community families selling their children to the peoples, but the book presents him as dealing with the same problem of an illegitimate mixing with foreigners as Ezra 9–10, which does use הושיב. Despite what some in the community believe, a royal tax does not lie at the root of their problem in this regard, and Nehemiah himself does not mention the tax at all; the real issue is that some community members exhibit little respect for the boundaries of identity that should distinguish them from the peoples.[61] And as we

---

60. Lisbeth S. Fried, "Exploitation of Depopulated Land in Achaemenid Judah," in *The Economy of Ancient Judah in its Historical Context*, ed. Marvin Lloyd Miller, Ehud Ben Zvi, and Gary N. Knoppers (Winona Lake, IN: Eisenbrauns, 2015), 151–64 (158–60); Peter Altmann, *Economics in Persian-Period Biblical Texts: Their Interactions with Economic Developments in the Persian Period and Earlier Biblical Traditions*, FAT 109 (Tübingen: Mohr Siebeck, 2016), 232.

61. See Janzen, "The Cries of Jerusalem," 131. Nehemiah himself admits to charging interest on loans to fellow Judeans (5:10), but he does not claim any responsibility for taking land given in pledge by the debtors (5:11), the sort of thing that

will see in Nehemiah 8–10, this disregard on the community's part to safeguard the borders that Ezra–Nehemiah has drawn around it, its refusal to live up to the identity it ought to have, goes beyond the problems raised in Nehemiah 5 and 6:17-19.

The problems with community identity in Nehemiah 8–10 are preceded by a reiteration of the group's genealogical boundaries in Nehemiah 7, where we see a near-verbatim repetition of the list of Ezra 2 of those of the first post-exilic generation who migrated to Judah, as if the author of Ezra–Nehemiah wanted to contrast the two generations. This genealogical boundary is still in force, for as God moves Nehemiah to enroll the people in genealogies, he turns to this "book of the genealogy of the ones going up at the first" (7:5), apparently as the basis for updated records he wants to create. So 7:6-72 [73] returns readers to the original post-exilic community, "the ones going up from the captivity of the exile" (7:6), who gave so generously to found the temple (7:69-71 [70-72]). The claim of Ezra 2:59 that some migrants "were not able to make known their ancestral house or their seed, if they were from Israel," is repeated in Neh. 7:61, and 7:64 says, as Ezra 2:62 does, that some of the priests who moved to Judah were not enrolled in written genealogies. Close readers will notice that the report of the community's donations to the construction of the temple in Neh. 7:69-71 [70-72] is somewhat different than that of Ezra 2:68-69, and perhaps that simply makes the point that documents not composed by the kings will not always be entirely reliable, rather as Ezra–Nehemiah privileges royal over prophetic speech.[62] But 7:6-72 [73]

would have caused people to sell their children into slavery. In regard to charging interest in 5:10, he says "let us stop" doing this, but when it comes to returning land, he addresses the community in 5:11 with a verb in the second person. His claim to be innocent of impoverishing his fellow community members even while admitting to taking interest from them may seem disingenuous—and this is not the only place in the Memoir that might raise questions in regard to Nehemiah's honesty, as David Clines points out in "The Nehemiah Memoir: The Perils of Autobiography," in *What Does Eve Do to Help? and Other Readerly Questions*, JSOTSup 94 (Sheffield: Sheffield Academic Press, 1990), 124–64—but this is the stance that Nehemiah, and so Ezra–Nehemiah as a whole, maintains.

62. The differences between Ezra 2:1–3:1 and Neh. 7:6-73 are minor, but they are noticeable enough to suggest that the author of Ezra–Nehemiah worked with two somewhat different versions of the list. Arguments as to whether the list originally appeared in Neh. 7 (e.g., Williamson, *Studies in Persian Period History*, 245–6) or Ezra 2 (e.g., Blenkinsopp, *Ezra–Nehemiah*, 43–4), then, overlook the point that the two lists are different enough that it was not copied from one place to another by a different author or redactor. The list simply existed in two somewhat different forms, like the list of Neh. 11:3-19 and that of 1 Chron. 9:2-17 (e.g., H. G. M. Williamson,

is close enough to the version in Ezra 2 that it is clear the genealogical boundaries of the community have not changed, or at least they are not supposed to change, even if some members of Ezra and Nehemiah's generation act as if that is not true as they intermarry with foreigners and force their kin to sell their children to the peoples in order to survive. The narrative of Ezra–Nehemiah does no more at this point of the story than it did in Ezra 1–6 to resolve the problem of those who could not prove their descent from Israel, so again the genealogical border privileges migration from Babylonia in establishing genealogical identity for the group.

Nehemiah 8–10, however, tells readers that the genealogical boundary will not matter unless those inside of it can keep the law. Ezra reappears in the narrative to teach Torah, and now the law clearly involves more than just an imperative of separation from the peoples. "All the people" themselves request the teaching of "the book of the law of Moses that Yhwh commanded Israel" (8:1), and Ezra and the Levites embark upon a process of helping the people בין "understand" it (8:7), and understanding results (8:2, 3, 8). The response of "all the people" to their new understanding is to weep (8:9), assumedly because they now realize they had not been obeying the law, and perhaps also because, given the content of the upcoming prayer of 9:6-37, they have been reminded of the grave consequences of this failure. They discover they must celebrate Sukkoth (8:14), a notable contrast with the first post-exilic generation who kept that festival "as it is written" upon arrival in Judah, offering the proper sacrifices for it and all the other "holy festivals of Yhwh," and doing so "according to the regulation" (Ezra 3:4-5), without any need for anyone to teach them about the commandments written in the law. Clearly, however, that law had been forgotten for some time, and only after this teaching does "all the assembly, the ones returning from the captivity" (8:17) again act "according to the regulation in regard to Sukkoth" (8:18) like their ancestors in Ezra 3.

1 and 2 Chronicles, NCBC [Grand Rapids, MI: Eerdmans, 1982], 87–8; James T. Sparks, *The Chronicler's Genealogies: Towards an Understanding of 1 Chronicles 1–9*, SBLAB 28 [Leiden: Brill, 2008], 348–9). The differences between the two versions are minor, however, and the names of the ancestral houses are virtually identical. So although בני in Ezra 2:10 is בנוי in Neh. 7:15, יורה in Ezra 2:18 is חריף in Neh. 7:24, and the name Magbish in Ezra 2:30 is missing from Neh. 7 (although it does appear in LXX[ASL] Neh. 7:33), the point the text is making about an unchanging genealogical identity for the community is not compromised. Of the thirty-nine lay ancestral houses named in Ezra 2:3-35, thirty-six names in Neh. 7:8-38 remain the same, and all of the priestly and Levitical ancestral houses are identical in both chapters.

The king may have commanded Ezra to teach the law throughout the entire satrapy, but in the narrative of Nehemiah 8–10 the law is something that affects only Israel; it is "written in the law Yhwh commanded Israel" that "the Israelites" should celebrate Sukkoth (8:14), and failure in obedience to the law is, as far as we can tell in 9:6-37, something that affects only Israel. The law distinguishes Israel from the peoples not only because it mandates separation from them, but also because it is the key aspect of God's covenant with the descendants of Abraham, the figure whom God chose (9:7-8, 13-14), and so as a reaction to understanding the law, and as they "confessed their sins and the iniquities of their ancestors" in 9:6-37, "the seed of Israel were separated from all the foreigners" (9:2). And what the Levites confess on the people's behalf in the prayer of 9:6-37[63] reflects to some degree Ezra's prayer of Ezra 9:6-15: the community's ancestors were sinful and repetitively refused to keep the law, and so God consistently handed them over to "the peoples of the lands" (Neh. 9:26-31); because the ancestors לא עבדוך "did not serve you" in the land God so generously gave them (9:35), אנחנו עבדים "we are servants/slaves" in that same land (9:36), since a failure to serve God results in slavery to foreigners.[64] The land's "great yield belongs to the kings whom you set over us because of our sins," the Levites confess, and so "we are in great distress" (9:37). As in Ezra 9, a key aspect of the community's identity is its tendency to sin, something that has resulted in the group's current status as עבדים, and if it is going to be the people it truly should be, this must come to an end, which is the point of the community's agreement to keep the law in Nehemiah 10. It is no wonder that some readers see Nehemiah 8–10, or even Nehemiah 9 itself, as the climax of the book,[65] since it appears to point to a key shift in the community's understanding of the law and how they must change so that adherence to it becomes the central aspect of their identity.

But as much as the prayers of Ezra 9 and Nehemiah 9 seem to have in common—and Michael Duggan has identified thirty-two words and

---

63. According to the OG, Ezra rather than the Levites is responsible for the prayer of Neh. 9:6-37 (see 2 Esd. 9:6), but the MT and the other Versions present this prayer as a continuation of the Levites' speech that begins in 9:5. The opening phrase that we see in LXX 9:6, καὶ εἶπεν Εσδρας, is a later insertion that links an important speech in the book to the well known character who in Neh. 8 taught the law, the significance of which Neh. 9:6-37 reflects upon.

64. Williamson, *Studies in Persian Period History*, 290.

65. E.g., Rolf Rendtorff, "Noch einmal: Esra und das 'Gesetz,'" *ZAW* 111 (1999): 89–91; Tamara Cohn Eskenazi, "Nehemiah 9–10: Structure and Significance," *JHS* 3 (2001): art. 9 (18–19).

phrases that they share⁶⁶—there are important differences, perhaps the most significant being the frequently noted fact that in Ezra 9 the community's status as "slaves" is portrayed as the result of divine mercy, whereas in Nehemiah 9 this is not a positive aspect of the community's identity, since as a result of it the group finds itself "in great distress." And because "the kings whom you set over us" are the immediate cause of this distress, the prayer thus appears to portray the Persian kings negatively, something we see nowhere else in the book,[67] except perhaps in Ezra 4:17-22, when Artaxerxes has been misled by officials in Across-the-River and orders a halt to the construction of the wall. This being said, both Ezra 9 and Nehemiah 9 identify the community's state of slavery as part of the punishment for the sins of the ancestors and as an act of divine mercy on God's part, since that sin could have led to complete annihilation, and the Levites refer to Yhwh's "great mercies" and "grace" in this regard (Neh. 9:31).[68] In the contexts in which we find them, both prayers indict the current generation along with the ancestors, since that of Ezra 9 reacts to the unlawful intermarriages and the prayer of Nehemiah 9 appears after the community realizes they have not been keeping the law, yet the pattern established in Neh. 9:26-31, in which sin and punishment are always followed by forgiveness, leaves readers with a much more hopeful vision of the future than Ezra 9 does. This pattern can lead readers to expect that God will relent from the punishment that has made the community slaves to the foreign kings and put them in great distress, and so to believe also that God might restore independence to them from the Achaemenids.[69]

66. Michael W. Duggan, "Ezra 9:6-15: A Penitential Prayer within its Literary Setting," in *Seeking the Favor of God*, ed. Mark J. Boda, Daniel K. Falk, and Rodney A. Werline, SBLEJL 21-23 (Atlanta: Society of Biblical Literature, 2006–2008), 1:165–80 (175–6).

67. See, e.g., Waldemar Chrostowski, "An Examination of Conscience by God's People as Exemplified in Neh 9,6-37," *BZ* 34 (1990): 253–61 (261); Duggan, *The Covenant Renewal in Ezra–Nehemiah (Neh 7:72B–10:40)*, 231–2; Armin Siedlicki, "Contextualizations of Ezra–Nehemiah," in Boda and Redditt, eds, *Unity and Diversity in Ezra–Nehemiah*, 263–76 (271–2); Klaas A. D. Smelik, "Nehemiah as a 'Court Jew,'" in Kalimi, ed., *New Perspectives on Ezra–Nehemiah*, 61–72 (71–2).

68. See also Manfred Oeming, "'See, we are serving today' (Nehemiah 9:36): Nehemiah 9 as a Theological Interpretation of the Persian Period," in Lipschits and Oeming, eds, *Judah and the Judeans in the Persian Period*, 571–88 (580–1).

69. So, e.g., Blenkinsopp, *Ezra–Nehemiah*, 307–8; Rodney Alan Werline, *Penitential Prayer in Second Temple Judaism: The Development of a Religious Institution*, SBLEJL 13 (Atlanta: Scholars Press, 1998), 58–9; Harm van Grol, "'Indeed, servants we are': Ezra 9, Nehemiah 9 and 2 Chronicles 12 Compared," in *The Crisis of Israelite Religion: Transformation of Religious Tradition in Exilic and Post-Exilic*

God, after all, had saved the ancestors who had been in עבדה "slavery" in Egypt (9:17), before Israel became a sinful people, and so can do the same for this generation if it repents.[70]

Nehemiah 9 does not explicitly state that independence will be the reward for repentance, but a reasonable reader could conclude that if the community makes obedience to the law central to their identity then they can expect an end to their current distress. Just as the prayer says in regard to Abraham that לבבו נאמן "his heart was faithful" (9:8), the community resolves in light of its confession to make an אמנה "agreement" (10:1 [9:38]),[71] as they attempt to identify with faithful Abraham and against their sinful ancestors.[72] The agreement describes the community as "all who are separated from the peoples of the lands to the law of God" (10:29 [28]), emphasizing yet again that obedience to the law is not only part of the community's ideal identity but also distinguishes them from outsiders. The community swears to keep God's law (10:30 [29]), which means the following: they must not intermarry with "the peoples of the land" (10:31 [30]) or buy goods from them on the Sabbath (10:32a [31a]); they must observe the Sabbath year (10:32b [31b]); and they must also faithfully fill the לשכות "chambers" (10:38, 39, 40 [37, 38, 39]) of the temple to provide for the cult and its personnel (10:33-40 [32-39]), which involves specific matters such as supplying the temple with the wood offering (10:35 [34]) and first fruits (10:36 [35]). This list of legal duties is preceded by a long series of signatories to the agreement in 10:2-28 [1-27], beginning with Nehemiah and including many of the family names of the lay ancestral houses that appear in the genealogy of Ezra 2 and Nehemiah 7 (10:15-20 [14-19]) and in the list of the wall builders of Nehemiah 3 (10:21-28 [20-27]). In 10:2-9 [1-8] we also see some of the priestly names that will appear in the lists of Neh. 12:1-7, 12-21, and in 10:10-14 [9-13] we find

---

Times, ed. Bob Becking and Marjo C. A. Korpel, OTS 42 (Leiden: Brill, 1999), 209–27 (217–18); Richard J. Bautch, *Developments in Genre between Post-Exilic Penitential Prayers and the Psalms of Communal Lament*, SBLAB 7 (Atlanta: Society of Biblical Literature, 2003), 135; H. G. M. Williamson, "The Temple and History in Presentations of Restoration in Ezra–Nehemiah," in *Reading the Law: Studies in Honour of Gordon J. Wenham*, ed. J. G. McConville and Karl Möller, LHBOTS 461 (New York: T&T Clark International, 2007), 156–70 (168–9).

70. Volker Pröbstl, *Nehemia 9, Psalm 106 und Psalm 136 und die Rezeption des Pentateuchs* (Göttingen: Cuvillier Verlag, 1997), 27–8.

71. Eskenazi, "Nehemiah 9–10," 17–18.

72. Katherine E. Southwood, "'But now…do not let all this hardship seem insignificant before you': Ethnic History and Nehemiah 9," *SEÅ* 79 (2014): 1–23 (20–1).

names of Levites who appear in Neh. 9:4-5. The list of signatories here, that is, acts rather as the list of Ezra 10:18-44, which named the men who had agreed to send away their foreign wives, and becomes the portrait of a community newly purified from past sinful habits and dedicated to a law-abiding future.

Only now is the community worthy to enter "the holy city" (11:1), and so the lists of names in Neh. 11:1-24[73] of community members who relocate to Jerusalem might remind readers of the lists of those who migrated to Judah. The community we now see appears truly linked to the first generation of returnees, not just descended from them but separated from the peoples as that generation was, their group identity protected by genealogies, the divine law the king promotes, and Jerusalem's new wall, which provides protection from the disloyal coercion that evil local figures like Sanballat and Tobiah might try to exert against the community, and which the priests and Levites now purify along with the people (12:30). On the same day the wall is dedicated, offerings are established to collect the income of the temple personnel the group had promised in Nehemiah 10 to provide (12:44),[74] "and all Israel in the days of Zerubbabel and in the days of Nehemiah"[75] delivered to the temple what they owed (12:47). This generation may not have been law-abiding until this point, but the work of the two leaders sent by Artaxerxes has returned the community to its ideal state, and so it acts just as the ideal generation did at the beginning of the book. In the final reference to what happened "on that day" of the purification of the wall, the community finds it "written in the book of Moses" that Ammonites and Moabites cannot be part of the assembly (13:1), and so "upon hearing the law, they separated out from Israel all those who had mixed with them (כל ערב)"[76] (13:3). Following upon what

---

73. As Chapter 1 mentions, the OG has the shorter and original version of the text in this part of the book; see Fulton, *Reconsidering Nehemiah's Judah*.

74. The LXX says here that the people brought "the portions for the priests and Levites," but the MT says that they brought "the portions of the law for the priests and the Levites," an even more obvious connection to Neh. 10.

75. LXX[B] omits "and in the days of Nehemiah" here, but this phrase was likely original to the text and omitted by the copyist of Vaticanus, who altered the text to have it correspond to the situation in Neh. 13, where it becomes clear that the community did not always support the temple in the days of Nehemiah.

76. The noun ערב is used so infrequently in biblical Hebrew that it is difficult to determine its precise sense, but in places such as Jer. 25:20, 24; 50:37 it appears to refer to people regarded as foreigners who have mixed into a group understood to be natives; for that sense of the word here, see Schunck, *Nehemia*, 374–5, and Laird, *Negotiating Power*, 215.

one might infer from the prayer of Neh. 9:6-37, the case may be that the community has returned to the purity of identity that God intended, and so liberation from Persia could be near at hand.

4. *Nehemiah 13:4-34: The Epigone, Conclusion*

If Ezra–Nehemiah ended with Neh. 13:3, readers would have come full circle, from one ideal generation to one that, having sinned, resolves to change its ways and act in accord with the identity it should have. Nehemiah's prayer in Neh. 1:5-11 and the success of his wall-building suggested the community was putting the shame of their earlier punishment behind them, and Nehemiah 8–10 points in the same direction. But in the conclusion of the book in 13:4-34, which takes place twelve years later, upon Nehemiah's return to Jerusalem after attending upon Artaxerxes in Babylon (13:6), Nehemiah finds the community has failed to keep the specific aspects of the law they agreed to uphold in Neh. 10:29-40 [28-39]. The bulk of that agreement was dedicated to filling the לשכות "chambers" of the temple with provisions for its services and personnel (10:33-40 [32-39]), yet upon his return, Nehemiah finds that Eliashib the high priest has installed Tobiah, who in the narrative has sought only evil for the community, in a לשכה that was meant to store the offerings for the temple (13:4-5). Moreover, the community had not supplied the temple chambers as they swore in Nehemiah 10 they would, and so the Levites were forced to leave Jerusalem and return to their settlements (13:6-7), with the result that Nehemiah finds the temple "abandoned" (13:11). Tobiah, moreover, is an Ammonite (Neh. 2:10; 3:35 [4:3]), one of the peoples whom the law insists must be expelled from the assembly (13:1-3). In the worldview of Ezra–Nehemiah, of course, it does not matter that Tobiah is a Yahwist, because Yahwism is not a way the book distinguishes the "holy seed" who belong in the "holy city" from impure outsiders. From the author's point of view, it is disturbing that the high priest in charge of the temple chambers is קרוב "close"[77] to an Ammonite (13:4) who has no place in the assembly, let alone in the temple, and that he appears to value this relationship over the proper functioning of the cult. It is left to Nehemiah to expel Tobiah from the temple, and he then orders the purification of the chamber Tobiah had occupied (13:8-9). Like Ezra, Nehemiah uses the language of purity in the context of discussing outsiders, and he takes the language seriously

---

77. קרוב indicates a close relationship that could be one of blood (e.g., Lev. 21:2, 3; 25:25; Num. 27:11; Ruth 2:20), geographical proximity (e.g., Gen. 45:10; Exod. 12:4; 32:27; Deut. 13:8 [7]), or friendship (e.g., Job 19:14; Ps. 38:12 [11]).

enough that he employs cultic professionals to ritually purify the space occupied by Tobiah, an impure foreigner.[78] Nehemiah must also bring the Levites back to the temple (13:11), and in order to distribute the rations to the cultic personnel he establishes new figures whom he describes as נאמנים "faithful" (13:13), precisely what the community and its native leadership have otherwise proven not to be. He had to re-establish the duties of the cultic personnel as a whole, he says, and he was responsible for the resumption of the wood and first fruits offerings (13:30-31), two of the specific matters the community had claimed the law made it their duty to provide (10:35-36 [34-35]).

This is not the community's only legal failing in the book's conclusion, because they are also purchasing goods from foreigners in Jerusalem on the Sabbath (13:16), something they had also agreed not to do, since they understood the law as prohibiting this (10:32a [31a]). "Your ancestors acted this way," Nehemiah warns them, "and God brought upon us and upon this city all of this evil" (13:18).[79] The evil God brought upon Jerusalem was assumedly its destruction and depopulation, which Nehemiah's efforts have reversed. So Nehemiah can now use his wall to physically separate foreigners who want to trade on the Sabbath from the temple community inside of the city (13:19-22), and if one can see it as a symbol of the separation that the community should have from foreigners,[80] it is also a functional border that reinforces the boundary of the law that defines community identity and that nullifies the threats of violence from evil outsiders like Sanballat who may wish to force the community to act disloyally. Yet the wall provides no defense against the decision of some community members to marry foreign women (13:23), a violation of another major aspect of the law they agreed to uphold (10:31 [30]), and even a grandson of the high priest has married into the family of Sanballat (13:28). The children of these marriages did not know how to speak the language of Judah, Nehemiah says (13:24), but the main problem he identifies in this regard is that foreign women made even

---

78. Hannah Harrington points out that the notion that rooms can become impure and need purification derives from Lev. 14:33-53 and Num. 19:18, but there is no sense in either of those passages that foreigners in and of themselves transmit impurity to a space ("The Use of Leviticus").

79. The OG has a somewhat different reading here: "our God brought upon them and upon us and upon this city all these evil things." This likely reflects a secondary expansion that demonstrates a more exact theodicy of God punishing the evildoers themselves, as well as later generations.

80. So, e.g., Esler, "Ezra–Nehemiah as a Narrative," 421–4; Janzen, "The Cries of Jerusalem," 129–32.

a great king like Solomon sin. Nehemiah refers to these marriages as a "great evil," and says that "to cause foreign women to dwell (להשיב)" in the community is "to rebel (למעל) against our God" (13:27), thereby reusing the language of Ezra 9–10 in regard to marriages to outsiders (Ezra 9:2, 4; 10:2, 10, etc.) and so emphasizing the community's tendency to remain in disobedience. In fact, of all the specific aspects of the law the community saw as necessary to uphold in Nehemiah 10, the only one of which Nehemiah does not find them in violation upon his return to Judah is the observance of the law of the Sabbath year (10:32b [31b]), and that may simply be because the odds of Nehemiah's return in such a year were only one in seven.

Whatever hope Nehemiah 8–10 might have raised in regard to a better future for the community, perhaps even independence from Persia, is dashed in Nehemiah 13. Particularly when it comes to Nehemiah's reference to the destruction of Jerusalem for the people's past sin in 13:18, we see here the same fear that we do in Ezra 9:6-15 of a potential annihilation of the community and the city for the failure to keep the law, rather than the more hopeful future that readers can infer from Neh. 9:6-37. The community cannot keep the law, not without leadership of the kind that Ezra and Nehemiah bring, and leaders not sent by the Achaemenid from the center of the empire have failed them; the high priest privileges his links to Tobiah over a functioning temple cult and does not prevent his grandson from marrying outside of the group into the family of a man who has never acted in this narrative except to lie and endanger the community. Things are now no different than they were when Ezra arrived at the beginning of the story of this generation, where descendants of the high priest Jeshua were also guilty of intermarriage (Ezra 10:18). As Chapter 1 discusses, Nehemiah 8 mainly refers to Ezra as scribe when he teaches the law along with the Levites who have migrated with him from Babylonia, but he also does so in his role as priest (8:2, 9). Because the people do not understand the law before the teaching of Nehemiah 8, however, this means the priests born in Judah had failed to do their job in this regard. The community may wish to avoid acting like their evil ancestors whose failure in regard to the law brought about disaster and a near annihilation of Judah, but they are congenitally unable to do so, and so this failure is, unhappily, part of their identity. They should be like the ideal migrant generation of Ezra 1–6, devoted to the temple and the decrees of the king who is led by God, and their nature as a group should be defined by the law that guards their holy community from impure peoples not descended from Babylonian Judeans. Their only hope lies in the leadership the Achaemenids send to them, for left to their own devices the community can never be righteous enough to earn independence from Persia. They depend upon the Achaemenid to send them leaders who will curb their natural tendency to court disaster as they defy divine law, something that also makes them disloyal subjects of the king, for the community leadership born in Judah has failed to do this. Whatever leadership this later generation has that the king has not sent from the center of the world is corrupt and fails to keep the law (Ezra 9:2; Neh. 5:7; 6:17), even after those leaders swear in a solemn written agreement they will act rightly (Neh. 13:4-5, 11, 17, 28).

The ideal generation of Ezra 1–6 is distinguished by genealogical and cultic boundaries, although observance of them really reflects loyalty to the king who has chosen this community to rebuild the temple. As the genealogical boundaries fail in Ezra 9–10, a legal boundary is invoked to distinguish the community from outsiders, as are holiness and purity boundaries that derive from the law. Yet the emphasis on obedience to the law as a way to define the ideal community is itself related to loyalty to the king in Ezra–Nehemiah, since he promulgates the law and demands it be obeyed, and he enforces it within the judicial system that also deals with royal law. To fail to be a good member of the post-exilic temple assembly is also to fail to be a good subject of the king, and is to be like the disloyal people of the land who live around the exilic community. And since this failure has become the actual identity of the epigone of Ezra 7–Nehemiah 13, they need the leadership the Achaemenid sends to force them to remain loyal to king and God. For Ezra–Nehemiah, the community is fortunate to have Achaemenid rule that brings them the law and the leadership to enforce it that they need, and they are also fortunate that Judeans remain in diaspora, close to the center of the world, with a pool of faithful leaders who can teach the law and help the community in Judah be the sort of people they should. The generation of Ezra 1–6 came from the diaspora and so acted out that ideal identity, but the generation of Ezra and Nehemiah had lived for too long away from the center of the empire, and so needs the correction that group can provide with the support of the Persian king.[81] This, at least, is the perspective of

---

81. As scholars often point out, in Ezra–Nehemiah the diaspora is where the true knowledge of the law resides; see, e.g., Peter R. Bedford, "Diaspora: Homeland Relations in Ezra–Nehemiah," *VT* 52 (2002): 147–65; Bustenay Oded, "Exile–Homeland Relations during the Exilic Period and Restoration," in *Tᵉshûrôt LaAvishur: Studies in the Bible and the Ancient Near East, in Hebrew and Semitic Languages*, ed. Michael Heltzer and Meir Maul (Tel Aviv-Jaffa: Archaeological Center Publications, 2004), 153*–60*; Japhet, *From the Rivers of Babylon*, 166–7; Kessler, "Images of Exile," 335–7; Gary N. Knoppers, "The Construction of Judean Diasporic Identity in Ezra–Nehemiah," *JHS* 15 (2015): art. 3.

Ezra–Nehemiah's author, but if some within the Judean temple community did marry outside of the genealogical boundaries that the author understood as defining the group, or befriended figures such as Tobiah whom Ezra–Nehemiah portrays as their enemy, then different groups within the post-exilic temple community likely held incompatible views as to how the group should define itself.[82] The very existence of a prayer such as Neh. 9:6-37, which, outside of the larger context of Nehemiah 8–13, could be construed by Persian-period readers as anti-Persian, suggests that not everyone in the community was as pro-Achaemenid as the author of Ezra–Nehemiah.[83] Before we address this issue, however, we turn in the following two chapters to show how the key aspects of group identity Ezra–Nehemiah creates was one largely, although not entirely, shaped by Achaemenid ideology.

---

82. Gary N. Knoppers, *Jews and Samaritans: The Origins and History of their Early Relations* (Oxford: Oxford University Press, 2013), 160–5; Southwood, *Ethnicity and the Mixed Marriage Crisis*, 185–9.

83. See David Janzen, "Yahwistic Appropriation of Achaemenid Ideology and the Function of Nehemiah 9 in Ezra–Nehemiah," *JBL* 136 (2017): 839–56.

Chapter 3

The Beneficent King in Achaemenid Ideology and in Ezra–Nehemiah

1. *Introduction: The Background of Achaemenid Ideology*

The identity Ezra–Nehemiah constructs for its community, particularly its picture of a group that fails to live up to its ideal self as a community of loyal Persian subjects, is one that acknowledges the superiority and necessity of the Achaemenid kings who ruled them and accepts the ways in which they presented themselves and their colonized peoples. Ezra–Nehemiah, as we will see in this and the following chapter, creates community identity through a combination of Achaemenid ideology and a Yahwism that is amenable to it, and so the author's worldview accepts the inherent goodness of the king and the necessity of his dynasty's rule. It accepts that the Judean temple community is better off with Achaemenid leadership, since it also accepts the imperial claim that the God of creation has made them kings, and that they act according to divine will to the benefit of all the peoples they rule. As we have seen in Chapter 2, an important aspect of the community's ideal identity in Ezra–Nehemiah is loyalty to the king, and so in the author's worldview they should always do what the king commands, since this is also what God commands. To show the specific ways in which the worldview of the author of Ezra–Nehemiah has been shaped by Achaemenid ideology as he or she constructs an identity for the community, we turn to a discussion of that ideology, and this chapter focuses on the dynasty's claims surrounding their abilities to improve the lives of their colonized peoples, and even to be able to reestablish the paradise on earth the creator god originally intended for humanity. The world needs them to rule, the Achaemenids say, because without their leadership it descends into a violent chaos. The second part of the chapter examines the Achaemenids' claims of beneficence in some detail, and the third section explores how those claims are reflected by the author of Ezra–Nehemiah, who, in accepting them, has the core of his or her community's identity mimic the Achaemenids' portrayal of the nature of the colonized peoples they rule.

We begin, however, with a brief discussion of some of the background of the Achaemenid worldview, particularly in regard to points of contact that it might have had with Zoroastrian thought, in order to provide some context for the discussion that follows. Achaemenid ideology was designed to legitimate the dynasty's rule, and in a largely non-literate world it was broadcast in many different ways, including through imperial architecture, coins, seal impressions, and the variety of imperial gardens referred to as paradises. The imagery of Achaemenid imperial art as produced in Persia is often referred to as the court style,[1] and we find reflections of it in artistic material produced elsewhere in the empire that combines court style with local traditions to create various kinds of artistic *koinē*s. Regional workshops from Western Anatolia to Edom to the Caucasus produced local imitations of Persian ceramics,[2] and at a satrapal capital such as Daskyleion in Anatolia, almost three-quarters of the seals used an Achaemenid *koinē* or Persianizing imagery,[3] and even cities less central to the imperial project produced art reflecting Achaemenid iconography, although there tends to be more variation in the artistic styles of the work created in such places.[4]

The materials produced in the court style conveyed messages about the king, his goodness, his power, and the necessity of his rule, as this and the next chapter will discuss, and local variations of these messages helped the colonized make sense of them. It is true that we know of little in the way of objects from Persian-period Judah that reflect even Persianizing imagery as conveyed through *koinē* iconography, let alone material of the court style.[5] Persian-period Judean coins often adopt Athenian imagery,

---

1. For a discussion of the definition, see Deniz Kaptan, *The Daskyleion Bullae: Seal Images from the Western Achaemenid Empire*, 2 vols, AchHist 12 (Leiden: Nederlands Instituut voor het Nabije Oosten, 2002), 1:2-5.

2. Margaret C. Miller, "Luxury Toreutic in the Western Satrapies: Court-Inspired Gift-Exchange Diffusion," in *Der Achämenidenhof/The Achaemenid Court*, ed. Bruno Jacobs and Robert Rollinger, CeO 2 (Wiesbaden: Harrassowitz, 2010), 853–97 (862–8).

3. Elspeth Dusinberre, *Empire, Authority, and Autonomy in Achaemenid Anatolia* (Cambridge: Cambridge University Press, 2013), 65–7.

4. Elspeth R. M. Dusinberre, "Anatolian Crossroads: Achaemenid Seals from Sardis and Gordion," in *The World of Achaemenid Persia: History, Art and Society in Iran and the Ancient Near East*, ed. John Curtis and St John Simpson (London: I. B. Tauris, 2010), 323–35.

5. Persian-period seals and sealings, for example, were rare in Palestine, and almost entirely absent, as far as the archaeological record makes us aware, in Judah.

some even portraying the head of Athena, since Athenian coins were used throughout the Eastern Mediterranean in the fifth and fourth centuries BCE. The iconography of Judean coinage simply reflects that of the province's main trading partners,[6] although it is possible that the heads that appear on some Judean coins are meant to represent the Achaemenid.[7] This does not mean, however, that Achaemenid ideology was not broadcast in Judah, for Darius claims on the Bisitun Inscription that "I set forth this inscription everywhere among the lands" (DB 4.91-92), a claim supported by discoveries of an Akkadian translation of it in Babylon and an Aramaic copy at Elephantine, the latter written a century after the text was first composed.[8] Those who transmit the *hamdugā* "written record" of the inscription and tell of what he has done will prosper, Darius says (4.52-56), and so we should assume, as Robert Rollinger has argued, that the Achaemenid inscriptions of which we know circulated widely through the empire,[9] and that some of them were known in Judah.[10]

See Christoph Uehlinger, "'Powerful Persianisms' in Gyltpic Iconography of Persian Period Palestine," in Becking and Korpel, eds, *The Crisis of Israelite Religion*, 134–82.

6. E.g., Meshorer, *A Treasury of Jewish Coins*, 7–8; Stephen N. Gerson, "Fractional Coins of Judea and Samaria in the Fourth Century BCE," *NEA* 64 (2001): 106–21 (109).

7. E.g., Haim Gitler, "Identities of the Indigenous Coinages of Palestine under Achaemenid Rule: The Dissemination of the Image of the Great King," in *More than Men, Less than Gods: Studies on Royal Cult and Imperial Worship*, ed. Panagiotis P. Iossif, Andrzej S. Chankowski, and Catherine C. Lorberf, StHel 11 (Leuven: Peeters, 2011), 105–19 (108–10); Patrick Wyssman, "The Coinage Imagery of Samaria and Judah in the Late Persian Period," in *A "Religious Revolution" in Yehûd? The Material Culture of the Persian Period as a Test Case*, ed. Christian Frevel, Katharina Pyschny, and Izak Cornelius, OBO 267 (Fribourg: Academic Press, 2014), 221–66 (249).

8. Jonas C. Greenfield and Bezalel Porten, *The Bisitun Inscription of Darius the Great: Aramaic Version*, CII 1/5/1 (London: Lund Humphries, 1982), 2–3.

9. Robert Rollinger, "Royal Strategies of Representation and the Language(s) of Power: Some Considerations on the Audience and the Dissemination of the Achaemenid Royal Inscriptions," in *Official Epistolography and the Language(s) of Power: Proceedings of the First International Conference of the Research Network Imperium and Officium*, ed. Stephan Procházka, Lucian Reinfandt, and Sven Tost, PapVin 8 (Vienna: Österreichischen Akademie der Wissenschaften, 2015), 117–30 (120–3).

10. So also Gard Granerød, "'By the favour of Ahuramazda I am king': On the Promulgation of a Persian Propaganda Text among Babylonians and Judaeans," *JSJ* 44 (2013): 455–80 (478–80).

In the Persian period, a monumental administrative building was located at Ramat Rahel, close to Jerusalem, and assumedly functioned as the administrative capital of the small province of Judah,[11] and among its features was a garden with native as well as imported flora, including the Persian walnut tree, the cedar of Lebanon, the *Juglans regia*, native to Northern Iran, and the earliest known example in the Levant of the citron, native to India.[12] The Persians, it would appear, constructed a paradise at Ramat Rahel, and as the next section of the chapter discusses, such parks also conveyed important aspects of Achaemenid ideology. The administrative building itself was constructed before the Persian period, but the Achaemenids did add a massive extension to the existing palace, a project that involved construction techniques new to the region.[13] Achaemenid architecture also broadcast imperial messages, and examples of it were found elsewhere in Palestine. There appears to have been a Persian-style palace at Sidon,[14] and such palaces were constructed throughout the empire,[15] perhaps even at Samaria, where an Achaemenid-style throne was found.[16] Judah is never mentioned in the Achaemenids' lists of their subject peoples, and it may have been too

---

11. See the discussions in Oded Lipschits et al., "Palace and Village, Paradise and Oblivion: Unraveling the Riddles of Ramat Rahel," *NEA* 74 (2011): 2–49; Oded Lipschits, "Shedding New Light on the Dark Years of the 'Exilic Period': New Studies, Further Elucidation, and Some Questions Regarding the Archaeology of Judah as an 'Empty Land,'" in *Interpreting Exile: Displacement and Deportation in Biblical and Modern Contexts*, ed. Brad E. Kelle, Frank Ritchel Ames, and Jacob L. Wright, SBLAIL 10 (Atlanta: Society of Biblical Literature, 2011), 57–90.

12. O. Lipschits, Y. Gadot, and D. Langgut, "The Riddle of Ramat Rahel: The Archaeology of a Royal Persian Period Edifice," *Transeu* 41 (2012): 57–79 (71–2).

13. Because the Persian-period wing was later dismantled down to the foundations, we know little about it, but the excavators write that techniques new to the region were used in the construction of the foundations and floors. See Oded Lipschits et al., *What Are the Stones Whispering? Ramat Rahel: 3000 Years of Forgotten History* (Winona Lake, IN: Eisenbrauns, 2017), 101–5.

14. John Curtis, "The Archaeology of the Achaemenid Period," in *Forgotten Empire: The World of Ancient Persia*, ed. John Curtis and Nigel Tallis (Berkeley: University of California Press, 2005), 30–49 (41–2).

15. John Curtis and Shahrokh Razmjou, "The Palace," in Curtis and Tallis, eds, *Forgotten Empire*, 50–5 (50).

16. For the four fragments of the throne that have been discovered, see Miriam Tadmor, "Fragments of an Achaemenid Throne from Samaria," *IEJ* 24 (1974): 37–43 and Avner Raban, "A Group of Objects from a Wreckage Site at Athlit," *Michmanim* 6 (1992): 31–53 [Hebrew].

poor and unimportant to have garnered much attention from the dynasty,[17] but it was part of the empire, it was administered from Ramat Rahel, and at least the local imperial administration would have been interested in monitoring the taxes and labor owed to the king. Colonization involves the dissemination of imperial ideology, the empire's explanation as to why the colonized benefit from empire and thus why they should support imperial rule, and given that the administration cared enough about this to create a paradise attached to their center of administration in Judah suggests that the imperial apparatus saw it necessary to broadcast Achaemenid ideology even here, at least to elite Judean figures with whom it came into contact.[18] Owning physical objects with hybrid artistic styles reflecting this ideology was a sign of membership in the elite elsewhere in the Persian Empire,[19] and allowed local populations to negotiate between imperial ideology and their own traditions to make sense of their social locations as Achaemenid subjects.[20] It is not unreasonable to believe that this sort of ideological work of creating group identity within the context of Achaemenid rule went on among the elite of Judah, as well, even though in this small and impoverished province there is little physical evidence of it.

The Achaemenid ideology we are about to discuss, even in its more central expressions of the official inscriptions and the iconography of the court style, was itself a hybrid development of royal iconography from earlier empires. The paradises the next section of the chapter

17. So, e.g., Lester L. Grabbe, "The Law of Moses in the Ezra Tradition: More Virtual than Real?," in Watts, ed., *Persia and Torah*, 91–113 (110–11); Eskenazi, "The Missions of Ezra and Nehemiah," 524–6.

18. For a discussion of all the places in the empire where Judeans could have come into contact with Persians, including in Palestine, see Jason M. Silverman, "Iranian–Judaean Interaction in the Achaemenid Period," in *Text, Theology, and Trowel: New Investigations in the Biblical World*, ed. Lidia D. Matassa and Jason M. Silverman (Eugene, OR: Pickwick Publications, 2011), 133–68.

19. Elspeth R. M. Dusinberre, *Aspects of Empire in Achaemenid Sardis* (Cambridge: Cambridge University Press, 2003), 145–56; Amélie Kuhrt, "Achaemenid Images of Royalty and Empire," in *Concepts of Kingship in Antiquity: Proceedings of the European Science Foundation Exploratory Workshop*, ed. Giovanni B. Lanfranchi and Robert Rollinger, HANEM 11 (Padua: S.A.R.G.O.N., 2010), 87–105 (98–9); Miller, "Luxury Toreutic," 867; Briant, *Kings, Countries, Peoples*, 239–41.

20. Henry Colburn, "Art of the Achaemenid Empire, and Art in the Achaemenid Empire," in *Critical Approaches to Ancient Near Eastern Art*, ed. Brian A. Brown and Marian H. Feldman (Boston: W. de Gruyter, 2014), 773–800.

discusses, for example, were not the first royal parks in the ancient Near East.[21] The atlantid pose that consistently appears in Achaemenid iconography, in which figures representing the colonized peoples of the empire are portrayed with cupped hands and slightly bent arms raised above their heads, supporting with little effort the king who stands above them,[22] is present in Western Semitic art by the second millennium BCE, and sometimes appears on Achaemenid glyptic art that has strong ties to Assyrian iconographic traditions.[23] Use of cylinder seals, on which Achaemenid imperial art appeared, had largely died out in Mesopotamia by the Persian period, but the Achaemenids adopted it from the Elamites.[24] The architecture of Achaemenid royal palaces, which themselves communicated important messages to those who visited them, reflects Assyrian and Babylonian influence,[25] but key aspects of those messages were sent through the construction of the pillared hall, which is Urartian in origin.[26]

21. For evidence of gardens associated with Mesopotamian palaces from the Middle Assyrian to the Neo-Babylonian dynasties, see Irene Winter, "'Seat of Kingship'/'A Wonder to Behold': The Palace as Construct in the Ancient Near East," *ArsOr* 23 (1993): 27–55, and Amélie Kuhrt, "The Palace(s) of Babylon," in *The Royal Palace Institution in the First Millennium BC: Regional Development and Cultural Interchange between East and West*, ed. Inge Nielsen, MDIA 4 (Athens: The Danish Institute of Athens, 2001), 77–93 (82–4).

22. See Margaret Cool Root, *The King and Kingship in Achaemenid Art: Essays on the Creation of an Iconography of Empire*, ActIr 19 (Leiden: E. J. Brill, 1979), 147–53.

23. Mark B. Garrison, "*By the Favor of Auramazdā*: Kingship and the Divine in the Early Achaemenid Period," in Iossif, Chankowski, and Lorberf, eds, *More than Men, Less than Gods*, 15–104 (43–7).

24. Margaret Cool Root, "The Legible Image: How Did Seals and Sealing Matter in Persepolis?," in *L'Archive des Fortifications de Persépolis: État des questions et perspectives de recherches*, ed. Pierre Briant, Wouter F. M. Henkelman, and Matthew W. Stolper, Pers 12 (Paris: De Boccard, 2008), 87–148 (96–7).

25. Rémy Boucharlat, "Susa under Achaemenid Rule," in *Mesopotamia and Iran in the Persian Period: Conquest and Imperialism 539–331 BC*, ed. John Curtis (London: British Museum Press, 1997), 54–67 (60); David Stronach, "From Cyrus to Darius: Notes on Art and Architecture in Early Achaemenid Palaces," in Nielsen, ed., *The Royal Palace Institution in the First Millennium BC*, 95–111 (99–102); Curtis and Razmjou, "The Palace," 54

26. Aminia Kanetsyan, "Urartian and Early Achaemenid Palaces in Armenia," in Nielsen, ed., *The Royal Palace Institution in the First Millennium BC*, 145–53; Lori Khatchadourian, *Imperial Matter: Ancient Persia and the Archaeology of Empire* (Oakland, CA: University of California Press, 2016), 87–99.

The Achaemenids combined elements of many different cultural traditions to create an ideology unique to the ancient Near East, which we will begin to examine in the next section of the chapter. This uniqueness is not due only to the wide variety of cultures from which they drew their artistic inspiration, for their ideology reflects elements of thought associated with Zoroastrianism, something we do not see in messages broadcast by earlier Near Eastern empires. It is not clear that the Achaemenids were themselves Zoroastrians, and scholarship has reached no consensus on the matter.[27] They obviously were Mazdeans, for they worshiped Ahura Mazda, the "Wise Lord" of the Avestan texts of Zoroastrianism, but it is difficult to say if they adopted enough of the other tenets of that religion to be considered adherents. This is not an issue we need to resolve, since our focus is on the ideology the Achaemenids broadcast, but Zoroastrianism is an Iranian religion—Avestan represents the Central branch of Old Iranian, and Old Persian, the language of the Achaemenids, the Southwestern one[28]—and there are enough similarities between Achaemenid and Zoroastrian thought to suggest that ideas associated with the latter were part of the cultural background that influenced Achaemenid thinking about the relationship between the divine, creation, humanity, and the king.

The central religious texts of Zoroastrianism can largely be divided into two groups. The older of these is the Avesta, named after the language in which the texts were written, and the later is the material composed in Pahlvai (Middle Persian), beginning with commentaries on the Avesta from the Sasanian period (third to seventh centuries CE), although most important Zoroastrian texts in Pahlavi were assembled in the eighth

---

27. For some of the arguments that the Achaemenids were Zoroastrians, see Mary Boyce, "The Religion of Cyrus the Great," in *Achaemenid History III: Method and Theory*, ed. Heleen Sancisi-Weerdenburg (Leiden: Nederlands Instituut voor het Nabije Oosten, 1988), 15–31; P. O. Skjævrø, "The Achaemenids and the *Avesta*," in *Birth of the Persian Empire, Volume I*, ed. Vesta Sarkhosh Curtis and Sarah Stewart (London: I. B. Tauris, 2005), 52–84; Andrew G. Nichols, "The Iranian Concept of *aša* and Greek Views of the Persians," *SCO* 62 (2016): 61–86 (63–4). For some of those who argue that there is not enough evidence for this claim, see Pierre Briant, *From Cyrus to Alexander: A History of the Persian Empire*, trans. Peter T. Daniels (Winona Lake, IN: Eisenbrauns, 2002), 93–4; Bruce Lincoln, "Religion, Empire, and the Spectre of Orientalism: A Recent Controversy in Achaemenid Studies," *JNES* 72 (2013): 253–65 (253–5); Khatchadourian, *Imperial Matter*, 11.

28. Gernot Windfuhr, "Dialectology and Topics," in *The Iranian Languages*, ed. Gernot Windfuhr (London: Routledge, 2009), 5–42 (12).

through tenth centuries.²⁹ Zoroastrian scholarship generally agrees the Avesta was not committed to writing before the fourth century CE, but there is also consensus that these texts had an extremely long history of oral transmission. The language of the earliest parts of the Avesta is so close to the Sanskrit of the Rigveda that their origin is often dated to about 1000 BCE, and if this is correct then certainly oral versions of the earlier parts of the Avesta existed by the time the Achaemenid dynasty began, although there is no unanimity on this point.³⁰ At the core of this earlier Avestan material are the *Gatha*s "songs," which Zoroastrian tradition and some scholars attribute to Zoroaster himself.³¹ The *Gatha*s now make up part of the *Yasna* "sacrifice," an Avestan collection of texts related to sacrificial rituals. The text of the *Yasna* is divided into seventy-two chapters, each referred to as a *Yasna*, and the *Gatha*s include *Y.* 28-34; 43-51; and 53, while *Y.* 27 and 35-41, like the *Gatha*s, appear to have originally developed in an early dialect of Avestan.³² Yet even if no part of the Avesta existed in oral form by the time the Achaemenids came to power, this material does have much in common with Achaemenid ideology and provides us with important cultural context to help make sense of it.

Zoroastrianism attributes creation to Ahura Mazda, whose name in Pahlavi is Ohrmazd. Creation is not an important focus of the *Gatha*s, although they do refer to Ahura Mazda as creator (*Y.* 31.7, 11; 44.3-5), but later Avestan material provides readers with the order of Ahura Mazda's creation—sky, water, earth, animal, plant, fire, and human (*Y.* 19.2)—that appears largely unchanged in Pahlavi writings (e.g., *GBd* 1.54). The Avesta describes this creation as ruled first by Yima, the first son of the first human, and during his time humans and animals were free

---

29. For brief descriptions and dates of key Zoroastrian texts, see Miguel Ángel Andrés-Toledo, "Primary Sources: Avestan and Pahlavi," in *The Wiley Blackwell Companion to Zoroastrianism*, ed. Michael Stausberg and Yuhan Sohrab-Dinshaw Vevaina (Chichester: John Wiley & Sons, 2015), 519–28.

30. Abolala Soudavar ("The Formation of Achaemenid Ideology and its Impact on the *Avesta*," in *The World of Achaemenid Persia: History, Art and Society in Iran and the Ancient Near East*, ed. John Curtis and St John Simpson [London: I. B. Tauris, 2010], 111–38) and Albert de Jong ("Religion at the Achaemenid Court," in Jacobs and Rollinger, eds, *Der Achämenidenhof*, 533–58), for example, argue that the Achaemenids were responsible for shaping important aspects of Zoroastrian thought, including ideas that now appear in the Avesta.

31. For a discussion of scholarly positions, see Helmut Humbach, "Gathas I: Texts," *EIr* (online edition, 2012, available at http://www.iranicaonline.org/articles/gathas-i-texts; accessed 13 January 2020).

32. Garrison, "*By the Favor of Auramazdā*," 21–2.

from death, and plants and waters free from drought, and there was no heat, cold, ageing, or death (*Y.* 9.4-5; *Vd* 2.5-19). Ahura Mazda's good creation, however, was opposed by the evil creations of Angra Mainyu, called Ahriman in Pahlavi. The Avestan *Vīdēvdād* describes Ahura Mazda as creating sixteen different lands, but the creation of each is followed by Angra Mainyu's construction of something evil—the serpent and winter (*Vd* 1.2-3), the locust (1.4), sin (1.5), and so on. The Pahlavi texts provide a similar picture, and there Ahriman is responsible for the creation of evil and dangerous things such as the serpent, scorpion, ant, fly, and locust (see, e.g., *GBd* 22-23). So we see here a dualism at the heart of Zoroastrianism, present from its earliest traditions, in which good and evil are "fundamental twins," as the *Gatha*s put it (*Y.* 30.5), and what is evil and harmful to Ahura Mazda's good creation is the work of Angra Mainyu.

Besides being associated with the evil aspects of creation, Angra Mainyu/Ahriman is also associated with the Lie, called *druj* in Avestan. The Lie is the evil counterpart of *aša* "Truth" (e.g., *Y.* 30.5), which is the creation of Ahura Mazda (e.g., 31.8), who endowed humans with *aša* (10.7), something they can embody (30.7). The Avestan word *aša* refers, of course, to that which is true, but it is cognate with Sanskrit *r̥ta*, a word that in the Rigveda refers to the order that gods like Mithra—who is named also in the Achaemenid inscriptions (e.g., A²Sa 4-5; A²Ha 5-6) and in the Avesta (e.g., *Yt* 10)—use to govern the world (e.g., *RV* 5.63.7).[33] The words derive from Indo-European **ar-* "fit, order,"[34] and so what is true is what fits together properly and is correctly ordered. We can see this Truth that the *Gatha*s laud and associate so firmly with Ahura Mazda, "the father of Truth" (*Y.* 44.3; 47.2), as that which provides the right order for humanity and the world to function as they should. In Pahlavi texts, Truth is one of the seven Aməša Spəntas, the "Bounteous Immortals," who include Ohrmazd and six quasi-divine beings created by him who join him in the struggle against the Lie (e.g., *GBd* 1.53; *MX* 43), and in the *Gatha*s one can call upon Truth (*Y.* 31.4) and sacrifice to it (34.3).

Ethically, then, human life is a struggle against the Lie (*GBd* 3.23; *Dk* 3.124; 6.1), and each aspect of creation, including the non-human

---

33. See Mary Boyce, *A History of Zoroastrianism. Volume I: The Early Period*, HOS 8/1, 3rd ed. (Leiden: E. J. Brill, 1996), 27–8.

34. Julius Pokorny, *Indogermanisches etymologisches Wörterbuch* (Bern: Francke, 1959–1969), 1:56–7; Thomas V. Gamkrelidze and Vjačeslav V. Ivanov, *Indo-European and the Indo-Europeans: A Reconstruction and Historical Analysis of a Proto-Language and a Proto-Culture*, trans. Johanna Nichols, 2 vols, TLSM 80 (Berlin: W. de Gruyter, 1995), 1:710.

ones, is involved in the war against it (*GBd* 6). Ahriman is the Lie, says Pahlavi material (*IBd* 2.11), and the *Gatha*s say that non-Zoroastrian gods (*daēva*s) wrongly chose the Lie (*Y.* 30.6). Thanks to Ahura Mazda's Truth, however, humans have the ability to choose rightly. Ahura Mazda has provided them with a law in accordance with Truth to guide their behavior (*Y.* 21.1; 46.15), and good human action should extend to the treatment of the earth. They should care for it by planting crops, watering dry ground and draining wet ground, and they should kill the dangerous animals Angra Mainyu created (*Vd* 3.23-24), actions that help make the world more like Ahura Mazda's good creation that existed in the beginning. In Pahlavi material, each of the four classes of humans—priests, warriors, farmers, and artisans—has its own duty to perform in the service of Truth: the priests tell people of the good works they should enact; the warriors maintain quiet and peace in their countries; the farmers cultivate the earth; and the artisans engage only in the work they understand (*MX* 31-32). The Lie also has commandments, the *Gatha*s say, but those are aimed at destroying the followers of Truth (*Y.* 31.1), and the Lie-follower fights against Ahura Mazda (44.12) and devastates others' houses and lands (31.18). The Lie is clearly very dangerous, as Ahriman constantly works to destroy the welfare of the creatures Ohrmazd made (*IBd* 28.1-2), and a Pahlavi passage warns that one can come under the power of the Lie and so be unable to control one's own actions (*Dk* 6.1).

The fight between Ahura Mazda and Angra Mainyu is not an equal one, however, and the world of the Lie will be destroyed (*Y.* 30.10), while Lie-followers will be punished in the afterlife for their actions. Even at creation Ahura Mazda determined the appropriate rewards for good and evil (*Y.* 43.5); he is "all-seeing" (45.4), aware of all actions (31.13) and of what every person deserves (32.6). At death, the righteous cross the *čīnvatō pərətu* "bridge of judgment/separation"[35] (*Y.* 46.10; 51.13) with the help of Zoroaster (46.10) or Ahura Mazda (19.6), but the evil enter *drūjō dəmānā* "the house of the Lie" (46.10-11; 51.13-14), a fate the *Gatha*s contrast with arrival in *garō dəmānā* "the House of Welcome" (51.15).[36] In the *Gatha*s, these rewards and

---

35. Or potentially "the bridge of the compiler," a reference to the builder of the bridge who piled up stones; see Jean Kellens, "Yima et la mort," in *Languages and Cultures: Studies in Honor of Edgar C. Polomé*, ed. Mohammed Ali Jazayery and Werner Winter (Berlin: Mouton de Gruyter, 1988), 329–34.

36. See Michael Stausberg, "Hell in Zoroastrian History," *Numen* 56 (2009): 217–53 (220–3), for a review of material from the *Gatha*s that discusses the House of the Lie and the House of Welcome.

punishments appear to be eternal (45.7; 46.11), but in Pahlavi texts, some of which, like *Ardā Wīrāz Nāmag*, describe the rewards of heaven and punishments of hell in detail, a final defeat of Ahriman and the Lie coincides with a resurrection of all of the dead and the purification of sinners for eternal life in an eschatological world (*GBd* 34; *IBd* 30; *DD* 32.12-15). Avestan texts associate the eschatological defeat of evil with a figure named Saoshyant (*Yt* 19.89, 92-93; *Vd* 19.5), and one Pahlavi text refers to him as the last figure who will bring true religion from Ohrmazd, since after the eschatological victory there will be no more need for further teaching (*Dk* 3.35). In the eschatological age, according to the Pahlavi tradition, there will be no evil, disease, tyranny, or death (*Dk* 7.11.4), and winter and mountains will disappear as the earth becomes a great and perfect plain (*IBd* 30.33), descriptions reminiscent to some degree of Avestan portrayals of Ahura Mazda's original creation.

2. Achaemenid Ideology, Part 1: The Beneficent King

The evidence of the Persepolis Fortification Archive tells us that Ahura Mazda, or Auramazda as the god is called in Old Persian, was not widely worshiped in Persia during the Achaemenid dynasty, or at least not in comparison with the other traditional deities of Persia and Elam,[37] but Auramazda clearly was the chief god of the Achaemenids, and had perhaps been newly introduced to Persia from Eastern Iran.[38] Darius was the first of the Achaemenid kings, and he set the ideological agenda for the dynasty,[39] breaking to some degree with that of the Teispid dynasty of Cyrus and Cambyses, kings who did not compose inscriptions in Old Persian or refer to Auramazda as their patron god.[40] Cyrus refers to himself as King of Anshan (as we see, for example, on the Cyrus Cylinder

---

37. Wouter F. M. Henkelman, "Humban and Auramazdā: Royal Gods in a Persian Landscape," in *Persian Religion in the Achaemenid Period/La religion perse à l'époque achéménide*, ed. Wouter F. M. Henkelman and Céline Richard, CeO 16 (Wiesbaden: Harrassowitz, 2017), 273–346 (318).

38. So Matt Waters, "Cyrus and the Achaemenids," *Iran* 42 (2004): 91–102 (98–9).

39. M. B. Garrison, "Seals and the Elite at Persepolis: Some Observations on Early Achaemenid Art," *ArsOr* 21 (1991): 1–29.

40. Bruno Jacobs, "From Gabled Hut to Rock-Cut Tomb: A Religious and Cultural Break between Cyrus and Darius?," in Curtis and Simpson, eds, *The World of Achaemenid Persia*, 91–101 (93–4).

[AOAT 256 K2.1.12]), a traditional title of the Elamite kings,[41] and it is perhaps better to describe the Teispids as an Elamite or Perso-Elamite dynasty rather than a Persian one.[42] Darius never claims to be Cambyses' son, and so is generally understood by scholars to be a usurper,[43] but he does say he is related to the Teispids,[44] and he incorporates them into what he calls "our family" (DB 1.8), tracing his ancestry and that of Cyrus back to a common forebear, *Haxāmaniš* "Achaemenes" (1.3-6), the ancestor after whom he names his dynasty (1.6-7).[45] Elamite culture helped to shape developing Persian identity in the eighth and seventh centuries BCE,[46] and its influence did not disappear during Darius's reign. Elamite is one of the three languages in which the Achaemenid inscriptions were typically rendered during the reigns of Darius and his son Xerxes, and

---

41. D. T. Potts, "Cyrus the Great and the Kingdom of Anshan," in Sarkhosh, ed., *Birth of the Persian Empire, Volume I*, 7–28 (13–15); Hanspeter Schaudig, "The Magnanimous Heart of Cyrus: The Cyrus Cylinder and its Literary Models," in *Cyrus the Great: Life and Lore*, ed. M. Rahim Shayegan (Boston: Ilex Foundation, 2019), 67–91 (86).

42. For Cyrus's connection to Elam, see, e.g., Potts, "Cyrus the Great"; Lloyd Llewellyn-Jones, *King and Court in Ancient Persia 559 to 331 BCE*, DDAH (Edinburgh: Edinburgh University Press, 2013), 24–5. It is likely best to refer to Cyrus as a Perso-Elamite (so Margaret Cool Root, "Achaemenid Imperial Architecture: Performative Porticoes of Persepolis," in *Persian Kingship and Architecture: Strategies of Power in Iran from the Achaemenids to the Pahlavis*, ed. Susan Babaie and Talinn Grigor [London: I. B. Tauris, 2015], 1–63 [3]), since he bore the title King of Persia (as we see in the Nabonidus Chronicle [*ABC* 7.ii.15]) as well as King of Anshan. For a list of his titles, see Waters, "Cyrus and the Achaemenids," 94.

43. Potts, "Cyrus the Great," 23.

44. Cyrus, unlike Darius, never refers to Achaemenes as an ancestor. On the Cyrus Cylinder, he calls himself a descendant of *Šišpiš* "Teispes" (AOAT 256 K2.1:20-22), and so the Old Persian inscriptions on which Cyrus claims to be an Achaemenid (CMa, CMb, and CMc) are thus regarded as forgeries by Darius; see, e.g., Waters, "Cyrus and the Achaemenids," 91; Potts, "Cyrus the Great," 20; Thomas Harrison, *Writing Ancient Persia*, CIE (London: Bristol Classical Press, 2011), 13.

45. It is possible to read these lines at the opening of the Bisitun Inscription as saying that Cyrus and Darius actually come from two different families, however; see Enrique Quintana, "Elamitas Frente a Persas: El Reino Independiente de Anšan," in *Elam and Persia*, ed. Javier Álvarez-Mon and Mark B. Garrison (Winona Lake, IN: Eisenbrauns, 2011), 167–86.

46. Wouter F. M. Henkelman, "The Achaemenid Heartland: An Archaeological-Historical Perspective," in *A Companion to the Archaeology of the Ancient Near East*, ed. D. T. Potts (Chichester: Blackwell, 2012), 931–62 (933).

the first language in which the Bisitun Inscription was carved,[47] while Elamite remained an important administrative language during the time of those two kings,[48] who borrowed from Elamite artistic traditions.[49] Under Darius's leadership, however, the Persian Empire draws on other cultural sources, including those discussed in the previous section of the chapter, to broadcast a new royal ideology, and this part of the chapter focuses on the aspects of this ideology that present the Achaemenid as a necessary figure, the king the world needs to reestablish Auramazda's perfect creation and whose reign thus benefits all of humanity.

A key aspect of Achaemenid ideology is the central place of Auramazda as creator, an idea that appears to be much more important for the Achaemenids than the *Gathas*. Seventy percent of the Achaemenid inscriptions longer than a paragraph contain a reference to creation, and these references are always the inscriptions' first element, preceding even the king's first-person introduction.[50] Almost all of these references follow precisely the same formula, such as this one that opens Darius's burial inscription: "The great god (*baga vazraka*) is Auramazda, who established (*adā*) this earth, who established that sky, who established humanity, who established the happiness (*šiyātim*) of humanity,[51] who made (*akunauš*) Darius king, one king of many, one lord of many" (DNa 1-8). The inscriptions consistently use the verb *dā-* to refer to Auramazda's creative acts—and only Auramazda is ever the subject of that verb in the Achaemenid inscriptions—but, like its Greek cognate τίθημι, Old Persian

---

47. For the chronology of the stages of the creation of the inscription at Bisitun, see Rykle Borger, *Die Chronologie des Darius-Denkmals am Behistun-Felsen* (Göttingen: Vandenhoeck & Ruprecht, 1982), 103–32.

48. The trilingual inscriptions that include Elamite versions disappear almost entirely after the time of Xerxes (Jennifer Finn, "Gods, Kings, Men: Trilingual Inscriptions and Symbolic Visualizations in the Achaemenid Empire," *ArsOr* 41 [2011]: 219–75 [217–18]), and official Achaemenid records cease to appear in Elamite after c. 460 (Joseph Wiesehöfer, *Ancient Persia from 550 BC to 650 AD*, trans. Azizeh Azodi [London: I. B. Tauris, 2001], 10).

49. Root, "Achaemenid Imperial Architecture," 3–4.

50. Bruce Lincoln, *"Happiness for Mankind": Achaemenian Religion and the Imperial Project*, ActIr 53 (Leuven: Peeters, 2012), 173.

51. The word *martiyahyā* in the phrase *hya šiyātim adā martiyahyā* is normally read as a dative of reference—"who established happiness for humanity" (Roland Kent, *Old Persian: Grammar, Texts, Lexicon*, AOS 33, 2nd ed. [New Haven, CT: American Oriental Society, 1953], §250h)—but since the word is in the genitive it can also be read as a simple possessive.

dā- can mean "to set up, establish,"[52] and so Auramazda establishes or sets up creation in order.[53] Such a systematic and repetitive reference to creation is unique to the Achaemenids among ancient Near Eastern royal inscriptions,[54] and this standard creation formula links Auramazda's primal act of establishing or ordering creation to the appointment of the Achaemenid as king. The formula uses a different verb (*kar-*) to refer to Darius's appointment to office, perhaps to distinguish this act from Auramazda's creation of the world. On two inscriptions, however, Darius makes himself (DSf 8-9) and his position as king (DPd 2-3) the object of the verb *dā-*. The first of those inscriptions opens with the standard creation formula and its repetitive use of the verb (DSf 1-5), and so there Darius suggests that he too is an integral part of Auramazda's original plan for the cosmos.

Yet even without those two uses of *dā-*, the creation formula by itself makes it clear that Achaemenid rule is key to the order Auramazda established at creation, something that Darius explains in a number of writings. On his burial inscription, for example, he writes that Auramazda bore "this earth" to him because the god "saw this earth in turmoil (*yaudantim*)" (DNa 32). He makes the same point on another inscription, one that also opens with the standard creation formula: "Much that was poorly done, that I made good. The lands were in turmoil (*ayaudan*), one fought another" (DSe 31-34). Constant violence was not the desired result of the creative act of the great god Auramazda, something that included humanity's original happiness (*šiyāti*), and so Auramazda bore this earth to Darius so he could return it to its original goodness and make humanity happy once more. There may be nothing in the Achaemenid inscriptions that makes the original creation sound exactly like the deathless realm free of heat, cold, and drought that we encounter in the Avestan material, but when Darius asks Auramazda and "the gods of the court" to save Persia from invasion, famine, and the Lie (DPd 12-24), we can assume he believed that happiness excludes such things, and that in the world Auramazda planned for humans there is no fear of warfare,

52. Pokorny, *Indogermanisches etymologisches Wörterbuch*, 1:235–6.
53. See Bruce Lincoln, *Religion, Empire, and Torture: The Case of Achaemenian Persia with a Postscript on Abu Ghraib* (Chicago: University of Chicago Press, 2007), 51–2; Prods Oktor Skjævrø, "Zarathustra: A Revolutionary Monotheist?," in *Reconsidering the Concept of Revolutionary Monotheism*, ed. Beate Pongratz-Leisten (Winona Lake, IN: Eisenbrauns, 2011), 317–50 (338–9).
54. Albert de Jong, "Ahura Mazdā the Creator," in Curtis and Simpson, eds, *The World of Achaemenid Persia*, 85–9.

no lack of food, and no Lie,[55] the entity that, as we will see, is aligned against Auramazda's goodness in Achaemenid ideology, just as it is in Zoroastrian literature.[56]

An obvious link between the king and the happiness of humanity that Auramazda created, then, is the Achaemenid's role in re-creating it. Darius says that he encounters a world where things are "poorly done," but he makes them "good," and in the Bisitun Inscription he describes how he went about doing so. The world, as Darius says, was "in turmoil" before Auramazda established him as king to set it right, and in the first four columns of Bisitun, which were carved some time before column 5, and so which originally constituted the entirety of the writing, Darius describes his struggle against nine opponents he had to overcome in the first year of his rule to secure his control over the empire. Some of these rebels who declared themselves king he defeats quickly; in 1.81-83, for example, Darius does not have to fight a single battle to defeat the Elamite Açina, for the Elamites surrender him to Darius without risking a military conflict. Others Darius defeats over the course of multiple battles, and it takes four of them to subdue the Persian rebel Vahyazdata and his forces in 3.21-75, for example. Despite this sort of variety in Darius's account of his fight to secure the empire, however, the stories of his victories in the Bisitun Inscription are repetitive, for he wins every battle, and only the names of the antagonists, dates, and battle sites change. Every description of every military encounter opens the same way: "Auramazda bore me support; by the will (*vašnā*) of Auramazda my army struck that rebellious army greatly" (2.24-26, 34-36, 39-41, 45-46, etc.). This sort of repetition certainly makes rebellion seem futile, as does the final result in every case, the death of the man who began it (1.83; 2.4-5, 13, 76, 90-91, etc.).

In the fourth column of the inscription, Darius summarizes his victories, and in 4.2-36 repetitively states that each of the nine rebels *adurujiya* "lied" (4.8, 10-11, 13, 16, etc.), claiming to be someone he was not, such as Bardiya, the son of Cyrus (4.8-9, 27), Nebuchadrezzar, the legitimate son of Nabonidus, the last king of Babylon (4.14, 29-30), and so on. With these lies, each one *hamiçiyam akunauš* "made rebellious" a particular land (4.9-10, 12, 15, etc.). Lying, says Darius in 4.33-36, which is really a summary of the summary, is what leads to rebellion: "the Lie made them

---

55. Lincoln, *Religion, Empire, and Torture*, 55.
56. Clarisse Herrenschmidt, "Vieux-perse *šiyāti-*," in *La religion iranienne à l'époque achéménide*, ed. Jeans Kellens, IrAntSup 5 (Leuven: Iranica Antiqua, 1990), 13–21; Jeans Kellens, "L'âme entre le cadavre et le paradis," *JA* 283 (1996): 19–56 (34–8); Lincoln, *"Happiness for Mankind"*, 12.

rebellious (*drauga diš hamiçiya akunauš*), so that they lied (*adurujiyašan*) to the people." Happily, however, "Auramazda made them into my hand (*auramazdā manā dastayā akunauš*); according to my desire thus I did (*akunavam*) to them." What the Lie *akunauš* "made, did," manifested in what each rebel "did" in making a land rebellious, is what Auramazda undid through Darius, who then "did" to each rebel as he pleased. The Achaemenid's fight to bring an end to the world's violent turmoil is really a struggle between Auramazda and *drauga* "the Lie," the same sort of binary view of the cosmos that we see in Zoroastrian texts beginning with the *Gatha*s.[57] In the Bisitun Inscription, as in later Zoroastrianism, the Lie is apparently so strong that it can control human will; "the Lie made them rebellious," Darius says in his summary, just as earlier in the inscription he writes that the world's recent problems began when Cambyses went to Egypt, allowing the Lie to control the peoples, stating that "after that, the people became hostile; after that, the Lie became great (*vasiy*) in the land" (1.33-34). The word *vasiy* comes from the same Indo-European root (*$wek̂$- "wish") as the noun *vašna* "will,"[58] suggesting that the Lie became great as it did what it wished. Old Persian *vašna* appears thirty-six times at Bisitun, and only Auramazda is ever said to have a "will" in this or any other Achaemenid inscription, and his will is always exercised in favor of the king. Darius is king by Auramazda's will (1.11-12), and by his will rules a vast empire (1.13-14), and, as noted above, Darius attributes victory in every battle to "the will of Auramazda." So the history Darius relates in this inscription is ultimately one of a struggle between the greatness or wish of the Lie and the wish or will of Auramazda, but it is Auramazda's will that always prevails, resulting in the Achaemenid's victories and rule over a great empire.

In the Achaemenid worldview, the choice of Darius and his descendants to rule is not accidental, for the kings have just the qualities one needs to end turmoil and reinstate humanity's happiness. Darius and Xerxes are excellent rulers, each explains in virtually identical language, because they are friends of *rāsta*, what is "right, just," but not of evil (DNb 5-8; XPl 5-8), and as a result they are not friends of the Lie-follower (DNb 12-13; XPl 13-14). They exercise great willpower so they can judge rightly and so that their subjects do not harm each other (DNb 13-15; XPl 14-17); the kings, apparently, would never harm their subjects, unless they were meting out deserved punishment. The result, then, is that they properly

---

57. See, e.g., Boyce, "The Religion of Cyrus the Great," 24–5; Lincoln, *Religion, Empire, and Torture*, 95.

58. Pokorny, *Indogermanisches etymologisches Wörterbuch*, 1:1135.

reward those who "cooperate, work with" (*ham-taxš-*) them, but punish those who do harm (DNb 16-19; XPl 17-21). In control of themselves and enemies of the Lie and its adherents, it is no wonder that these and other Achaemenids each refers to himself as *xšayaθiya vazraka* "the great king," appointed by *baga vazraka* "the great god." Their inscriptions otherwise use the adjective *vazraka* only to describe the *būmi* "earth," the first of Auramazda's creations that he bore to the Achaemenids to rule, and the *xšaça* "kingdom" where the Achaemenid exercises this rule in the world. Yet the standard creation formula never describes the earth as great, and the Achaemenids refer to it as such only where the king introduces himself as "the great king" and states that he rules *būmiyā vazrakayā* "in this great earth" (e.g., DNa 11-12; XPa 9; A¹Pa 13-14). The earth is not "great," that is, until the Achaemenid rules in it, and so the "kingdom" is also "great" (DSf 11-12; DSm 3-4; DZc 3-4) because this is the part of the world that the king can make most like himself and his god.[59] Here alone in the earth we find a king who successfully struggles against and defeats the Lie that aims to destroy human happiness.

Since the Achaemenid works to restore happiness to humanity, and has the proper skills to complete such a task, it is to everyone's benefit that they follow his command. Those who work with the Achaemenids do Auramazda's will, because, rather like Jesus in the Fourth Gospel, the Achaemenid acts only according to the will of god, and he accomplishes his goals only because his god acts for him. "Auramazda bore me support," writes Darius. "What I commanded to do, he made well done. That which I did, all by the will of Auramazda I did" (DSf 19-22). "This which I did," write Darius and Xerxes in virtually identical language,[60] "all by the will of Auramazda I did. Auramazda bore me support until I did the work" (DNa 48-51; XPh 43-46). So it is important that the people the king rules work with him, since he is only doing what Auramazda wants, and can only act because Auramazda supports him, and thus when the king writes that the people did what he commanded (e.g., DB 1.19-20, 23-24; DSe 19-20), or that the people acted "according to my desire" (e.g., DB 4.35-36; DNa 36-38), they work with him in establishing a world free from the Lie and full of happiness. Those who refuse to work with the

---

59. Cl. Herrenschmidt, "Désignation de l'empire et concepts politiques de Darius Iᵉʳ d'après ses inscriptions en vieux-perse," *StIr* 5 (1976): 33–65 (42–5).

60. In this case, this part of Darius's inscription begins with the words "this which has been done," but otherwise the inscriptions of the two kings are identical here. At this point in Darius's burial inscription, "this which has been done" is a reference back to the earlier parts of DNa where Darius refers to his actions as king.

Achaemenid thus oppose the desire of both god and king, and are like Gaumata, the first rebel Darius defeated, who was aligned with the Lie and who acted rather like the Lie-follower of the *Gatha*s, stealing other peoples' houses and land (DB 1.64-66). Liars like Gaumata take what does not belong to them, but the Achaemenids stress that they reward the righteous, who are those who *ham-taxš-* "work with" them.

Darius refers to his *kāma* "desire" as that to which his colonized peoples must conform, and in the inscriptions only the Achaemenid and Auramazda are ever said to have a "desire," and there does not appear to be any difference between what god and king want, since they both desire the original order that Auramazda created. Darius says something about this order at the beginning of the Bisitun Inscription, where, after he describes his assassination of Gaumata, who he says was a usurper, he writes in regard to the kingdom that "I set it down in place (*gāθavā*)" (DB 1.62-63). The Achaemenids almost always use *gaθu* "place" in the sense of the proper order of things that they restore, and so when Darius writes that he restored to the people what Guamata had stolen from them, he says that "I set the people down in place" (1.66). "By the will of Auramazda I did this; I cooperated (*hamataxšaiy*) until I set down our house in place" (1.68-69). Darius cooperates (*ham-taxš-*) with Auramazda, assumedly, to realize the god's will for his family, his house, and all the people, setting all things and people down in their proper places, so that his house rules the people and everyone enjoys what truly belongs to them, just as Auramazda intended. He works with Auramazda, and so the people should work with him to realize his desire for them, so that they can experience true happiness once more.

The cosmological hierarchy in Achaemenid ideology that makes obedience to royal command the basis of an ethical life is expressed most clearly in the Bisitun Inscription, where the Achaemenid acts only according to Auramazda's will and everyone else does what the Achaemenid commands. In this hierarchy of god, king, and everyone else,[61] Darius uses the term *bandaka* "subject" to refer to everyone else,

---

61. This tripartite hierarchy, argues Jack Balcer, was widespread among Indo-European peoples, and so likely derives from proto-Indo-European culture ("Ancient Epic Conventions in the Bisitun Text," in *Achaemenid History VIII: Continuity and Change*, ed. Heleen Sancisi-Weerdenburg, Amélie Kuhrt, and Margaret Cool Root [Leiden: Instituut voor het Nabije Oosten, 1994], 257–64 [258]). The inscriptions do refer to other gods on whom the Achaemenids depend for aid, as Chapter 4 discusses in more detail. Darius says that "Auramazda, and the other gods who are, bore me support" (DB 4.60-61, 62-63), and asks for help from Auramazda and "the gods of the court" (DPd 21-22, 23-24). Achaemenid kings sometimes ask Auramazda and

so that the totality of his empire's population is *bandaka* (DB 1.19), as are the generals of his armies (e.g., DB 2.19-20, 29-30, 49-50, 82), one of whom holds the rank of satrap (3.56). Achaemenid reliefs broadcast this three-tiered cosmic hierarchy as well, and on the relief on Darius's tomb, for example, a figure in a winged disk, who represents Auramazda,[62] is portrayed above all the other characters. On the level below him is Darius, and below Darius are figures representing the peoples of the empire.[63] The word *bandaka* derives from the Old Persian root *band-* "bind," and it is perhaps because the word suggests the king's subjects are bound by or to him that the Akkadian translation of the Bisitun Inscription renders the word as *qallu*, and the Aramaic translation as עלים, both of which, like Hebrew עבד, mean "slave."[64] Serving as slaves for the Achaemenid is to everyone's benefit, however, for in this way the colonized peoples can realize the happiness Auramazda intended for them. In reality, the Achaemenids distinguished between their Persian subjects and everyone else in the empire, for only Persian nobility could serve as officers in

---

"the gods" for protection (e.g., DSe 50-51; XPb 27-29; A¹Pa 22-23), although Artaxerxes II specifically calls upon Auramazda, Anahita, and Mithra for this (e.g., A²Sa 4-5; A²Sd 3-4). So we could subdivide the first tier of this cosmic hierarchy into two parts, with Auramazda occupying its higher level and the other gods who support the Achaemenids the lower one.

62. Not all scholars believe the figure in the winged disks of Achaemenid art represents Auramazda—see, e.g., Alireza S. Shahbazi, "An Achaemenid Symbol II: Farnah '(God-Given) Fortune' Symbolized," *AMI* 9 (1980): 119–47; Garrison, "*By the Favor of Auramazdā*," 26—but it seems more likely that Auramazda is indeed the figure we see there. As Ursula Seidl has noted, the version of the Bisitun Inscription discovered in Babylon replaces the image in the winged disk with representations of Babylonian gods ("Ein Monument Darius' I. aus Babylon," *ZA* 89 [1999]: 101–14 [107–8]), suggesting the figure at Bisitun represents a divinity. Root points out that the figure in the winged disk at Bisitun and elsewhere wears a divine headdress with the star of Shamash, symbols that also indicate the figure is to be understood as a god (*The King and Kingship*, 169–74), and Abolala Soudavar points out that Neo-Assyrian and Neo-Babylonian art represents divinities within winged disks (*The Aura of Kings: Legitimacy and Divine Sanction in Iranian Kingship*, BibIr 10 [Costa Mesa, CA: Mazda Publishers, 2003], 90–1).

63. See also the discussion in Khatchadourian, *Imperial Matter*, 6–9.

64. For the appearance of *qallu* as the translation of *bandaka* on the Akkadian version of the Bisitun Inscription, see CII 1/2/1.44, 48, 53, 62, 69, 73, 79, 86. For the translation of *bandaka* by Aramaic עלים, see *TAD* C2.1.19 (where it is misspelled as עילם). עלים was assumably used at other places in the original Aramaic text to translate *bandaka*, but because of the scroll's fragmentary nature this is the only place where the word has been preserved.

court,⁶⁵ and the Achaemenids evinced no interest in acculturating the colonized elites into the Persian world.⁶⁶ There is certainly nothing odious or difficult about the place of the colonized as servants bound to or by the Achaemenid, something that is clear in the dynasty's reliefs that portray figures that represent the colonized peoples in the atlantid pose, with their arms upraised and supporting the king, but doing so with little effort and with joy.⁶⁷ The loyalty and tribute the colonized owe to the king is the proper response for the good the empire has done for them, and as humanity brings the Achaemenid their tribute, they work with the king to construct the empire for their own benefit. Of course, everyone, including Persians, bore tribute to the king, and everyone was expected to adhere to the king's *dāta* "law," a word that reflects both individual royal commands and the general concept of law,⁶⁸ and something Xerxes says Auramazda set down (XPh 49-50, 51-53), just as the Avesta refers to the *dāta* of Ahura Mazda (*Y.* 21.1; 46.15). Achaemenid ideology, of course, makes no distinction between the law of Auramazda and the law of the king, as Chapter 4 discusses.

The Achaemenid worldview includes a geographical hierarchy as well, and the kings believed that the colonized on the margins of the world benefitted from the goodness the dynasty brought from the world's center. It is because the colonized at the margins of the empire benefit from the king's rule that "a Persian has fought battle far from Persia" (DNa 46-47),

---

65. Plutarch claims the Athenian politician and general Themistocles, who entered the service of Artaxerxes I after having been ostracized from Athens, was treated like a member of the Persian nobility (*Them.* 29.4). If this makes Themistocles the exception that proves the rule that only Persians held positions in the Achaemenid court, the exception was made, Thucydides writes, because of the brilliance of Themistocles' counsel (1.138.2-3).

66. See, e.g., Josef Wiesehöfer, "The Achaemenid Empire in the Fourth Century B.C.E.: A Period of Decline?," in Lipschits, Knoppers, and Albertz, eds. *Judah and the Judeans in the Fourth Century B.C.E.*, 43–73.

67. For a discussion of this iconographic element, see Root, *The King and Kingship*, 147–53.

68. Contra Lisbeth Fried ("'You shall appoint judges': Ezra's Mission and the Rescript of Artaxerxes," in Watts, eds, *Persia and Torah*, 63–89 [81–4]), who argues that Old Persian *dāta* refers only to the word of the king. Chapter 4 discusses the Achaemenids' understanding of the word, but for evidence that Old Persian *dāta* was understood to extend beyond individual royal commands, see Christopher Tuplin, "The Justice of Darius: Reflections on the Achaemenid Empire as a Rule-Bound Environment," in *Assessing Biblical and Classical Sources for the Reconstruction of Persian Influence, History and Culture*, ed. Anne Fitzpatrick-McKinley, CeO 10 (Wiesbaden: Harrassowitz, 2015), 73–126.

as Darius writes on his burial inscription, which lists the lands and peoples he rules (22-30), those who do what he says and who are held by his law (20-22). The statement reflects the Achaemenid understanding of peace and order radiating out from the imperial center, and their ideology claimed that the rest of the world could benefit from what is at its center in Persia, since this was the best part of the earth. Herodotus writes that the Persians honor most those who live closest to them and think the least of those who live farthest away (1.134.2), and Achaemenid ideology does make a distinction between the part of the earth the kings understood to be central—Persia, particularly, and to some extent nearby regions that had been imperial centers in the past—and the other parts of their empire. When the Achaemenids list the lands and peoples they rule, Persia is always named first (e.g., DB 1.14-17; XPa 16-28), and Darius says that he is king "in Persia," the king's true space, as Bruce Lincoln puts it.[69] The only exceptions in this regard are the lists that do not mention the Persian people, and these only begin with the Medes (DNa 22; DSe 21; XPh 19), Elamites (DPe 10), or Babylonians (DSf 29-30), the nearby homes of powerful kingdoms that preceded the Achaemenids' own. These Achaemenid lists of the peoples they rule move from areas at or near the centers of empire to lands and peoples located progressively farther away from Persia. This picture of a good center of the world, from which the Achaemenids can bring the rule that benefits people far away, corresponds to the Avestan notion that the first perfect lands created by Ahura Mazda were in Iran (*Vd* 1).[70] Xenophon writes that Cyrus the Younger claimed that the Persian Empire included all the habitable lands of the earth, and that outside of it are areas that are only too hot or too cold for humans to live (*Anab.* 1.7.6), and we can see here a reflection of a Zoroastrian understanding of hell in which one part is extremely cold and another extremely hot (e.g., *MX* 7.27-28; *AWN* 55.1),[71] and so we perhaps see in Xenophon's report an Achaemenid belief that life outside of the empire is literally hell-ish.

So if Persia and, to some degree, other central parts of the empire—Media, Elam, and Babylonia, specifically—are central and best, those colonized peoples farther away need the goodness the king can create, and as he provides them with peace and happiness from the center of the world,

---

69. Lincoln, *Religion, Empire, and Torture*, 22.
70. Lincoln, *Religion, Empire, and Torture*, 127.
71. Avestan texts evince little interest in describing hell (Stausberg, "Hell in Zoroastrian History," 220–7), but insofar as they address its climate, the emphasis falls on its coldness (*HN* 2.25). According to *Vd* 19.1, the cold north is also the dwelling place of Angra Mainyu.

they in turn bring tribute to the imperial center, a process we can see on the reliefs originally located in the apadana or audience hall at Persepolis. The panels depict representatives of different colonized groups, each distinguished by their dress,[72] in their final moments as individual peoples before being absorbed into empire as they wait in a long line to meet the king and present him with gifts.[73] The Achaemenid palaces themselves were built with the gifts and tribute of the colonized, as the Achaemenids take care to note; one of Darius's inscriptions from Susa (DSf) describes different groups from throughout the empire bringing exotic materials used to construct the palace there, and the columns in various palaces, including the one at Susa, had components brought from different parts of the empire.[74] Achaemenid palaces were distinguished by the pillared hall, and this hypostyle construction with its many identical columns supporting the roof broadcast the message that the empire sheltered its many colonized peoples from the Lie even as they helped the king to create that shelter.[75] The palace, then, becomes a microcosm of empire, the perfect place that the colonized and king build together with the empire's tribute as the peoples "work with" the king. It is a *fraša* "wonder" (DSa 5; DSf 56-57; DSj 6; DSo 4), a word the Achaemenids otherwise use only to describe Auramazda's creation (DSs 1; DNb 1-2; XPl 1-2).[76] The latter is restored in the empire the kings build with the colonized who work with them, symbolized in the construction of the palace, and so Darius's use of *fraša* to describe the one at Susa (DSf 56-57), a microcosm of the good original creation he restores with his colonized peoples and for their benefit, parallels the *Gathas*' use of *fraša* to describe the restoration through sacrifice of the original order Auramazda brought to the world (*Y.* 30.9; 50.11).[77]

The inscriptions provide no details as to how the Achaemenids rewarded those colonized peoples who worked with them, but we can gather from Classical sources that the dynasty became renowned for its beneficence to its loyal subjects. Greek writers describe the kings rewarding soldiers for great deeds in battle (Herodotus 8.85.3; 8.90.4), administrators for

---

72. Margaret Cool Root, "Reading Persepolis in Greek: Gifts of the Yauna," in *Persian Responses: Political and Cultural Interaction with(in) the Achaemenid Empire*, ed. Christopher Tuplin (Swansea: The Classical Press of Wales, 2007), 177–224 (186-7).

73. Lincoln, *"Happiness for Mankind"*, 186.

74. Boucharlat, "Susa under Achaemenid Rule," 59.

75. Khatchadourian, *Imperial Matter*, 110–17.

76. See Lincoln, *"Happiness for Mankind"*, 357–74.

77. Skjærvø, "The Achaemenids and the Avesta," 74–5.

their proper governance of agricultural land (Xenophon, *Oec.* 4.8), client rulers for their loyalty (Xenophon, *Anab.* 1.2.27), spies for providing them with information (Xenophon, *Cyr.* 8.2.10), and the list could go on. These rewards were themselves a way to broadcast their largesse to the loyal, but another more systematic way that the Achaemenids communicated the benefit of their rule was through the paradises. Xenophon claimed that they could be found in every satrapy (*Cyr.* 8.6.12), and, as mentioned above, the Persians established one at Ramat Rahel, the administrative center close to Jerusalem. Old Persian **paridaisa*[78] refers to a walled enclosure, and Classical sources say they were known for containing every kind of plant (e.g., Xenophon, *Anab.* 1.4.10; *Oec.* 4.13), including non-native species, and, as the previous section of the chapter discusses, the paradise at Ramat Rahel contained flora not native to Palestine. Some paradises were associated with satrapal residences (e.g., Xenophon, *Hell.* 4.1.15; *Anab.* 1.4.10), rather as the one in Judah was associated with the province's administrative building, and there is evidence that some of them were used for hunting (e.g., Xenophon, *Anab.* 1.2.7; *Cyr.* 8.6.12) or for growing fruit and wood (e.g., Aelian, *Var. hist.* 1.33; Strabo 16.1.11). The variety of uses to which they appear to have been put[79] suggests that different paradises likely had different functions, and that a single one could have multiple functions.[80] Lincoln argues they were a ubiquitous model of *šiyāti*, the original happiness Auramazda intended for humans that the Achaemenids claimed to re-create,[81] a conclusion bolstered by the fact that a paradise near Persepolis was called **vispa-šiyātiš* "all

---

78. The word is not extant in Old Persian, but it was borrowed as a loanword in languages used by people in the empire, including Greek (παράδεισος), Akkadian (*pardēsu*), and Hebrew (פרדס). It is unclear as to precisely how the Old Persian word was pronounced; it has the meaning of "walled enclosure," but Old Persian presumably adopted it as a loanword, or else we would expect a different final consonant that reflected Old Persian *didā* "wall." Avestan has *pairidaēza* "wall, enclosure," but this word may also be borrowed; see Angela Della Volpe, "Wall," in *Encyclopedia of Indo-European Culture*, ed. J. P. Mallory and Douglas Q. Adams (London: Fitzroy Dearborn, 1997), 628–9. For suggestions as to the original form of the Old Persian word, see Christopher Tuplin, *Achaemenid Studies*, Hist 99 (Stuttgart: Franz Steiner, 1996), 93–6.

79. For a discussion of the Classical and Akkadian literature that refers to the paradises, see Tuplin, *Achaemenid Studies*, 96–131.

80. Rémy Boucharlat, "Gardens and Parks at Pasargadae: Two 'Paradises'?," in Rollinger, Truschnegg, and Bichler, eds, *Herodot und das Persische Weltreich*, 557–74 (557).

81. Lincoln, *Religion, Empire, and Torture*, 1–2.

happiness."[82] The paradises, writes Diodorus, contained "plants and other costly items artistically arranged for luxury and the enjoyment in peace of good things" (14.80.2), and each could function as a microcosm of a world of fertility and wealth, perhaps reflecting some of the aspects of the perfect creation the Avesta describes, the original period in which plants as well as humans and animals existed in a state of perfect well-being.

The paradises model the world as it was intended to be, the world the Achaemenids reestablish, and given that at least one was destroyed as the first act of a rebellion in Phoenicia (Diodorus 16.41.5), they could be closely associated with Achaemenid rule.[83] They provided those who saw and entered them with a picture of a fertility that exists because of the dynasty's efforts. The excavators at Ramat Rahel, for example, argue that the paradise there made an effective medium to broadcast the Achaemenids' ability to mold nature to their will: "The well-watered imperial Persian garden must have left a lasting impression on the viewers in this relatively arid environment. Its imported trees from far-off lands, aromatic plants and impressive fruit trees, together with its aesthetic architectural features, symbolized the power and affluence of the Persian-period rulers."[84] Plutarch describes a paradise leaving a similar formidable impression when he writes that the soldiers of Artaxerxes II were so awestruck by the size and beauty of the trees in one they encountered while on campaign with the king that they hesitated to cut any of them down to warm themselves during the night, even after royal permission had been given (*Art.* 25.1-2). The message the paradises broadcast of the fertility, plenty, and wealth the Achaemenid restores to the world was echoed in the dynasty's iconography, and Achaemenid art abounds with images associating the king with the fertility that he brings to the world. The apadana that Darius built in the palace at Persepolis is full of such imagery, such as rosettes, cone-laden fir trees, and pomegranates,[85] and the many pillars that support the roof of the apadana, where the emissaries of the colonized peoples would meet the king, use floral and faunal motifs suggesting that, like the paradises, the palace displayed a model of the

---

82. P. O. Skjævrø, "Achaemenid *Vispašiyātiš*, Sasanian *Wipšād*," *StIr* 23 (1994): 79–80.

83. Llewellyn-Jones, *King and Court in Ancient Persia*, 93.

84. Lipschits, Gadot, and Langgut, "The Riddle of Ramat Rahel," 72.

85. Margaret Cool Root, "The Lioness of Elam: Politics and Dynastic Fecundity at Persepolis," in *A Persian Perspective: Essays in Memory of Heleen Sancisi-Weerdenburg*, ed. Wouter Henkelman and Amélie Kuhrt, AchHist 13 (Leiden: Nederlands Instituut voor het Nabije Oosten, 2003), 9–32 (21–2).

fertile and perfect world the Achaemenids were reestablishing.[86] The Greeks certainly associated the Achaemenid with fertility and agriculture, argues Pierre Briant,[87] and Xenophon describes the king as laboring to ensure the productivity of land throughout the empire (*Oec.* 4.8, 12) and spending most of his time in the paradises (4.13). Briant suggests that the image of a Persian figure guiding an ox with a plow, which appears on cylinder seals and Cilician coins, might depict the king as guaranteeing fertility for his subjects.[88]

Yet fertile agricultural land is of no value if it has no one to protect it, agree the characters Socrates and Cristobulus in Xenophon's *Economist* (4.4-17), and that is why, they say, the Persians pay equal attention to agriculture and the craft of warfare. Official Achaemenid ideology downplayed the massive military power available to them—the following chapter will discuss this point in more detail—but this does not mean that it was absent in the imperial imagery the dynasty sanctioned. The whole focus of the first four columns of the Bisitun Inscription is Darius's defeat of various violent manifestations of the Lie, but descriptions of such specific military encounters are unique to Bisitun among all the Achaemenid inscriptional material. The imagery of the Persian hero engaged in some sort of combat, however, is much more common on cylinder seals and coins from the Persian Empire. In such depictions, a figure in Persian dress is in combat with or, more frequently, controlling in his outstretched arms animals or monsters, and this is, in fact, the most common image on the glyptic art from Persepolis.[89] It is common as well among the seal images produced elsewhere in the empire; the Persian hero appears on fourteen percent of the seal images from Daskyleion, thirty-five percent of the seals from the Achaemenid palace at Memphis, and at least fifteen percent of the seals discovered at Wadi ed-Daliyeh in

---

86. Khatchadourian, *Imperial Matter*, 115–16.
87. Briant, *Kings, Countries, Peoples*, 272–4.
88. Briant, *Kings, Countries, Peoples*, 271–85.
89. Of the more than three hundred seals from Persepolis with the hero image, two-thirds portray the control situation and one-third the combat situation; see Mark B. Garrison and Margaret Cool Root, *Seals on the Persepolis Fortification Tablets. Volume I: Images of Heroic Encounter*, UCOIP 117 (Chicago: The Oriental Institute of the University of Chicago, 2001), 59. For discussions and reproductions of these and other common scenes on Persepolitan glyptic, see Mark B. Garrison, *The Ritual Landscape at Persepolis: Glyptic Imagery from the Persepolis Fortification and Treasury Archives*, SAOC 72 (Chicago: The Oriental Institute of the University of Chicago, 2017), 78–100.

Samaria.⁹⁰ At Daskyleion, the hero is normally wearing a crown, and thus is a representation of the Achaemenid, and when portrayed in combat he is always pictured just before he plunges his dagger into the animal or monster he opposes, at which point his defeat of the enemy is not complete but guaranteed.⁹¹

It is possible that some of the Achaemenids' subjects found such imagery threatening, but if we read it through the lens of the Bisitun Inscription, for example, we can see that at least part of its purpose is to point to the king's beneficence, portraying him as using his military might to save his colonized peoples from attacks by manifestations of the Lie that work against the king's reestablishment of the perfection of creation. The portraits of the crowned archers on Achaemenid coinage reflect the military power available to the king as well,⁹² but in the larger context of Achaemenid ideology this is a benefit to the loyal colonized subjects whose happiness is both provided and defended by the king. The most common depiction of the Persian archer in Achaemenid glyptic art is, in fact, that of the archer protecting domesticated animals,⁹³ and while there may be many depictions at Persepolis of the Persian hero in the act of stabbing a rampant lion, the reliefs in the Palace of Darius in that royal complex also include a depiction of the hero holding a lion cub in one hand, while the other holds a dagger down at his side,⁹⁴ as he cares for the world he defends. On PFS 7*, a seal from the Persepolis Fortification Archive, the king appears in the center of the seal as the Persian hero with Auramazda directly above him, while in each extended arm he controls a beast, and flanking the beasts on the outer edges of the scene are date palms,⁹⁵ the agricultural bounty that exists because the Achaemenid, with Auramazda's will and support, defends the empire from danger. The king combats the Lie by defeating violent incarnations of it, and the imagery

---

90. Garrison and Root, *Seals on the Persepolis Fortification Tablets*, 55.

91. See the analyses in Root, *The King and Kingship*, 310–11; Kaptan, *The Daskyleion Bullae*, 1:57–71.

92. See the analysis in Cindy L. Nimchuk, "The 'Archers' of Darius: Coinage or Tokens of Royal Esteem?," *ArsOr* 32 (2002): 55–79.

93. Mark B. Garrison, "Achaemenid Iconography as Evidenced by Glyptic Art: Subject Matter, Social Function, Audience and Diffusion," in *Images as Media: Sources for the Cultural Hero of the Near East and the Eastern Mediterranean (1st Millennium BCE)*, ed. C. Uehlinger, OBO 175 (Göttingen: Vandenhoeck & Ruprecht, 2000), 115–63 (135–6).

94. Root, "Achaemenid Imperial Architecture," 27.

95. See a discussion of the seal in Finn, "Gods, Kings, Men," 232–4.

3. The Beneficent King

of PFS 7* links the Achaemenid's defense of the world to the fertility and prosperity, represented by the date palms, that his subjects experience as a result of this work.

So focused are the messages of Achaemenid ideology on the person of the king that they have no room for beneficent actors besides him. Avestan texts, like the later Pahlavi material, divide humanity into the four classes of priests, warriors, farmers, and artisans (e.g., *Y.* 19.17), but in the dynasty's self-presentation, the king fills all of those roles except for the last. The magi were the traditional clergy of Zoroastrianism, and in the Sasanian period had priestly, administrative, and legal roles.[96] During the Achaemenid period, the Persepolis Fortification Archive makes it clear that magi received rations in order to conduct the cults of various gods (e.g., PF 757-759; 769; 1798; 1951), and Greek texts identify them as officiants at sacrifices and religious rituals associated with the Achaemenids (e.g., Xenophon, *Cyr.* 8.1.23; 8.3.11; Herodotus 1.132; Strabo 15.3.14) and connect them with Zoroastrian teaching.[97] The magi, however, are conspicuously absent from the ideology the Achaemenids broadcast,[98] and the only one who is ever mentioned in their inscriptions is Gaumata, the first manifestation of the Lie in Achaemenid literature, and Darius repetitively refers to him as "the Magian" (DB 1.36, 44, 46, 50, etc.). Whatever roles the magi actually performed in the empire were not important for Achaemenid royal ideology, and since Darius apparently found it convenient to identify one of them as a conduit for the Lie, Achaemenid self-presentation could apparently do without them. Nor does there appear to be a need for priests to act as intermediaries between the king and Auramazda as the Achaemenids portrayed things, since some

---

96. So, e.g., Franz Grenet, "Where Are the Sogdian Magi?," *BAI* 21 (2007): 159–77 (159).

97. Plato, for example, refers to "royal tutors" instructing the king's children in "the Magian teaching of Zoroaster," which he describes as "service for the gods" (*Alc.* 121e-122a), and in *On Philosophy*, Aristotle wrote that the Magi taught of a good spirit called Zeus or Ὠρομάσδης and an evil one called Hades or Ἀρειμάνιος (Diogenes Laertius 1.8), names that reflect Auramazda/Ohrmazd and Ahriman. Herodotus claims that the Magi kill ants, snakes, and reptiles (1.140.3), reflecting the Zoroastrian belief in Angra Mainyu/Ahriman's evil creation and the necessity to destroy manifestations of it.

98. The Achaemenids may have underwritten some of the sacrifices the magi performed, at least in the region around Persepolis (the area covered by the Persepolis Fortification Archive), but that is not the same thing as claiming that their royal ideology presented the magi as important figures.

of their iconography depicts the king as standing alone before the altar, without the need for magi as cultic officiants.[99] We have just seen that the Achaemenids portrayed themselves as the warriors and farmers *par excellence*, protecting the land and ensuring its fertility, and since they also depicted themselves acting as priests, they claimed the roles of the first three classes of humanity, leaving their subjects to fill the fourth one, that of the artisans who, as Pahlavi texts present them, are to do only the work they understand (*MX* 32.5-6). This self-presentation fits the three-tiered cosmic hierarchy of the inscriptions that divides the world into Auramazda, the king, and everyone else, and everyone else must act as loyal subjects who obey the king's command and not presume that they know better as to how to farm, govern, and defend the empire, or how best to interpret the divine will.

Auramazda is dependent upon the king to restore happiness, just as the king is dependent upon Auramazda as he acts to do so,[100] and this close and unmediated connection between god and king may explain why the art of both the court style and colonized *koinē* sometimes associates the Achaemenid with divinity. In the reliefs originally located in the apadana at Persepolis, different groups of representatives from the colonized peoples are being led to the king, a Persian noble holding the hand of the first member of each group, reflecting Mesopotamian iconography of worshipers being led before a god.[101] Greek writers, in fact, insisted that the kings' subjects had to prostrate themselves and do obeisance (προσκύνησις) before him (e.g., Plutarch, *Them.* 27.4; Arrian, *Anab.* 4.11.8), reflecting the Greek belief that the Persians regarded the king as a god, something they insisted was antithetical to their understandings of human freedom and divinity (e.g., Herodotus 7.136.1; Xenophon, *Hell.* 4.1.35). Aeschylus's *Persians* relies on this Greek understanding of the Achaemenid worldview, and the Persian characters in the play refer to Darius as θεῖον "divine" (651), θεομήστωρ "divine counselor" (654-655), and "like a god" (711). This may say more about Greek perceptions than

---

99. Clarisse Herrenschmidt, "Writing between Visible and Invisible Worlds in Iran, Israel, and Greece," in *Ancestor of the West: Writing, Reasoning, and Religion in Mesopotamia, Elam, and Greece*, ed. Jean Bottéro, Clarisse Herrenschmidt, and Jean-Pierre Vernant, trans. Teresa Lavender Fagan (Chicago: The University of Chicago Press, 2000), 69–146 (116–17).

100. Skjævrø, "The Achaemenids and the *Avesta*," 57–8.

101. Margaret Cool Root, "Defining the Divine in Achaemenid Persian Kingship: The View from Bisitun," in *Every Inch a King: Comparative Studies on Kings and Kingship in the Ancient and Medieval Worlds*, ed. Lynette Mitchell and Charles Melville, RE 2 (Leiden: Brill, 2013), 23–65 (56–7).

Achaemenid self-presentation, however, since evidence from the royal reliefs tells us the king's subjects did not prostrate themselves when in his presence.[102] Nonetheless, the fact that cultic rites were performed at royal tombs[103] and before a statue of Darius in Sippar,[104] and the fact that the king and Auramazda physically resemble each other on Achaemenid reliefs,[105] tell us Achaemenid ideology portrayed the king as merged with the divine or as Auramazda's "doppelganger."[106] The Achaemenids reworked iconography from different parts of their empire to associate themselves with local depictions of divinities, writes Elspeth Dusinberre, and so the Persepolis seals portray the king as standing on animals who bear him, as gods are sometimes depicted in Eastern Anatolian and Mesopotamian art.[107] Some Anatolian coins of the Persian period place images of the head of the king where those of divinities had traditionally appeared,[108] while some of the images of the king on Samarian coins seem to portray a cult statue, potentially pointing to local worship of him.[109]

---

102. See the discussion in Josef Wiesehöfer, "'Denn ihr huldigt nicht einem Menshen als eurem Herrscher, sondern nur den Göttern': Bemerkungen zur Proskynese in Iran," in *Religious Themes and Texts of Pre-Islamic Iran and Central Asia: Studies in Honour of Professor Gherardo Gnoli on the Occasion of his 65th birthday on 6th December 2002*, ed. Carlo G. Cereti, Mauro Maggi, and Elio Provasi, BzI 24 (Wiesbaden: Reichert, 2003), 447–52.

103. See, e.g., Arrian, *Anab.* 6.29.7; Wouter Henkelman, "An Elamite Memorial: The *šumar* of Cambyses and Hystapes," in Henkelman and Kuhrt, eds, *A Persian Perspective*, 101–72.

104. Robert Rollinger, "Herrscherkult bei Teispiden und Achaimeniden: Realität oder Fiktion?," in *Studien zum vorhellenistischen und hellenistischen Herrscherkult*, ed. Linda-Marie Günther and Sonja Plischke, Oik 9 (Berlin: Verlag Antike, 2011), 11–54; Caroline Waerzeggers, "A Statue of Darius in the Temple at Sippar," in *Extraction and Control: Studies in Honor of Matthew W. Stolper*, ed. Michael Kozuh et al., SAOC 68 (Chicago: The Oriental Institute of the University of Chicago, 2014), 323–9.

105. Llewellyn-Jones, *King and Court in Ancient Persia*, 20–1.

106. That the Achaemenids portrayed kingship as merged with the divine is the conclusion in Root, "Defining the Divine," 60; the description of the king as Auramazda's "doppelganger" is that of Llewellyn-Jones in *King and Court in Ancient Persia*, 20.

107. Elspeth R. M. Dusinberre, "King or God? Imperial Iconography and the 'Tiarate Head' Coins of Achaemenid Anatolia," in *Across the Anatolian Plateau: Readings in the Archaeology of Ancient Turkey*, AASOR 57 (Boston: ASOR, 2002), 157–71 (157, 159–61).

108. Dusinberre, *Empire, Authority, and Autonomy*, 241–4.

109. Gitler, "Identities of the Indigenous Coinages," 110–11.

The Achaemenid inscriptions do not suggest the kings understood or portrayed themselves as the equals of Auramazda or "the other gods who are," the traditional deities of Persia and Elam whose cults they supported.[110] In Achaemenid ideology, however, the kings are god-like as far as their subjects are concerned, uniquely linked to Auramazda, needing no intermediary, Magian or otherwise, to worship and communicate with their god, and providing their peoples with fertility and defense. They are god-like, certainly, in the way they can convey the truth about the divine will for the world. Their inscriptions make no references to the important Avestan concept of *aša* "Truth"—its Old Persian cognate **arta*[111] never appears in the inscriptions[112]—although this is not because they were unaware of the concept, which occurs frequently enough in names of figures associated with the empire, such as *arta-xšaça* (Artaxerxes), "one whose reign is through Truth," *arta-banu* (Artabanus), "glory of Truth," *arta-sūras* (Artasyras), "powerful through Truth," and so on.[113] Unlike the *Gathas*, the Achaemenids never claim that Auramazda endowed humans with Truth, or that Auramazda is "the father of Truth," or that Truth is an entity to which one can sacrifice.[114] Life is not a struggle between Auramazda and Truth on one side and Angra Mainyu (who is never mentioned in the inscriptions) and the Lie on the other, it is a struggle between Auramazda and his agent, the Achaemenid, on one side and the Lie and humans who manifest it on the other. In the inscriptions,

---

110. Darius refers to "the other gods who are" (DB 4.61, 62-63); Chapter 4 discusses the Achaemenid concept of *baga* "god," which the dynasty limited to the traditional deities of Persia and Elam.

111. Pokorny, *Indogermanisches etymologisches Wörterbuch*, 1:56; Gamkrelidze and Ivanov, *Indo-European and the Indo-Europeans*, 1:710.

112. In one of his inscriptions, Xerxes uses the word *artācā* in the context of referring to the worship of Auramazda (XPh 41, 50–1, 53–4), but the meaning of the word and the phrase in which it appears are disputed. Some see it as related to Old Persian **arta*, but others to **artu* "time, season"; for a brief discussion, see Nichols, "The Iranian Concept of *aša*," 64. In the same inscription, Xerxes writes that those who worship Auramazda will be *artāvan* "blessed" in the afterlife (XPh 48, 55). This Old Persian word is a cognate of Avestan *ašavan* "one who has Truth," and in Avestan material it is the *ašavan* who enters a blessed afterlife (*Vd* 19.30-31; *HN* 2.16).

113. See E. Benveniste, *Titres et noms propres en iranien ancien*, TIEIUP 1 (Paris: C. Klincksieck, 1966), 83–5, 102, 107–8.

114. Shahrokh Razmjou maintains that the appearance of **arta* in so many Old Persian names of the Achaemenid period means that Arta was worshiped as a god at the time ("Religion and Burial Customs," in Curtis and Tallis, eds, *Forgotten Empire*, 150–80 [151]). Even if that is true, however, Achaemenid ideology never portrays Truth as a divine or quasi-divine figure.

truth is the creation of the Achaemenids, and most inscriptions that have more than one paragraph begin most of the paragraphs with the verb *θanh-* followed by a royal name—*θāntiy dārayavauš* "thus says Darius," for example—a verb from the same Indo-European root as words like Avestan *sənghaiti* "proclaims" and Sanskrit *śaṃsati* "vows, recites," as well as Latin *censere* "to judge, proclaim solemnly." Achaemenid inscriptions generally represent themselves as royal speech, and as the kings speak through the inscriptions they solemnly proclaim the way things are, defining the truth of the world for their empire.[115] What is true is what they say is true, and it is important for the colonized to believe this because they must act in accordance with what the Achaemenid says, since he commands according to his desire, which is also Auramazda's desire. What is true, what is best for humanity, is the word of the Achaemenid, who directly represents and speaks for Auramazda.

If we wanted to compare the Achaemenids to a figure from the Avesta, then perhaps the parallel should be Saoshyant, the individual associated with the eschatological defeat of evil, for the world the Achaemenids depict is one that they have largely rid of evil and restored to its pristine paradisiacal state. The comparison is not precise, since there is no eschatology in Achaemenid ideology, although we could say that history has largely come to an end as far as the kings portray things through their official media, since each king continues the rule of a world freed from turmoil. They must continue to fight to root out the Lie and its evil effects from the world, and the next chapter discusses the ways in which they justify this violence in the context of the rest of their ideology, but we turn first to the ways Ezra–Nehemiah reflects the picture of the beneficent king the Achaemenids broadcast to their empire.

3. *Community and Beneficent King in Ezra–Nehemiah*

As we turn to read Ezra–Nehemiah in light of these aspects of Achaemenid self-presentation, with a particular focus on the book's depiction of community identity, we will see that it presents the kings largely as they present themselves, and that it portrays the community much as the Achaemenids portray the colonized peoples in the media that reflected

---

115. É. Pirart, "Le mazdéisme politique de Darius Ier," *IIJ* 45 (2002): 121–51 (130 n. 50); Lincoln, *"Happiness for Mankind"*, 34–5. Old Persian *θanh-* is from the Indo-European root **k̑ens-* "to speak solemnly"; for the cognates mentioned above, see Pokorny, *Indogermanisches etymologisches Wörterbuch*, 1:566 and Douglas Q. Adams and J. P. Mallory, "Speak," in Mallory and Adams, eds, *Encyclopedia of Indo-European Culture*, 534–6 (536).

their worldview. In Ezra–Nehemiah, the king of Persia is appointed by God and acts according to divine will, needing no intermediary to interpret it, and so he is able to announce the truth. It is the king's goal to make the world better for the peoples he rules, and so long as the colonized obediently work with him, keeping the law sent by God and authorized by the king, their lives will become better, as the king rewards their loyalty and ensures their prosperity. As Chapter 2 demonstrates, Ezra–Nehemiah depicts the first generation of the post-exilic community as a colonist-like group sent by the king from Babylon at the center of the world, and makes loyalty to the king the key aspect of their identity, but the longer they remain at the margins of the empire the more they struggle to maintain that ideal, a reflection of the geography of Achaemenid ideology, in which goodness is found at the empire's center. The epigone of Ezra 7–Nehemiah 13, however, has lived far from the king and this good center for so long that without Achaemenid leadership it will destroy itself, having abandoned its ideal identity and become disloyal to the God who has given the rule of the earth to the Persian kings. In this longer second part of the book, readers see that anomism has unfortunately become the defining characteristic of the community's identity, and as a result they are just like the colonized peoples the Achaemenids describe, utterly dependent on the dynasty's rule to save them from destruction and provide for their happiness and prosperity.

This sort of reading of Ezra–Nehemiah does not account for all of its features, in part because there are other aspects of Achaemenid ideology that Chapter 4 discusses, and in part because the author's worldview was shaped by things such as his or her elite social location within the Judean temple assembly, a matter Chapter 5 takes up. And one obvious and seemingly important point of disconnection between the theology of Ezra–Nehemiah and that of the Achaemenids is that they look to two different deities to ground important claims of their worldviews, for in the former Yhwh and not Auramazda is the God who governs the world. Yet based on evidence from elsewhere in the Persian Empire, we would expect that the Achaemenids' theological message about creation and the divine control of history would have been expressed in terms acceptable to a Judean worldview. One example of such evidence is the Chalouf Stela from Egypt, which commemorates Darius's construction of a canal between the Nile and the Red Sea. On one side it bears a trilingual inscription in Old Persian, Elamite, and Akkadian with language and thought shared with the inscriptions the previous section of the chapter discusses, referring to Auramazda as creator (DZc 1-3) and as bearing the kingship to Darius (3-4). Darius presents himself as in complete command of the construction of the canal, ordering its creation (8-9) so that ships could go from Egypt to Persia, "as was my desire" (12). On the stela's other side, however, is a hieroglyphic text, and while it is fragmentary it obviously represents a very different worldview. The iconography on this side is distinctly Egyptian, and it refers to Ra, not Auramazda, as giving Darius rule over Egypt and ordering him to construct the canal.[116]

To take another example of the Achaemenids' willingness to translate their ideology into ideas acceptable to local worldviews, a statue of Darius discovered at Susa, but originally carved in Egypt and located in the temple of Ra-Atum at Heliopolis,[117] portrays the king in a style typical of that of the Saite Dynasty that Cambyses overthrew when he conquered Egypt, and the general iconography of the statue is Egyptian,[118] and was obviously carved by Egyptian artists.[119] The statue's hieroglyphic text uses language typical of the royal inscriptions of the Saite period, and refers to Darius as "the living image of Ra," "the supreme lord of the earth," "the perfect god, master of the Two Lands," and so on.[120] Auramazda is never mentioned in the Egyptian text, and so it is Ra, not Auramazda, who is named as creator, supporting and authorizing Darius's reign as a pharaoh.[121] Yet the statue of Darius, like the Chalouf Stela, also has a trilingual inscription in Old Persian, Elamite, and Akkadian that refers to Auramazda as creator (DSab 1) and in which Darius introduces himself in a manner common to the dynasty's inscriptions—"I am Darius, the

---

116. For a drawing of the Egyptian side of the stela and discussions of its iconography and what can be read of the hieroglyphic text, see J. Ménant, "La stele de Chalouf," *RTRPA* 9 (1897): 131–57; Briant, *Kings, Countries, Peoples*, 244–7.

117. Petrographic analysis indicates the stone from which the statue was carved was from Egypt (Jean Trichet and Pierre Poupet, "Étude pétrographique de la roche constituant la statue de Darius découverte à Suse en décembre 1972," *CDAFI* 4 [1974]: 47–59), and so scholars generally accept it was originally located in the temple of Ra-Atum before being relocated to Susa (Shahrokh Razmjou, "Assessing the Damage: Notes on the Life and Demise of the Statue of Darius from Susa," *ArsOr* 32 [2002]: 81–104 [86–7]).

118. For a description of the iconography and its cultural influences, see David Stronach, "Description and Comment," *JA* 260 (1972): 241–6.

119. Jean Yoyotte, "Les inscriptions hiéroglyphiques: Darius et l'Égypte," *JA* 260 (1972): 253–66 (253–4).

120. For a translation and discussion of the Egyptian text, see Yoyotte, "Les inscriptions hiéroglyphiques."

121. As Alan Lloyd argues, there could be no Egyptian state without a pharaoh, and so Darius found it necessary to present himself as one. See his "Darius I in Egypt: Suez and Hibis," in Tuplin, ed, *Persian Responses*, 99–115.

great king, king of the lands, king in this great earth" (2-3)—and asks for Auramazda's protection (4), making no mention of any Egyptian god. The statue form of Darius is posed in Egyptian style, but he is also dressed in a Persian robe with Persian bracelets;[122] on the block of stone that serves as the statue's foundation, human figures representing the peoples subject to the king are carved in what is Egyptian style, but they adopt the atlantid pose of Achaemenid reliefs, their hands raised to support the king with little effort, rather than bound as in the Egyptian iconographic tradition.[123] So the statue of Darius, like the Chalouf Stela, provides a local audience with depictions of Achaemenid ideology that appropriate important aspects of their native worldviews and iconography, something the dynasty undoubtedly hoped would make their basic imperial claims understandable and acceptable. Like the Persianizing imagery of the *koinē* art forms elsewhere in the colonies, these sorts of adaptations of royal ideology helped local populations negotiate between their worldviews and their place as subjects to the Persians.

We find official representations of Achaemenid ideology accommodating itself to local worldviews in other parts of the empire, as well. The iconography on the copy of the Bisitun Inscription in Babylon, for example, replaced the figure of Auramazda, who appears in the relief Darius had carved along with the inscription on Mount Bisitun in Iran, with figures of Babylonian gods.[124] Throughout the Persian period, in fact, the Babylonian elite emphasized the role of Marduk in bestowing kingship,[125] and so in Babylon, as in Egypt, we see an accommodation of official Achaemenid imagery to local worldviews and vice versa. On the Chalouf Stela, Achaemenid ideology literally has two faces, one phrased in the language of the central imperial message and the other in language that translated that message into a worldview understandable by local

---

122. Stronach, "Description and Comment," 245.

123. For a discussion of the statue's iconography, see Root, *The King and Kingship*, 146, and Razmjou, "Assessing the Damage," 85. For a longer discussion of Achaemenid appropriation of Pharaonic ideology and iconography in Achaemenid self-presentations in Egypt, see Melanie Wasmuth, "Political Memory in the Achaemenid Empire: The Integration of Egyptian Kingship into Persian Royal Display," in *Political Memory in and after the Persian Empire*, ed. Jason M. Silverman and Caroline Waerzeggars, ANEM 13 (Atlanta: SBL Press, 2015), 203–37.

124. Seidl, "Ein Monument Darius' I. aus Babylon," 107–8.

125. John P. Nielsen, "'I overwhelmed the king of Elam': Remembering Nebuchadnezzar I in Persian Babylonia," in Silverman and Waerzeggars, eds, *Political Memory in and after the Persian Empire*, 53–73.

populations. It is hardly unreasonable, then, to suggest that officials in Judah who represented the Achaemenids and who found themselves in a position of justifying the dynasty's rule to the local elite would have found ways of accommodating those justifications to a Judean worldview, something that would have presented Yhwh rather than Auramazda as "the God of the heavens" (Ezra 1:2).

Cyrus's speech that opens Ezra–Nehemiah and places Yhwh in this role, then, likely reflects an imperial attempt to accommodate Achaemenid ideology to Judean worldviews. Here, just as in the Achaemenid inscriptions, it is the king who speaks the truth in order that the divine will might be manifested, and he does not need the Magi or Judean prophets or anyone else to act as an intermediary between himself and the divine. So although Ezra 1:1 refers to Cyrus's announcement as the fulfillment of "the word of Yhwh from the mouth of Jeremiah," royal rather than prophetic speech appears in the text. Ezra–Nehemiah never reports direct divine speech from the mouths of the prophets, and so if it is simply not clear as to which oracle(s) from Jeremiah the author may have in mind at this point,[126] that is because, in his or her view, prophetic oracles are not overly important, at least not in comparison with royal speech, and the author refuses to privilege the prophetic word over the royal one. It obviously does matter to the author that Yhwh be presented as in control of the world, and so the opening verse asserts that Yhwh foretold the end of the exile, but the king interacts with God directly to convey the divine will, and just as in the Achaemenid inscriptions he speaks the truth: the God of the heavens has given him all the kingdoms of the earth and ordered him to build a temple. And Cyrus's interpretation of the divine will is one supported by God, as Chapter 2 notes, since he decides on his own initiative to order those among Yhwh's people to go to Jerusalem and build (1:3), and God supports this order by rousing this people (1:5), thereby demonstrating the truth of Cyrus's claims and the trustworthiness of his decisions and actions.

---

126. Scholars have suggested a range of plausible possibilities, such as Jer. 25:11 or 29:10-14, which refer to seventy years of exile in Babylon (e.g., Gunneweg, *Esra*, 41; Serge Frolov, "The Prophecy of Jeremiah in Esr 1,1," *ZAW* 116 [2004]: 595–601), or to Jeremiah's call narrative, which refers to God's word in Jeremiah's "mouth" concerning the destruction and rebuilding of nations, reflected in the rebuilding of Judah in Ezra–Nehemiah (so Laird, *Negotiating Power in Ezra–Nehemiah*, 80–1), or to passages like Jer. 30–33 that refer to a new covenant and Davidic king (see Karrer-Grube, "Scrutinizing the Conceptual Unity of Ezra and Nehemiah," 135–59 [150–7]; Fried, *Ezra: A Commentary*, 50).

Cyrus was not an Achaemenid, but since Darius retroactively incorporated him into the dynasty, the author of Ezra–Nehemiah likely thought of him as such. He clearly appears in Ezra 1 as the Achaemenids portrayed themselves, chosen by the divine to rule the whole earth and speaking the truth of these matters to his peoples. His generosity to the Judean community in Babylonia is immediately on display, ordering that they should receive gifts from "the people of their place" (1:4, 6), while he brings to them the vessels from the first temple (1:7-11) so they can be used in the cult in Jerusalem. The community itself is located near the center of the world, in Babylonia, one of the good lands in Achaemenid ideology. Readers first encounter Cyrus in Babylon as he personally conveys the temple vessels to the people who will journey to Jerusalem, and Nehemiah refers to Artaxerxes as "the king of Babylon" (Neh. 13:6),[127] and this tells us that the author of the book understands Babylon to be an imperial center, and portrays the community as being like a group of colonizers migrating from the center to the margins of empire on the king's orders, as Chapter 2 discusses.[128] Beginning in Ezra 1:11, and then continually throughout the book, they are הגולה "the exile," linked to a people still literally in exile in Babylonia, and so their identity is to some extent rooted at the center of the empire, which is where colonizers come from. As we saw in Chapter 2, some of the migrants are unable to prove that they are descended from Israel, but this does not result in their exclusion from the community, for what matters is that they originally come from the center of the world. The community is loyal to the king, as his subjects should be, and the king guards their welfare, clearly demonstrated in the fact that the gifts he urges others to provide them result in the vast donations the community itself can give to restart the temple cult (2:69). They work with the king, as the Achaemenids said the colonized peoples should, following the divine command he truly communicates so they can make their own lives better. If they are subjects of the great king, they are like the peoples as represented in the atlantid pose on the Achaemenid reliefs, supporting the king with little effort. In

---

127. A title that Artaxerxes I, like Xerxes, actually used; see Robert Rollinger, "Xerxes und Babylon," NABU 1999–8, online: http://www.achemenet.com/pdf/nabu/nabu1999-008.pdf (accessed 13 January 2020).

128. So simply because Ezra 1–6 portrays Babylonia as central is not evidence for this material as written relatively early in the post-exilic period, contra Juha Pakkala, "Centers and Peripheries in the Ezra Story," in *Centres and Peripheries in the Early Second Temple Period*, ed. Ehud Ben Zvi and Christoph Levin, FAT 108 (Tübingen: Mohr Siebeck, 2016), 295–314 (299–304). This is just a reflection of Achaemenid ideology.

Ezra–Nehemiah, the community defines themselves through their loyalty to the king upon their arrival in the colonies, not only as they obey his order to build, but also insofar as this order defines them over against the other Yahwists in Palestine whom they do not permit to join them since, they say, Cyrus the king of Persia has commanded them alone to construct the temple (4:3).

The distinction between this first generation of the community and the Yahwists and others described as the "adversaries" of "the descendants of the exile" (4:1) can be better appreciated once we have some sense as to how the Achaemenids broadcast the truth of the world to their peoples. It is not just that "the people of the land" (4:4) are outside of the genealogical boundaries of the community whom the king has ordered to migrate from the good center of the world, and that their actions in Ezra 4 that portray them as thwarting a royal order place them outside the boundaries of loyalty that also define that group. The letter of 4:11-16, something the local population has bribed officials to send to the king, contains lies, and so it makes them the natural enemy of the Achaemenid who punishes Lie-followers, those who oppose his work to reestablish humanity's happiness. The letter contains three notable falsehoods: in a rebuilt Jerusalem, the community will not pay its taxes (4:13); Jerusalem was originally destroyed because it was a "rebellious city, causing harm to kings" (4:15); and so if the king allows the construction of the city walls, he can expect a rebellion in Across-the-River (4:16).[129] Readers even vaguely familiar with other Judean writings that would have existed in some form by the time Ezra–Nehemiah was composed, such as the books of Kings, Jeremiah, and Ezekiel, would have seen the second statement as false, since in these works it is a failure to obey their God rather than insurrection that leads to the destruction of Jerusalem, a matter of which Ezra–Nehemiah informs readers as soon as Ezra 5:12 and then repeats at numerous points (Ezra 9:6-15; Neh. 1:5-11; 9:6-37; 13:17-18). The people of the land are, at this point, trying to convince the king that the community and not they themselves are his disloyal subjects, but once the walls are constructed later in the narrative there is no hint of rebellion in Judah, the people of the land's third lie of the letter, nor any attempt to reduce the payment of tax to the king, their first lie, not even in Nehemiah 5 where, as Chapter 2 notes, some of the people claim a royal tariff has been a factor in their impoverishment (Neh. 5:4).

---

129. See Janzen, "A Colonized People," 37. MT 4:16 says that "no portion in Across-the-River will remain to you" if Jerusalem is rebuilt; 2 Esd. 4:16 says that "you will not have peace" under that circumstance; and the parallel verse in 1 Esd. 2:20 says "you will not have a way down to Coele-Syria and Phoenicia."

One reason to place the correspondence of Ezra 4:11-22 in its current achronological location is to emphasize that the people of the land are liars, in clear distinction from the loyal ideal community of Ezra 1–6. For the Achaemenids, lies stand at the root of rebellion, and the king is the implacable foe of the Lie; the author may well intend readers to see this correspondence about the wall as demonstrating the way in which the people of the land went about opposing the construction of the temple, but by immediately presenting these people as liars, these foils of the first generation of the temple community push readers to associate their own group more closely with the king and his devotion to the truth. In 4:17-22 the king is misled by these lies, as Chapter 4 will discuss, but when in Ezra 5 imperial officials confront the community directly about the construction of the temple during the reign of Darius, the community's elders have a chance to speak the truth to the king. They tell him that their ancestors angered God, who had the temple destroyed and the people exiled, but Cyrus made a decree to rebuild it and even gave the vessels that belonged to it to Sheshbazzar (5:12-16). Their explanation follows the narrative of Ezra 1–3, and so readers know they speak the truth, unlike the people of the land.[130] This truth-telling is supported by a written record of Cyrus's order that Darius discovers in the royal archives, one that says that the crown would even pay for the temple's construction (6:1-4). Darius enforces this order of royal generosity, and then adds to it by insisting the empire will fund the temple's sacrifices (6:9-10), and so the truthful community reaps the rewards of loyalty to the good rulers, as the טעם "decree" of Cyrus and Darius (6:3, 8), their true royal speech, allows the temple to be completed, resulting in the

---

130. The only part of the elders' explanation not explicitly supported by the narrative is that Sheshbazzar laid the temple's אשׁיא "foundation" (5:16), since Sheshbazzar disappears from the narrative after Ezra 1, while Ezra 3 refers to a return led by Zerubbabel and Joshua, and 3:8-13 portrays the temple as being founded under their leadership. The author may have decided to retain the explanation of 5:16 (or may have added that explanation him- or herself) in order to reinsert Sheshbazzar into the narrative of the return since 1:8-11 describes him as interacting with Cyrus and leading the journey to Judah. As James VanderKam points out, one can understand the Aramaic word אשׁיא, from Akkadian *uššu*, as referring to a sub-foundation, something that would support the foundation Zerubbabel and Jeshua lay in Ezra 3, where the Hebrew root יסד is used (3:6, 10, 12) (*From Joshua to Caiaphas*, 8–9). The appearance of Aramaic אשׁיא in Ezra is the earliest occurrence of the word of which we are aware; in Akkadian, *uššu* is commonly used to refer to the very bottom of a structure, and is frequently used to designate the opposite of a building's *gabadibbû* "parapet"; see *CAD* 20.304–7.

people's חדוה "happiness, joy" (6:16), what the Achaemenids consistently maintained they could provide for the world. In this context, it matters that the loyal subjects whom the king has sent from the center of the empire remain distinct from the colonized who are native to the margins of the world. Such peoples are unlike the king and are "in turmoil," as the Achaemenids put it, and they manifest the Lie. They are, as a result, the antithesis of goodness, and a genealogical boundary, one that has the sanction of royal order, since Cyrus chose this Babylonian community alone to build, helps the king's loyal subjects remain separate from the colonized, who are liars and disloyal to the king.

The author of Ezra–Nehemiah could have translated 4:8–6:18 from Aramaic into Hebrew, and could have turned the correspondence that makes up the bulk of this section into a narrative, but chose to leave a series of letters[131] in Aramaic, the bureaucratic language of the Persian Empire. The focus here is on the interaction with empire, demonstrating that one must loyally work with the king and interact with his bureaucracy by telling the truth to his representatives and appealing to royal orders, something that is rewarded with royal beneficence and results in the happiness the Achaemenids promise. Frank Polak and Timothy Hogue argue that the letters of Ezra 4:8–6:18 are written in an official and Eastern Aramaic, while the narrative sections that connect them are in a Western Aramaic spoken in Palestine, a code-switching between the official language of the empire and that of the community that interacts with it.[132] To engage the empire and fulfill the divine will one must literally speak the empire's language, and if the case is that the community completes the temple "by the decree of the God of Israel and by the decree of Cyrus and Darius and Artaxerxes, the king of Persia" (6:14), it is important that the Aramaic section says nothing more about divine involvement in the temple's construction, not even in regard to inspiring the prophets mentioned in 5:1 and 6:14, and not even when 4:24 reports that the temple construction Yhwh had ordered was brought to a halt. The use of Aramaic in official letters allows readers to see this as an imperial project that, while it was a response to divine command, is carried out under Achaemenid orders and completed through official imperial channels and the kings' protection and generosity. It allows readers to see the project

---

131. See Williamson, "The Aramaic Documents in Ezra Revisited," 47.
132. Frank H. Polak, "Sociolinguistics and the Judean Speech Community in the Achaemenid Empire," in Lipschits and Oeming, eds, *Judah and the Judeans in the Persian Period*, 589–628 (592–6); Timothy Hogue, "Return from Exile: Diglossia and Literary Code-Switching in Ezra 1–7," *ZAW* 130 (2018): 54–68 (62–6).

from the standpoint of imperial actors,[133] who eventually respond with the truth and beneficence the Achaemenids promise. This process is not entirely unproblematic, since 4:11-22 shows readers the imperial bureaucracy can be corrupted and the king misled, a matter Chapter 4 discusses, but in the end the community's truth-telling reaches the king who acts as the Achaemenids say they will in regard to loyal subjects who work with them.[134]

We see in Ezra 1–6 a community ensconced in empire, a group who seems like colonists, but who at the very least may be described as loyal subjects, sent from the imperial center to work with the king and combat the corruption and lies they encounter at the empire's periphery, and so as the language switches from Aramaic back to Hebrew in 6:19, the change has a very different effect than the same switch from Aramaic at the end of Daniel 7 to Hebrew at the beginning of Daniel 8, which Anathea Portier-Young argues is a way to urge readers of that book to "dis-identify" with empire.[135] In Ezra–Nehemiah, part of the community's ideal identity is its place as a loyal group of colonists within empire rewarded by the king's generosity, and so the community and king, like Hebrew and Aramaic, work together. The speech of Cyrus and Darius in 6:1-12, communicated through imperial documents through which they speak in the first person, defines the truth and conveys their generosity without any divine action, and prophetic speech is avoided, even though prophets are mentioned in 6:14, so that readers can see that history conforms to the Achaemenids' will, who are the kings they always claimed to be. It is true that the whole project began under a divine order, but no divine speech is reported here or anywhere else in Ezra–Nehemiah, for it is up to the Achaemenids to truthfully relate, interpret, and enact Yhwh's will. For the community to be loyal to the king, to cooperate and work with him, is not any different

---

133. Diana Edelman, "Identities within a Central and Peripheral Perspective: The Use of Aramaic in the Hebrew Bible," in Ben Zvi and Levin, eds, *Centres and Peripheries in the Early Second Temple Period*, 109–31 (125–8).

134. Lisbeth Fried argues that Ezra 1–6 has been structured according to the standard three-act form of Greek rhetoric, and that Haggai and Zechariah take the place of the *deus ex machina* in act three that reverses the negative fortunes of the protagonists ("*Deus ex Machina* and Plot Construction in Ezra 1–6," in *Prophets, Prophecy, and Ancient Israelite Historiography*, ed. Mark J. Boda and Lissa M. Wray Beal [Winona Lake, IN: Eisenbrauns, 2013], 189–207). In Ezra 5–6, however, it is the king and the imperial apparatus that are responsible for the completion of the temple. The author does not bother to give any specific sense as to what the prophets said.

135. Anathea E. Portier-Young, "Languages of Identity and Obligation: Daniel as a Bilingual Book," *VT* 60 (2010): 98–115 (113).

than to be loyal to their God. They certainly should not be like the disloyal liars who live around them in Palestine and who oppose the divine will the kings enact, and so a genealogical boundary that distinguishes them from other peoples in the land can be as important as one that defines them as loyal subjects of the king.

The longer the community remains far away from the empire's center, however, the greater the danger it runs of being contaminated by the peoples of the land—literally, according to Ezra 9—who lie, are disloyal, and who do not work with the king. Having surveyed the Achaemenids' understanding of geography, we now see that Ezra–Nehemiah has adopted it, and this is why the book portrays individuals and groups that come from the center of the world as good and those whose native land is far away from it as evil. In the Achaemenid view of the world, centers like Persia, Media, Elam, and, importantly for Ezra–Nehemiah, Babylonia, are the best parts of the world, while regions further away are worse, since at the world's edges life is closer to Zoroastrian understandings of the place of punishment in the afterlife. In the case of the Judean group that migrated from Babylonia, it simply becomes less like a community of loyal colonists and more like the colonized at the periphery of empire the longer they remain far from the center of the world. Even the fact that Jerusalem is almost always the center of action in Ezra–Nehemiah, not to mention the site of Yhwh's temple, does not alter this vision of the world for a narrative that continually identifies the community as "the exile" and "captives," as if they were somehow still located in Babylonia, which remains their spiritual home, as it were.[136] And so when the narrative jumps ahead by three generations in Ezra 7–8, where we find Ezra and his fellows in Babylonia, preparing for their journey to Judah, it returns readers yet again to a group at the center of the world who interacts with the king and who sends members to travel to the colonies under royal direction. Like the group of Ezra 1, they are on the receiving end of great royal generosity in regard to the temple, and Artaxerxes' letter to Ezra in 7:12-26 largely emphasizes the royal gifts to the temple and its personnel that Ezra is to convey. Beyond the donations of the king and his nobles (7:15), Artaxerxes authorizes his treasurers in Across-the-River to give Ezra goods for the temple, as well as one hundred talents

---

136. Erhard Gerstenberger argues the Babylonian diaspora exercised a kind of "spiritual power" in post-exilic Judaism; see his *Israel in the Persian Period: The Fifth and Fourth Centuries B.C.E.*, trans. Siegfried S. Schatzmann, SBLBE 8 (Leiden: Brill, 2012), 124–5. There is likely some truth to this, but in Ezra–Nehemiah, influenced by Achaemenid thought, it is the simple geographic location of the group in Babylonia that results in its goodness and its importance for its daughter community in Judah.

of silver (7:21-23), an amount of money that, by itself, would constitute almost thirty percent of the annual tribute that Herodotus said was owed by the entire satrapy (3.91.1), and the total amount of gold and silver that Ezra claims to bring to Judah as gifts from the king and "all Israel" in Babylonia vastly outstrips even that (8:25-27).[137] The picture of the imperial center that we see here is a place of unbelievable prosperity, where a loyal group of Judeans live and where, at divine prompting, the king gives Ezra "all that he sought from him" (7:6; see also 7:27). The Achaemenids are so generous here that it might seem as if the normal flow of tribute from margins to center has been reversed,[138] and this is a picture that corresponds to Achaemenid ideology in which the kings ensure fertility and prosperity to those who are loyal and so who work with them to fulfill the divine will.

As Chapter 2 discusses, however, by Ezra 9 the community in Judah to which Ezra and his fellows migrate can no longer be described as loyal, and if their failure in loyalty is one in regard to divine law, Artaxerxes has adopted Torah as royal law in his letter to Ezra in 7:12-26, since he orders Ezra to teach "the law of your God" throughout the satrapy of Across-the-River, where he is also to appoint judges to enforce דתא די אלהך ודתא די מלכא "the law of your God and the law of the king" (7:25-26). These two kinds of law now exist in the same judicial system, and can be discussed as if they are the same thing, just as the Achaemenids say their *dāta* "law" was "set down" by Auramazda (XPh 49-50). Yahwistic law does not replace a pre-exilic monarchy in Ezra–Nehemiah[139] so much as it acts as an extension of royal will, which is also divine will, just as the Achaemenids claim. Chapter 4 discusses this issue in more detail, but we can at least say here that, in light of Ezra 7, a failure in loyalty to God is now a failure in loyalty to the king, because his judges and justice system throughout the satrapy are responsible for enforcing Torah along with royal law. The specific failure in regard to the law in Ezra 9–10 are

---

137. Parts of the text of 8:26-27, which refers to the value of the silver, gold, and vessels that Ezra and his group transported to Judah, are corrupt, but even the numbers and measures that can be read with certainty, such as the 650 talents of silver and one hundred talents of gold in 8:26, amount to more than five times the annual tribute Herodotus claimed was due from the entire satrapy. See the discussion of Ezra 2:69 in Chapter 2 in regard to the weights involved and the trustworthiness of Herodotus in his discussion of the Achaemenids' taxation system.

138. So Knoppers, "The Construction of Judean Diasporic Identity in Ezra–Nehemiah," 11–13.

139. Contra Thomas B. Dozeman, "Geography and History in Herodotus and Ezra–Nehemiah," *JBL* 122 (2003): 449–66 (457–64).

the marriages with "the peoples of the lands" community members have entered into, something that is very dangerous, not only because this failure might result in the destruction of the community (9:10-15), but also because the narrative has portrayed the peoples as a group that lies and is disloyal to the king. The very act of intermarrying with them itself reflects disloyalty to the law for which the king has accepted responsibility, and despite the very positive portrayal of the ideal generation of migrants in Ezra 1–6, and of the new group from the center of empire in Ezra 7–8, the Judeans have a long history of disloyalty, a point Ezra raises in light of the community's illicit marriages to foreign women (9:6-9). It is because their ancestors acted just as they do now, he says, that עבדים אנחנו "we are slaves" (9:9) and that the community exists in עבדה "slavery" (9:8). Of course, as Chapter 2 discusses, in the context of the prayer as a whole the very fact that the community still exists at all, even as slaves to Persia, is itself an act of תחנה "grace" (9:8-9), since the community's earlier failure in the law exposed them to punishment "through the sword, through captivity, and through plundering, and through shame" (9:7), and could have led to its complete annihilation.

This description of the community's past and current situation accords with the Achaemenids' view of their colonized peoples: in the past, the peoples suffered turmoil and violence until the Achaemenids were able to put everyone in their place—under Achaemenid rule, that is—and make them *bandaka*s "subjects," as Darius puts it (DB 1.19), who are bound to or by the king. Given the translations of *bandaka* we see in the Akkadian and Aramaic versions of the Bisitun Inscription with words that mean "slave," עבד seems a reasonable Hebrew translation of the term,[140] and in Ezra's prayer it is simultaneously the result of divine punishment and divine mercy. But there is no sense here that there is any alternative to it except the annihilation Ezra fears (9:13-15), and this too reflects Achaemenid ideology, which sees no fate better than serving as colonized subjects to the king; the alternative, as Chapter 4 discusses, is disloyalty that the Achaemenids punished with horrifying reprisals, and Ezra 7 erases any distinction between disloyalty to God and disloyalty to the king. As far as Ezra represents matters in his prayer, the community's identity as "slaves" is the only sort of existence that is still possible, since

---

140. So also Oeming, "'See, we are serving today' (Nehemiah 9:36)," 579, and see also Christine Mitchell, "Achaemenid Persian Concepts Pertaining to Covenant and Haggai, Zechariah, and Malachi," in *Covenant in the Persian Period: From Genesis to Chronicles*, ed. Richard J. Bautch and Gary N. Knoppers (Winona Lake, IN: Eisenbrauns, 2015), 291–306 (295–8).

the pre-exilic independence of their ancestors nearly led to their complete destruction, and their place as *bandaka*s to the Persians is also the result of divine will and grace, just as the Achaemenids asserted that they could only act to conquer the world because Auramazda wanted and allowed them to do so, thereby improving humanity's lot.

By the time we reach Ezra 9, generations after the loyal group of Ezra 1–6 migrated from the center of the empire, the community's sin demonstrates that it is no longer the case that the law distinguishes them from the peoples, and since they do not keep the law the king has authorized, they are disloyal subjects, just as the peoples of the land are. The community now needs the king to continue to send it leaders from the imperial center, since their local leadership has failed along with the rest of the community to maintain the group's distinctive identity in the colonies as a loyal and law-abiding group genealogically distinct from the peoples. Ezra is told that השרים והסגנים "the leaders and the officials"[141] were the first to intermarry with outsider women (9:2), just as Nehemiah must contend with the חרים "freepersons,"[142] figures whom the Nehemiah Memoir treats as influential community members,[143] and who in Neh. 6:17-19 collaborate with Tobiah, a dangerous enemy of the community.

---

141. The term סגן is a loanword from Akkadian *šaknu*, which could be used for someone who oversaw professional groups dependent on the state, or even someone serving as governor. Chapter 5 will discuss the significance of the word in more detail, but we can note here that the term also appears in reference to functionaries of the Persian administration in Elephantine; see Thierry Petit, "L'évolution sémantique des termes hébreux et araméens *pḥh* et *sgn* et accadiens *pāḥatu* et *šaknu*," *JBL* 107 (1988): 53–67 (58–60); Rainer Albertz, "The Thwarted Restoration," in *Yahwism after the Exile: Perspectives on Israelite Religion in the Persian Era*, ed. Rainer Albertz and Bob Becking, STAR 5 (Assen: Royal Van Gorcum, 2003), 1–17 (12).

142. Muhammad Dandamaev rightly points out that Northwest Semitic *ḥr* refers to freepersons (M. A. Dandamaev, "Babylonian Popular Assemblies in the First Millennium B.C.," *BCSMS* 30 [1995]: 23–9 [26–7]). In inscriptional material, the word mainly appears in Arabian dialects of Aramaic in references to individuals as belonging to households of freepersons (e.g., *CIS* 2.161.i.2; 2.990.2; 2.4000.3-4); in rabbinic Hebrew חור is used to distinguish freepersons from slaves (e.g., *m. Giṭ.* 4.4, 5; *m. B. Qam.* 1.3); and in Qoh. 10:16-17, חר is the opposite of נער "servant."

143. The חרים appear together with the priests and/or other officials as an important group within the people as a whole in Neh. 2:16; 4:8, 13 [14, 19]; 5:7; 7:5 (although 7:5 may not have originally been part of the Nehemiah Memoir). In passages like 6:17 and 13:17 Nehemiah depicts the חרים as leaders among the people, and those who appear to wield local power in the province; in 5:7 Nehemiah portrays them as among the economic elite, for he blames them for taking interest from others in the community, driving them into poverty.

Ezra teaches the law to the community in his role as priest (Ezra 10:10, 16; Neh. 8:2, 9), and the fact that his generation of the community does not know the law means, as Chapter 2 discusses, that the priests born in Judah have not been acting as good leaders in this regard, which explains why Ezra finds them in violation of the law(s) that forbid(s) intermarriage (Ezra 10:18-22). Nehemiah blames "the freepersons and the officials" in Neh. 5:7 for impoverishing their kin and so forcing Judeans to send their own children as slaves among the peoples, he blames the freepersons for violating the law of the Sabbath (Neh. 13:17), and he says the high priest prefers accommodating Tobiah to ensuring a functioning temple cult (13:4-14) and allows his grandson to marry outside of the community into the family of one of its enemies (13:28).

The leaders of the community who were born in Judah, in short, seem little different than Sanballat, Tobiah, and Geshem, leaders of neighboring peoples who oppose the king's will and with whom native Judean leaders forge alliances through marriage. The only remedy, then, is leadership the king sends from the center of the empire. Luckily for the Judeans in Palestine, they have kin who remain at the imperial center, a group whom the narrative never criticizes,[144] and who can provide law and leadership to the Judeans in the colonies. Nehemiah is not even a member of that Babylonian community, since readers first encounter him in Susa, not Babylon. Not only is he someone who can converse with the king at the center of the world, but his office as royal cupbearer (Neh. 1:11) is one traditionally held by the Persian nobility,[145] and so he is as close to the imperial center as one can be without being the king.[146] It does not

---

144. John Kessler, "The Diaspora of Zechariah 1–8 and Ezra–Nehemiah: The Role of History, Social Location, and Tradition in the Formulation of Identity," in *Community Identity in Judean Historiography: Biblical and Comparative Perspectives*, ed. Gary N. Knoppers and Kenneth A. Ristau (Winona Lake, IN: Eisenbrauns, 2009), 119–45 (134). To be fair, Ezra–Nehemiah actually says very little about the diaspora—so Japhet, *From the Rivers of Babylon*, 115–16—since its focus remains on the temple community in Judah.

145. Maria Brosius, "New out of Old? Court and Court Ceremonies in Achaemenid Persia," in *The Court and Court Society in Ancient Monarchies*, ed. A. J. S. Spawforth (Cambridge: Cambridge University Press, 2007), 17–57 (26–9). For the appearance of Persian nobility in the role of the king's cupbearer in the Persepolis fortification archive, see Wouter F. M. Henkelman, "'Consumed before the king': The Table of Darius, that of Irdabama and Irtaštuna, and that of his Satrap Karkiš," in Jacobs and Rollinger, eds, *Der Achämenidenhof*, 667–775 (672).

146. So, historically speaking, it is very unlikely that Nehemiah actually held this position. Herodotus refers to precisely that office (οἰνοχόος, which is the translation of Hebrew משקה in LXX^A Neh. 1:11) as held by a Persian noble (3.34.1), and

matter that he does not come from the diaspora community in Babylonia, because, like that group, he comes from the center of empire, and from an even more central position—the presence of the king—than the Judeans in Babylonia occupy. Under his leadership, the community can once again work with the Achaemenid as they construct Jerusalem's wall, building with the royal work groups (פלכים) mentioned in Nehemiah 3 to complete a task authorized by the king and God.

Sara Japhet writes that Ezra 1–6 focuses on the people without emphasizing their leadership, and describes this view of the community as "democratization," while Michael Duggan sees a "growth of democracy" in Nehemiah 8–9, as the law passes from Ezra (8:2-6) to the Levites (8:7-8) to the ancestral heads (8:13) and finally to all Israel (9:1-3).[147] But as central as the community may be to Ezra–Nehemiah's narrative, democracy is not desirable for it as far as the author is concerned. The community of Ezra 1–6 does have leadership that is fairly prominent in the text—Zerubbabel and Jeshua the high priest, as well as the ancestral heads and elders—and what is important about them is their loyalty to king and God. Zerubbabel and Jeshua restart the sacrificial cult upon the community's arrival in Jerusalem "as it is written in the law of Moses" (Ezra 3:2), and work with and are loyal to the king as they begin the construction on the temple that he has commanded (3:8) and insist on following his orders precisely when, along with the ancestral heads, they refuse to allow Yahwists from outside of the community to build with them (4:3). The community of Ezra and Nehemiah's generation needs

---

that is otherwise always the case for positions in court like this. Darius himself, for example, was quiver-bearer to Cyrus (Aelian, *Var. hist.* 12.43), Darius III had been a previous king's letter-bearer (Plutarch, *Alex.* 18.7), DNc and DNd refer to Persians as spear- and clothes-bearer to Darius I (see Rüdiger Schmitt, *The Old Persian Inscriptions of Naqsh-i Rustam and Persepolis*, CII 1/1/2 [London: School of African and Oriental Studies, 2000], 45–6 for discussions of these translations), and so on. These were ceremonial positions at court, so there is no connection between the role Nehemiah claimed to have and the Neo-Assyrian *rab šāqê*, a term that literally means "cupbearer" but that referred to someone with administrative functions (contra Fitzpatrick-McKinley, *Empire, Power and Indigenous Elite*, 185–6). One could see the position of cup-bearer to which Nehemiah refers as simply that of a waiter (so Lester Grabbe, "The Terminology of Government in the Septuagint—in Comparison with Hebrew, Aramaic, and Other Languages," in *Jewish Perspectives on Hellenistic Rulers*, ed. Tessa Rajak et al., HCS 50 [Berkeley, CA: University of California Press, 2007], 225–37 [231]), but one hardly imagines figures like these had the sort of close personal relationship to the king Neh. 2 portrays.

147. Japhet, *From the Rivers of Babylon*, 66–75; Duggan, *The Covenant Renewal in Ezra–Nehemiah (Neh 7:72B–10:40)*, 296–7.

leadership like this, but the narrative shows us none is forthcoming from within the community itself, which explains the necessity for the king to send leaders from the center of the world to protect the wayward group from engaging in actions that would only endanger its existence by provoking violent divine wrath. The Achaemenids act in Ezra–Nehemiah, as they do according to their own inscriptions, to save the colonized peoples from harming themselves.

The Achaemenid understanding of geography, then, in which humanity needs leadership from the good center of the world to be happy, appears to be a key aspect of the worldview of Ezra–Nehemiah's author. Goodness and true leadership radiate out from the empire's core, providing prosperity and protection for the colonized. In Ezra–Nehemiah's story of the construction of Jerusalem's wall, for example, Artaxerxes follows the divine will, just as the Achaemenids claimed they consistently did, in authorizing and paying for the construction (Neh. 2:8).[148] The story of this building project, as Chapter 2 mentions, sounds rather like that of Ezra 1–6, for once more the king sends someone from the center of the world to undertake work sanctioned by God, only to find it opposed by the local population who lie and accuse the builders of rebellion (Neh. 2:19; 3:34 [4:2];[149] 6:6-7). One of the things this pattern accomplishes both in Ezra 1–6 and Nehemiah 1–6 is to contrast those sent by the king from the center of the world with those who are from the empire's margins and who thus appear disloyal by nature. To adopt the Achaemenids' binary distinction between a good center and naturally corrupt margins that must be properly ruled for their own good means adopting the Achaemenids' portrayal of their colonized, and Ezra–Nehemiah does just that, because the righteous and loyal generation of Ezra 1–6 is replaced by an inherently disloyal one in Ezra 7–Nehemiah 13, and this is the picture of community identity that dominates the book. Even the Persian officials in Ezra 4, who write on behalf of the people of the land, lie and so are disloyal to the king, and apparently the longer one remains distant from the king and the imperial center the more corrupt one becomes. This is certainly true in regard to the temple community, and by the time of Nehemiah even their prophets cannot be trusted to speak for God, for, just like the Persian officials of Ezra 4, they can be bribed to lie (Neh. 6:10-14). The community by this point fails to recognize the royal beneficence that is providing them with a temple and a walled city, and blame the king's tax for their poverty (Neh. 5:4), when in fact it is their own greed that has resulted in their

---

148. See also the discussion in Oeming, "The Real History," 138–43.

149. For the translation of היעזבו להם in 3:34 [4:2] as "Will they free themselves?," see Chapter 2.

dire financial situation. Nehemiah is able to convince them of this and so he changes how they act (5:6-13), and as the representative of the king he is responsible for feeding one hundred and fifty people every day with amounts of food so vast that they would have taken much of it away to their families (5:14-18),[150] a manifestation of the prosperity the Achaemenids bestow on their subjects.

The Levitical prayer of Neh. 9:6-37 appears to challenge this connection between the Achaemenids and community prosperity, however, and the end of the prayer portrays the community's status as עבדים "slaves" or "subjects"—*bandaka*s, in other words—to the Persians as something that denies them access to the fertility of the land the Achaemenids claimed to provide. The Levites state in 9:36-37 that "we are slaves" upon the land God gave to the ancestors, as "its great yield[151] belongs to the kings whom you set over us because of our sins," and so "we are in great distress," and, as Chapter 2 discusses, the prayer suggests that the community could win control of its land back from the Persians if it can remain faithful to the law.[152] By including these verses from the source material, the author of Ezra–Nehemiah acknowledges that Israel's history, as he or she understands it, is governed by a covenant in which God intended them to live in independence on the land (9:22-25), but that their basic character is one of rebelliousness and lawlessness (9:26-30) that does not make this ideal possible. Nehemiah 13 makes clear, as Chapter 2 also explains, that

---

150. For the amounts of food involved, and this passage's reflection of Achaemenid demonstrations of royal largesse, see Lisbeth S. Fried, "150 Men at Nehemiah's Table? The Role of the Governor's Meals in the Achaemenid Provincial Economy," *JBL* 137 (2018): 821–31.

151. The OG omits the end of 9:36 (everything in the verse after the word פריה in the MT, or καρπὸν αὐτῆς in the LXX) and the first words of 9:37 (ותבואתה מרבה in the MT). LXX[L] has restored the missing words following the tradition behind the MT, and it has translated ותבואתה מרבה as οι καρποι αυτης. This suggests the OG received a Hebrew text with the same wording in 9:36-37 as the MT, but that the words were eventually omitted in the Greek textual tradition because of haplography in a Greek text as a scribe's eye jumped from καρπὸν αὐτῆς in 9:36 to καρποι αυτης in 9:37.

152. This is the consensus scholarly reading of the passage. The alternative reading proposed by Manfred Oeming (in "'See, we are serving today'") does not really work. His argument that the community's distress in 9:37 is caused not by being subjects to the Persians but because they are "about to" reject Torah (p. 582) skips over the community's reference in that verse to "our sins." The community is already sinful in this confession, and they are already suffering in their servitude to the Persians, since they refer to the תלאה "hardship" that they endure "to this day" (9:32). In this prayer, life as subjects to the Persians involves hardship that is part of the punishment for the community's sins and those of their ancestors.

this is still the character of the group that lives generations removed from the imperial center, and that they are incapable of keeping the law when the king's representative is absent, which is why they are in need of the Achaemenid to send them leaders from that center. As a result, when the final clause of the prayer—"we are in great distress"—is read in light of the end of the book, it can be understood as referring to the community's distress in regard to their inherently rebellious nature that demands Achaemenid rule so that they do not commit actions that would lead God to annihilate them. The produce of the land does belong to "the kings whom you set over us," but at numerous points in Ezra–Nehemiah the prosperity created by the land and sent to the king as taxes returns to the community many-fold through great royal largesse (Ezra 1:6-11; 6:5, 8-9; 7:15-24; 8:25-27; Neh. 2:8; 5:17-18; 7:70), reflecting the Achaemenids' claims of their ability to provide fertility and prosperity for their subjects. This reflects the idea the dynasty communicated when it represented the colonized on its reliefs as supporting the king with ease and in joy. As long as the Achaemenids exist to send proper leadership to Judah, the community will continue to reap the benefits of prosperity the king guarantees his loyal subjects.

In the end, the result of Nehemiah's leadership on behalf of the king—at least before his absence in Nehemiah 13 leads to chaos within the community—is happiness and joy, just as the Achaemenids promised it would be. Having led the completion of Jerusalem's walls, the city can be re-inhabited in Nehemiah 11, so that, at the end of the story of the dedication of the wall in 12:27-43, the community "rejoiced because God made them rejoice with great joy, and the women and children also rejoiced, and the joy of Jerusalem was heard far away" (12:43). Joy has also been the community's response to the completion of the temple (Ezra 6:16), to the first celebration of the pilgrimage festival of Unleavened Bread there (6:22), to the law that Ezra brings and teaches (Neh. 8:9-12), and to the community's celebration of Sukkoth in accordance with that law (8:17).[153] Life lived in obedience to the law authorized and promoted by the Achaemenids results in celebrations of happiness, the result of royal beneficence that derives from loyalty to the king and God. The community cannot afford to be completely joyful, given the danger their identity as habitual sinners poses to their own well being, and so when they understand the law Ezra and the Levites teach in Nehemiah 8, their first reaction is to weep (8:9), assumedly because they understand they have repeatedly violated it. Yet the kings of Persia have been indispensable to any

---

153. Karrer-Grube, "Scrutinizing the Conceptual Unity," 156–7.

happiness the community has experienced, for they enact the divine will and provide the group with prosperity and the leadership that keeps them faithful, and so there can be no joy without them. In Ezra–Nehemiah, then, there is no real distinction between the Achaemenids' leadership that provides happiness for the community and the local leadership they have sent to the colonized community in Judah to enforce Torah, since that local leadership is completely dependent on the will of the king.[154]

4. *Conclusion: From Colonizers to Colonized*

In Ezra–Nehemiah, the Achaemenids are the beneficent kings they claim to be in the picture of the world they broadcast to their empire, appointed by the God who created the world, and who interact with the divine without intermediary. The book never reports direct prophetic speech, and Neh. 6:10-14 even portrays prophets as figures who can be bribed to lie. The Achaemenid alone speaks for and interprets divine commands, and prophetic figures who, like those in Nehemiah 6, attempt to obstruct royal orders are liars. The Achaemenids thus act to restore the happiness God intended humans—or, in Ezra–Nehemiah, Judeans—to experience, and they work with their subjects to realize their royal desire, which is also divine desire, and so make the lives of the colonized better as they prevent the peoples from harming themselves. The center of the world truly is where the Achaemenids said it was, in Persia and the nearby regions that had once been imperial centers, and so the first-generation community, "the captives from the exile" who originally migrated from such a place, was good, just as the Judeans who remain in Babylonia continue to be. Ezra 1–6 portrays that generation as emissaries sent by the king to work with him and enact the divine will that he mediated, a very different group than the peoples of the lands they encountered in the colonies who are inherently disloyal and liars. This community needed to be aware of its genealogical borders that could prove if one was descended from Israel or, more importantly, if one had migrated from Babylonia, for the king chose

---

154. Ehud Ben Zvi argues that post-exilic Judah did in general make such a distinction, and saw the Achaemenid as responsible for human happiness and local leadership as responsible for enforcing Torah ("Memory and Political Thought in the Late Persian/Early Hellenistic Yehud/Judah: Some Observations," in *Leadership, Social Memory and Judean Discourse in the Fifth-Second Centuries BCE*, ed. Diana V. Edelman and Ehud Ben Zvi, WANEM [Sheffield: Equinox Publishing, 2016], 9–26 [20–1]), but if that truly was the case for some community members, it was not a distinction endorsed by the author of Ezra–Nehemiah.

them alone to work with him and accomplish the royal and divine will. Their loyalty to the king, manifested as they cooperated in the building project God had ordered the king to undertake, a work that royal decree specified was only for this community to complete, distinguished them from the peoples who lived around them.

This ideal community of loyal subjects changes, however, as it spends more time away from the center of the world, and it needs the Achaemenid to renew its leadership to keep it loyal to the law of God that the king has authorized, so that its own actions do not lead to the complete destruction of the group. Happiness and prosperity are now the result of the leaders the Achaemenid sends, and they are responsible for preventing the community from assimilating completely with the peoples around them. If they were like a group of colonizers in Ezra 1–6, generations in the colonies have made them more and more like the natives of the land they find there. The king now sends Ezra to bring the law the Achaemenid authorizes and enforces, which Ezra uses first to protect the genealogical distinctiveness of the community, and later to teach them loyalty to God. The king sends Nehemiah to build the wall and Jerusalem, and as governor he is the representative of the king who enforces the boundaries that are meant to distinguish the group from the peoples around them. These are imperial representatives who help the community live up to its ideal identity, restoring the genealogical, legal, purity, and spatial boundaries between themselves and other groups, and so turning them once again into loyal subjects of the king, who commanded that such distinctions be observed. Because "the law of your God" exists within the same justice system as "the law of the king," the restoration of social boundaries mandated in the law makes the community the loyal subjects of the king they should be, which allows them to partake of the royal largesse that creates their prosperity and happiness. In Ezra 7–Nehemiah 13, then, the temple community no longer seems like a group of colonizers but another colonized people who depend upon Achaemenid leadership to survive and prosper.

Achaemenid ideology obviously formed an important part of the worldview of Ezra–Nehemiah's author, and while his or her worldview was also clearly shaped by Yahwism, it is a Yahwism permeated by Achaemenid ideology, colonized by it, we could say, since the true Yahwists are the ones associated with the center of empire, who understand that the king speaks for God and so who are loyal to the king, conforming themselves to his law, something that sits side-by-side with Torah in the royal judicial system. The empire is not perfect in Ezra–Nehemiah, for its local agents can be bribed and can lie and oppose the work of the king, and in the case of Ezra 4:11-22 the king can even be convinced by their lies. The next chapter examines how Ezra–Nehemiah portrays the imperfections of empire even as it maintains the essential goodness of the Achaemenid, but we turn first to the way the book follows Achaemenid ideology in justifying the violence the king could use to destroy the temple community.

Chapter 4

THE KING, GOD, AND TORTURE

1. *Achaemenid Ideology, Part 2: The Necessity of Torture*

If Ezra–Nehemiah broadcasts the superiority of Achaemenid rule over any alternative, as the dynasty itself did, the book also reflects the assertion of Achaemenid ideology that the king has a right to inflict torture and horrible violence on the colonized when their actions threaten the happiness the king labors to establish for them. In this matter, as in that of the Achaemenids' beneficence, the author of Ezra–Nehemiah defines the community's identity in a manner wholly compatible with Achaemenid ideology, creating a picture of them that mimics the dynasty's portrayal of the colonized as peoples who need to be controlled through their fear of the consequences of violating royal law. It is possible for the author to depict the community in this way because, as Chapter 3 has discussed, he or she already believes that Yhwh's will is aligned with that of the kings, that loyalty to the Achaemenid should be central to the definition of community identity, and that Torah was administered by a royal judicial system. This chapter begins, however, by examining messages broadcast from Persia, although our focus in this regard now turns to the Achaemenids' justifications for their punishment and torture of the disobedient, and the manner in which they managed to maintain both that the king is the representative of Auramazda restoring the perfect happiness of creation and that he sometimes should slaughter and maim his subjects. This discussion creates the context for a return in the chapter's second section to Ezra–Nehemiah's creation of community identity, now as part of an examination of the ways in which Achaemenid justifications of imperial violence shaped the author's depictions of the Judean temple community, a discussion that builds on observations made in

Chapter 3. The second part of this chapter says more about Yhwh's role as enabler of empire within the context of Achaemenid ideology and further investigates the consequences of Ezra–Nehemiah's claim that Torah became part of an imperial justice system. Neither Yhwh nor Yhwh's law could ever threaten Achaemenid sovereignty in the author's worldview, and he or she borrows the Achaemenid notion that the king's law is really divine law. This is why Ezra–Nehemiah can maintain that Torah is part of a foreign legal system, with the result that divine and royal law appear entirely complementary. If the identity of the temple community should be defined primarily by their loyalty to the Achaemenid, as Chapter 3 argues, since loyalty to Yahwistic law is loyalty to a law the dynasty has adopted, the community's repetitive failures in this regard make it just like the other colonized peoples whom the Achaemenids describe. Their natural immorality leads them to rebel against the king who speaks for and administers divine law, so an important aspect of their continued well-being is their fear of Persian reprisals for disloyalty. In Ezra–Nehemiah, as in Achaemenid ideology, imperial violence is always justified because the inherently disloyal temple community, like all of the dynasty's colonized peoples, needs the fear of such righteous violence to remain loyal to the divine will and the king who enforces it.

Despite such legitimation of imperial violence, however, Ezra–Nehemiah does not maintain that everything the empire does is justifiable, as the third section of the chapter discusses, but on the rare occasions when the book criticizes Persia it is the empire's bureaucracy and not the king who is to blame. The empire's imperfections in Ezra–Nehemiah stem not from the Achaemenid and his decisions to slaughter and torture his subjects, even though the book presents exile and destruction as possible fates of the Judean temple community, but from the king's bureaucrats acting in disloyalty to him. Ezra–Nehemiah is not entirely pro-empire, but it is steadfastly pro-Achaemenid, and the book is also clear that there is no better future that is possible for the community than to live in this imperfect kingdom because they are like all the other colonized peoples as the Achaemenids conceived of them, fortunate that they can be ruled by a king who threatens them with destruction if they violate the divine law he oversees.

The Achaemenids did not make violence a central aspect of the ideology they broadcast, a sharp contrast with Neo-Assyrian royal inscriptions, which are dominated by kings' accounts of their victories and scenes of their torture of rebellious leaders, and on their inscriptions the Neo-Assyrian kings describe blinding and mutilating captured enemies, burning their children, destroying entire cities, and slaughtering large proportions of defeated populations.[1] This is not the tone of the Achaemenid inscriptions nor the imagery that dominates in their iconography. There are fifty-three Achaemenid inscriptions that postdate the Bisitun Inscription, and not one of them refers to a specific armed struggle or to any specific rebellion,[2] and although Bisitun describes Darius's punishment of his enemies, such passages are brief indeed when compared with equivalent examples from Neo-Assyrian inscriptions.[3] In Achaemenid iconography, the king is almost never portrayed in combat against humans; only the Bisitun relief represents him as triumphant over enemies,[4] and only a small number of seals depict bound captives.[5] It is true, as the previous chapter discusses, that the king can be portrayed as the Persian hero in combat with animals or monsters or, more frequently, controlling them in his outstretched arms to either side, and it is also true that he can be pictured as an archer, but this was imagery intended to point toward the king as maintaining order as he controls his animal or animal-like foes or, when depicted in combat with them, as establishing order, since he is in the act of killing them.[6]

Nonetheless, such imagery demonstrates that the Achaemenids were not opposed to alluding to the military power available to them, as is also the case, for example, with the long lines of archers depicted on the walls of the Achaemenid palace at Susa,[7] and on occasion the king, or at least a distinctly Persian figure, can be represented in combat against humans. For example, a scene painted in a Persian-period tomb in Anatolia depicts a group of warriors led by a commander in Persian dress defeating a group

---

1. For discussions and specific examples of some of the horrific actions the Neo-Assyrian kings narrate on their inscriptions, see Charlie Trimm, *Fighting for the King and the Gods: A Survey of Warfare in the Ancient Near East*, RBS 88 (Atlanta: SBL Press, 2017), 355–64, 373–7, 385–8.

2. Lincoln, *Religion, Empire, and Torture*, 12–14. If there is an exception to this it is XPh 28-35, where Xerxes refers to some sort of rebellion, but this inscription provides no details as to where or when it happened, making it difficult to use the adjective "specific" to describe it.

3. Margaret Cool Root, "Imperial Ideology in Achaemenid Persian Art: Transforming the Mesopotamian Legacy," *BCSMS* 35 (2000): 19–27 (23).

4. Kaptan, *The Daskyleion Bullae*, 1:87–9.

5. Root, *The King and Kingship in Achaemenid Art*, 182–4.

6. See Root, *The King and Kingship*, 310–11; Garrison, "Seals and the Elite at Persepolis," 17–18; Garrison and Root, *Seals on the Persepolis Fortification Tablets. Volume I*, 58–9; Harrison, *Writing Ancient Persia*, 86–8.

7. Stronach, "From Cyrus to Darius," 102–3.

of poorly arrayed Scythians.⁸ Seals in the court style only rarely illustrate warriors killing humans, although those from Anatolia more frequently present figures in Persian dress as warriors.⁹ Xin Wu identifies three different groups of seals and stamps produced in court and *koinē* styles that depict Persians fighting enemies of non-Persian ethnicities, and these impressions would have circulated among the empire's elites.¹⁰

So even if the Achaemenids did not emphasize their ability to exercise military power, it was still part of the ideology they broadcast and was, in fact, a necessary part that fit with their self-presentation as beneficent kings. As Chapter 3 discusses, Darius maintains on the Bisitun Inscription that the Lie manifests itself in armed rebellion against his rule, and so interferes with and attempts to overthrow his work to restore the original happiness of humanity that Auramazda created. Little of what Darius accomplishes according to that inscription is possible without his command of powerful armies, and martial prowess is an important reason why the Achaemenid makes a good king, as both Darius and Xerxes claim in nearly identical language. Each composed an inscription that provides long lists of the qualities that make them excellent rulers, and both begin with references to creation and humanity's happiness, for it is that happiness which Auramazda first bestowed that they mean to restore and maintain through their leadership. They begin their inscriptions by asserting that Auramazda *adadā ima frašam* "established this wonder," a reference to creation, and "established the happiness of humanity" (DNb 1-3; XPl 1-3), and then both go on to refer to the *xraθu* and *aruvasta* that Auramazda "set down" upon them (DNB 3-4; XPl 3-4). Old Persian *xraθu* is cognate with Sanskrit *kratu* "power" and Greek κρατύς "strong," and *aruvasta* with Avestan *aurvant* "brave, hero,"¹¹ and so the words appear to point to the kings' strength and martial ability, especially as both Darius and Xerxes refer later in these inscriptions to their *aruvasta* when they introduce their skill in warfare (DNb 32-33; XPl 36-37). Avestan *xratu*, a cognate of *xraθu*, refers to mental power that achieves desired ends, and so involves the notions of will, skill, and aptitude,¹² and the Akkadian

---

8. Lâtife Summerer, "Picturing Persian Victory: The Painted Battle Scene on the Munich Wood," in *Achaemenid Culture and Local Traditions in Anatolia, Southern Caucasus and Iran*, ACSS 13 (Leiden: Brill, 2007), 3–30.

9. Dusinberre, *Empire, Authority, and Autonomy*, 93–5.

10. Xin Wu, "'O young man...make known of what kind you are': Warfare, History, and Elite Ideology of the Achaemenid Persian Empire," *IrAnt* 49 (2014): 209–99 (247–53, 259–62).

11. Kent, *Old Persian*, 170, 180.

12. Amir Ahmadi, "Avestan *xratu-*," *IrSt* 47, no. 6 (2014): 1–11.

version of Darius's inscription translates "*xraθu* and *aruvasta*" with the phrase *ṭēme ḫissatu itbārūtu* "understanding, intelligence, (and) skill" (*CAD* 7.295). None of these three Akkadian words necessarily refers to skill as a warrior, but this translation and the context of these Old Persian words in the inscription suggest *xraθu* and *aruvasta* refer to power in battle skillfully and intelligently applied. The kings also use *aruvasta* in a more general sense of skill or intelligence as they act in "both court and war camp" (DNb 27-32; XPl 31-36), and so readers of the inscriptions can see that they are good kings in part because they can rightly judge their subjects, properly rewarding and punishing them (DNb 5-27; XPl 5-31), but also because they are skilled in battle (DNb 32-45; XPl 36-50). Good kings must possess talent in both of these realms, according to the inscriptions, and the notion that the Achaemenids were renowned warriors was broadcast widely enough that it shows up in Classical sources (e.g., Herodotus 1.136; Diodorus 17.6.1-2; Strabo 15.3.8).[13]

The notion that the kings re-create the happiness Auramazda intended for humanity means not only that they must be able to suppress rebellions by liars who want to eliminate such happiness, but also that the farther they can extend their rule the better off the world is. As Chapter 3 discusses, the Achaemenids thought of the empire as the only place worth living, and may have conceived of life outside of it as literally hell-ish, and so on Darius's burial inscription the king lists the lands and peoples he rules (DNa 22-30), and then refers positively to the fact that "a Persian has fought battle far from Persia" (46-47), since warfare is the cause of having such a great empire.[14] That inscription begins with the standard creation formula (DNa 1-8), and so it alludes to the idea that Darius uses this warfare to restore the happiness of humanity that Auramazda originally created to many peoples far beyond the borders of Persia. We can see the same idea broadcast on the relatively small number of seals of the court and Persianizing styles that represent the king in battle against human foes, for they almost always depict these enemies as at the margins of the

---

13. For a discussion of the Classical material that treats the Achaemenids' martial ability, see Lincoln, *"Happiness for Mankind"*, 335–45.

14. Christopher Tuplin points out that the Type III darics, first issued between 490 and 480 BCE, are the first Achaemenid royal coins to portray a figure with spear as well as bow, and he suggests there may be a connection with Darius's statement from the previous lines of the burial inscription that "the spear of a Persian has gone forth far" (DNa 43-44); see "The Changing Pattern of Achaemenid Persian Royal Coinage," in *Explaining Monetary and Financial Innovation: A Historical Analysis*, ed. Peter Berhnholz and Roland Vaubel, FMPS 39 (Cham: Springer, 2014), 127–68 (142-3).

empire. They are Greeks, Egyptians, and Central Asians,[15] suggesting the king works to expand imperial borders and include even more peoples in the happiness he provides.[16] The Achaemenids were even willing to admit that such efforts came at a human cost, and the Akkadian and Aramaic translations of the Bisitun Inscription, which vary in some minor ways from the Old Persian text, list the numbers of soldiers Darius's forces killed in some of the different military encounters he narrates, and the sum of the enemy dead amounts to about one hundred and twenty thousand.[17] The Achaemenids broadcast the story of Darius's victories long after his time, since the copy of the Aramaic translation of Bisitun of which we are aware was produced in Elephantine a century after the text was originally composed, while Herodotus, writing in the middle of the fifth century, seems to know the basic story of Darius's overthrow of Gaumata narrated in DB 1 (see Herodotus 3.61-88), and even knows most of the names of the nobles whom Darius says helped him to come to power (compare DB 4.83-86 and Herodotus 3.68, 70). The Achaemenids were clearly not trying to conceal the vast military power they could wield against peoples they understood to be in rebellion, even if such references did not form a central part of their imperial message.

The kings also broadcast the necessity of their violence through another medium, that of their subjects' bodies. On the Bisitun Inscription, in

---

15. Christopher Tuplin, "War and Peace in Achaemenid Imperial Ideology," *Electrum* 14 (2017): 31–54 (38).

16. Tuplin suggests that the marginal locations of the enemy may also allude to the marginal place that the Achaemenids wanted imagery of warfare to play in their ideological self-presentation; see "War and Peace in Achaemenid Imperial Ideology," 39.

17. This, at least, is the sum of the numbers provided in the Akkadian translation; the Aramaic text is fragmentary, but follows the Akkadian closely (see Greenfield and Porten, *The Bisitun Inscription of Darius the Great*, 5–16, for a comparison of the Akkadian and Aramaic texts). Not all of the battle reports in the Akkadian version of Bisitun provide a number of the enemy soldiers that Darius's armies killed, and the state of the text means that not all of the numbers are fully visible. It is not clear that these casualty figures are historically reliable since, according to the text, far more enemy soldiers were killed in battles led by Darius himself than in conflicts where he had assigned leadership of his armies to his generals; for the question of the historical reliability of the casualty figures and the ideology they communicate, see John O. Hyland, "The Casualty Figures in Darius' Bisitun Inscription," *JANEH* 1 (2014): 173–99. From our perspective, however, what matters is the Achaemenids' assertion that they were able to kill so many enemy soldiers in so many places over such a short period of time.

which Darius says "I set forth (*frāstāyam*) this inscription everywhere among the lands" (DB 4.91-92), he discusses the torture of the leaders of the rebellions he defeated. He claims to have killed all of them, as Chapter 3 mentions, but that is not all he did to them. "I impaled him," he says in regard to three of those men (2.76, 91; 3.52), and at another point, when he executes one of the liars and that man's followers among the Babylonian nobility, Darius writes that "they were impaled" (3.92). In two of these cases, the rebel was first mutilated and kept bound at the entrance of Darius's palace, so that "all the people saw him" (2.73-76, 88-90), and in one case Darius writes as well that *frāhanjam* "I hung forth" the bodies of the rebel's followers (2.76-78). Messages can be broadcast on the bodies of rebels, just as they can be circulated through texts and art, and if Darius set forth (*fra-stā-*) his inscriptions throughout his empire, he could also hang forth (*fra-hanj-*) the bodies of the rebels who are inevitably defeated and executed because they are on the wrong side of Auramazda's battle against the Lie, their torture and death carried out by the king who only does the divine will. The display sends a vivid message, as does the mutilation of the rebels who are *basta* "bound" before their execution (DB 1.82-83; 2.75, 89-90; 3.88; 5.26). Old Persian *basta* is a passive participle of the verb *band-*, and the noun *bandaka* "subject" derives from the same root. One can be bound as a loyal subject to the Achaemenid or bound by him in preparation for torture and death,[18] becoming a text on which the king carves a message.

The specific tortures to which the king subjected liars and rebels before their executions were not arbitrary, but were part of the message he sent. Darius describes removing rebels' noses, ears, and eyes, and, in one case, a tongue, and his enemies were seen bound in this manner by "all the people" before their execution. As Bruce Lincoln observes, Darius deliberately chose to remove the parts of the body through which the Lie may enter and leave a person,[19] and so the torture broadcasts the king's ability to control the spread of the Lie. The nose may seem anomalous in this list—it is obvious to us how one can speak a lie, and use one's ears to hear it and eyes to see manifestations of it—but in Zoroastrian tradition evil and the Lie are connected to foul smells. Stench is part of the punishment of hell (e.g., *HN* 2.25; *DD* 27.2-3; *IBd* 28.47; *AWN* 17.10-11; 18.3-10), and *DD* 72.10-12 says that those who stink in this life are sinners and welcome the presence of demons. Lincoln notes as well that the Achaemenids use the word *gasta* "stench" to refer to evil (e.g.,

---

18. See Janzen, "Yahwistic Appropriation of Achaemenid Ideology," 848–9.
19. Lincoln, *"Happiness for Mankind"*, 222–4.

DNa 52; XPh 57-58; A²Sa 5),²⁰ rather as Latin *odium* "hatred" comes from the same root as *odor* "smell."²¹ In this sort of mutilation, Darius demonstrates that he can stop the Lie from spreading and so defeat it and, of course, he demonstrates to "all the people" how much better it is to be *bandaka* than *basta*.

The Achaemenids describe their ability to inflict such torture on those who manifest the Lie as one of the virtues of their rule. "The one who was hostile, him I punished well (*ufrastam aparsam*)," writes Darius (DB 1.22), and both he and Xerxes state that "the one who causes harm, according to the harm I punish (*parsāmiy*)" (DNb 17-19; XPl 19-21). All three words—*ufrastam, aparsam,* and *parsāmiy*—come from the Old Persian root *fraθ-*, which in these cases has the sense of "punish," but its cognate roots in Avestan and Sanskrit refer to inquiry,²² something reflected in the Akkadian version of the Bisitun Inscription, which translates the verb *fraθ-* with *šâlu* "to ask, investigate" (CII 1/2/1.9, 97, 105). One reason why torture is necessary, according to the logic of Achaemenid ideology, is because it sometimes functions as trial by ordeal, and the Achaemenids are good kings who employ their *aruvasta* "skill, intelligence" in judgment as well as in war, because they use such trials to investigate and determine the guilt of the accused. The guilty, of course, will suffer torture and die through the ordeal, and in these cases the investigation is simultaneously a punishment. For example, Plutarch relates a story of Artaxerxes II executing a soldier who claimed to have killed Cyrus the Younger in battle after the king had publicly taken credit for the act himself, and the king had the soldier's eyes gouged out and molten metal poured in his ears until he died (*Art.* 14.5). The removal of his eyes symbolized how the Lie had made him fail to see the world in accordance with the truth the king announces, but, as Lincoln argues, the use of the molten metal reflects some version of a Zoroastrian belief in which the resurrected dead cross a river of molten metal at the eschaton that will purify the wicked but feel only like warm milk to the righteous (*GBd* 34.16-19; *DD* 32.12-13; *IBd* 30.17-20, 29-32).²³ The Achaemenid

20. Lincoln, *Religion, Empire, and Torture*, 93–4.
21. Kent, *Old Persian*, 183.
22. The Indo-European root **perk̂-* means "to ask"; German *fragen* derives from this root, as does Old Persian *fraθ-* "to ask," as well as Avestan *frasā* "question," *pərəsaiti* "ask," and Sanskrit *pṛṣṭhā-* "legal inquiry." See Pokorny, *Indogermanisches etymologisches Wörterbuch*, 1:822, and Douglas Q. Adams, "Ask," in Adams and Mallory, eds, *Encyclopedia of Indo-European Culture*, 33.
23. See the analysis of the passage from Plutarch in Lincoln, "Religion, Empire, and the Spectre of Orientalism," 259–60.

inscriptions say nothing about any sort of eschatological beliefs, but this cultural background sheds some light on the actions Artaxerxes authorized in Plutarch's story. Had the man not been controlled by the Lie, he would have, according to the worldview through which the Achaemenids saw things, survived this trial by molten metal, but his death demonstrated he was guilty after all. Artaxerxes thus tries and punishes him "according to the harm" he caused through his manifestation of the Lie. Those who see and hear in accordance with the Lie do not deserve to see or hear at all, and in this case Artaxerxes removed the liar's ability to see and, with a trial by ordeal that focused attention on his faulty hearing, proved that he was controlled by the Lie. Punishing criminals "according to the harm" they caused also went beyond cases tried directly by the king, and as Xenophon writes approvingly of the work of Cyrus the Younger as satrap of Lydia, Phrygia, and Cappadocia, he says that it was not uncommon there to come across those who had lost feet, hands, or eyes to the Persian justice system Cyrus oversaw (*Anab.* 1.9.13), each mutilated body bearing a message about the importance of loyalty to the king and the law.

The Achaemenids thus fit these sorts of tortures into their worldview that presents them as beneficent kings because they portray such punishment as corresponding to the wrong done by evil persons, who are controlled by the Lie and so who fight the king's efforts to reinstate humanity's happiness. The kings could also paint such messages on canvases much larger than individual bodies, and Diodorus, for example, refers to Artaxerxes III slaughtering hundreds of Sidonian nobles as they came to him to make peace during the Tennes Rebellion (16.45.1-2), while Herodotus says the Persians killed most of the men of Miletus in retaliation for that city's participation in the Ionian Rebellion, made the women and children of the city slaves, and burnt the temple at Didyma (6.19). The Persians sometimes razed rebellious cities (e.g., Strabo 11.11.4), massacred their leaders and horribly maimed the leaders' wives (Herodotus 4.202), and, as at Miletus, enslaved their populations (e.g., 6.101). The Persians continued the Mesopotamian empires' practice of exiling rebellious peoples, including the survivors of Miletus (Herodotus 6.20) and Sidon (*ABC* 9.1-8), to Iran and Mesopotamia (and see also, e.g., Herodotus 4.204; 5.15; 6.119; Diodorus 1.46.4; 17.69.2; Pliny, *Nat. hist.* 6.29).[24] Given the Achaemenids' understanding of geography that Chapter 3 discusses, they would have believed that such forced migrations were

---

24. For a discussion of this topic and further evidence from primary sources of the Persian practice of exiling rebellious populations, see R. J. van der Spek, "Cyrus the Great, Exiles, and Foreign Gods: A Comparison of Daskyleion and Persian Policies on Subject Nations," in Kozuh et al., eds, *Extraction and Control*, 233–64.

beneficial for the rebellious, since bringing them to the good lands at the center of the world would make them better people, or at least expose them to peoples who were by nature better than they. There is no reason to doubt that the temple community in Judah would have been aware of the real threat of Persian power that could be directed against them as a group, just as the other colonized peoples were. The *Economics* of Pseudo-Aristotle, for example, says that Mausolus, the satrap of Caria, invented the claim of an imminent Persian attack because he wanted to take resources from the satrapy's elite (1348a), and the fact that his lie was successful—the local nobility immediately gave Mausolus the funds he said he needed to strengthen his defenses—demonstrates that the empire's subjects saw the threat of imperial violence as very real. Judeans lived near the border of Egypt, which the Persians invaded on multiple occasions following Egyptian rebellions, and so Judeans could hardly have been unaware of the massive military power available to the Achaemenid.

The possibilities of exile, destruction, loss of land, and military attack are key issues of concern in the parts of Ezra–Nehemiah we now turn to examine, but the book, like Achaemenid ideology, sees no contradiction between the horrors its author believed the empire was quite capable of inflicting and the goodness of the dynasty's rule. As the next section of the chapter discusses, the author's reliance on Achaemenid ideology, and especially on the dynasty's portrayals of their subject peoples, allows him or her to create a portrait of a monarchy that does not just faithfully adhere to Yhwh's commands but even administers Yhwh's law, and that could also subject the community to terrible torture. The author can justify the threat of a Persian annihilation of the community because he or she adopts the Achaemenid depiction of the colonized when constructing the identity of his or her own community, a people who need to live in fear of imperial violence to be good, just as the Achaemenids claimed.

2. *The Community and Imperial and Divine Violence in Ezra–Nehemiah*

One might imagine that a book produced by a people subject to empire would send an anti-imperial message, at least a covert one, when it comes to responding to the imperial violence that threatens the colonized, but that was not the approach taken by Ezra–Nehemiah's author. He or she instead mimics the Achaemenids' claim that the violence they inflicted on the colonized was legitimate, not by referring to the king as a skillful and intelligent judge who punishes through trial by ordeal, but by adapting to a Yahwistic worldview the dynasty's claim that the colonized must live in fear of imperial retaliation for disobedience of royal law, which is also divine law. So firmly is Yhwh's will aligned with royal will in Ezra–Nehemiah, as this section of the chapter discusses in more detail, that Torah poses no threat to Achaemenid rule. It is easy to see, then, how the author could appropriate the Achaemenid equation of royal and divine law when urging readers to remain faithful to Torah. In doing so, the book portrays the community in the way the Achaemenids depict their colonized peoples, nations who would live in immorality were it not for their fear of the king's power to punish violations of Auramazda's law that he administers. Ezra–Nehemiah is hardly the only writing in the Hebrew Bible to justify imperial violence, and many others describe Yhwh as using foreign kings to execute judgment on Israel and Judah, but no other such writing has foreign kings administer and enforce Torah, an idea adapted from the Achaemenids. In the author's worldview, imperial violence is always legitimate, for the temple community of Ezra–Nehemiah shares the identity of the colonized of Achaemenid ideology. Like them, they are inherently disobedient and must live in fear of imperial violence for their failures to keep divine law.

Ezra–Nehemiah is able to appropriate the Achaemenid claim that the king administers and enforces God's commands because the book portrays Yhwh in the role Auramazda takes in the Achaemenids' inscriptions, as Chapter 3 mentions. The dynasty, however, did not always portray non-Persian deities in a positive light. In an inscription at Persepolis, Xerxes writes that, in one of the lands he rules, *daivā ayadiyan* "(false) gods were worshiped," but, he says, "by the will of Auramazda I destroyed that sanctuary" and ended the cult of those gods, worshiping Auramazda there instead (XPh 35-41). It is best not to take this as an example of Achaemenid intolerance of the worship of deities besides Auramazda, since there is no evidence that this was widespread imperial policy,[25] but instead to understand the passage as an allusion to a violent suppression of a rebellion that appealed to divine support, and that refers to the destruction of the sanctuaries of the divinities believed to have authorized

---

25. The exception to this is the claim of Berossus that Artaxerxes II erected statues of Anahita in different cities in the empire and required even some non-Persians to participate in the cult (according to Clement of Alexandria, *Exhortation to the Heathen* 5). This seems so out of character with everything else we know about the Achaemenids' approach to cult that scholars have explained Berossus's statement as misconstruing an attempt by Artaxerxes to establish a cult for Persians in the diaspora (so Briant, *From Cyrus to Alexander*, 678–9) or as a move on the king's part to tie non-Persians more closely to the empire (so Amélie Kuhrt, "Can We Understand how the Persians Perceived 'Other' Gods/'the Gods of Others'?," *AfR* 15 [2013]: 149–65 [152–3], following G. De Bruecker).

the revolt.[26] The *daivā* "(false) gods" in Xerxes' inscription reflect the *daēva*s of the Avesta whom, as Chapter 3 mentions, the *Gatha*s accuse of having chosen the Lie rather than Truth. The Lie as we encounter it in Achaemenid ideology is rebellion against the king who always acts in accordance with Auramazda's will, and so for the Achaemenids a *daiva* is a god who supports insurrection against the king and opposes the happiness with which he provides humanity, a god who, rather like the *daēva*s of the Avesta, has chosen the Lie instead of the truth the king proclaims. Following a failed Babylonian revolt against Xerxes, for example, the worship of Marduk and Nabu was sharply curtailed in Uruk, where Anu then became the most venerated god, since the rebels had assumedly claimed that the other two deities, whose cults in Uruk had been more prominent than Anu's, supported this rebellion, leading Xerxes to number them among the *daiva*s and so to attack their cults.[27] Similarly, when Darius writes that the Elamites and Scythians "were hostile, and by them Auramazda was not worshiped" (DB 5.15-16, 31-32), his point is that their hostility to his rule is the equivalent of a failure to worship Auramazda, since they ignore the legitimacy of god's earthly representative and so are under the control of the Lie. Darius, on the other hand, does worship Auramazda, and because of that, "by the will of Auramazda, according to my desire thus I did to them" (5.16-17, 32-33); specifically, that is, Darius was able to crush the Elamite and Scythian armies and execute their leaders (5.10-14, 25-30).

26. This is certainly the consensus understanding of the passage; see, e.g., Wouter F. M. Henkelman, *The Other Gods Who Are: Studies in Elamite–Iranian Acculturation Based on the Persepolis Fortification Texts*, AchHist 14 (Leiden: Nederlands Instituut voor het Nabije Oosten, 2008), 10; Harrison, *Writing Ancient Persia*, 80–1; Josef Wiesehöfer, "Achaemenid Rule and its Impact on Yehud," in Jonker, ed., *Texts, Contexts and Readings in Postexilic Literature*, 171–85 (180).

27. The worship of Anu at Uruk had ancient roots, but by the time of Cyrus's capture of Babylonia, Anu's sanctuary was of secondary importance. For the rise in Anu's prominence at Uruk as a result of Achaemenid reprisals for a Babylonian revolts, see Karlheinz Kessler, "Urukäische Familien versus babylonische Familien: Die Namengebung in Uruk, die Degradierung der Kulte von Eanna und der Aufstieg des Gottes Anu," *AoF* 31 (2004): 237–62. Paul-Alain Beaulieu points out that evidence suggests a rise in Anu's popularity at Uruk even during the time of Nabonidus, but he also argues that, after the revolts in Babylonia during Xerxes' reign, the Persians promoted Anu's cult as a counterbalance to those of more widely worshiped Babylonian gods, including but not limited to Marduk and Nabu. See his "Uruk before and after Xerxes: The Onomastic and Institutional Rise of the God Anu," in *Xerxes and Babylonia: The Cuneiform Evidence*, ed. Caroline Waerzeggers and Maarja Seire, OLA 277 (Leuven: Peeters, 2018), 189–206.

The Achaemenids never identify Auramazda as *daiva*, referring to him only as *baga* "god," but he is not the only divinity who receives this title in their inscriptions. Artaxerxes III also refers to Mithra as *baga* (A³Pa 25), and Darius says *aniyāha bagāha tyaiy hantiy* "the other gods who are" bore him support along with Auramazda (DB 4.61, 62-63). Like other Achaemenids, Darius states that Auramazda is *maθišta bagānām* "the greatest of the gods" (e.g., DPd 1-2; XE 2; A²Hc 1-2), implying that there were other divinities upon whom the dynasty was willing to bestow the title *baga*, assumedly "the gods of the court" who worked with Auramazda (e.g., DPd 13-15; and see also, e.g., DSt 7-8; XPb 27-29; A¹Pa 22-23).[28] The Achaemenids, then, worshiped divinities besides Auramazda, and Artaxerxes II, for example, calls upon the help of Anahita and Mithra as well as Auramazda (e.g., A²Sa 4-5; A²Ha 6-7), while in his *Babyloniaca*, Berossus claims that the same king erected statues of Anahita (so Clement of Alexandria, *Exhortation to the Heathen* 5).[29] The Persepolis Fortification Archive tells us the Achaemenids supported the cults of deities popular in Elam and Persia,[30] and Classical authors refer to them sacrificing horses to Mithra (Xenophon, *Anab.* 4.5.34-35; Strabo 11.14.9). When Darius invokes "the other gods who are" and "the gods of the court," then, he has traditional Elamite and Indo-Iranian deities in mind,[31] so gods besides Auramazda were not necessarily *daiva*s; that is a

---

28. In DPd 13–15, Darius writes, *manā auramazdā upastām baratuv hadā viθaibiš bagaibiš* "bear me support, O Auramazda, with the gods of the court." An Achaemenid asks that Auramazda act *hadā viθaibiš bagaibiš* only in this inscription (see also DPd 21-22, 23-24), but in other inscriptions of Darius and other kings, unnamed *baga*s are invoked along with Auramazda.

29. Berossus does not appear to have been particularly well informed about Persian religious practices, but there is little reason to doubt his basic claim that statues of Anahita were erected at a number of places in the Persian Empire; see Bruno Jacobs, "Berossos and Persian Religion," in *The World of Berossos: Proceedings of the 4th International Colloquium on "The Ancient Near East between Classical and Ancient Oriental Traditions*, ed. Johannes Haubold et al. (Wiesbaden: Harrassowitz, 2013), 123–35. Plutarch appears to refer to Artaxerxes II as participating in a coronation ritual in a temple dedicated to Anahita (*Art.* 3.2); see the discussion of the passage in Briant, *From Cyrus to Alexander*, 676–7.

30. Henkelman, *The Other Gods Who Are*, 254–304.

31. It is unlikely that the Achaemenids had the gods of subject peoples in mind when they used phrases like these on their inscriptions, contra Lucas L. Schulte, *My Shepherd, though You Do Not Know Me: The Persian Royal Propaganda Model in the Nehemiah Memoir*, CBET 78 (Leuven: Peeters, 2016), 80–1. When the Achaemenids broadcast messages for the colonized through media such as the Chalouf Stela, they simply adopt local depictions of regional deities, but Old Persian *baga* almost

term reserved for those divinities whom rebels say support their struggle against the king and the happiness he provides for the colonized.

The author of Ezra–Nehemiah makes it clear that Yhwh is no *daiva*, since at no point in the book does Yhwh ever oppose a king's desire. It is Yhwh who gives Cyrus "all the kingdoms of the earth" (Ezra 1:2), and Yhwh never supports rebellion. Even when Ezra 4:24 implies in the context of 4:1-24 as a whole that a royal command puts a stop to the temple construction Yhwh had ordered, Yhwh does nothing to contradict the king. It is important in regard to this total divine support for the Achaemenids that Ezra–Nehemiah never quotes divine speech from prophetic figures, even though it names Jeremiah, Haggai, and Zechariah (Ezra 1:1; 5:1; 6:14), and that it says prophets can be bribed to lie (Neh. 6:10-14). Prophetic speech is not as important in the book as royal speech is, and, because the book claims that prophets are sometimes untrustworthy, Ezra–Nehemiah makes it possible for readers to doubt the veracity of any prophet whose speech would contradict the book's message and who might proclaim, for example, that Yhwh opposed Achaemenid rule or planned to bring it to an end. Haggai and Zechariah actually allude to such ideas in the Book of the Twelve (Hag. 2:20-23; Zech. 2:1-4 [1:18-21], 10-13 [6-9]), as Chapter 5 discusses, but Ezra–Nehemiah silences them, and so they appear in its narrative only as supporters of the temple construction the kings authorize and fund. In the Neo-Assyrian context, writes Martti Nissinen, false prophecy was understood to be prophecy that urged or supported rebellion against the king,[32] and one imagines the author of Ezra–Nehemiah would have said the same in the fourth century.

---

certainly had a more limited reference. And while there is evidence that non-Persians, such as Babylonians, lived in Persia in the Achaemenid period, the cults of gods not traditionally worshiped in Elam and Persia did not receive state support; see Wouter F. M. Henkelman, "Parnakka's Feast: *šip* in Pārsa and Elam," in *Elam and Persia*, ed. Javier Álvarez-Mon and Mark B. Garrison (Winona Lake, IN: Eisenbrauns, 2011), 89–166 (96–8).

32. Martti Nissinen, "Falsche Prophetie in neuassyrischer und deuteronomistische Darstellung," in *Das Deuteronomium und seine Querbeziehungen*, ed. Timo Veijola, SEFJ 62 (Göttingen: Vandenhoeck & Ruprecht, 1996), 172–95. He refers to texts such as the Vassal Treaty of Esarhaddon (SAA 2.6.108-118) and the prophecy in regard to Sasi (SAA 15.69.rev2-5). In one Neo-Assyrian case, a diviner wrote to Esarhaddon to tell him that he had been forced to perform divination in regard to the question as to whether someone else would become king, and says that he provided a positive answer only to save his own life (SAA 10.179). But his response, he assures Esarhaddon, was *alla šāru mehû* "only wind (and) storm," where *šāru* "wind" also has the sense of "falsehood" (*CAD* 17.2, 139–40).

One could say that Yhwh's voice is carefully controlled in Ezra–Nehemiah, since we never encounter direct divine speech through the narrative or the prophets, although Cyrus can announce the divine plan to build the temple in Ezra 1:2 on God's behalf. And despite the good work of Ezra and Nehemiah, or indeed of the community itself in Ezra 1–6, the divine will in the book always depends entirely on the royal response to it, which is no different than the way the Achaemenids write about their relationship to Auramazda on their inscriptions, which describe king and god as mutually dependent.[33] The kings can act only because they receive divine support, but Auramazda's *vašna* "will" for the world is accomplished only through their actions. The kings of Persia loyally carry out Yhwh's will in Ezra–Nehemiah, and so, as Chapter 2 explains, Cyrus obeys the divine command of Ezra 1:2 to build the temple, but must arrange on his own initiative precisely how to execute the order in 1:3-11. We see Yhwh influencing the Achaemenids to enact the divine will at other points in the book, as well, although it is sometimes difficult to tell just what form that influence takes. It is not precisely clear what the author means when he or she writes that Artaxerxes gave Ezra all that he sought from him כיד יהוה אלהיו עליו "according/corresponding to the hand of Yhwh his God that was upon him" (Ezra 7:6), a phrase much like the one that appears when Nehemiah explains the king's generosity in response to his plan to rebuild Jerusalem and its wall as כיד אלהי הטובה עלי "according/corresponding to the good hand of my God that was upon me" (Neh. 2:8).[34] In both cases, Artaxerxes responds to the divine will, and

---

33. P. O. Skjærvø, "The Achaemenids and the Avesta," in *Birth of the Persian Empire, Volume 1*, ed. Vesta Sarkhosh Curtis and Sarah Stewart (London: I. B. Tauris, 2005), 52–84 (57–8).

34. For the preposition -כ as having the sense of "corresponding to," see *IBHS* §11.2.9b. Lucas Schulte argues that -כ at the beginning of the phrase points to Artaxerxes' actions as resembling those produced by God's hand rather than as motivated by the divine (*My Shepherd, though You Do Not Know Me*, 163–4), and that is a grammatically possible reading. But Ezra directly says that God moved the king to act (Ezra 7:27), and Nehemiah prays before making his request to Artaxerxes (Neh. 2:5), while Maria Häusl points out that Nehemiah's prayer of Neh. 1:5-11 has the effect of portraying all of his actions as receiving divine support ("'So I prayed to the God of heaven' [Neh 2:4]: Praying and Prayers in the Books of Ezra and Nehemiah," in *Prayers and the Construction of Israelite Identity*, ed. Susanne Gillmayr-Bucher and Maria Häusl, SBLAIL 35 [Atlanta: SBL Press, 2019], 53–82 [77]). Context, then, suggests that both Ezra 7:6 and Neh. 2:8 refer to the king's actions as corresponding to what God ordered or moved Artaxerxes to do. In fact, LXX Ezra 7:6 reflects Hebrew כי יד אלהיו עליו (so LXX[B]; LXX[A] has the same reading, except that it adds κυρίου

the phrases used in regard to that action in Ezra 7:6 and Neh. 2:8 could refer to anything from a divine command that the king obeys to a direct manipulation of an unwitting monarch. The introductory story of Cyrus in Ezra 1 suggests the former reading, but even the latter interpretation reflects well on Achaemenid kings—who can also be generous entirely on their own initiative, as Cyrus and Darius are in Ezra 6:1-12—for it portrays them as extensions of the divine will.

Given this particular conflation of Yahwistic and imperial ideas, it is very difficult to see how the author of Ezra–Nehemiah could ever believe Yhwh would ask Judah to rebel against the Achaemenids, and we can also see that the author would never be able to condemn a Persian exile or annihilation of the community as illegitimate or as contradicting God's will. The author never directly addresses that second issue, however, except insofar as he or she discusses the possibility of punishment for violations of the law, and as we turn to that issue we can note first that, given the author's understanding of Yhwh, it is hardly a surprise to find that his or her understanding of Yhwh's law is just as amenable to Achaemenid interests. Much of what the book says about the law corresponds to other Yahwistic writings available by the fourth century: it is specifically Yhwh's law (e.g., Ezra 7:10; Neh. 8:8, 18; 9:3, 26; 10:30 [29]), given through Moses (e.g., Ezra 3:2; 6:18; 7:6; Neh. 8:1; 9:14; 10:30 [29]) at Mount Sinai (Neh. 9:13), and the people's very survival depends on adherence to it (Ezra 9:6-15; Neh. 9:6-37; 13:18). However, the presentation of the law is somewhat different in Ezra–Nehemiah than in other biblical writings, in part due to the particular aspects of the law the author chooses to emphasize, and he or she carefully controls the significance of that law, just as he or she carefully controls Yhwh's voice. If the community's existence hangs in the balance when they fail to keep Torah, as Ezra says is the case when he proclaims that "we have abandoned your commandments" (Ezra 9:10), that situation can be entirely rectified by having community members send away their foreign wives, the solution of Ezra 10. If Israel has repetitively disobeyed the law since God gave it to them at Sinai, as the Levites announce (Neh. 9:26-32), the community can correct this matter by agreeing "to walk in God's law" (10:30 [29]), something that amounts to banning marriages to outsiders (10:31 [30]), observing the Sabbath, which consists of not trading with foreigners on

---

before θεοῦ), and if this text is original and MT's כיד reflects parablepsis of an original כי יד, then the narrator says that Artaxerxes grants Ezra's request "because the hand of his God was upon him."

that day (10:32a [31a]),³⁵ observing the Sabbath year (10:32b [31b]), and properly supplying the needs of the temple and its personnel (10:33-40 [32-39]). As far as a reader of Ezra–Nehemiah can tell, nothing else about the law is significant, except perhaps the proper observance of sacrifice (Ezra 3:2) and festivals (Ezra 3:4; Neh. 8:13-18), and maintaining the proper order of priests and Levites (Ezra 6:18). Whatever form of the Pentateuch the author associated with Aramaic דת and Hebrew תורה,³⁶ the concept of Yahwistic law, insofar as Ezra–Nehemiah presents its essential aspects, is as unthreatening to Achaemenid rule as the book's concept of Yhwh.³⁷

35. In Neh. 13:15-18, Nehemiah implies that agricultural work on the Sabbath also violates that law (see his use of חלל in 13:17-18), but he never actually refers to the law there, and so Neh. 10:32 [31] is the only verse in the book that clearly provides specific guidance in regard to what the law demands in regard to the observance of the Sabbath.

36. Scholars do not agree as to whether the authors of Ezra–Nehemiah and its original sources were aware of the final form of the Pentateuch or of some earlier stage of its composition, but Aramaic דת in Ezra 7 is, like the word תורה in the Hebrew sections of the book, mainly understood to refer to the Pentateuch in some form. David Carr, for example, argues the Persians likely authorized the final form of the Pentateuch (*The Formation of the Hebrew Bible: A New Reconstruction* [Oxford: Oxford University Press, 2011], 204–24), while H. G. M. Williamson (*Ezra, Nehemiah*, xxxvii–xxxix) and Joseph Blenkinsopp (*Ezra–Nehemiah*, 155) see Ezra's Torah as a combination of Priestly and Deuteronomic material. Sara Japhet argues there is enough evidence in Ezra–Nehemiah to demonstrate the entire Pentateuch was known in Judah by the time the book was written ("What May Be Learned from Ezra–Nehemiah about the Composition of the Pentateuch?," in *The Formation of the Pentateuch: Bridging the Academic Cultures of Europe, Israel, and North America*, ed. Jan C. Gertz et al., FAT 111 [Tübingen: Mohr Siebeck, 2016], 543–60), although Philip Yoo (*Ezra and the Second Wilderness*, OTRM [Oxford: Oxford University Press, 2017], 31) believes different authors of the different sources used in the final version of Ezra–Nehemiah were aware of the Pentateuch at different stages of its development. Frank Crüsemann (*Torah: Theology and Social History of Old Testament Law*, trans. Allan W. Mahnke [Minneapolis: Fortress Press, 1995], 334–9), on the other hand, maintains that Ezra's law was likely some form of the Pentateuch, but that it is impossible to say what point of development it had reached.

37. Some scholars argue, in fact, that the emphasis on separation from outsiders, to the point of demanding that community members divorce their foreign spouses, conformed to an imperial directive (so Kenneth G. Hoglund, *Achaemenid Imperial Administration in Syria-Palestine and the Missions of Ezra and Nehemiah*, SBLDS 125 [Atlanta: Scholars Press, 1992], 236–40) or was meant to solidify the community's bond to the imperial administration (so John Kessler, "Persia's Loyal Yahwists:

Had the author merely wanted to make the point that God's law poses no threat to Achaemenid interests, perhaps these sorts of depictions of it would have been enough, but he or she goes further and composes or includes from an earlier source a passage in which a foreign king takes responsibility for authorizing and enforcing Yahwistic law. Artaxerxes orders Ezra to appoint judges to enforce "the laws[38] of your God" throughout the entire satrapy, and to teach the people in Across-the-River who do not know these laws (Ezra 7:25), and the king also announces a list of punishments for those who do not obey דתא די אלהך ודתא די מלכא "the law of your God and the law of the king" (7:26). As far as Ezra–Nehemiah presents things, the law that Judeans understand as given by Yhwh is now an integral part of the imperial justice system in Across-the-River, and not just religious law that the temple community in Judah alone will use. According to 7:25-26, the judges the king orders Ezra to appoint throughout the satrapy will enforce the laws given by Yhwh,[39] since 7:25 specifically refers to "the laws of your God" that those officials will adjudicate. Moreover, the law Ezra is ordered to bring is not only for the Yahwists in Across-the-River,[40] for in 7:25 Artaxerxes specifically commands Ezra to teach "the laws of your God" throughout the satrapy to those who do not know them. It is not historically possible that Pentateuchal law was a primary legal standard by which an entire Persian satrapy was governed,[41] but that is the claim of 7:25-26, and perhaps because the Pentateuch was used in Samaria as well as Judah it may

Power Identity and Ethnicity in Achaemenid Yehud," in *Judah and the Judeans in the Persian Period*, ed. Oded Lipschits and Manfred Oeming [Winona Lake, IN: Eisenbrauns, 2006], 91–121 [111]). Chapter 5 returns to Ezra–Nehemiah's suspicion of marriages of community members to those outside of the group.

38. The Old Greek, Vulgate, and Syriac reflect an original text in 7:25 that has the singular form of the word דת (although LXX[L] has corrected to the tradition of the MT, which reads דתי אלהך), but that is likely the influence of the phrase דתא די אלהך "the law of your God" from the following verse, where דת is in the singular.

39. Lisbeth Fried, for example, argues that if Artaxerxes truly did order Ezra to appoint judges, then they would have been Persian judges applying Persian and not Judean concepts of justice; see her "'You shall appoint judges': Ezra's Mission and the Rescript of Artaxerxes," in *Persia and Torah: The Theory of Imperial Authorization of the Pentateuch*, ed. James W. Watts, SBLSymS 17 (Atlanta: Society of Biblical Literature, 2001), 63–89. There is some sense to this as a historical argument, but that is not actually what the text says, and the text is our concern here.

40. Contra, e.g., Gary N. Knoppers, "Beyond Jerusalem and Judah: The Mission of Ezra in the Province of Transeuphrates," *EI* 29 (2009): 78*–87* (83*).

41. So, e.g., H. G. M. Williamson, *Studies in Persian Period History and Historiography*, FAT 38 (Tübingen: Mohr Siebeck, 2004), 42–3.

have sounded convincing to some in the temple community. By choosing to include Ezra 7:25-26, however, the author makes the Achaemenids responsible for punishing violations of the law. Artaxerxes refers to the satrapal judges who will enforce it, and the list of punishments they are authorized to impose includes the death penalty and corporal punishment (7:26),[42] but the real fear expressed in passages such as Ezra's prayer (Ezra 9:6-15) is of the destruction or exile of the group for a communal failure to obey the law. Readers would have been well aware of what the Achaemenids could do when it came to violent punishments of the colonized, and in the author's worldview imperial violence exercised against the community could only be the result of the divine will.

The claim that Yhwh's law existed in the same justice system overseen by the king fits the worldview of Ezra–Nehemiah's author quite well, for in his or her understanding God does not contradict the king but works through him to accomplish the divine will, and since divine and royal desires are in accord, the law codes that reflect those desires will be also. Given Ezra 7:25-26, the imperial apparatus will be in charge of punishing disobedience of the law, including violations of the law of the king, which complements divine law. All of these ideas reflect similar claims from Achaemenid ideology, where the law is a key aspect of the dynasty's rule that restores humanity's happiness. It has a divine origin, as Xerxes says when he urges his subjects to "go around in that law which Auramazda set down" (XPh 49-50),[43] paralleling the Avestan notion that Ahura Mazda has provided humanity with a law (*Y.* 21.1; 46.15).

---

42. The OG translates Aramaic שרשי (שרשו according to the *kĕtîb*) in 7:26 as παιδείαν, a general word for punishment, which may indicate the translator was not clear as to how to make sense of it. Some see it as deriving from the Semitic root *šrš*, and so understand it as having the sense of being uprooted or exiled; e.g., Rudolph, *Esra und Nehemia*, 74; Gunneweg, *Esra*, 128. Franz Rosenthal sees it as a loanword from Old Persian *srauśya "corporal punishment" (*A Grammar of Biblical Aramaic*, 7th ed., PLO 5 [Wiesbaden: Harrassowitz, 2006], §189), which is the more likely conclusion, since the Aramaic noun סרשיתא appears at Elephantine (*TAD* A6.3.6) with a similar meaning.

43. A Greek inscription from Sardis might refer to Auramazda as Zeus Baradates or Zeus Legislator (SEG 29-1205.4-5), and if the inscription truly does use Βαραδατεω as a way of describing Auramazda, then it points to a widespread association of this god with the concept of law. It is not clear, however, that the inscription refers to Auramazda, or that Baradates is a divine title rather than the name of the ancestor of the individual who dedicated the statue to which the inscription refers. See competing arguments in M.-L. Chaumont, "Un nouveau gouvernour de Sardes à l'époque achéménide d'après une inscription récemment découverte," *Syria* 67 (1990): 579–608 (580–1), and Briant, *From Cyrus to Alexander*, 677–8.

Going around in Auramazda's law, says Xerxes, is the key to realizing the happiness Auramazda intended for humans (XPh 46-50), the restoration of creation to which the opening of that inscription refers (1-6). Both Xerxes and Darius mention the law in inscriptions that open with the standard Achaemenid creation formula (DNa 1-8; DSe 1-7; XPh 1-6)[44] and that list the many lands and peoples they rule (DNa 22-30; DSe 22-30; XPh 19-28), and in each case, they introduce these lists by saying, "that which was said by me, that they did; my law held them" (DNa 20-22; DSe 19-21; XPh 17-19), a claim Xerxes makes on the same inscription in which he refers to the law as set down by Auramazda. The king's law from Auramazda, that is, holds the peoples so their happiness can be restored. On the Bisitun Inscription as well, after listing the lands he rules (DB 1.12-17), Darius writes that "these lands went around in my law; that which was said by me, thus it was done" (1.23-24). Darius and Xerxes clearly link *dāta* "law" to "that which was said by me," so it is clear that the concept of law does not contradict royal command. Law exists to rule the colonized, who must do the king's will, which is also Auramazda's will, and to achieve the happiness that both god and king desire for them they must adhere to what the king calls "my law," which is also "that law which Auramazda set down."

The law that Auramazda set down is not limited to the concept of specific royal commands,[45] however, as we see when the Akkadian version of DNa 20-22 translates Old Persian *dāta* with *dīnātu* "laws," since here the translator understood *dāta* as referring to the laws or legislation in general and not specific royal commands. Some decades later, when Xerxes borrowed the language from Darius's burial inscription and also wrote in reference to his colonized peoples that "my law held them" (XPh 17-19), the Akkadian translation of his inscription used not *dīnātu* but *dātu* as a loanword, and so the *dātu/dāta* is also Akkadian *dīnātu*, the laws in general, which is why other Akkadian writings of the Persian period use *dātu* to refer to royal tax regulations, as well as criminal and civil law.[46] Xenophon discusses the βασιλικοὶ νόμοι "royal laws" of the Persians (*Oec.* 14.6-7) in the same context in which he writes about the seventh- and sixth-century law codes of Draco and Solon (14.4-7),

---

44. Darius also uses the word *dāta* in the plural in DNb 58, but the text is broken at this point. One of Xerxes' inscriptions (XPl) closely parallels DNb, but it has nothing equivalent to the closing lines of DNb where the word *dāta* appears.

45. Contra Fried, "'You shall appoint judges,'" 81–4.

46. For the use of Akkadian *dātu* in those latter senses, see M. Jursa, J. Paszkowiak, and C. Waerzeggers, "Three Court Records," *AfO* 50 (2003/2004): 255–68 (259).

and that suggests he understood there to be some sort of Persian legal code that received royal authorization. Christopher Tuplin argues that Old Persian *dāta* and **dātabara* (literally, "one who bears *dāta*," and so referring to varieties of legal offices) were borrowed so widely throughout the empire as loanwords in contexts that refer to general legislation going beyond individual royal commands that when we encounter *dāta* in Old Persian or as a loanword—such as in the Aramaic word דת that appears in Artaxerxes' letter to Ezra (Ezra 7:14, 25, 26)—it refers to the general concept of law.[47]

In Achaemenid ideology, then, royal law and command are a necessary and beneficial part of the rule of the colonized, since doing what Auramazda and the king desire results in their happiness, and so the Achaemenids referred to their law as they explained how they made the world a better place. On Darius's burial inscription, the king lists his colonized peoples whom, he says, his law "held," and then goes on to say that "Auramazda, when he saw this earth in turmoil (*yaudantim*), after that he bore it to me, he made me king" (DNa 31-34) so that Darius could "put it down in place (*gāθavā*)" (35-36). As a result, he says in regard to the peoples he rules, "that which I said, that they did, according to my desire" (36-38), which is how he described the peoples' obedience to the law earlier in the inscription (20-22). Auramazda gave "this earth" that he established (1-2) to Darius so the king could quell its turmoil and have the world act according to his desire, his command, which accords with the law Auramazda set down. In an inscription from Susa, Darius again refers to his use of the law to make life better for the colonized. After listing the peoples he rules, he goes on to say that "much that was poorly done, that I made good" (DSe 31-32). It was his job to create a good world "by the will of Auramazda," writes Darius, because the lands were in turmoil (*ayaudan*) as "one struck (*ajan*) another" (32-34). This is the normal Achaemenid description of the pre-Achaemenid world, and Darius writes that he ensured this violence did not continue, so that now "all are in place" (35-37), and he accomplished this because the peoples he conquered "fear my law, so that the stronger does not strike (*naiy jantiy*) nor destroy the weak" (37-41). Darius's law, which originates with Auramazda, makes the world a better place, putting an end to violence and injustice among the inherently immoral peoples who are afraid of the consequences of disobedience, and so who are "in place," working with the king and obeying his commands to restore their own peace and happiness.

47. Tuplin, "The Justice of Darius."

In Achaemenid ideology, it is important that the colonized fear the king's law Auramazda has set down, since this makes their lives better. Such fear is inspired by the king's power, wisdom, and ability—his *xraθu* and *aruvasta*—to properly punish those whose actions manifest the Lie. Imperial violence, we could say, is represented only at the margins of Achaemenid ideology, but it is still important that the colonized be aware of the frightening consequences of acting in opposition to royal law and command. The author of Ezra–Nehemiah agreed with this position, for it fit his or her understanding of the relationships between the divine, the king, the law, and his or her colonized community, an understanding that depends to a large degree on Achaemenid ideology. Ezra–Nehemiah's Yhwh never acts against the king's command, and the Achaemenid is largely an extension of the divine will, while the epigone of Ezra 7–Nehemiah 13 is inherently immoral, just like all of their ancestors, except for the generation of Ezra 1–6, which was lucky enough to emerge from the imperial center. The epigone, on the other hand, is no different than their ancestors who violated God's law as soon as they received it at Sinai (Neh. 9:16-17) and repetitively thereafter (9:26-30). So before there was Cyrus of Persia, Ezra–Nehemiah says, there was Nebuchadnezzar of Babylon (Ezra 2:1; 5:12, 14; 6:5; Neh. 7:6), who created "the captivity of the exile" as God's punishment for their ancestors' sins. By identifying the community in Judah as "the exile," Ezra–Nehemiah not only creates continuity with a group that lives at the good center of the world, as Chapter 3 explains, but also makes captivity and exile key to the community's self-understanding, so that a central aspect of group identity is as the deserving recipients of divine punishment enacted through imperial violence,[48] a basic fact of their history in the book,[49] something that never

---

48. For some scholars, the post-exilic emphasis on exile as a paradigm of the people's historical experience is the result of the failure of earlier prophecies of a great restoration to be fulfilled; e.g., Bradley C. Gregory, "The Postexilic Third Isaiah: Isaiah 61:1-3 in Light of Second Temple Hermeneutics," *JBL* 126 (2007): 475–96 (490–1). This may help explain the focus on exile in some post-exilic texts, but as Ezra–Nehemiah presents things, full restoration has been achieved.

49. And this shared history of exile distinguishes the community from all the peoples around it in Palestine, for no other group in the region shares the community's history of divine punishment, not even the other Yahwists in Palestine who are not descended from the group that migrated from Babylonia. See Dalit Rom-Shiloni, *Exclusive Inclusivity: Identity Conflicts between the Exiles and the People Who Remained (6th–5th Centuries BCE)*, LHBOTS 543 (New York: Bloomsbury, 2013), 46–7; Rom-Shiloni, "From Ezekiel to Ezra–Nehemiah," 131–3; and Southwood, "The Holy Seed," 204–5.

really comes to an end, insofar as it is always part of the way Ezra–Nehemiah identifies the community.[50] Already by Ezra 5, readers learn that "because our ancestors angered the God of the heavens, he gave them into the hand of Nebuchadnezzar the king of Babylon, the Chaldean, and this house he destroyed and the people he exiled to Babylon" (5:12), and when the book arrives at the time of the epigone in Ezra 7–Nehemiah 13, it returns at numerous points to the sins of the ancestors and the divine punishments they received (Ezra 9:7; Neh. 1:7-8; 9:16-30; 13:18, 26).

Accounts such as those of Ezra 9–10 and Nehemiah 13, as well as the prayers of Ezra and the Levites, make it clear that the current version of the community is no different than their ancestors. "From the days of our ancestors, we have been in great guilt, to this day," says Ezra in his prayer (Ezra 9:7), and this guilt continues to this day "because we have abandoned your commandments" (9:10) through the sin of intermarriage. The Levites' prayer in Nehemiah 9 focuses particularly on the sins of the ancestors; God provided them with "just regulations, true laws, good statutes and commandments" at Mount Sinai (9:13), but according to this prayer there was no point at which the ancestors kept the law. Despite God's provision for them in the wilderness (9:19-21), "they did not obey your commandments; they refused to obey" (9:16-17). Despite God's gift of a rich land (9:22-25), "they were disobedient[51] and rebelled against

---

50. So Kessler, "The Diaspora in Zechariah 1–8 and Ezra–Nehemiah," 135–7; Southwood, *Ethnicity and the Mixed Marriage Crisis in Ezra 9–10*, 156–61. Mark Boda argues that the general interpretation of history in Ezra–Nehemiah is that the exile has come to an end, and only the prayer of Neh. 9:6-37 presents the matter differently (*Praying the Tradition: The Origin and Use of Tradition in Nehemiah 9*, BZAW 277 [Berlin: W. de Gruyter, 1999], 189–95). But if we take the continued identification of the community as "the exile" and "the captivity" seriously, then the text is consistently linking community identity to the punishment of exile. It is certainly possible that many members of the post-exilic temple community believed a new beginning for the cult in Jerusalem indicated divine punishment had come to an end, but that is not the picture we see in Ezra–Nehemiah. See also Jill Middlemas, "The Future of the 'Exile,'" in Ahn and Middlemas, eds, *By the Irrigation Canals of Babylon*, 63–81.

51. The OG here has ἤλλαξαν "they changed," reading וימרו as from the root מור rather than מרה as pointed in the MT (LXX^L reads it as from מרר "to be bitter"). But since the preceding verses focus on Yhwh's good actions in providing Israel with a good land, no attitude of the people toward God and the law while in the land has been previously expressed for the people to change at this point in the story. They maintain the same disregard toward the law that we see in 9:16-17, and so nothing has changed in terms of their disobedience. As a result, the MT and not the OG has more likely interpreted וימרו in accordance with the author's intentions.

you, and cast your law behind their back" (9:26). Despite punishment for this disobedience—"you gave them into the hand of their adversaries"—followed by a merciful alleviation of it (9:27), something that happened more than once (9:28), the people learned no discernible lesson from this pattern of events and "they did not obey your commandments and they sinned against your regulations" (9:29). Moreover, the Levites confess, "we have done evil" (9:33), and readers see this evil continue in Nehemiah 13, a story of yet another manifestation of the group's inherent inability to keep the law, and a repudiation of the belief the community expresses in Nehemiah 10 that, left to their own devices, they could do otherwise.

One further point can be made about the creation of community identity in light of Ezra–Nehemiah's portrayal of the law, although it is one the book never makes explicitly: if Torah and the king's law can exist in the same legal system overseen by the same satrapal judges, then it would seem as if they would be entirely complementary. After all, it is hard to see how someone responsible for judging both "the law of your God and the law of the king" could arrive at a ruling if someone had acted in accordance with one of those law codes but was in violation of the other. This implies, then, that one should always be loyal to the king's law, as this will never contradict Torah. If other incentive were needed to reinforce such a message, stories of Persian military actions and the presence of those mutilated by the Persian justice system would have provided it.

The notion that God could use foreign kings and armies to punish a disobedient people was hardly the invention of the author of Ezra–Nehemiah, for that had been grounded in Yahwistic tradition for centuries. The author of Ezra–Nehemiah, however, presents this Yahwistic tradition in a worldview shaped by Achaemenid ideology so that the Judean temple community is just one more colonized people who are far from the good center of the world who should be defined by their loyalty to the king. This means they must obey the king's law, which includes Yhwh's law, and their fear of the destruction that God would otherwise order the Achaemenid to carry out helps to motivate such obedience. In Ezra–Nehemiah the real existential threat to the community is their own worst impulses, rooted in their very nature, and so the essence of their identity is as a colonized people as the Achaemenids would have understood that concept. As a result, there is no better state in which the community can exist than the one they are in now, as Ezra says in his prayer, where he describes them as עבדים, *bandaka*s or "subjects" to the Persians, the פליטה "survivor" that God has השאיר "caused to remain" through divine

תחנה "grace" (Ezra 9:8). Before the punishment of Nebuchadnezzar's exile, Judah had been independent, the book reports, but, the Levites say, there was no point after God gave them the law during which their ancestors were faithful (Neh. 9:26-30), and the community now exists only because Yhwh is אל חנון ורחום "a gracious and merciful God" (9:31). As Chapters 2 and 3 explain, even here in Nehemiah 8–13 the book presents no future for the community who cannot do what is right without "the kings whom you set over us because of our sins" (9:37). These kings are necessary because the Judean temple community of Ezra–Nehemiah is just like the colonized peoples of the Achaemenid inscriptions, while the kings act on God's behalf, have ordered the law to be sent to Judah, have taken responsibility for a legal system that will enforce it, supply the leadership that keeps the community obedient, and are the source of the community's fear of the consequences of disobedience.

3. *The End of History and the Last King, Part 1*

If the author of Ezra–Nehemiah is willing to accept Achaemenid ideology, even to the point where the threat of imperial violence has a good and necessary role to play in his or her theology and understanding of community identity, then it might seem that, from the author's point of view, the Persian Empire can do no wrong. That conclusion is not strictly accurate, however, since there are points where the book portrays imperial officials as corrupt and evil, and so it is best to describe Ezra–Nehemiah as pro-Achaemenid, although not always pro-empire. The book can justify imperial violence because it creates a group identity that corresponds to the Achaemenids' portrayal of the colonized, and as a result the community itself is more frequently the source of problems they must overcome; if they lament in Neh. 9:36-37 that they are "slaves" or subjects to the kings who take the produce of the land, that is their fault, since the prayer of 9:6-37 as a whole blames the community's sin for this state of affairs.[52] If some of them believe a royal tax is responsible for their financial woes (Neh. 5:4), the problem is really other Judeans who have been charging them interest and taking their land when they default on the loans (5:6-11).[53] And if community members live in fear of some

---

52. See also, e.g., Werline, *Penitential Prayer in Second Temple Judaism*, 58; Oeming, "'See, we are serving today' (Nehemiah 9:36)," 581–2.

53. So contra Smelik, "Nehemiah as a 'Court Jew,'" 71–2, Neh. 5 does not portray the Achaemenids negatively. Nor does Nehemiah admit culpability here (contra Eskenazi, *In an Age of Prose*, 148–9), for although he does say that he and

sort of violent intervention on the part of the Persians that could damage or even annihilate the group, then that, says Ezra 9:6-15, is the result of their own failings as well, since any such violence would be the result of the community's sin. Yet not every setback or threat in Ezra–Nehemiah can be laid at the door of the community, and while this conclusion to the chapter discusses the book's suspicion of the imperial officials in regions near Judah, it emphasizes again Ezra–Nehemiah's insistence that there is no future for the people except under Achaemenid rule. The empire may be flawed due to the corruption of some of its administrators in Palestine, as the author sees it, but existence within the empire is as good as things will get for the community, and this is why they must strive to remain loyal Persian subjects. References to such flaws make up the single aspect of Ezra–Nehemiah that contradicts Achaemenid ideology, but the dynasty, like Ezra–Nehemiah's author, believed that there was no better future for the colonized than to continue to live within the empire. In Achaemenid ideology, there was no way in which the happiness of the present could be exceeded, and in that worldview, history had basically come to an end after the time of Darius, for there were no historical events worth reporting after the first Achaemenid had set everything and everyone down in place, so that each king after him was, in essence, the last king.

For the author of Ezra–Nehemiah, however, the dynasty's perfection does not extend to all of its representatives in Palestine, and he or she is suspicious of imperial officials who operate in the regions around Judah. One of the two places where readers encounter such suspicion is Ezra 4, which opens with the community of Persia's loyal Yahwists adhering to the order given to them by Cyrus and so rejecting the offer of the people of the land to participate in the temple construction (4:1-3), with the result that the latter group pays "counselors" to frustrate the project (4:5). As Chapter 2 discusses, the correspondence that follows between royal officials and Artaxerxes in 4:11-22 concerns the construction of Jerusalem's wall, but assumedly shows readers how the people of the land had worked earlier with royal officials whom they had bribed to put a stop to the construction of the temple, as well. If the achronological material of 4:11-22 lets readers know near the beginning of the book that the people of the land were liars who acted in disloyalty against the will of king and God, it also gives readers a sense of the problems posed by working

---

his kin have been lending money at interest (5:10), his exhortation that the assembly return the land and property they have taken is directed at others (5:11). One may see Nehemiah as disingenuous here, but he claims no responsibility for the taking of land that has caused community members to sell their children into slavery.

4. The King, God, and Torture

with the imperial bureaucracy in the colonies.[54] The authors of the letter to the king in 4:11-16 may be "the people of Across-the-River," but the preceding verses specify the involvement of royal officials (4:8-9)—in the context of Ezra 4, these are the "counselors" bribed by the people of the land—and those officials are the recipients of the letter Artaxerxes sends in response (4:17). The case those bureaucrats make to the king, as Chapter 3 explains, is based on lies, and although the Achaemenids insist that they are not Lie-followers, nor friendly to those who are (DB 4.63; DNb 12-13; XPl 13-14), Artaxerxes ends up parroting the language of his lying officials in his response of 4:17-22. Like them, he refers to Jerusalem's מרד "rebellion" and אשתדור "insurrection" that occurred in יומת עלמא "days of old" (compare 4:15 and 19), to the problem of maintaining the flow of tax (מדת בלו והלך) in the region should the city be rebuilt (4:13, 20), and to the notion that Jerusalem's wall will damage (נזק in the Haphel) royal rule (4:15, 20). The officials tell Artaxexes that he should search (יבקר) in "the book of the annals of your ancestors" if he wishes to discover the truth about Jerusalem (4:15), and the king responds that "they searched (בקרו) and found" information about the city (4:19), and while all of that information is true, as fourth-century Judean readers would understand it—Jerusalem was once governed by mighty kings who controlled all of the current satrapy of Across-the-River, and the city did rebel against imperial rulers (4:19-20)[55]—Artaxerxes's interpretation of it has been shaped by the lies his officials have told him, causing him to see the temple community in Jerusalem as inherently disloyal, even though, up to this point in the narrative, it is his own officials and not the community who have manifested the Lie.

Officials in the colonies, readers discover, can be corrupted by disloyal groups of the colonized, who work against the will of God and king, and the author seems to believe this idea is important enough that he or

---

54. See also on this point Grätz, "The Adversaries in Ezra/Nehemiah," 77.
55. That is to say, biblical narratives with which fourth-century readers might be familiar tell stories like these. On David and Solomon's control of a vast kingdom, see 2 Sam. 8–10 and 1 Kgs 4:7-18, and note as well that Chronicles, a work roughly contemporaneous with Ezra–Nehemiah (see Chapter 5), includes a tradition of a large Davidic empire in 1 Chron. 18–19. For the idea that Jerusalem rebelled against imperial rulers, see 2 Kgs 24:1; 2 Chron. 36:13, and sections of Jeremiah that link the city's destruction of its kings' failures to remain loyal to Babylon (e.g., Jer. 27). Yet, as Chapter 3 discusses, the Judean literature of which we are aware ultimately attributes the city's destruction to the people's failure to remain loyal to their God, as, for example, 2 Kgs 21–25 makes abundantly clear. This is the position of 2 Chron. 36 as well, and of the elders in Ezra 5:12.

she puts a series of correspondence out of chronological order so that readers encounter the problem early in the narrative. In the context of Ezra 4:1-24, the lies of the officials in the correspondence of 4:11-22 in regard to Jerusalem's wall are portrayed as having some bearing on the construction of the temple, since 4:24 says it was brought to a halt, and the chapter implies this was the result of corrupt officials influencing the king. Since Yhwh ordered the construction of the temple, this may appear to challenge Ezra–Nehemiah's portrayal of divine and royal wills that never diverge, yet it is notable that Yhwh declines to intervene here, unwilling to contradict what the text implies was a royal decision. The problem as Ezra–Nehemiah presents it has been caused by a disloyal bureaucracy in the colonies, and the matter is rectified in Ezra 5–6 by the king through bureaucratic means, as further official correspondence in Aramaic and royal records stored at the center of the empire resolve the issue. So while the Achaemenid eventually does deal with the problem by means of imperial institutions, the empire is a flawed entity in Ezra 4 because it contains corrupt officials who can endanger a project the king has ordered to be completed. Readers encounter the same problem in the narrative of the construction of the wall in Nehemiah 1–6, for, as Chapter 1 discusses, Sanballat, Tobiah, and Geshem, the opponents of the wall, are all part of the local leadership of regions surrounding Judah, and lying and disingenuousness are their main characteristics in the story. The real reason they oppose the wall, according to Neh. 2:10, is that "they found it very evil that someone had come to seek the good of the Israelites," but they lie about their motivations and plan on lying to the king. Like the officials of Ezra 4, they claim that the Judeans will rebel, and they even state they will lie to Artaxerxes and say that Nehemiah will announce that he is king once Jerusalem's wall is rebuilt (Neh. 6:5-7). Of course, the community of Nehemiah's generation only compounds the problem when they intermarry with the families of these corrupt officials (Neh. 6:17-19; 13:28) and privilege their presence in the temple over ensuring the functioning of the cult (13:4-12), acting as if they wanted God to destroy them (see Ezra 9:6-15).

Yet because the epigone acts just like its ancestors, those of the first post-exilic generation excepted, Ezra–Nehemiah leaves readers with no option except Achaemenid rule, even if the author is willing to criticize local imperial officials. Beyond threatening the Judeans with destruction for failing to keep Torah, the Achaemenid can also send good leaders from the imperial center, as Artaxerxes sends Ezra and Nehemiah, and so the book suggests the problem with the local imperial bureaucracy is that some of its members, like the Judean temple community, have lived too long away from the king and the good part of the earth. For the community, however, this means that, like all the other colonized peoples, it needs the Achaemenids to continually renew their local leadership, because the leaders who emerge from the community itself are, as Chapter 3 explains, as unreliable as those among the other colonized peoples in Palestine. The community needs the Achaemenids, Nehemiah 8–13 tells readers, because they cannot keep the law without the leadership the king sends, and without that leadership destruction will result. Even the threat of Persian destruction is a boon as far as the author of Ezra–Nehemiah is concerned, so that the people can live in fear of the law of God and the law of the king. As Ezra–Nehemiah presents things, life as עבדים or subjects to the Achaemenids is as good as their existence can be, even if the empire is not perfect. Judah may once have been independent, but, given the community's nature, they will survive only if they live under Achaemenid rule.

The idea that life in the empire is as good as things can get is one that derives from Achaemenid ideology, as well, for the kings portrayed themselves not only as members of the dynasty that is necessary to keep the colonized peoples in place to restore their happiness, but as the last dynasty, in which every king effectively acts as the one before him, maintaining the perfection that Darius restored. For all intents and purposes, Achaemenid ideology presents the dynasty's rule as timeless, since they have brought history to Auramazda's intended end. We see this worldview reflected in the Achaemenid inscriptions' increasing lack of interest in historical events; as both Heleen Sancisi-Weerdenburg and Robert Rollinger have pointed out, the later an Achaemenid inscription is, the more likely it is that it will have nothing to say about such things.[56] The earliest Old Persian inscription is the first four columns of Bisitun (the fifth and final column was added only some time later),[57] and no other Achaemenid text provides the sort of historical specificity DB 1-4 does. In that first part of the Bisitun Inscription, Darius provides the names of the rebels he fights and of his generals who defeated them, as well

---

56. Heleen Sancisi-Weerdenburg, "The Persian Kings and History," in *The Limits of Historiography: Genre and Narrative in Ancient Historical Texts*, ed. Christina Shuttleworth Kraus, Mnemosyne (Leiden: Brill, 1999), 91–112; Robert Rollinger, "Thinking and Writing about History in Teispid and Achaemenid Persia," in *Thinking, Recording, and Writing History in the Ancient World*, ed. Kurt A. Raaflaub, AWCH (Malden, MA: John Wiley & Sons, 2014), 185–212.

57. For the chronology of the stages of the creation of the inscription at Bisitun, see Borger, *Die Chronologie des Darius-Denkmals*, 103–32.

as the precise dates and places of each military encounter. But in DB 5, the later addition, he is not entirely specific as to even the year in which he engaged in each of the two conflicts he narrates there,[58] and he says nothing about where they were fought. Xerxes imitates language from his father's inscriptions in regard to his descriptions of Auramazda's act of creation (e.g., XPa 1-6; XPb 1-11), his self-introduction as the great king (e.g., XPc 6-9; XPd 8-14), the list of the peoples he has colonized (XPh 13-28), and the attributes that make him an excellent ruler (XPl), but his inscriptions include nothing that rivals the historical specificity of DB 1-4. As the previous section of the chapter discusses, one of Xerxes' inscriptions mentions a rebellion he associates with the worship of *daivā* "(false) gods" whose sanctuary he destroys (XPh 35-41), but he says nothing about where or when the rebellion took place, or even the names of the *daiva*s who supported it. The preceding lines on the same inscription refer to one of the colonized peoples he ruled who rebelled or, as Xerxes puts it, *ayauda* "was in turmoil" (28-35), and while his language in regard to his response to this rebellion mimics that of his father when he refers to his victories on the Bisitun Inscription—"Auramazda bore me support; by the will of Auramazda that people I struck, and I set them down in place" (XPh 32-35; compare DB 2.24-26, 34-36, 39-41, etc.)—unlike Darius he makes no mention of the antagonist, the place or date (or even year) of the struggle, or the name of the colonized people who were "in turmoil." After Xerxes, Achaemenid inscriptions become even shorter, and say nothing at all about geopolitical events. The Achaemenids came to believe that historical details do not matter, conclude Sancisi-Weerdenburg and Rollinger, and portray the king and empire as part of the timeless happy order Auramazda originally intended the world to experience.[59] After Darius put the peoples down in place and realized the original divine goal for creation, there are, in this worldview, no more historical events worth discussing, for history has effectively come to an end.

This move to a lack of historical specificity is anticipated in the summary of Darius's victories that he provides in the fourth column of Bisitun. As Chapter 3 discusses, in DB 4.33-36 he summarizes all of the work he did to become king and defeat his rivals by attributing rebellion to the Lie and

---

58. DB 5 opens with Darius saying that he is about to relate "what I did in both the second and third year after I became king" (5.2-4), but he does not specify in the following narrative of his battles against the Elamites and Scythians the year in which each of the conflicts took place. There are also no references here to the specific months and dates of battles as is the case in DB 1-4.

59. Sancisi-Weerdenburg, "The Persian Kings and History," 109–10; Rollinger, "Thinking and Writing about History," 200–201.

his victories to Auramazda, so that the outcome of every encounter with a rebel is exactly the same. This struggle between Auramazda and the king on one side and the Lie on the other is at the core of Achaemenid ideology, and it can ultimately explain everything that happens. This is also the ahistorical picture portrayed on the relief carved at Bisitun to reflect the events Darius narrates in the first four columns, on which viewers see all of Darius's enemies bound in a line before him, as if they were all led captive to him at the same time. This contradicts the narrative of DB 1-4, in which each is killed at a different point, but the goal of this relief is not to depict what happened in Darius's understanding of history but what happens in his understanding of theology:[60] the Achaemenid, who does Auramazda's will, is always victorious, because Auramazda will always defeat the Lie, and so the king always has and always will defeat and kill those who oppose him and his god. It is a timeless message, and the particulars of any given rebellion do not matter since the outcome is always the same.

The inscription of Xerxes from Persepolis in which he refers to a rebellion is the last one in which the Achaemenids refer to a military struggle of any sort. At numerous points in his inscriptions Xerxes puts emphasis instead on what he has built, and so on another inscription from Persepolis, for example, he opens with the standard creation formula (XPa 1-6) and then refers to one of his constructions in that city (11-13). "Much other good (*naibam*) was done (*kartam*) in Persia that I did and that my father did" (13-15), he continues, and this "good" may refer to other construction projects—where the verb *kar-* "to do, make," appearing here as the passive participle *kartam*, can be understood as "to build"—but it need not be so narrowly construed. "Whatever good work (*kartam... naibam*)[61] that is seen," Xerxes goes on to say in that inscription, "all by the will of Auramazda we did" (15-17), and so in this inscription we see Xerxes describing himself as continuing Darius's work of doing good things. The only specific act he refers to is his extension of Darius's palace at Persepolis, but Chapter 3 points out that the Achaemenids could use their palaces as microcosms of their kingdom, and so it would hardly be a contradiction to see the maintenance of a palace, the locus of imperial rule and the place of the king, as a symbol of the work that a king does throughout the empire, as both replicate the original paradise of creation. Darius writes that he encountered a whole world where things were

---

60. Peter Calmeyer, "Textual Sources for the Interpretation of Achaemenian Palace Decorations," *Iran* 18 (1980): 55–63 (56).

61. As a passive past participle of the verb *kar-*, *kartam* is used here as a substantive, with the sense of "thing that is done, work." See Kent, *Old Persian*, §283.

duš-karta "poorly done," but says that he made it *naiba* "good" (DSe 31-32). The latter adjective is one the inscriptions apply only to the work of Auramazda and the king. Persia is naturally "good," as are the people who live there (DPd 6-9; DSp 2-3), and Darius uses *naiba* as a general description of his rule; "all I did was good," he writes (DSi 4). Like the world Auramazda creates, the kings' work is *naiba* "good," something accomplished as they act (*kar-*) according to Auramazda's will.

After Darius, then, royal inscriptions stop emphasizing armed conflict and avoid specific dates, and focus instead on the building projects the kings accomplished. This does not mean that Darius's binary view of the world disappears from Achaemenid ideology; the Bisitun Inscription was still being copied a century after Darius composed it, as we know from the Aramaic version from Elephantine, and it was still on display in Babylon,[62] and other inscriptions that he authored were still extant and circulating throughout the empire as well.[63] Yet while Classical sources that describe the fifth and fourth centuries tell us there were many military encounters the Achaemenids could have discussed, the kings excise such events from their ideological constructions of their reigns, and in their presentations of things the world appears at rest, having been ordered and put in place by Darius, so that all that is left for his successors is to maintain the happiness he restored to humanity by making the world "good." So, in yet another inscription from Persepolis, Xerxes writes that "what was done (*kartam āha*) by my father, that I protected, and I added other work (*kartam*)" (XPf 38-40), and all of this work was done "by the will of Auramazda" (40-43). Xerxes simply protects what his father did (*kar-*), and he does (*kar-*) more of the same. He does not refer to any specific work in this inscription, and so one can take it as referring to his father's royal work in general that he guards and completes.[64] Inscriptions of later Achaemenids can

---

62. Greenfield and Porten, *The Bisitun Inscription*, 2–3.

63. The copy of the Bisitun Inscription from Elephantine actually contains some lines from Darius's burial inscription—*TAD* C2.1.66-69 corresponds to a version of DNb 50-60—and indicates that at least one version of the burial inscription was circulating through the empire, as well. Hassan Rezai Badghbidi argues that DB 4.88-92 suggests that Darius circulated both DNa and DNb ("Darius and the Bisotun Inscription: A New Interpretation of the Last Paragraph of Column IV," *JPerSt* 2 [2009]: 44–61).

64. One could make a distinction between Xerxes' inscriptions and those of the kings who follow him, as Rollinger does ("Thinking and Writing about History," 201–2), since, among other differences, those of the latter group are shorter and say nothing at all about historical events, but they share Xerxes' emphasis on maintaining and completing earlier royal work.

focus specifically on their maintenance of earlier royal building projects, and Artaxerxes I, for example, after opening an inscription at Persepolis with the standard creation formula (A¹Pa 1-8), says *adam akunavam* "I made" the palace on which Xerxes had previously worked, thanks to the will of Auramazda (17-22), and he asks for divine protection of him, his kingdom, "and that which was made/done (*kartam*) by me" (22-24). At Susa, Artaxerxes II refers to the palace Darius made (*akunauš*) that later burned, but says that "by the will of Auramazda, Anahita, and Mithra, I made (*akunām*) this palace" (A²Sa 3-4), and he asks these three gods not to harm "what I made" (5).

The Achaemenids after Darius's time emphasize the work they do, and while this normally specifies a particular building project, sometimes repairing or restoring the work of earlier kings, it can refer simply to work in general, as in the example of Xerxes's inscription from the preceding paragraph. No Achaemenid after Darius ever makes a figure besides a king the subject of the verb *kar-* "to do, make, build"—outside of references to Auramazda's work of creation, at any rate—and so in this world it is the king alone who acts; at the very least, we could say, it is the king's actions alone that matter. The kings can assume that those who read or are told of the inscriptions' contents already know the ideology broadcast by Darius, in which the Lie is always defeated and the king always acts to benefit the colonized; the very fact that Darius and Xerxes use virtually identical language to refer to the virtues that make them good kings (compare DNb and XPl) suggests the Achaemenids saw these as timeless and possessed by all of the dynasty's rulers.[65] If fifth- and fourth-century Greek sources tend to depict a depersonalized and generic Great King of Persia,[66] that in part reflects Achaemenid self-presentation after the time of Darius. Each king after him is, in essence, the last king, since with Darius's reign history has largely reached Auramazda's desired goal. His inscriptions were still visible, and at least some of them were made available throughout the empire, while coins and seal impressions depicting the royal hero controlling or in combat with animals and monsters still circulated,[67] but those who reign after him need take no major steps to alter the world. Achaemenid ideology after the time of Darius can ignore what modern historians consider to be important historical events because, for the Achaemenids, history has largely come

65. Kuhrt, "Achaemenid Images of Royalty and Empire," 97–8.
66. For examples and discussion, see Llewellyn-Jones, "The Great Kings of the Fourth Century," 317–46.
67. Xin Wu argues that seals and stamps depicting combat art increased in popularity after the time of Darius ("'O young man,'" 267–71).

to an end and those events are of no consequence. The later kings maintain and repair Darius's work, and they build palaces, representations of the perfect world Darius restored, just as he did, and their actions alone matter, since no one else accomplishes anything worth comparing to the happiness they maintain for the colonized.

Since Ezra–Nehemiah is willing to condemn corrupt imperial officials who live far away from the king and the good center of the earth, the author obviously believed that what other imperial actors did mattered, since they could act against the king's wishes. As good as the kings may be according to the book, and as faithfully as it presents them following divine leadership, their imperial apparatus is flawed, and thus the empire has imperfections Achaemenid ideology refuses to acknowledge. Wilda Gafney writes that, in Ezra–Nehemiah, "the empire is God,"[68] and there is some truth to this in the sense that the book never portrays Yhwh as challenging a royal decision, so that the royal will largely is divine will. The author, however, is not as confident that the imperial bureaucracy always works with the king as faithfully as Ezra and Nehemiah do, or as the loyal version of the temple community does in Ezra 1–6, and these corrupt officials ultimately suffer from the same problem the community does, for away from the good center of the world they act counter to divine and royal will. But that being said, there is no future for the community without Achaemenid rule in Ezra–Nehemiah, and the community ultimately is who the Achaemenids say their colonized are, inherently evil subjects who need the kings' rule and who remain loyal because of their fear of the dynasty's power to punish those who disobey the royal and divine law. To be fair, the author of Ezra–Nehemiah, unlike the Achaemenids, can imagine a future different from that which exists in his or her present, but this alternative would be the destruction or exile of the community for their failure to do what the king commands, which includes adherence to Torah. Try as the community might to act like the generation of Ezra 1–6 and work in complete loyalty to the king and to God, such loyalty is not possible without the Achaemenids, and so they will not be able to avoid exile and destruction without continuing to be a colonized people in the imperfect empire ruled by the perfect dynasty, where each king simply maintains the world Darius has set down in place.

---

68. Wilda Gafney, "A Prophet-Terrorist(a) and an Imperial Sympathizer: An Empire-Critical, Postcolonial Reading of the No'adyah/Nechemyah Conflict," *BITh* 9 (2011): 161–76 (165).

Chapter 5

EMPIRE AND IDEOLOGY IN PERSIAN-PERIOD JUDAH

1. *Ezra–Nehemiah within the Temple Community's Factions*

Wilda Gafney writes that "the empire is God" in Ezra–Nehemiah as part of an ethical critique of a book in which, she says, Judah's God becomes a colonized subject along with the Judean characters of the narrative, since they all function in the work to serve Persian interests.[1] Ezra–Nehemiah's depiction of the temple community clearly has drawn so much from Achaemenid ideology that the book obviously justifies imperial rule to the temple assembly in Judah, and from a contemporary perspective, the lengths to which the book goes to support the imperial project, including the violence the Achaemenids were more than willing to visit upon those whom they deemed to be followers of the Lie, makes the work problematic, to say the least. Moreover, the author has constructed an exclusive identity for the community, one that links it by genealogy to a group at the center of the empire, and claims that attempts to ignore this social boundary will result in their destruction. This sort of exclusive community identity that privileges descent from colonists sounds uncomfortably like the miscegenation laws of apartheid-era South Africa and pre-civil rights-era United States that banned marriages between those of African and European descent, write Makhosazana Nzimande and Cheryl Anderson;[2] indeed, says Willa Johnson, Ezra 9–10 is still used in the United States to support

---

1. Gafney, "A Prophet-Terrorist(a) and an Imperial Sympathizer," 171.
2. Makhosazana K. Nzimande, "*Imbokodo* Explorations of the Prevalence of Historical Memory and Identity Contestations in the Expulsion of the *Nāšîm Nokriyyōt* in Ezra 9–10," in Jonker, ed., *Texts, Contexts and Readings in Postexilic Literature*, 269–94 (290–2); Anderson, "Reflections in an Interethnic/Racial Era," 47–8.

racist behavior and to argue against interracial marriage.³ Jean-Pierre Ruiz points out that Nehemiah's opposition to foreign marriages on the grounds that the children of such unions were not able to speak the local language "sounds frighteningly familiar" to Latin American immigrants in the U.S., since they are often excluded from constructions of national identity that are based on one's facility in speaking English.⁴ The book's construction of a community identity grounded in imperial ideology and exclusivist understandings of the group is one that silences the voices of those who are excluded, writes Nāsili Vaka'uta, and an ethically responsible reading of Ezra–Nehemiah is one that provides a voice to those whom the work classifies as outsiders.⁵

In order to face the ethical problems with which Ezra–Nehemiah leaves us, Vaka'uta's approach of restorying the book from the perspectives of those it excludes is one option; this chapter will explore another, and compare Ezra–Nehemiah's adoption of imperial ideology in its construction of social identity with the portrayal of empire and community in other biblical writings from the Persian period. Based on what works commonly dated to that time can tell us about the community associated with the temple in Jerusalem, this chapter argues, most of its members had very different views of empire and group identity than those held by the author of Ezra–Nehemiah. Because the book is the only writing from the Persian period that is devoted to relating events that took place in that era in a history-like manner, it can be easy to take some of its claims for granted, and believe that the temple community really did rigidly define itself by descent from Babylonian immigrants, something reinforced in the book's focus on the need to prevent marriages with outsiders,⁶ and that its members generally were content with Achaemenid rule.⁷ The next section of the chapter, however, will consider other Persian-period biblical texts that give us at least some sense of the range of opinions that existed in the temple community in regard to their sense of identity. Some of these

3. Johnson, *The Holy Seed Has Been Defiled*, 96.
4. Jean-Pierre Ruiz, *Readings from the Edges: The Bible and People on the Move*, SLC (Maryknoll, NY: Orbis Books, 2011), 109.
5. Nāsili Vaka'uta, *Reading Ezra 9–10 Tu'a-Wise: Rethinking Biblical Interpretation in Oceania*, SBLIVBS 3 (Atlanta: Society of Biblical Literature, 2011), 161–78.
6. E.g., Hoglund, *Achaemenid Imperial Administration in Syria-Palestine*, 236–40; Fröhlich, "*Mamzēr* in Qumran Texts," 103–15; Kessler, "Persia's Loyal Yahwists," 111.
7. E.g., Ehud Ben Zvi writes that the post-exilic community "accepted the present reality of the Great King as the overarching monarchy of their *oecumene* and most likely did not conceive of an alternative" ("Memory and Political Thought," 21).

views are far more inclusivist than that broadcast by Ezra–Nehemiah, just as we will see that most other Persian-period biblical texts are entirely dismissive of imperial claims, and so portray empire and community very differently than Ezra–Nehemiah does. The way in which Ezra–Nehemiah uses imperial ideology to portray the temple community as a group of imperial subjects who depend on Achaemenid rule to survive was not, as far as we can tell, widely shared among the members of the temple assembly. And while the book casts doubts upon the validity of prophecy, the third section of the chapter discusses prophetic voices from the Persian-period temple community that spoke against the claims of empire.

This first section of the chapter creates the groundwork for those investigations by examining some of the factions or groups within the temple assembly for whom Ezra–Nehemiah was written. The most important reason why Ezra–Nehemiah's views of empire were not widely shared within the Persian-period community, this part of the chapter argues, is because it was produced by the governor's office or by a faction within the assembly closely associated with and dependent upon it, a group of people who benefitted from the political status quo and were willing to accept Achaemenid claims about the colonized peoples' need for their rule and the legitimacy of the violence they visited upon their disloyal subjects. But the temple community consisted of a number of different factions, each with a somewhat different worldview, something that is evident from Ezra–Nehemiah itself, although from the author's perspective those who held competing understandings of group identity and the community's relationship to the Achaemenids were disloyal to both God and king and would lead the temple assembly to destruction if no one acted to curb their heretical impulses. Nonetheless, in the Levitical prayer of Neh. 9:6-37 we can see a text that, in isolation from the rest of the book, portrays "the kings whom you set over us" in quite negative terms, since they are condemned as those who take the produce of the land and leave the community "in great distress" (9:37). In its current context in Nehemiah 8–13, the prayer functions as part of the author's argument that the community cannot do without Achaemenid rule, but given that it originally existed independently of the book,[8] it makes us aware that some

---

8. It is universally accepted in scholarship that Ezra–Nehemiah's author did not write this prayer, given that it seems to contradict the otherwise positive presentation of the Achaemenids in the book. Dates for its composition range from the pre-exilic period (e.g., Gili Kugler, "Present Affliction Affects the Representation of the Past: An Alternative Dating of the Levitical Prayer of Nehemiah 9," *VT* 63 [2013]: 605–26 [622–3]) to the Hellenistic period (e.g., Jacques Vermeylen, "The Gracious God, Sinners and Foreigners: How Nehemiah 9 Interprets the History of Israel,"

in the temple community had a very different view of that issue. And the book's emphasis on the need to avoid marriage outside of the immigrant community, as well as the scenes in Ezra 9–10 and Neh. 13:23-28 that focus on the necessity to divorce foreign women, tell us that not everyone in the assembly agreed with the specific genealogical boundary that the book's author drew around the temple community; the author would have had no need to construct or include such scenes if no one in the assembly believed that marriages with outsiders (as Ezra–Nehemiah defines them) were acceptable. The Nehemiah Memoir itself refers to marriage alliances between assembly members and the families of Tobiah and Sanballat (Neh. 6:17-19; 13:28), and this tells us that not everyone saw these Yahwists as an existential threat to the community, despite the book's portrayal of them. There were obviously members of the temple assembly who did not believe that community boundaries prohibited such unions, and, as Gary Knoppers argues, if Nehemiah numbers prophets among his opponents, that may be due to the fact that they held a more inclusive vision of the community than he did.⁹

It follows, then, that not everyone in the Persian-period temple assembly held precisely the same worldview as the very elite group out of which Ezra–Nehemiah emerged, and to set the stage for this discussion we turn first to a brief explanation of the development and governance of the temple community and then to some examples of factions within it, including the one from which Ezra–Nehemiah emerged. The temple community in Judah would have had some authority to manage its own affairs, so long as its interests did not conflict with those of the Persian administration. The בית אבות or "ancestral house" replaced the pre-exilic בית אב "father's house" as the basic level of social organization in

---

in *History and Identity: How Israel's Later Authors Viewed its Earlier History*, ed. Núria Calduch-Benages and Jan Liesen, DCLY 2006 [Berlin: W. de Gruyter, 2006], 77–114 [105–11]), although it is mainly dated to the exilic and Persian periods (e.g., Pröbstl, *Nehemia 9*, 103–4; Boda, *Praying the Tradition*, 189–95; Lena-Sofia Tiemeyer, "Abraham—A Judahite Perspective," *ZAW* 120 [2008]: 49–66 [62–3]; Mark Leuchter, "Inter-Levitical Polemics in the Late 6th Century BCE: The Evidence from Nehemiah 9," *Bib* 95 [2014]: 269–79 [272]). There are no obvious signs that suggest a date as late as the Hellenistic period (see Oeming, "'See, we are serving today' [Nehemiah 9:36]," 578), and so given that the author of Ezra–Nehemiah was aware of its existence in the fourth century, we would imagine that other community members knew of it also, and that some of them had encountered it in contexts much less positive in regard to Achaemenid rule than Ezra–Nehemiah.

9. For hints in Ezra–Nehemiah that there were divisions within the community based on such disagreements, see Knoppers, "Nehemiah and Sanballat," 305–31.

Babylonia during the exile,[10] as Chapter 1 mentions. In the post-exilic period, these ancestral houses—or their leaders, at least—played some role in governing the קהל "assembly," a group Ezra–Nehemiah mentions and equates with "the ones going up from the captivity of the exile" and "the people of Israel" (compare Ezra 2:1-2 and 2:64, as well as Neh. 8:1 and 8:2), as well as with "the descendants of the exile" and "all the people of Judah and Benjamin" (compare Ezra 10:7, 9 and 10:12, 14). The assembly is the totality of Ezra–Nehemiah's community, and in the book we see it act with Ezra and Nehemiah to help them reach important decisions (e.g., Ezra 10:8, 14; Neh. 5:13; 8:2, 17), and it is likely that, as the Judeans in exile searched for a form of local organization and governance to replace the pre-exilic one based in monarchical rule, they adopted one they encountered in Babylonia, where each temple and city was governed by a *puḫru* "assembly" of elders, the heads of the prominent families, that judged local matters such as theft of temple property, leasing of temple lands, family disputes, criminal cases, and so on.[11] Foreigners in Babylonia who lived in groups defined by ethnicity established their own assemblies, and Israel Ephʻal, noting the existence of a *puḫur šībūtu ša miṣira* "assembly of the elders of the Egyptians" in a Neo-Babylonian document, points to the way biblical texts refer to the exilic community in Babylonia as "the elders of Judah/Israel/the exiles" (e.g., Jer. 29:1; Ezek. 8:1; 14:1; 20:1), and to the way Ezra–Nehemiah refers to "the elders of the Judeans" (e.g., Ezra 5:5, 9; 6:7), who are the ראשי אבות "ancestral heads" (e.g., Ezra 2:68; 3:12; 4:2; Neh. 7:70; 8:13).[12] The sixth-century

---

10. See the discussions in, e.g., Weinberg, *The Citizen-Temple Community*, 49–61; Williamson, "The Family in Persian Period Judah"; Blenkinsopp, *Judaism: The First Phase*, 81; Albertz, "More and Less than a Myth," 31.

11. See discussions in M. A. Dandamaev, "The Neo-Babylonian Elders," in *Societies and Languages of the Ancient Near East: Studies in Honour of I. M. Diakonoff*, ed. M. A. Dandamaev et al. (Westminster: Aris & Phillips, 1982), 38–41; Dandamaev, "The Neo-Babylonian Popular Assembly," in *Šulmu: Papers on the Ancient Near East Presented at International Conference of Socialist Countries*, ed. Petr Vavroušek and Vladimír Souček (Prague: Charles University, 1988), 63–71; Dandamaev, "Babylonian Popular Assemblies," 23–9; Marc Van De Mieroop, *The Ancient Mesopotamian City* (Oxford: Clarendon Press, 1997), 121–38. As some of these works point out, kings through the Neo-Babylonian period began to take more control over temple affairs and finances, and in some judicial matters royal judges rather than the assembly began to exercise more authority in arriving at legal rulings. What is important for our purposes, however, is the existence of such assemblies as models for the Judean exiles to imitate.

12. Ephʻal, "The Western Minorities in Babylonia," 76–9.

Judean exiles were resettled in Babylonia in a place that became known as "the city of Judah";[13] the Judean ancestral house and assembly likely developed there, and was then brought by emigrants from that community to Judah and established as the assembly's form of local self-governance in the Persian period.

The high priest exercised power in Judah's local government, as demonstrated by the fourth-century Judean coin that bore the legend יוחנן הכוהן "Johanan the priest" and that had precisely the same iconography as ones reading יחזקיה הפחה "Hezekiah the governor."[14] This does not necessarily mean that a high priest of the name Johanan served as governor, but it at least points to an elevated status for the office of the high priest in fourth-century Judah, a conclusion supported by the late fourth-century work of Hecataeus of Abdera, which draws on Judean sources from Egypt in claiming that the high priest is the leader of Judaism.[15] Josephus's picture

---

13. Laurie E. Pearce, "New Evidence for Judeans in Babylonia" in *Judah and the Judeans in the Persian Period*, ed. Oded Lipschits and Manfred Oeming (Winona Lake, IN: Eisenbrauns, 2006), 399–410; Pearce, "'Judean': A Special Status in Neo-Babylonian and Achaemenid Babylonia?," in Lipschits, Knoppers, and Oeming, eds, *Judah and the Judeans in the Achaemenid Period*, 267–77; Pearce, "Identifying Judeans and Judean Identity in the Babylonian Evidence," in *Exile and Return: The Babylonian Context*, ed. Jonathan Stökl and Caroline Waerzeggers, BZAW 478 (Berlin: W. de Gruyter, 2015), 7–32.

14. For discussions of the coin with Johanan's name, including when in the fourth century it might have been minted, see John Betlyon, "The Provincial Government of Persian Period Judea and the Yehud Coins," *JBL* 105 (1986): 633–42; Dan Barag, "Silver Coin of Yohanan the High Priest and the Coinage of Judea in the Fourth Century B.C.," *INJ* 9 (1986–87): 4–14; Meshorer, *A Treasury of Jewish Coins*, 14; Fried, "A Silver Coin of Yoḥanan Hakkôhēn." For discussions of the Hezekiah coins, see Peter Machinist, "The First Coins of Judah and Samaria: Numismatics and History in the Achaemenid and Early Hellenistic Periods," in *Continuity and Change: Proceedings of the Last Achaemenid History Workshop*, ed. Heleen Sancisi-Weerdenburg, Amélie Kuhrt, and Margaret Cool Root, AchHist 8 (Leiden: Nederlands Instituut voor het Nabije Oosten, 1994), 365–79 (369–71); Meshorer, *A Treasury of Jewish Coins*, 15–18.

15. Scholars generally agree that at least the material attributed to Hecataeus in Diodorus 40.3.1-8 truly does come from the author; see Bezalel Bar-Kochva, *Pseudo-Hecataeus, On the Jews: Legitimizing the Diaspora*, HCS 21 (Berkeley, CA: University of California Press, 1996), 25–39; Lester L. Grabbe, "Hecataeus of Abdera and the Jewish Law: The Question of Authenticity," in *Berührungspunkte: Studien zur Sozial- und Religionsgeschichte Israels und seiner Umwelt*, ed. Ingo Kottsieper, Rüdiger Schmidt, and Jakob Wöhrle, AOAT 350 (Münster: Ugarit-Verlag, 2008), 613–26. Deborah Rooke (*Zadok's Heirs: The Role and Development of the High Priesthood in Ancient Israel*, OTM [Oxford: Oxford University Press, 2000], 246–50)

of the local Judean administration in the later Persian period presents both the high priest and an assembly of elders as exercising power,[16] an arrangement that continued into the Hellenistic and Hasmonean periods.[17] It would appear, then, that in the Persian period the assembly and high priest worked together to govern the community in regard to matters that fell outside of immediate imperial interests. And as the next section of the chapter discusses, although Chronicles is devoted to a portrayal of the pre-exilic past, it anachronistically portrays the assembly as involved in the governance of pre-exilic Judah and Israel.

Different factions or groups in the assembly, however, prioritized different concerns and had somewhat different worldviews. Persian-period biblical writings make us aware of at least some of these factions, and to introduce the idea we can take as an example the different groups of temple personnel and briefly examine the ways in which various biblical writings reflect the interests of particular factions from this part of the assembly. The list of migrants in Ezra 2 refers to priests, Levites, musicians, gatekeepers, temple servants, and Solomon's servants (2:36-57), although normally the book mentions only priests and Levites when discussing temple personnel (e.g., Ezra 3:8; 6:16; 10:18-43; Neh. 10:1-28

---

and Russell E. Gmirkin (*Berossus and Genesis, Manetho and Exodus: Hellenistic Histories and the Date of the Pentateuch*, LHBOTS 433 [New York: T&T Clark International, 2006], 34–71) argue otherwise, but Hecataeus as represented by Diodorus seems so familiar with Jewish tradition that we have little reason to doubt the basic aspects of his knowledge of fourth-century Judaism.

16. *Ant.* 11.317, 329–39 says the high priest acted as Judah's representative in the region's dealings with Alexander on his campaign through Palestine. In 11.306-308, however, Josephus says "the elders of Jerusalem" demanded that the high priest's brother either divorce his foreign wife or abandon his priestly duties, and this points to an assembly of elders who have some say in regard to temple affairs; see also VanderKam, *From Joshua to Caiaphas*, 82–3.

17. The Tobiad Romance (*Ant.* 12.154-236) refers to the third-century high priest Onias as in charge of sending tribute to the Ptolemies (12.156-159) and as exercising "the leadership of the people" (12.163). And while 1 Macc. 14:27-49 refers to the second-century high priest Simon as governor, ἡγούμενος "leader," and ethnarch, the high priests did not exercise power alone after the Persian period. The high priest and γερουσία "council of elders" jointly send a letter to Sparta in 1 Macc. 12:6, and both are addressed by the letter Sparta sends in return (14:20), while a letter from the Seleucid Demetrius II is addressed to the high priest and the elders (πρεσβύτεροι) of Judah in 1 Macc. 13:36. In fact, in a letter from Antiochus III recorded in *Ant.* 12.138-144, the king writes that, upon entering Jerusalem after taking Coele-Syria from the Ptolemies, the Judeans met him "with their council of elders," but he says nothing about the presence of a high priest at this event.

[9:38-10:27]). In Chronicles, the temple musicians and gatekeepers are understood to be Levites (e.g., 1 Chron. 9:33; 15:16-23; 23:2-5), and the same is true for Josephus and Tannaitic sources (e.g., *Ant.* 7.363-382; 20.216-217; *m. Sukkah* 5.4; *m. Mid.* 2.5-6), and so it would seem that at some point in the Persian period these groups were absorbed into the Levites. In the Deuteronomistic History, however, we read only of the "Levitical priests" or "the priests, the descendants of Levi" (e.g., Deut. 17:9; 18:18; 21:5; Josh. 3:3; 8:3; and see 1 Kgs 12:31), and there is no sense there that pre-exilic Judah made any distinction between priests and Levites. Perhaps the greater specificity of temple offices that we see in Ezra 2 reflects the exiles' experience of Babylonian temples; eighth- to fifth-century texts from the Ezida temple at Borsippa, for example, allow us to identify twenty-eight different groups of cultic personnel based on their duties, including priest (*šangu*), doorkeeper, musician, fisherman, barber, scribe, boatman, and so on, a fairly common composition known from other Babylonian temples.[18] More frequently in post-exilic biblical texts, however, the temple personnel consist only of priests, understood to be descended from Aaron, and the rest of the tribe of Levi. Based on the claim of Ezekiel 40–48, there was a different group of priests who saw themselves as descended from Zadok and who claimed the sole right to minister at the altar, limiting the other Levites to secondary cultic roles (40:46; 43:19; 44:10-16; 48:11), and this suggests that, at least in the exilic and/or early Persian periods, there were Zadokite and Aaronide factions within the priesthood.[19] The dispute over the right to officiate

18. Caroline Waerzeggers, *The Ezida Temple of Borsippa: Priesthood, Cult, Archives*, AchHist 15 (Leiden: Nederlands Instituut voor het Nabije Oosten, 2010), 38–40.

19. Ezekiel 40–48 is often described as a post-exilic addition to the book, but if that is the case then it is almost certainly from the early Persian period, since its utopian vision of cult was never realized. For arguments for exilic or early post-exilic datings of the chapters see, e.g., Antti Laato, *A Star Is Rising: The Historical Development of the Old Testament Royal Ideology and the Rise of Jewish Messianic Expectations*, ISFCJ 5 (Atlanta: Scholars Press, 1997), 168–9; Andrew Mein, *Ezekiel and the Ethics of Exile*, OTM (Oxford: Oxford University Press, 2001), 142–3; Joseph Blenkinsopp, "Bethel in the Neo-Babylonian Period," in *Judah and the Judeans in the Neo-Babylonian Period*, ed. Oded Lipschitz and Joseph Blenkinsopp (Winona Lake, IN: Eisenbrauns, 2003), 93–107 (104); Paul M. Joyce, *Ezekiel: A Commentary*, LHBOTS 482 (New York: T&T Clark International, 2007), 219–20. It is also possible that the passages that refer to the Zadokites alone as altar priests were inserted later—e.g., Risto Nurmela, *The Levites: Their Emergence as a Second-Class*

as altar priests, however, was resolved in favor of the Aaronides,[20] who make up the priesthood in the Priestly material from the Pentateuch (and some of this material may well be post-exilic),[21] Chronicles, and

Priesthood, SFSHJ 193 (Atlanta: Scholars Press, 1998), 95–7—which would mean that the dispute between the Zadokites and Aaronides continued throughout the first part of the Persian period.

20. Scholarship has made sense of Ezek. 40–48's exclusivist claims for the Zadokites in different ways. One popular assumption is that the Zadokites formed the late pre-exilic priesthood, were taken into exile, and then, in these chapters, assert their sole right to be the altar priests of the post-exilic cult against the Aaronides, a priestly group that had not gone into exile. For some reconstructions of this struggle, see Joseph Blenkinsopp, *Sage Priest Prophet: Religious and Intellectual Leadership in Ancient Israel*, LAI (Louisville: Westminster John Knox Press, 1995), 89–93; Joachim Schaper, *Priester und Leviten im achämenidischen Juda: Studien zur Kult- und Sozialgeschichte Israels in persischer Zeit*, FAT 31 (Tübingen: Mohr Siebeck, 2000), 174–94; Reinhard Achenbach, *Die Vollendung der Tora: Studien zur Redaktionsgeschichte des Numeribuches im Kontext von Hexateuch und Pentateuch*, BZABR 3 (Wiesbaden: Harrassowitz, 2003), 93–110. Others argue the Aaronides and Zadokites were, or eventually merged into, the same group; see, e.g., Nurmela, *The Levites*, 107–39; Min, *The Levitical Authorship of Ezra–Nehemiah*, 63–5. There is little evidence for a pre-exilic Zadokite priestly dynasty, however. As some scholars note, only one of Zadok's descendants ever appears in a narrative functioning as a priest (1 Kgs 4:2), and otherwise there is no sense in the Deuteronomistic History that the Zadokites were recognized as a priestly house, while not one of the priestly houses in the many lists of Ezra–Nehemiah is linked to Zadok; see Alice Hunt, *Missing Priests: The Zadokites in History and Tradition*, LHBOTS 452 (New York: T&T Clark International, 2006), 81–104. Since there was no pre-exilic Zadokite dynasty, it is unclear why a priestly group claiming Aaron as their ancestor would also refer to themselves as descendants of Zadok, and so it is likely that the Aaronides and Zadokites were two different groups. More discussion of the Zadokites follows below.

21. Scholarship on P tends to distinguish between an original narrative, referred to as Pg, which many argue originally existed independently of the other parts of the Pentateuch rather than as a redactional layer. See, e.g., Philippe Guillaume, *Land and Calendar: The Priestly Document from Genesis 1 to Joshua 18*, LHBOTS 391 (New York: T&T Clark, 2009), 6–10; Thomas Römer, "The Exodus Narrative According to the Priestly Document," in *The Strata of the Priestly Writings: Contemporary Debate and Future Directions*, ed. Sarah Shectman and Joel S. Baden, ATANT 95 (Zurich: Theologischer Verlag Zürich, 2009), 157–74 (158); Suzanne Boorer, *The Vision of the Priestly Narrative: Its Genre and Hermeneutics of Time*, SBLAIL 27 (Atlanta: SBL Press, 2016), 34–47. This material is often dated to the exilic period, or at least to the part of the Persian period that pre-dates Darius (e.g., Carr, *The*

Ezra–Nehemiah (Ezra 7:5; Neh. 10:39 [38]; 12:47).[22] Chronicles does refer at one point to a priestly house named after Zadok (2 Chron. 31:10), and we see an important priest of this name in Chronicles' stories of David (e.g., 1 Chron. 15:11; 16:39; 18:16), but in Chronicles, Zadok is a descendant of Aaron (1 Chron. 5:34 [6:8]), as is the case in other Second Temple priestly genealogies,[23] and so Chronicles reflects a point when Zadokite claims have been subordinated to Aaronide ones. Chronicles

---

Formation of the Hebrew Bible, 297–8; Boorer, *The Vision of the Priestly Narrative*, 100–103), although there are some who date it later (e.g., Kratz, *The Composition of the Narrative Books*, 229–47; Konrad Schmid, "How to Identify a Persian Period Text in the Pentateuch," in *On Dating Biblical Texts to the Persian Period: Discerning Criteria and Establishing Epochs*, ed. Richard J. Bautch and Mark Lackowski, FAT 2/101 [Tübingen: Mohr Siebeck, 2019], 101–18). If we want to discuss the totality of Priestly material in the Pentateuch, then we must also deal with the legal material that most scholars believed was added in the post-exilic period (e.g., Christophe Nihan, *From Priestly Torah to Pentateuch: A Study in the Composition of the Book of Leviticus*, FAT 2/25 [Tübingen: Mohr Siebeck, 2007], 562–75; Lester L. Grabbe, "The Last Days of Judah and the Roots of the Pentateuch: What Does History Tell Us?," in *The Fall of Jerusalem and the Rise of the Torah*, ed. Peter Dubovsky, Dominik Martl, and Jean-Pierre Sonnet, FAT 107 [Tübingen: Mohr Siebeck, 2016], 19–45 [39–40]), although it is sometimes dated earlier (e.g., Jacob Milgrom, *Leviticus 17–22: A New Translation with Introduction and Commentary*, AB 3A [New York: Doubleday, 2000], 1361–4; Carr, *The Formation of the Hebrew Bible*, 298–303). So there is no consensus as to whether or not the Priestly material, either in whole or in part, is exilic or post-exilic.

22. And see also Ezra 8:2, 33, where Ezra refers to an ancestral house by the name of Phinehas, which is Aaronide, since in biblical tradition Phinehas is the name of one of Aaron's grandsons (Exod. 6:25; 1 Chron. 5:29-30 [6:3-4]). The notion that these references to the Aaronides in Ezra–Nehemiah are later insertions (e.g., Joseph Blenkinsopp, "The Mystery of the Missing 'Sons of Aaron,'" in *Exile and Restoration: Essays on the Babylonian and Persian Periods in Memory of Peter R. Ackroyd*, ed. Gary N. Knoppers and Lester L. Grabbe, LSTS 73 [London: T&T Clark, 2009], 65–77 [67–8]) is based on the assumption that only later texts refer to the Aaronides as priests. P, however, is earlier than Ezra–Nehemiah since, as Chapter 4 mentions, the author is aware of a Pentateuch that includes P, and given the additional evidence of Chronicles, in which the priesthood is clearly Aaronide, Ezra–Nehemiah's depiction of the priesthood as descended from Aaron reflects the situation of the fourth-century temple.

23. For comparisons of these genealogies, see Gary N. Knoppers, *1 Chronicles 1–9: A New Translation with Introduction and Commentary*, AB 12 (New York: Doubleday, 2004), 410; Ralph W. Klein, *1 Chronicles: A Commentary*, Hermeneia (Minneapolis: Fortress Press, 2006), 178.

recognizes "the house of Zadok" as part of the priesthood, in other words, but only insofar as the Zadokites are one branch of the Aaronides. Later Second Temple-period texts, most notably those from Qumran, do refer to Zadokites, and it is possible that some Zadokites, dissatisfied with a secondary status within the priesthood, joined the Qumran community.[24] At some point, likely early in the Persian period, the Aaronides won the battle for the priesthood in Jerusalem, allowing the Zadokites to continue serving as priests so long as they put themselves under Aaronide authority, and by the time the temple at Gerizim was constructed in the fifth century, the priesthood there was understood to be Aaronide also.[25]

By the later Persian period, then, the two main factions within the assembly's cultic personnel were the Aaronide priests and the Levites, where the priests largely corresponded to the group that would be referred to in the context of a Babylonian temple as the *ērib bīti* "temple enterer," those allowed access to the divine image and at the highest rank of the temple

---

24. Past arguments that Zadokites founded Qumran have largely been abandoned, however, since scholars realized that the earliest versions of the *Rule of the Community* from Cave 4 lacked any references to the priests as Zadokites, and that these must have been added to the more complete version of that text from Cave 1; see, e.g., Sarianna Metso, *The Textual Development of the Qumran Community Rule*, STDJ 21 (Leiden: Brill, 1997), 105–6; Martha Himmelfarb, *A Kingdom of Priests: Ancestry and Merit in Ancient Judaism*, JCC (Philadelphia: University of Pennsylvania Press, 2006), 125–6. The Dead Sea Scrolls do refer to the Zadokites, but not as often as they mention the Aaronides (Charlotte Hempel, "Do the Scrolls Suggest Rivalry between the Sons of Aaron and the Sons of Zadok and if so Was It Mutual?," *RevQ* 24 [2009]: 135–53 [136]). And since post-exilic writings outside of Ezek. 40–48 (assuming that these chapters are post-exilic) otherwise witness to the existence of an Aaronide priesthood, it is possible that, as Nathan MacDonald puts it, the Zadokites were simply the creation of post-exilic exegesis (*Priestly Rule: Polemic and Biblical Interpretation in Ezekiel 44*, BZAW 476 [Berlin: W. de Gruyter, 2015], 146–8). Combined with the evidence from Chronicles, however, Ezek. 40–48 suggests that the Zadokites were an actual priestly group, but one eventually subsumed by the Aaronides.

25. We know this not only because of Josephus's claim that Gerizim was founded by priests from Jerusalem (*Ant.* 11.302-324), but also from the inscriptions at Gerizim, where common personal names include Aaronide ones such as Amram, Eleazar, and Phinehas (Ger. 1; 24; 25; 32; 61; 149; 384; 389; 390); see Gary N. Knoppers, "Aspects of Samaria's Religious Culture during the Early Hellenistic Period," in *The Historian and the Bible: Essays in Honour of Lester L. Grabbe*, ed. Philip R. Davies and Diana V. Edelman, LHBOTS 530 (New York: T. & T. Clark International, 2010), 159–74 (165–6). The only legible name that appears with the word "priest(s)" at Gerizim is Phinehas (Ger. 24; 25; 389).

personnel.[26] This hierarchical ordering of Aaronides and Levites was not a settled matter as far as Persian-period Levites were concerned, but pro-Aaronide writings take the priests' prominence for granted. Whether the Priestly material is exilic or post-exilic, it was part of the Pentateuch the temple community used in the Persian period, and P is clear as to the superiority of the Aaronides over the Levites. In P, the priests are holy (e.g., Exod. 28:42; 29:1; Lev. 8:12, 30) while the Levites are not, so while the priests offer sacrifices in the holy sanctuary (e.g., Lev. 1:5-9; 2:1-3; 3:1-5; 4:16-21), the Levites cannot touch or even look at holy things associated with the sanctuary or they will die (Num. 4:15, 20; 18:3), and so they are not temple enterers and are excluded from work at the altar. In P, the Levites have been given to the Aaronides to serve them (Num. 3:5-10; 18:1-7), and so are clearly of a lower rank, and this suggests that P is an Aaronide document promoting priestly interests. But this is not the only perspective on the hierarchy of the temple personnel in the Persian period, and in Chronicles, for example, the Levites are holy (2 Chron. 23:6; 29:33; 30:15; 35:3, 6), and so can enter the temple just as the Aaronides do (23:6). Both Levites and priests have been chosen by God to work in the cult (1 Chron. 15:2; 2 Chron. 29:11), and both teach the law (2 Chron. 17:7-9) and act as judges (19:8-11), and Levites are also involved with sacrifice (29:34; 30:16-17). Chronicles, in short, provides the Levites with a higher status in cult and civil society than the Pentateuch does,[27] and while the obvious conclusion might be that Chronicles emerged from a Levitical faction, enshrining the Levites' interests,[28] the book's focus on royal activities and the structuring of its material around the reigns of the

---

26. See Caroline Waerzeggers, "The Pious King: Patronage of Temples," in *The Oxford Handbook of Cuneiform Culture*, ed. Karen Radner and Eleanor Robson (Oxford University Press, 2011), 725–51 (735–7).

27. In Chronicles, then, Aaronides and Levites have equal but different cultic tasks to perform; see Louis C. Jonker, *Defining All-Israel in Chronicles: Multi-levelled Identity Negotiation in Late Persian-Period Yehud*, FAT 106 (Tübingen: Mohr Siebeck, 2016), 274; Janzen, *Chronicles and the Politics of Davidic Restoration*, 108–17.

28. So, e.g., von Rad, *Das Geschichtsbild des Chronistischen Werkes*, 88–115; Manfred Oeming, *Das wahre Israel: Die "genealogische Vorhalle" 1 Chronik 1–9*, BWANT 128 (Stuttgart: W. Kohlhammer, 1990), 46; Kim Strübind, *Tradition als Interpretation in der Chronik: König Josaphat als Paradigma chronistischer Hermeneutik und Theologie*, BZAW 201 (Berlin: W. de Gruyter, 1991), 23; Thomas Willi, "Leviten, Priester und Kult in vorhellenistischer Zeit: Die chronistische Optik in ihrem geschichtlichen Kontext," in *Gemeinde ohne Tempel: Zur Substituierung und Transformation des Jerusalemer Tempels und seines Kults im Alten Testament, antiken*

Davidides suggests it came from a pro-Davidic group. Some argue that Chronicles uses its narrative about the Davidides to provide a royal basis for post-exilic Levitical privilege, and so they maintain that the work did indeed emerge from a Levitical faction.[29] But if promoting the Levites through royal decree was the author's chief goal, then we would expect Chronicles to conclude with the story of David, who establishes Levitical cultic duties in the book, or we might imagine that such a pro-Levitical author would have chosen to retell not the story of Samuel–Kings in such a way that it focuses on David and his descendants, but that of the Priestly material from the second half of Exodus through Numbers in order to rework its pro-Aaronide stance.[30] The group or faction in the assembly to which the Chronicler belonged clearly did not believe, as P's group did, in the privileged position of the Aaronides in the temple, and Chronicles seems designed to appeal to a Levitical faction within the cultic personnel, even if the book did not emerge from such a group.[31]

In Chronicles, then, we see work produced by one faction of the assembly—and the next section of the chapter will discuss Chronicles and its pro-Davidic group—attempting to gain the support of another. On the other hand, Malachi, often dated to the fifth century BCE,[32] does appear to be a work produced by a Levitical faction that promotes their cause. It refers to those who work in the cult as "priests" (1:6; 2:1), but Aaron's name never appears in the writing, which says that God made a covenant with Levi, not Aaron (2:4, 8). Levi originally honored the covenant, God says in Malachi, by properly teaching the people, something the current group of priests does not do (2:4-9). The priests, moreover, have failed to sacrifice properly, and are warned their families will be removed from

---

Judentum und frühen Christentum, ed. Beate Ego et al., WUNT 118 (Tübingen: Mohr, 1999), 75–98 (90–5); Antje Labahn, "Antitheocratic Tendencies in Chronicles," in Albertz and Becking, eds, *Yahwism after the Exile*, 115–35.

29. E.g., P. Abadie, "Le fonctionnement symbolique de la figure de David dans l'œuvre du Chroniste," *Transeu* 7 (1994): 143–51; Jozef Tiňo, *King and Temple in Chronicles: A Contextual Approach to their Relation*, FRLANT 234 (Göttingen: Vandenhoeck & Ruprecht, 2010), 107–19.

30. See Janzen, *Chronicles and the Politics of Davidic Restoration*, 34–6.

31. Janzen, *Chronicles and the Politics of Davidic Restoration*, 95–117.

32. E.g., Andrew E. Hill, *Malachi: A New Translation with Introduction and Commentary*, AB 25D (New York: Doubleday, 1998), 80–4; Michael H. Floyd, *Minor Prophets*, 2 vols, FOTL 22 (Grand Rapids, MI: Eerdmans, 2000), 2:575; James D. Nogalski, *The Book of the Twelve*, 2 vols, SHBC (Macon, GA: Smyth & Helwys, 2011), 2:993; S. D. Snyman, *Malachi*, HCOT (Leuven: Peeters, 2015), 2. The next section of the present chapter will return to the question of the date of Malachi.

the priesthood (2:3).[33] Malachi has a very different view of the priesthood than P, where God's covenant of priesthood is with Aaron (Exod. 29:9; 40:15), not his ancestor Levi. Malachi, however, refers to the priests as בני לוי "Levites" (3:3) rather than בני אהרן "Aaronides,"[34] and to a covenant made with Levi, which includes all who have descended from this ancestor, rather than to a covenant specific to Aaron's descendants alone, and so makes it possible for readers to look for an alternative to the current Aaronide priesthood that the book deprecates. It is likely that Malachi is from a Levitical group, one arguing the Aaronides are unfit to continue as priests, and that they will be removed as altar priests when God purifies all the Levites (3:3), allowing non-Aaronide Levites to conduct worship at the altar.[35] The concept of a divine covenant with Levi, which can be understood as erasing the hierarchical boundary that separates Aaronides from Levites, is present already in Jer. 33:21-22, but Malachi is not the only work to mention it after the Aaronides took the office of priest, since the Nehemiah Memoir refers to "the covenant of the priesthood and the Levites" (Neh. 13:29), and Ezra–Nehemiah as a whole refers to the "Levitical priests" (Ezra 6:20; 8:29, 30; Neh. 12:1, 30, 44; 13:30), just as the Deuteronomistic History does. Nehemiah 10:39 [38]

33. In MT 2:3, God promises to rebuke (גער) the priestly families, but LXX's ἀφορίζω reads Hebrew גדע "cut off," in which case God is speaking of ending the lineage of the priests (although the end of the first line of the poetry in LXX 2:3 does not refer to the priests' "seed" as the MT does). Regardless of which text one follows at this point, the verse as a whole refers to the removal of the current priesthood. In both the MT and the text behind the LXX, God promises to spread פרש on the faces of the priests, a word normally used in ritual contexts to refer to animal excrement and entrails that must be removed from the ritual compound (Exod. 29:14; Lev. 4:11; 8:17; 16:27; Num. 19:5), and as a result of this contamination, writes David Petersen, the priests will have to be removed from their cultic service (*Zechariah 9–14 and Malachi: A Commentary*, OTL [Louisville: Westminster John Knox Press, 1995], 189).

34. For Malachi's use of "Levites" to refer to the priests, see Nurmela, *The Levites*, 84; Tiemeyer, *Priestly Rites and Prophetic Rage*, 127–9.

35. So also Paul L. Redditt, *Haggai, Zechariah, and Malachi*, NCBC (Grand Rapids, MI: Eerdmans, 1995), 151–2. Joachim Schaper argues that Malachi emerged from a group of dissident priests who held very different views of some aspects of cult than their Aaronide fellows did ("The Priests of the Book of Malachi and their Opponents," in *The Priests in the Prophets: The Portrayal of Priests, Prophets and Other Religious Specialists in the Latter Prophets*, ed. Lester L. Grabbe and Alice Ogden Bellis, JSOTSup 408 [London: T&T Clark International, 2004], 177–88 [186–7]), but if that is the case then this dissident group was clearly allied with the Levites, since 3:3 says the Levites will be involved with sacrifice.

and 12:47 specifically refer to the priests as descendants of Aaron, but since the priests are also "Levitical" and part of a covenant that embraces the Levites as well, there is no sense in Ezra–Nehemiah that one group is superior to the other.

This is not a sign that Ezra–Nehemiah was produced by a Levitical faction, however; as in the case of Chronicles, other evidence in the writing suggests a different social location for its author. Although Ezra–Nehemiah refers to "Levitical priests" and a single covenant with priests and Levites, the book gives no indication at all that the Levites should replace or join the Aaronides in their work at the altar. It is at points suspicious of the priests' ethical purity (Ezra 10:18; Neh. 13:4-9, 28-29) and, as Chapter 2 notes, the priests in Ezra–Nehemiah fail to teach the law, but Levitical interests do not dominate Ezra–Nehemiah, nor do Levitical characters. Levites are portrayed positively in Nehemiah 8, where they join Ezra in teaching the law, but the book indicts Levites along with the priests in the sin of intermarriage (Ezra 10:23). Ezra–Nehemiah has little interest in cultic issues, and priests rather than Levites are responsible for sacrifice (Ezra 3:2-3), so it appears unlikely that it was produced by a Levitical faction in the community.[36] In Ezra–Nehemiah, the solution to questionable priestly leadership is not a replacement of the Aaronides by the Levites at the top of the temple hierarchy but reliance on the Achaemenids to send people like Ezra and Nehemiah from the center of empire to force the temple's leadership to act properly.

The next section of the chapter will discuss some of the other factions of which we are aware within the Persian-period temple assembly, but we can learn from this brief overview that different Persian-period writings provide us with insight into at least some of the temple assembly's factions, and that the worldviews of those factions did not entirely agree, and as a result their views of identity and governance differed as well. In the case of the Levites and the Aaronides, the two factions did not agree as to whether or not Levites should be considered as holy, nor what sort of role they should have in the temple leadership. When we turn in the chapter's next section to the views of empire that different assembly factions held, then, we will not be surprised to find that different groups in the temple community as a whole did not agree with the way that Ezra–Nehemiah constructs community identity through a reliance on Achaemenid ideology, and an important reason why that is so has to do with the social location of the group that produced the book.

---

36. Contra Min, *The Levitical Authorship of Ezra–Nehemiah*, 72–87.

Ezra–Nehemiah's dominant voice, outside of that of the third-person narrator, is Nehemiah's, whose first-person narration takes up about a quarter of the work, so we would expect that Ezra–Nehemiah was written by someone associated with the governor's office, which would explain why it is so heavily dependent upon Achaemenid ideology and why it is willing to the take the first-person word of a governor at face value and devote so much of the work to it. Someone closely linked to the governor would be more likely than others to see the community's future as yoked to imperial rule, present loyalty to the crown as a key aspect of community identity, portray Yhwh as entirely supportive of Achaemenid rule, and willing to describe Torah as part of a royal judicial system, something that justifies the threat of imperial violence. The book is suspicious of leaders in the imperial apparatus elsewhere in Palestine, figures whose interests would not always have corresponded to those of Judah and its governor, and who had the power and influence to threaten projects such as Nehemiah's wall. The book is also very concerned that members of the temple community are willing to tie their families by marriage to such figures (Neh. 6:17-19; 13:28), something that weakens the governor's control over the local elite. To take one such case that Nehemiah mentions, as the result of marriages between Tobiah's family and elite families of the temple assembly, "many in Judah were bound by oath to him," and so provided Tobiah with information as to the inner workings of the governor's office in Judah, even while he was opposed to Nehemiah's initiatives (Neh. 6:17-19), a situation that Nehemiah would have experienced as threatening and destabilizing. Marriages to other elite families outside of Judah could have the same result, in fact, making all such unions problematic from the governor's perspective.[37] Ezra–Nehemiah insists the community needs the leadership the Achaemenid provides, and it largely devalues the assembly's own leadership and its

---

37. It is true that at the end of the fifth century Bagohi, the governor of Judah, and Delaiah, the governor of Samaria, jointly backed the rebuilding of the temple at Elephantine (*TAD* A4.9), something that points to concord rather than rivalry between the two governors' offices (so Knoppers, *Jews and Samaritans*, 167). The point here, however, is not that the governors of Judah bore an implacable hatred against all other Persian appointees in Palestine, but that they would be suspicious that such figures, especially Yahwists, would attempt to gain leverage in Judah through alliances with elite community members or otherwise interfere in their projects, which is Nehemiah's concern in Neh. 3:33–4:17 [4:1-23] and 6:1-19. Wolfgang Oswald also points to a concern reflected by Ezra–Nehemiah that outside groups might gain leverage within the community, and sees this as an explanation of the reaction against marriages to outsiders ("Foreign Marriages and Citizenship in Persian-Period Judah," 15–16), but he does not link the book to the governor's office.

general character, claiming that without the figures the king sends from the center of the empire the group fails to be the perfect subjects of God and king that they should. Such a claim makes a governor appointed by the Achaemenid indispensable, precisely the picture we see in Nehemiah 8–13, where the community's attempt to keep the law collapses as soon as Nehemiah goes to Babylon. Nehemiah as governor manifests the king's beneficence as he constructs Jerusalem and its wall with royal funds and work groups, and as the king's representative, the community must follow the governor's orders, since he speaks for the Achaemenid who speaks for God, and loyalty to the king and royal law amounts to loyalty to God and God's law. Nehemiah is not the only important and good leader we see in the book, for in Ezra–Nehemiah anyone sent by the king from the center of empire is portrayed positively; problems arise only when peoples and leaders have been contaminated by living too long at the margins of empire. In Ezra–Nehemiah, community leaders born in Palestine are no better than anyone else in the assembly, and the group needs figures from the center of the empire sent by the king himself.

It is also possible that the author of Ezra–Nehemiah wrote for a faction within the temple assembly close to the governor, one that understood continued Achaemenid rule to be of paramount importance. It is the sort of writing that would appeal to an elite faction that benefitted from the political status quo that had developed in fourth-century Judah,[38] one made up of individuals such as those who sat at the governor's table each day, the kind of scene Nehemiah describes in Neh. 5:14-18, where he daily demonstrates the empire's generosity by providing food for one hundred and fifty members of the elite, so much food, in fact, that the guests would have taken some of it home, likely as part of their rations from the governor.[39] In this scenario, Ezra–Nehemiah's group was willing to

---

38. Mark Brett is not wrong when he argues that Ezra–Nehemiah creates a horizontal model of solidarity that largely deemphasizes hierarchy within the community ("National Identity as Commentary and as Metacommentary," in *Historiography and Identity [Re]formulation in Second Temple Historiographical Literature*, ed. Louis C. Jonker, LHBOTS 534 [New York: T&T Clark International, 2010], 29–40), but that is because in Ezra–Nehemiah the status that really matters is the whole community's place as *bandaka*s or עבדים "subjects" to the Persians. This is the result of the creation of the three-tiered cosmic hierarchy of Achaemenid ideology discussed in Chapter 3, which places all of humanity on the lowest of those levels, subject to the king.

39. For an analysis of the text, including a discussion of the vast amount of food Nehemiah claims to provide, as well as the way in which it reflects Achaemenid demonstrations of largesse to their subjects, see Fried, "150 Men at Nehemiah's Table?," 821-31.

critique the assembly's leadership, even if in doing so they were indicting themselves, if that would convince others in the temple community that they had no future outside of the empire, a conclusion that would lead to a solidifying of the political status quo and the advantageous place of Ezra–Nehemiah's faction within it. Their link to and dependence upon the governor and his authority would mean that they would have had no more interest than he did in seeing his position weakened by marriages between community members and elite families in other imperial jurisdictions, if only because they wanted the governor to see them as his allies. They in particular would have been wanted to urge the community's adherence to the royal law and define its identity by its loyalty to the king, since as community leaders they would have been blamed and have had the most to lose if the Achaemenid suspected the temple community was acting in rebellion against his rule. The figures who sat at Nehemiah's table would have been associated with some cross-section of the Judean elite, assumedly including the influential heads of the lay, priestly, and Levitical ancestral houses. We would expect that some of those individuals also functioned as the סגנים "officials" whom Ezra–Nehemiah portrays as community leaders (e.g., Ezra 9:2; Neh. 2:16; 4:8 [14]; 5:7). The Hebrew word סגן was borrowed from Akkadian *šaknu*, which referred to various offices of leadership, including those of overseers of professional groups dependent on the state.[40] In the Murašû texts from Persian-period Babylonia, the *šaknu* is normally the head of a *ḫaṭru*, a group or district of landholders who had obligations to the king that they met by producing taxes and providing a military reserve and state-controlled workers.[41] There is some archaeological evidence that such institutions existed in Judah,[42] and if the סגנים of Ezra–Nehemiah were the heads of the Judean equivalent of the Babylonian *ḫaṭru*, then such individuals would have been influential figures in the temple assembly while also being linked to the Persian administration, and they would have interacted with the

40. Israel Eph'al, "Changes in Palestine during the Persian Period in Light of Epigraphic Sources," *IEJ* 48 (1998): 106–19 (117); M. A. Dandamaev, "Neo-Babylonian and Achaemenid State Administration in Mesopotamia," in Lipschits and Oeming, eds, *Judah and the Judeans in the Persian Period*, 373–98 (375–6).

41. See Matthew W. Stolper, *Entrepreneurs and Empire: The Murašû Archive, the Murašû Firm, and Persian Rule in Babylonia*, UNHAII 54 (Leiden: Nederlands Instituut voor het Nabije Oosten, 1985), 70; Stolper, "The *šaknu* of Nippur," *JCS* 40 (1988): 127–55 (130–1).

42. Fried, "Exploitation of Depopulated Land in Achaemenid Judah"; Avraham Faust, "Forts or Agricultural Estates? Persian Period Settlement in the Territories of the Former Kingdom of Judah," *PEQ* 150 (2018): 34–59.

governor on a regular basis, given their obligations to the crown. They would have depended upon the governor's support to maintain such positions, and so would have taken care to align their interests with his.

Whether Ezra–Nehemiah was produced by the governor's office or by some group in the assembly associated with it and thus supportive of the political status quo, it derives from an elite group in the province, and so we cannot assume the beliefs of this group concerning empire and identity were necessarily widely shared within the community. Not all factions within the temple assembly were as enamored of Achaemenid rule and ideology as the author of Ezra–Nehemiah, who alone among biblical authors generally recognized as working in the Persian period wanted to define the community along the terms established by the empire, as the next section of the chapter points out. Nor, for that matter, were all assembly groups supportive of the author of Ezra–Nehemiah's exclusivist view of group identity that prohibits marriage outside of the community. The very opening of Ezra–Nehemiah provides readers with a rationale for that exclusivist understanding of community, and on the basis of Ezra 1–6 it can be easy to assume that events in early Persian-period Judah were driven by a conflict between migrants from Babylonia, who refused interaction with neighboring groups, and peoples native to the province, including Yahwists. However, Haggai and Zechariah 1–8, which were actually written in the period these chapters of Ezra–Nehemiah claim to document, offer no evidence for such a conflict.[43] Yet since Ezra–Nehemiah

---

43. The dates of Haggai and First Zechariah are discussed in the next section of the present chapter. For discussions of the absence of conflict between Babylonian immigrants and local groups in these works, see, e.g., Peter Ross Bedford, *Temple Restoration in Early Achaemenid Judah*, JSJSup 65 (Leiden: Brill, 2001), 27–34; J. A. Middlemas, "Going beyond the Myth of the Empty Land: A Reassessment of the Early Persian Period," in Knoppers and Grabbe, eds, *Exile and Restoration Revisited*, 174–94 (178–80); H. G. M. Williamson, "Welcome Home," in Davies and Edelman, eds, *The Historian and the Bible*, 113–23; Yigal Levin, "Judea, Samaria and Idumaea: Three Models of Ethnicity and Administration in the Persia Period," in Ro, ed., *From Judah to Judaea*, 4–53 (11); J.-D. Maachi and C. Nihan, "Le prétendu conflit entre exilés et non-exilés dans la province de Yehud à l'époque achéménide: Plaidoyer pour une approche différenciée," *Transeu* 42 (2012): 19–47 (25–31). Dalit Rom-Shiloni has argued that Haggai and Zechariah's failure to refer to people in the land who do not belong to the migrant community from Babylonia is a tacit endorsement of their exclusion; see *Exclusive Inclusivity*, 49–81. This argument from silence is unpersuasive, however, and it makes more sense to see a failure to condemn or demonize those outside of the migrant group as the result of a failure to see descent from this group as a marker of community identity. See the arguments of John Kessler in "Diaspora and Homeland in the Early Achaemenid Period: Community, Geography

advances the interests of those associated with the governor's office, which would want to limit the influence of non-assembly elites on the temple community, one can see why the author would create or accept a tradition in which Palestinian leaders and Yahwists from outside of the assembly opposed the community's attempts to carry out the orders of God and king from the very beginning of the work. This immediately defines groups and leaders outside of the governor's jurisdiction as the community's natural enemies, peoples with whom they should not want to make any kind of alliance. It is certainly true that we can see an exclusivist view of the exilic community on the part of Babylonian Judeans as early as Ezekiel,[44] but simply because some members of that group held such a view of communal identity does not mean that all of their descendants who moved to Judah did, as the next section of the chapter discusses. Chronicles, for example, raises no objections to marriages between Judeans and foreigners (e.g., 1 Chron. 2:3, 17, 35; 3:2; 4:18).[45] P, whether exilic or post-exilic, had a place in the Pentateuch that the Persian-period community used, and P places all of humanity in a covenant with Elohim (Gen. 9:1-17), and all the descendants of Abraham, including the non-Israelite ones, in a covenant with El Shaddai (Gen. 17:1-27), something that allows foreigners to live within Israel and even act in regard to some religious matters just as Israelites do (e.g., Exod. 12:19, 49).[46] Third Isaiah accepts foreigners into the community and says they

and Demography in Zechariah 1–8," in *Approaching Yehud: New Approaches to the Study of the Persian Period*, ed. Jon L. Berquist, SemeiaSt 50 (Atlanta: Society of Biblical Literature, 2007), 137–66, and in "'Is Haggai among the Exclusivists?' A Response to Dalit Rom-Shiloni's *Exclusive Inclusivity*," *JHS* 18 (2018): art. 1, 13–35.

44. Rom-Shiloni traces the development of this view from the exilic into the post-exilic period in *Exclusive Inclusivity*.

45. See the discussion in Gary N. Knoppers, "Intermarriage, Social Complexity, and Ethnic Diversity in the Genealogy of Judah," *JBL* 120 (2001): 15–30.

46. So in Gen. 17:26, then, Ishmael also enters into the covenant of circumcision, even though he becomes the ancestor of Arabian peoples in Gen. 25:12-18; his name may reflect *sumu'il*, a kingdom in Northern Arabia known from Neo-Assyrian inscriptions (see Ernst Axel Knauf, *Ismael: Untersuchungen zur Geschichte Palästinas und Nordarabiens im 1. Jahrtausend v. Chr.*, ADPV [Wiesbaden: O. Harrassowitz, 1985], 1–16). For discussions of the wider covenants with humanity in P, and the reflection of this in the openness to foreigners in P and H, see, e.g., Lisbeth S. Fried, "From Xeno-Philia to -Phobia—Jewish Encounters with the Other," in *A Time of Change: Judah and its Neighbours in the Persian and Early Hellenistic Periods*, ed. Yigal Levin, LSTS 65 (London: T&T Clark International, 2007), 179–204 (183–4); Konrad Schmid, "Judean Identity and Ecumenicity: The Political Theology of the

should be able to worship Yhwh in the temple (Isa. 56:1-8; 66:18-21).[47] For Ezra–Nehemiah, community identity is rooted in concerns pertinent to the governor and elite assembly members connected to his office, but that is not the case for any other Persian-period writing, even for ones that come from different elite factions in the temple assembly, and so we turn now to examine the variety of views of empire and identity held by various groups in the Persian-period assembly, none of whom articulated views on such matters that were as conservative as those of the elite faction who produced Ezra–Nehemiah.

2. Empire and Community Identity in the Persian-Period Temple Community

Prophetic works commonly dated to the early Persian period portray very different views of king and community identity than Ezra–Nehemiah does. While Ezra–Nehemiah silences prophets and presents some of them as liars, the involvement of Haggai and Zechariah in the temple-building project was apparently so entrenched in tradition that the author did not excise their names from Ezra 5:1 and 6:14, parts of the book's first Aramaic section, although they are never quoted. The common dating formulae used to structure Haggai 1–2 and Zechariah 1–8, as well as a common messenger formula, suggest that these writings once formed part of an independent document,[48] and the dates provided by the

Priestly Document," in Lipschits, Knoppers, and Oeming, eds, *Judah and the Judeans in the Achaemenid Period*, 3–26 (4–9, 18–26); Thomas Römer, "Conflicting Models of Identity and the Publication of the Torah in the Persian Period," in Albertz and Wöhrle, eds, *Between Cooperation and Hostility*, 33–51 (44–6).

47. For these passages as representing a very different view of foreigners than Ezra–Nehemiah, see, e.g., Andreas Schuele, "Who Is the True Israel? Community, Identity, and Religious Commitment in Third Isaiah," *Int* 73 (2019): 174–84 (177–8); Ulrich Berges, "Trito-Isaiah and the Reforms of Ezra/Nehemiah: Consent or Conflict?," *Bib* 98 (2019): 173–90.

48. There is some variation among the dating formulae and so, for example, we see a year–month–day sequence in Hag. 1:1 and 2:1, but a day–month–year sequence in Hag. 2:10 and Zech. 1:7. However, we see no such chronological specificity for oracles anywhere else in the Book of the Twelve, and there is enough commonality among the dating formulae to suggest that the ones in Haggai were added at the same time as those in Zech. 1–8 (contra Jakob Wöhrle, *Die frühen Sammlungen des Zwölfprophetenbuches: Entstehung und Komposition*, BZAW 360 [Berlin: W. de Gruyter, 2006], 367–74). And this is part of the reason why some argue that Haggai and First Zechariah were assembled as a composite work to celebrate the completion

redactor place their oracles in the second through fourth years of Darius's reign (520–518 BCE), early in the Persian period.[49] In Hag. 2:1-9, God promises to shake the cosmos so that all the nations will bring their treasures to Jerusalem for a glorious rebuilding of the temple, and in an oracle to Zerubbabel in 2:20-23, God refers not only to a coming cosmic shaking, but also says that "I will overturn the throne of kingdoms, and I will destroy the strength of the kingdoms of the nations."[50] "On that day," this prophecy concludes, "I will take you, Zerubbabel son of Shealtiel, my servant—the oracle of Yhwh—and I will make you like a signet ring, for

of the temple; see, e.g., Carol L. Meyers and Eric M. Meyers, *Haggai, Zechariah 1–8: A New Translation with Introduction and Commentary*, AB 25B (Garden City, NY: Doubleday, 1987), xliv–xlviii; Byron G. Curtis, *Up the Steep and Stony Road: The Book of Zechariah in Social Location Trajectory Analysis*, SBLAB 25 (Leiden: Brill, 2006), 111–13; Anthony R. Petterson, "A New Form-Critical Approach to Zechariah's Crowning of the High Priest Joshua and the Identity of the 'Shoot' (Zechariah 6:9-15)," in *The Book of the Twelve and the New Form Criticism*, ed. Mark J. Boda, Michael H. Floyd, and Colin M. Toffelmire, ANEM 10 (Atlanta: SBL Press, 2015), 285–304 (290). For the common messenger formula and other evidence that Haggai and Zech. 1–8 were once combined into a single document before they were incorporated into the Book of the Twelve, see Mark J. Boda, *The Book of Zechariah*, NICOT (Grand Rapids, MI: Eerdmans, 2016), 29–30.

49. See John Kessler, *The Book of Haggai: Prophecy and Society in Early Persian Yehud*, VTSup 91 (Leiden: Brill, 2002), 41–51. Not all scholars believe the dates are reliable—see Edelman, *The Origins of the "Second" Temple*, 80–150; Martin Hallaschka, "From Cores to Corpus: Considering the Formation of Haggai and Zechariah 1–8," in *Perspectives on the Formation of the Book of the Twelve: Methodological Foundations, Redactional Processes, Historical Insights*, ed. Rainer Albertz, James D. Nogalski, and Jakob Wöhrle, BZAW 433 (Berlin: W. de Gruyter, 2012), 171–90 (185–6); Louis Jonker, "Who's Speaking? On Whose Behalf? The Book of Haggai from the Perspective of Identity Formation in the Persian Period," in *History, Memory, Hebrew Scriptures: A Festschrift for Ehud Ben Zvi*, ed. Ian Douglas Wilson and Diana V. Edelman (Winona Lake, IN: Eisenbrauns, 2015), 197–214 (201–2). However, we have no good reason to doubt the veracity of the dates in Haggai and First Zechariah—see Ralph Klein, "Were Joshua, Zerubbabel, and Nehemiah Contemporaries? A Response to Diana Edelman's Proposed Late Date for the Second Temple," *JBL* 127 (2008): 697–701—and as Jason Silverman points out, no one who disputes the veracity of the dates has adequately explained why a much later redactor with no knowledge of the dates during which the oracles were delivered would have invented the specific ones the book provides (*Persian Royal–Judaean Elite Engagements in the Early Teispid and Achaemenid Empire: The King's Acolytes*, LHBOTS 690 [London: T&T Clark, 2020], 122–4).

50. This is the translation of the MT; the OG refers to God's destruction of "the thrones of kings" and of the strength of "the kings of the nations."

I have chosen you—the oracle of Yhwh of armies."⁵¹ Although Haggai never refers to Zerubbabel's Davidic lineage—in the Hebrew Bible, only 1 Chron. 3:19 makes such a connection—the prophet may have believed God would establish Zerubbabel as king after a divine overthrow of Persia. Some see the use of words such as עבדי "my servant" and חותם "signet ring" as hinting at a future royal status for Zerubbabel, for God refers to David as "my servant" (2 Sam. 7:5; 1 Kgs 11:32, 36), and the reference to a signet ring can be understood as a reversal of the prophecy of Jer. 22:24-30, where it appears as a symbol of God's rejection of the Davidides.⁵² It certainly is clear that, according to the prophet, God will

51. Some see 2:21b-22 as a later addition to the book; see, e.g., James Nogalski, *Literary Precursors to the Book of the Twelve*, BZAW 217 (Berlin: W. de Gruyter, 1993), 229–34; Wöhrle, *Die frühen Sammlungen*, 310, 322; Lena-Sofia Tiemeyer, "Death or Conversion: The Gentiles in the Concluding Chapters of the Book of Isaiah and the Book of the Twelve," *JTS* 68 (2017): 1–22 (5–6). It is unlikely, however, that an oracle to Zerubbabel in 2:21a, 23 was not originally linked to the cosmic shaking described in 2:21b-22. As discussed below, language in 2:23 such as עבדי and חותם may not necessarily indicate that the prophet believes Zerubbabel will be king, but it does suggest that he will be part of some great geopolitical work on Yhwh's part, the sort of thing that would involve cosmic shaking. Dating all of 2:20-23 to the early Hellenistic period, as Martin Hallaschka does (*Haggai und Sacharja 1–8: Eine redaktionsgeschichtliche Untersuchung*, BZAW 411 [Berlin: W. de Gruyter, 2011], 165–6), based on his argument that it reflects Alexander's overthrow of Persia, despite the book's claim that the oracle is from the second year of Darius (2:10, 20), is unnecessary. It simply is not clear why a Hellenistic redactor would create an oracle of a cosmic overthrow of an empire in the time of Zerubbabel that never came to pass. One assumes that the elite in Judah would have been aware to at least some degree that Darius was fighting to keep the empire together at the beginning of his rule, and since Haggai works with a worldview in which Yhwh controls all historical events, it makes perfect sense that the prophet and his faction could believe that such battles were the first step in a divine overthrow of Persia.

52. E.g., Paul L. Redditt, "The King in Haggai–Zechariah 1–8 and the Book of the Twelve," in *Tradition in Transition: Haggai and Zechariah 1–8 in the Trajectory of Hebrew Theology*, ed. Mark J. Boda and Michael H. Floyd, LHBOTS 475 (New York: T&T Clark, 2008), 56–82 (59); James Boswick, "Characters in Stone: Royal Ideology and Yehudite Identity in the Behistun Inscription and the Book of Haggai," in Knoppers and Ristau, eds, *Community Identity in Judean Historiography*, 87–117 (111–16); Antonios Finitsis, *Visions and Eschatology: A Socio-Historical Analysis of Zechariah 1–6*, LSTS 79 (New York: T&T Clark International, 2011), 119–20; Joseph Blenkinsopp, *David Remembered: Kingship and National Identity in Ancient Israel* (Grand Rapids, MI: Eerdmans, 2013), 79–81; Rom-Shiloni, *Exclusive Inclusivity*, 74–81.

overthrow the empire, although it is not as patent as some readers believe that Haggai thought this would result in the enthronement of Zerubbabel, since God calls many non-royal figures in the Hebrew Bible "my servant," and the word חוטם is not normally used to refer to kings.[53] A signet ring, however, is used to represent someone, and is a sign of their authority or an authorization of their message (1 Kgs 21:8), and combined with the reference to Zerubbabel as "my servant," the oracle vaguely points to some sort of formal role for Zerubbabel as a representative of Yhwh, even as he has previously been working up to that point as "governor" (Hag. 1:1, 14; 2:2, 21),[54] a representative of the empire, since with God's destruction of "the kingdoms of the nations," Persia will no longer have representatives in Judah or anywhere else. So, regardless of the specifics of the role Haggai envisions for Zerubbabel, the prophet clearly sees no future for the imperial status quo.

Isaiah 60–62, often described as the original late sixth-century core of Third Isaiah,[55] portrays a future in which the nations will voluntarily bring their wealth to rebuild all of Judah and to serve the community (60:1-16; 61:5-6), and God warns that the kingdom which does not do so will be

---

53. E.g., Wolter H. Rose, *Zemah and Zerubbabel: Messianic Expectations in the Early Postexilic Period*, JSOTSup 304 (Sheffield: Sheffield Academic Press, 2000), 208–43; John Kessler, "Haggai, Zechariah, and the Political Status of Yehud: The Signet Ring in Haggai 2:23," in *Prophets, Prophecy, and Prophetic Texts in Second Temple Judaism*, ed. Michael H. Floyd and Robert D. Haak, LHBOTS 427 (New York: T&T Clark International, 2007), 102–19 (110–17); Greg Goswell, "The Fate and Future of Zerubbabel in the Prophecy of Haggai," *Bib* 91 (2010): 77–90 (80–3); Jeremiah Cataldo, *Breaking Monotheism: Yehud and the Material Formation of Monotheistic Identity*, LHBOTS 565 (New York: Bloomsbury, 2012), 71–2.

54. This is the reading of the MT in those verses, but the OG never describes Zerubbabel as "the governor of Judah" in Haggai, only as ἐκ φυλῆς Ιουδα. Zerubbabel is also described as "from the tribe of Judah" in 1 Esd. 5:5 and *Ant.* 11.73, and both of these passages also claim he is descended from David. It is likely that the OG translator altered the original text as preserved in the MT in order to point to a Messianic lineage for Zerubbabel. A similar impulse is likely behind the Targum's זרבבל רבה דבית יהודה and the Syriac's *zrbbl rb' dyhwdh*; see Kessler, *The Book of Haggai*, 103 n. 2.

55. For summaries of the arguments for this dating, see Gregory, "The Postexilic Exile"; Jacob Stromberg, *Isaiah after Exile: The Author of Third Isaiah as Reader and Redactor of the Book*, OTM (Oxford: Oxford University Press, 2011), 11–13. Scholarship generally sees Third Isaiah as composed over the first few decades or the first century of the Persian period; see a discussion in John Goldingay, *A Critical and Exegetical Commentary on Isaiah 56–66*, ICC (London: Bloomsbury, 2014), 4–5.

destroyed (60:12).[56] There is no reference here to a great cosmic shaking, but 60:19-20 refers to a new creation in which Yhwh's brilliance will replace the light of the sun and moon, and this will be accompanied by the vast geopolitical change God is about to enact that will alter the empire's status to that of a people whose job is to serve the temple community, under pain of annihilation. First Zechariah, like Third Isaiah and unlike Haggai, does not definitively state God will overthrow the empire, but Zechariah is clear that God oversees and monitors the world (1:7-11;[57] 6:1-8), and will punish the nations that attacked Judah (2:1-4 [1:18-21],[58] 10-13 [2:6-9]), which may be a way of referring to divine punishment of Persia, given that Babylon had already been defeated.[59] Those exiles who remain in Babylonia are told in 2:10-11 [6-7] to flee to Zion to escape its destruction, a message concerning the divine punishment that strikes at

56. Some see this threat of violence against recalcitrant nations in 60:12 as so at odds with the overall tone of Isa. 60–62 that they argue the verse is a later addition—e.g., Sandra Labouvie, *Gottesknecht und neuer David: Der Heilsmittler für Zion und seine Frohbotschaft nach Jesaja 60–62*, FzB 129 (Würzburg: Echter Verlag, 2013), 34. This is not the only verse in this section of Third Isaiah that mentions divine violence, however, since 60:10 refers to God's punishment of Judah, so it would seem that just as Yhwh could strike Judah for disobedience in regard to divine commands, Yhwh can do the same to other disobedient nations.

57. Lena-Sofia Tiemeyer is correct to argue for an original unity to Zech. 1:8-11; see her *Zechariah's Vision Report and its Earliest Interpreters: A Redaction-Critical Study of Zechariah 1–8*, LHBOTS 626 (London: T&T Clark, 2016), 60–1. Attempts to argue that 1:8-11 was constructed through a process of redaction (e.g., Heinz-Günther Schöttler, *Gott inmitten seines Volkes: Die Neuordnung des Gottesvolkes nach Sacharja 1–6*, TTS 43 [Trier: Paulinus-Verlag, 1987], 49–59; Martin Hallaschka, "Zechariah's Angels: Their Role in the Night Visions and in the Redaction History of Zech 1,7–6,8," *SJOT* 24 [2010]: 13–27 [19–23]) fail to show that putative additions to reconstructed original versions of these visions actually enhance or explain them, as Tiemeyer argues.

58. We need not assume redaction in this passage, since there is no contradiction between 2:1-2 [1:18-19] and 3-4 [1:20-21] that indicates the presence of a redactional seam, contra Schöttler, *Gott inmitten seines Volkes*, 60–71; Hallaschka, *Haggai und Sacharja 1–8*, 166–77; the horns of 2:1-2 [1:18-19] are the same horns that readers see in 2:3-4 [1:20-21]. Nor need we argue that the explanation of 2:4b [1:21b] does not fit the vision (contra Tiemeyer, *Zechariah's Vision Report*, 81–4), since its focus is on the divine punishment of the "horns" that, in the vision, scattered Judah, and 2:4b [1:21b] explains the role of the workers introduced in 2:3 [1:20].

59. Mark J. Boda, "Terrifying the Horns: Persia and Babylon in Zechariah 1:7–6:15," *CBQ* 67 (2005): 22–41 (32–3).

one of the centers of empire. Like Haggai and Third Isaiah, First Zechariah never refers directly to Persia, but imperial rule is simply inconsequential in all three of these writings. First Zechariah is more specific than Haggai as to the kind of rule community members might imminently expect, since in 6:9-14 the prophet refers to the joint leadership of Joshua the high priest (called Jeshua in Ezra–Nehemiah) and a figure named the Branch (צמח), who may well be Zerubbabel, since God says that both Zerubbabel (Zech. 4:9) and the Branch (6:12) will build the temple.[60] The high priest and the Branch will each sit על כסאו "upon his seat/throne" (6:13), and the high priest will wear a עטרות "crown" (6:11).[61] Even if the Branch is not Zerubbabel,[62] in Zechariah's vision of the rule of Judah, the empire might as well not exist,[63] since First Zechariah retains no place at all for imperial leadership.

60. So, e.g., André Lemaire, "Zorobabel et la Judée à lumière de l'épigraphie (fin du VIᵉ s. av. J.-C.)," *RB* 103 (1996): 48–57 (48–52); Michael R. Stead, *The Intertextuality of Zechariah 1–8*, LHBOTS 506 (New York: T&T Clark International, 2009), 145–9; Finitsis, *Visions and Eschatology*, 130–1; Boda, *The Book of Zechariah*, 396–409.

61. The word עטרות in 6:11, 14 can be read as a feminine plural noun, but the verb in 6:14 (תהיה) suggests that we are to see it as a singular, which is how the same nominal form of the word should be read in Job 31:36. For some of the attempts to explain the Hebrew here, see Rose, *Zemah and Zerubbabel*, 46–8; Åke Viberg, "An Elusive Crown: An Analysis of the Performance of a Prophetic Symbolic Act (Zech 6:9-15)," *SEÅ* 65 (2000): 161–9 (164–5). Paul Redditt argues that we should understand עטרות as a plural, since the high priest could have different crowns to wear for different occasions ("King, Priest, and Temple in Haggai–Zechariah–Malachi and Ezra–Nehemiah," in *Priests and Cults in the Book of the Twelve*, ed. Lena-Sofia Tiemeyer, ANEM 14 [Atlanta: SBL Press, 2016], 157–72 [165]).

62. Zechariah 4:9 says that Zerubbabel has already laid the temple's foundation, while 3:8 and 6:12 refer to the Branch as a future figure who will build the temple, and some see this as indicating that Zerubbabel and the Branch are not to be understood as the same individual. See, e.g., Rose, *Zemah and Zerubbabel*, 140–1; Curtis, *Up the Steep and Stony Road*, 135–6; Anthony R. Petterson, *Behold your King: The Hope for the House of David in the Book of Zechariah*, LHBOTS 513 (New York: T&T Clark International, 2009), 114–20; Oded Lipschits, "'Here is a man whose name is Ṣemaḥ' (Zechariah 6:12)," in Davies and Edelman, eds, *The Historian and the Bible*, 124–36 (130–3).

63. Some readers see allusions to Persian rule in First Zechariah, however. Christine Mitchell, for example, argues that the Persians' administrative building and its paradise at Ramat Rahel form the background of Zechariah's visions ("A Paradise at Ramat Rahel and the Setting of Zechariah," *Transeu* 48 [2016]: 81–95), and Jason Silverman concludes that First Zechariah reflects divination that reports divine approval and imperial authorization necessary to begin temple construction (*Persian*

None of these early Persian-period writings links the community's identity to their relationship to the empire; as far as we can tell, identifying the community primarily as a colonized people within empire was simply not part of the worldview of the assembly groups from which these prophets emerged. The sharp contrast in this regard with Ezra–Nehemiah cannot be explained through positing a division within the temple community between theocrats who wanted to preserve the political status quo and prophetic visionaries who foresaw its destruction at God's hands, although such a split has been proposed.[64] If any of the works discussed so far in this section of the chapter might appear to promote a theocracy, it is First Zechariah, which points to a future in which the high priest will wear a crown, yet Zechariah clearly was a prophetic visionary. He portrays a joint rule of the high priest and Zerubbabel/the Branch, and while some argue that Zechariah uses language associated with kings when discussing the Branch—the Branch will משל "rule" and bear הוד "honor" as he sits on a כסא "throne/seat" (6:13)[65]—others point out that none of this vocabulary can be unambiguously connected with royalty,[66] and even if it could, in the oracle it is the high priest who receives the crown,[67] which

---

Royal–Judaean Elite Engagements, 189–93). Even if readers might have understood some of these visions to allude to the garden at Ramat Rahel, however, they may have seen such allusions as deprecating empire, in the sense that God could announce the divine control of the world and the coming punishment of empire in the imperial backyard, as it were. Also, First Zechariah does not clearly state at any point that the empire approves the construction of the temple. God does refer to temple construction in Zech. 4:9 and 6:12, but only in the context of assurance that it will be completed, not in the sense of approving the building process in the first place.

64. So Paul D. Hanson, *The People Called: The Growth of Community in the Bible* (San Francisco: Harper & Row, 1986), 215–311.

65. See, e.g., Redditt, "The King in Haggai," 60–2; Boda, *The Book of Zechariah*, 396–409.

66. See, e.g., Rose, *Zemah and Zerubbabel*, 63–4, 91–120, 129–30; Anthony R. Petterson, "The Shape of the Davidic Hope across the Book of the Twelve," *JSOT* 35 (2010): 225–46 (235–8). Michael Floyd refers to Zerubbabel as having "quasi-royal" status in Zech. 6:9-15 (*Minor Prophets*, 2:406).

67. Some argue that the original version of the oracle referred to the crowning of Zerubbabel/the Branch as well as the high priest, but that this was omitted from the passage when Zerubbabel died or was removed from office. See, e.g., Lemaire, "Zorobabel et la Judée," 55; Marvin A. Sweeney, *The Twelve Prophets*, 2 vols, BerO (Collegeville, MN: Liturgical Press, 2000), 2:629; Finitsis, *Visions and Eschatology*, 134–5; Jakob Wöhrle, "On the Way to Hierocracy: Secular and Priestly Rule in the Books of Haggai and Zechariah," in *Priests and Cult in the Book of the Twelve*, ed. Lena-Sofia Tiemeyer, ANEM 14 (Atlanta: SBL Press, 2016), 173–89 (183–4). This

6:14 says is kept in the temple.⁶⁸ In Zechariah 3–4, it is Zerubbabel who will build the temple, but it is the high priest who will have charge of it (3:7). Zechariah's vision of an empire-less future—or at least a future in which empire does not really matter—is likely one that comes from the elite of the temple personnel, a group invested in ensuring the power of the high priest but also one that means to work in concert with the rest of the assembly. It is notable, for example, that the crown the high priest will wear will be kept in the temple by laypersons who have arrived from Babylon and paid for the crown's construction (6:9, 14), something that suggests the high priest will wear it only with their consent.⁶⁹ There were some in the post-exilic community who looked for a Davidic restoration, as we will discuss below, and the faction that produced First Zechariah appears unwilling to alienate those people, so long as there can be agreement that the high priest will have an important role in governance, and so the work uses language that, with its references to Zerubbabel/the Branch, hints at Davidic restoration without directly confirming it. First Zechariah, however, refuses to link community identity and polity to empire in any way.

The same could be said for the faction that produced Third Isaiah, which comes from a group far more marginal in the community than First Zechariah's. Third Isaiah is concerned with the failure of social justice, and condemns those who heed cultic strictures but do not care for the poor (Isa. 58:1-14). It generally portrays the larger temple assembly negatively (59:9-15a; 64:6-7; 65:1-7), and although Third Isaiah holds the temple in high regard (56:7; 60:7, 13; 64:11; 65:11), it is suspicious of the priests who enact the cult within it (66:1-4).⁷⁰ The work indicts

---

conclusion, however, is guesswork, based on what readers conclude the prophet believed. The best evidence for what the prophet believed, however, lies in the text that is actually at our disposal.

68. The wording of LXX 6:14 is fairly different than that of the MT, not because the OG translator had a different text than the one we see in the MT, but because he or she chose to read the personal names in the verse as common nouns. So the original לחלם "to Helem" becomes τοῖς ὑπομένουσιν "to them that wait," as the translator made a connection with the root יחל, and so on. See Gunnar Magnus Eidsvåg, *The Old Greek Translation of Zechariah*, VTSup 170 (Leiden: Brill, 2016), 207–13.

69. This is why we need not argue that the crown which 6:14 says is stored in the temple cannot be the one the high priest wears in 6:11 (contra, e.g., Wöhrle, "On the Way to Hierocracy," 182–3). In 6:14, Zechariah is making a point about the sharing of power between lay and priestly authorities in the community.

70. By itself, 66:1-4 sounds like a rejection of temple cult altogether, but the positive view of temple elsewhere in the work suggests this section is attacking the governing priesthood; see, e.g., Brooks Schramm, *The Opponents of Third Isaiah:*

those who practice religious acts the group does not understand to be compatible with Yahwism (57:3-13; 65:1-7), people whom Third Isaiah calls "children of a sorceress" (57:3) yet who claim to be holy (65:5), and so who are likely part of the priestly leadership in the temple.[71] The writing does refer positively to a group of people whom God calls "my servants" and who are contrasted with those who commit cultic crimes, and God's servants will be vindicated even as the cultic criminals will be punished (65:1-16). We see a similar contrast between the חרדים, the "tremblers," and figures condemned for their cultic leadership (66:1-9), so those who call themselves the חרדים likely also referred to themselves as God's servants, and were the assembly faction from which Third Isaiah emerged. "You are our father," this group says to God, "for Abraham does not know us, and Israel does not acknowledge us" (63:16),[72] a statement that expresses their alienation from the mainstream community while

---

Reconstructing the Cultic History of the Restoration, JSOTSup 193 (Sheffield: Sheffield Academic Press, 1995), 166–9; Christophe Nihan, "Ethnicity and Identity in Isaiah 56–66," in Lipschits, Knoppers, and Oeming, eds, *Judah and the Judeans in the Achaemenid Period*, 67–104 (85–90); Joseph Blenkinsopp, "Trito-Isaiah (Isaiah 56–66) and the Gôlāh Group of Ezra, Shecaniah, and Nehemiah (Ezra 7–Nehemiah 13): Is There a Connection?," *JSOT* 43 (2019): 661–77 (671–2). Stefan Green argues that 65:17-25 describes "my holy mountain" as the true temple, and so sees 66:1-4 as a rejection of temple as conceived of by the elite ("The Temple of God and Crises in Isaiah 56–66 and *1 Enoch*," in *Studies in Isaiah: History, Theology and Reception*, ed. Tommy Wasserman, Greger Andersson, and David Willgren, LHBOTS 654 [London: T&T Clark, 2017], 47–66 [50–3]). For the original unity of 66:1-4, see Tiemeyer, *Priestly Rites*, 48–51; Stromberg, *Isaiah after Exile*, 61–3.

71. So, e.g., Lena-Sofia Tiemeyer, "'The Haughtiness of the Priesthood' (Isa 65,5)," *Bib* 85 (2004): 237–44.

72. This part of 63:16 begins with the word כי, and some prefer to take it as indicating a counterfactual statement—"if Abraham does not know us, and Israel does not recognize us…"—since 63:7–64:11 [12] as a whole appears to refer to the entire temple community, rather than a faction within it that understands itself to be unacknowledged by the rest of the group (e.g., Joseph Blenkinsopp, *Isaiah 56–66: A New Translation with Introduction and Commentary*, AB 19B [New York: Doubleday, 2003], 263). In this section of the writing, however, Third Isaiah does appear to be contrasting its faction with the larger temple community. God can say in regard to the whole assembly that "they are my people" (63:8), but also that "they" rebelled (63:10). Third Isaiah's own group, however, is able to refer to God as "our father" (63:16; 64:7), and says that they are made up of "your servants" (63:17), as opposed to "the wicked" (63:18), a designation of the larger assembly on the margins of which Third Isaiah's faction sits. Some argue that 63:16 should not be understood as the voice of Third Isaiah's group, since they would not refer to their opponents as "Israel"

also claiming that they are in an intimate relationship with God. Third Isaiah not only sides with the economically oppressed as it condemns the leadership of the temple, but also welcomes foreigners to participate in the temple cult (56:1-8; 66:18-24),[73] perhaps because its faction, at the margins of the assembly, identified with people whom their opponents claimed were entirely outside of the community's boundaries. Third Isaiah directs so much animus against the practice of cult that the writing likely derives from a group that was ostracized by the temple personnel,[74] and so stripped of the rations or wages with which the assembly had provided them (see Neh. 10:33-40 [32-39]; 13:10).[75] While this faction's vision of an imminent divine action parallels to some degree the great cosmic and

(e.g., Tiemeyer, *Priestly Rites*, 59–60), but Third Isaiah is simply acknowledging that its group does not make up the whole of "Israel," even if it does make up the righteous part of it.

73. Isa 66:18-24 is often described as a later addition written to conclude Third Isaiah or the Book of Isaiah as a whole; see, e.g., Wim Beuken, "Isaiah Chapters lxv–lxvi: Trito-Isaiah and the Close of the Book of Isaiah," in *Congress Volume: Leuven, 1989*, ed. J. A. Emerton, VTSup 43 (Leiden: E.J. Brill, 1991), 204–21; Blenkinsopp, *Isaiah 56–66*, 62–3; Goldingay, *A Critical and Exegetical Commentary*, 525. Given the passage's similarities to 56:1-8 and to other parts of Isa. 56–66—the reference to foreigners participating in the sanctuary, the creation of a new heavens and earth, the punishment of the rebellious—there is no reason to believe that this was not also the production of Third Isaiah's faction within the community. Jacob Stromberg argues persuasively that 66:18-24 has so much in common with 65:1–66:17 that 65:1–66:24 was written by the same person (*Isaiah after Exile*, 63–7).

74. So also, e.g., Hanson, *The People Called*, 281; Joseph Blenkinsopp, "The Social Roles of Prophets in Early Achaemenid Judah," *JSOT* 93 (2001): 39–58 (54–5).

75. In the ancient Near East, temple personnel were paid by means of rations from the temple or usufruct of its land; see Amélie Kuhrt, "Nabonidus and the Babylonian Priesthood," in *Pagan Priests: Religion and Power in the Ancient World*, ed. Mary Beard and John North (Ithaca, NY: Cornell University Press, 1990), 119–55 (151–4); Waerzeggers, *The Ezida Temple*, 38–40; M. Jursa, *Aspects of the Economic History of Babylonia in the First Millennium BC*, AOAT 377 (Münster: Ugarit-Verlag, 2010), 155–68. We have no evidence that Jerusalem's temple owned any land, so it would have relied entirely on the support of the assembly. Joseph Blenkinsopp's suggestion that the Jerusalem temple owned land depends on his reading of the word רכוש in Ezra 10:8 as referring to temple land, even though the word normally does not have this sense; see his "Did the Second Jerusalemite Temple Possess Land?," *Transeu* 21 (2001): 61–8. In fact, Nehemiah's claim in Neh. 13:10 that the Levites had to abandon their work at the temple when the assembly ceased providing them with rations shows how dependent the temple personnel were on those donations, an indication the temple itself had no land they could depend upon.

political changes in which Haggai's faction believed, it also involves a punishment of the elite opponents of Third Isaiah's group. Third Isaiah certainly does not come from the same faction as First Zechariah, but this very different group from the assembly's margins nonetheless shares the view of empire that we see from that work of the elite within the temple personnel, the group Third Isaiah condemns, for in both writings God is utterly sovereign and empire has no power at all, and certainly plays no role in determining the identity of the community.[76]

Haggai derives from an assembly faction much more like that of First Zechariah's than that of Third Isaiah's. First Zechariah points to a future in which the high priest will be an important leader and wear a crown, and Haggai is certainly pro-temple, for the bulk of it concerns prophetic exhortations to build the temple in the early years of Darius's rule and the community's positive response to that message. Like First Zechariah, Haggai's oracles, at least in the redacted form in which we encounter them, never discuss Joshua the high priest without also referring to Zerubbabel (or the Branch in Zech. 3:8 and 6:9-14),[77] but the prophecy of Hag. 2:20-23 is the exception to this, the point where the book returns to the theme of a coming divine shaking of the cosmos, something that has particular significance for Zerubbabel, according to Haggai, but not for

---

76. This is one important reason why attempts to link Third Isaiah to the worldview of Ezra–Nehemiah's author are unconvincing. Some maintain that Third Isaiah supports the reforms of Ezra and/or Nehemiah—e.g., Gregory, "The Postexilic Exile," 491–5; Karl William Weyde, "'For I am about to create new heavens and a new earth': Prophecy and Torah in Isaiah 65:17-25," in *New Studies in the Book of Isaiah: Essays in Honor of Hallvard Hagelia*, ed. Markus Zehnder, PHSC 21 (Piscataway, NJ: Gorgias Press, 2014), 209–29 (222–7); Marvin A. Sweeney, *Isaiah 40–66*, FOTL 19 (Grand Rapids, MI: Eerdmans, 2016), 28–30—but these arguments tend to point to very superficial or general points of similarity between the two writings, such as an interest in rebuilding and religious reform. Many post-exilic Judeans, we imagine, would have been interested in rebuilding Judah and Jerusalem, and the religious reforms Ezra–Nehemiah and Third Isaiah promote are not the same ones. The fact that the root חרד appears as a plural participle in only these two works to refer to a group called the "tremblers" is not evidence that these writings were produced by the same faction; as even Joseph Blenkinsopp notes, the חרדים of Isa. 66:2, 5 are poor and oppressed, while those of Ezra 9:4; 10:3 are associated with Ezra, near the very center of local power in the temple assembly ("Trito-Isaiah [Isaiah 56–66]," 672–3), so it would appear that two very different groups, who likely did not exist at the same time, decided to use the same word to refer to themselves.

77. Haggai 1:1, 12-15; 2:2, 4; Zech. 3:1-10; 4:1-14 (assuming that Joshua and Zerubbabel are the two anointed ones of 4:14); 6:9-14. See Rooke, *Zadok's Heirs*, 127–30; Cataldo, *Breaking Monotheism*, 67–70.

the high priest. As noted above, the language of these verses, like that of Zech. 6:9-14, may or may not allude to the notion that Zerubbabel will exercise royal rule in the future, but the fact that a non-priestly figure will act as Yhwh's representative in some fashion after God's great cosmic upheaval points to an origin for Haggai outside of the temple personnel. This suggests that the prophet spoke for an elite lay group with links to Zerubbabel the governor, but one that was willing to acknowledge the importance of the high priest, if not to the same extent that First Zechariah does. According to Hag. 1:1-2, the prophet addressed a community in 520 BCE who believed that it was not yet time to build the temple, perhaps because they were waiting for the end of a seventy-year period of destruction in awareness of an earlier oracle (see Jer. 25:11; 29:10),[78] or perhaps because their current poverty, which Haggai says God will alleviate if the temple is rebuilt (1:5-6, 9-11; 2:15-19), made the work seem impossible to some. If Haggai derives from an elite lay faction, this group may still have understood the temple to be the community's top priority because of its need for an institutional center for the community not associated with the Persian administration, which they believed God was about to bring to an end, or they may have wanted to maintain good relationships with the priests within the assembly. Zerubbabel, they believed, would have an important place in governance, no longer as a Persian appointee but in whatever role God saw fit to bestow upon him, and this positive portrayal of their current governor may have convinced him to tolerate the group's anti-imperial stance, a very different view of empire than Ezra–Nehemiah's. Haggai, just like Zechariah, considers the empire to be of little importance, and for Haggai it is a fleeting geopolitical reality that the prophet says God is about to overthrow.

The assembly factions who shared Haggai's and Zechariah's worldviews were from the elite strata of the community, but the marginalization of empire in these worldviews means that these elite groups did not understand the community's ideal identity to be as a colonized people placed in subjugation to Persia. The kind of leadership they emphasize

---

78. So, e.g., Peter Ross Bedford, "Discerning the Time: Haggai, Zechariah, and the 'Delay' in the Rebuilding of the Temple," in *The Pitcher Is Broken: Memorial Essays for Gösta W. Ahlström*, ed. Steven W. Holloway and Lowell K. Handy, JSOTSup 190 (Sheffield: Sheffield Academic Press, 1995), 71–94; Hayim Tadmor, "'The appointed time has not yet arrived': The Historical Background of Haggai 1:2," in *Ki Baruch Hu: Ancient Near Eastern, Biblical, and Judaic Studies in Honor of Baruch A. Levine*, ed. Robert Chazan, William W. Hallo, and Lawrence H. Schiffman (Winona Lake, IN: Eisenbrauns, 1999), 401–8; see also Elie Assis, "To Build or Not to Build: A Dispute between Haggai and his People (Hag 1)," *ZAW* 119 (2007): 514–27.

comes from within the community itself, and it will be established by God, just as Ezra–Nehemiah says the Persian Empire was. Third Isaiah critiques the leadership of the community from its marginalized social location, and says little about any sort of replacement of it, but empire is as inconsequential in this group's understanding of community identity as it is in those of the more central groups represented by Haggai and First Zechariah. All three of these writings were composed in the early part of the Persian period, and one could argue that such views of empire would inevitably have changed the longer the imperial status quo remained in place,[79] yet we see a similar picture in Malachi, a somewhat later writing,[80] which ignores empire altogether. Malachi gives a voice to a Levitical faction, as the first section of this chapter discusses,[81] a group located

---

79. So, e.g., David M. Carr, "Criteria and Periodization in Dating Biblical Texts to Parts of the Persian Period," in Bautch and Lackowski, eds, *On Dating Biblical Texts to the Persian Period*, 11–18 (16).

80. As n. 35 of this chapter mentions, Malachi is commonly dated to the fifth century BCE because it is seen as sharing some of the concerns of Ezra–Nehemiah, specifically the problem of intermarriage with foreign women and that of the community's failure to supply the cult properly. As discussed below, however, Malachi's concerns in regard to intermarriage are not those of Ezra–Nehemiah's author. And while Neh. 10:33-40 [32–39] and 13:10-13 point to the problem of supplying the temple cult, Hag. 1:5-6, 9-11; 2:15-19, from a period many decades earlier, refer to the poverty of the temple community, and that means that the time of Nehemiah's governorship was unlikely to have been the only one in the Persian period when a lack of good supplies for the temple and its personnel was an issue. Malachi was written after the temple and its cult had been restored, and so it reflects a period somewhat later than that of the prophecy of Haggai and Zechariah, but it is difficult to be more precise than this. One potentially helpful piece of information is Mal. 1:3-4, which claims that Edom is in ruins. If Alexander Fantalkin and Oren Tal are correct when they argue that, in the Persian period, the Negev and Shephelah show no real signs of rebuilding until the fourth century ("Redating Lachish Level I: Identifying Achaemenid Imperial Policy at the Southern Frontier of the Fifth Satrapy," in Lipschits and Oeming, eds, *Judah and the Judeans in the Persian Period*, 167–97), then this would suggest Malachi is a fifth-century work.

81. Some argue that Malachi was composed as a conclusion to the Book of the Twelve; e.g., James Nogalski, *Redactional Processes in the Book of the Twelve*, BZAW 218 (Berlin: W. de Gruyter, 1993), 210–12; Christophe L. Nihan, "Remarques sur la question de l''unité' des XII," in *The Book of the Twelve—One or Many?*, ed. Eleana Di Pede and Donatella Sciaola, FAT 2/91 (Tübingen: Mohr Siebeck, 2016), 145–65. Yet Malachi is more than a series of allusions to or reflections of earlier material from the book, and it is difficult to see why redactors who aimed only to conclude the Book of the Twelve would focus on issues such as the community's deficiencies in supplying temple offerings, Levitical condemnations of the priesthood, and the

between the more elite factions who produced Haggai and First Zechariah and the marginalized one that produced Third Isaiah. Malachi's picture of an ideal community is of one that properly supplies the temple cult (Mal. 1:6-14; 3:8-12), whose men do not marry women from outside of the community or divorce those inside of it (see the discussion on 2:10-16 below), whose purified Levitical priesthood properly instructs them and offers sacrifices (2:4-9), and who do what is right in the knowledge that God punishes the wicked (3:13-21 [4:3]). Malachi never refers to the empire or its understanding of the colonized, and its vision of coming divine action is one that affects the community alone, as God will purify Levitical-led worship in the temple (3:1-4) and punish those responsible for social injustice (3:5) and for evil in general (3:16-21 [4:3]). Perhaps the prophet's Levitical group simply accepted the existence and legitimacy of Persian rule, but even if that is the case this acceptance has left no imprint on Malachi's vision of community identity. The assembly the prophet discusses is defined by proper dedication to the cult and to social justice, not by their place as a colonized people who must remain loyal to Persia.

Post-exilic writings alert us to the existence of a group within the assembly associated with the house of David, as well. Ezra refers to someone belonging to the Davidic ancestral house of Shecaniah as travelling with him to Judah (Ezra 8:2; for בני שכניה, the house of Shecaniah, see also MT 1 Chron. 3:21), and Second Zechariah, from the later Persian or early Hellenistic period, refers to "the house of David" as a contemporary reality (Zech. 12:8, 10, 12), so there was a recognizable post-exilic Davidic group, which is why 1 Chronicles 3 can trace descent from David to individuals who lived in the early fourth century,[82] which is likely

---

problem of marriage to foreign women. Malachi is focused on concerns specific to its Persian-period community, and it is best to see it as an originally independent composition, formulated in light of texts its author knew; see Rainer Kessler, "The Unity of Malachi and its Relation to the Book of the Twelve," in *Perspectives on the Formulation of the Book of the Twelve: Methodological Formulations—Redactional Processes—Historical Insights*, ed. Rainer Albertz, James Nogalski, and Jakob Wöhrle, BZAW 433 (Berlin: W. de Gruyter, 2012), 223–36; Innocent Himbaza, "Les themes théologiques de Malachie et le concept du livre des XII Prophètes," in Di Pede and Sciaola, eds, *The Book of the Twelve*, 82–96.

82. The MT version of 1 Chron. 3:19-24 follows the genealogy of David for six generations after Zerubbabel in the post-exilic period, while the LXX creates a genealogy with eleven generations after Zerubbabel. If we assume about twenty years per generation, then the MT's genealogy takes us to about 400 BCE, but the LXX's to about 300. The LXX adds five generations to the more difficult MT in 3:21, where the MT has a string of personal names, each followed by בני, except for

when Chronicles was written.[83] The Davidides never returned to power at any sort of level in the Persian period, since Zerubbabel functioned as a Persian governor, not as a client ruler in a restored dynasty,[84] but this did not stop pro-Davidic factions in the assembly from promoting such a reinstatement, and Chronicles is one example of this, as the first section of this chapter mentions. Even so, the final chapters of the book provide positive portrayals of the foreign monarchs who ruled pre-exilic Judah as colonial suzerains. The Egyptian Neco, whom 2 Chron. 36:1-4 presents as Judah's suzerain, speaks like a prophet in 35:20-22, and part of the Chronicler's criticism of Zedekiah, the last Davidide to rule as king, is his rebellion against the Neo-Babylonian Nebuchadnezzar, "who made him [Zedekiah] swear by God" (36:13), thereby indicating that rebellion against this imperial king is rebellion against Yhwh, whom the suzerain

---

the final one. However, at each place where the MT has בני, the LXX reads בנו "his son/child," which solves the difficulty of how to read בני in this context by making each personal name the child of the previous one. The MT of 3:21, however, can be read as referring to a single generation, with emphasis placed on the fact that four of the figures named in this generation founded ancestral houses. Within MT 3:21, for example, we read of בני שכניה "the descendants of Shecaniah," the Davidic ancestral house to which Ezra 8:2 refers. So a translation of the more original version of 3:21 should read with the MT: "and the child of Hananiah, Pelatiah, and Jeconiah, the descendants of Rephiah, the descendants of Arnan, the descendants of Obadiah, the descendants of Shecaniah." The verse is providing readers with a list of ancestral houses that existed in the later Persian period and that claimed descent from David, and this suggests that the genealogy of 1 Chron. 3:19-24 ends around 400 BCE.

83. No other genealogy in Chronicles extends beyond the beginning of the exile, so the easiest way to explain why the Chronicler terminated the Davidic genealogy with the generation of 3:24, the children of Elioenai, is to conclude that this was the generation living in the Chronicler's own time. See also Kai Peltonen, "A Jigsaw without a Model? The Date of Chronicles," in *Did Moses Speak Attic? Jewish Historiography in the Hellenistic Period*, ed. Lester L. Grabbe, JSOTSup 317, ESHM 3 (Sheffield: Sheffield Academic Press, 2001), 225–71 (229); Klein, *1 Chronicles*, 14–15; Janzen, *Chronicles and the Politics of Davidic Restoration*, 10–13.

84. Contra F. Bianchi, "Le rôle de Zorobabel et de le dynastie davidique en Judée du VIᵉ siècle au IIᵉ siècle av. J.-C.," *Transeu* 7 (1994): 153–65; Lemaire, "Zorobabel et la Judée," 55–6; Herbert Niehr, "Religio-Historical Aspects of the 'Early Post-Exilic' Period," in Becking and Korpel, eds, *The Crisis of Israelite Religion*, 228–40 (230–1); Gabriele Boccaccini, *Roots of Rabbinic Judaism: An Intellectual History from Ezekiel to Daniel* (Grand Rapids, MI: Eerdmans, 2002), 49–56. For a brief explanation as to why we lack good evidence for any sort of Davidic restoration in the Persian period, see Janzen, *Chronicles and the Politics of Davidic Restoration*, 38–9.

appears to revere. Finally, Yhwh rouses Cyrus of Persia and, according to Cyrus, gives him "all the kingdoms of the earth" and entrusts him with the building of Yhwh's temple (36:22-23). This suggests that the Davidic party that produced Chronicles hoped for a Davidic restoration as a client monarchy to the Achaemenids, a type of local rule the Persians permitted for many colonized peoples,[85] and something that could be accomplished without divine intervention. Chronicles acknowledges that some Davidic kings sinned, some of them gravely (e.g., 2 Chron. 28), but it also maintains that God made a covenant with the Davidides which said that they would rule forever (1 Chron. 17:10b-14). When David speaks of this to Solomon in 1 Chron. 22:6-16, he refers to the eternal nature of this covenant (22:10), and says that Solomon will prosper (תצלח) if he observes the law (22:11-13), and Solomon does indeed prosper (ויצלח) during his reign (1 Chron. 29:23), for nowhere does the Chronicler claim that he failed to keep any aspect of the law. When the Chronicler does include statements that make Davidic rule appear conditional upon royal obedience (1 Chron. 28:6-7; 2 Chron. 7:17-18), it is always Solomon's obedience that will guarantee the eternality of the covenant, and the Chronicler's sinless portrayal of him means that, as far as the Chronicler and his or her pro-Davidic group are concerned, the eternal covenant with David and his descendants is never annulled.

Chronicles concludes in 2 Chron. 36:22-23 with almost exactly the same text as Ezra 1:1-3a, as the end of Jerusalem's punishment is fulfilled and Cyrus announces that God has appointed him to build the temple. In Ezra–Nehemiah, this is the beginning of the rule of a line of faithful imperial kings who work on God's behalf, but in Chronicles it signals the end of the seventy-year punishment for the sins of the people and kings narrated in 2 Chron. 36:11-21.[86] While Davidides may have sinned in the past, the work reveals to readers that each of them was punished in his lifetime, by invasion (e.g., 2 Chron. 12:1-12; 28:5) or disease (e.g., 21:18-19; 26:19-21) or assassination (22:8-9; 24:25) or exile (33:10-11;

---

85. For only a partial list of the peoples within the Achaemenid Empire who maintained their dynasts as a local level of administration under Persian rule, see Janzen, *Chronicles and the Politics of Davidic Restoration*, 15–23.

86. Gerrie Snyman asks if the final verses of Chronicles should be read as supporting the Persians' imperial cause ("Why Asa Was Not Deemed Good Enough: A Decolonial Reading of 2 Chronicles 14–16," in Jonker, ed., *Texts, Contexts and Readings in Postexilic Literature*, 241–68 [242]), but the question should be a bit more nuanced than that. Chronicles seems to acknowledge the inevitability of empire, but it does not portray it as overly important, and certainly not as important as Davidic leadership, as this section of the chapter discusses.

36:6, 10), a doctrine of immediate retribution[87] that explains to all future Davidic rulers how God responds to royal actions, so it is clear to them that they, like Solomon, must never sin. But even if the Chronicler seems convinced that future Davidides will rule as clients to the Achaemenids, imperial ideology does not define the people's identity in the work. Readers see instead a local dynasty ruling Judah with the help of the priests and Levites, who teach the law and act as judges (2 Chron. 17:7-9; 19:8-11), and where "the assembly" and "all the people" have a voice in placing new Davidic kings on the throne (e.g., 2 Chron. 23:3; 26:1), while kings will sometimes convene the assembly to help them make important decisions and carry out important cultic acts (e.g., 1 Chron. 13:1-5; 15:3; 2 Chron. 1:3; 5:2-6; 15:9; 34:29-33). The community Chronicles envisions is one in which empire is largely invisible, as the assembly and temple personnel work together with a Davidic king to enact cult rightly and to keep God's law. Chronicles does not entirely avoid references to Judah's colonized status in the late pre-exilic and early post-exilic periods, but this hardly defines the ideal community it portrays.

Chronicles, Haggai, First Zechariah, Third Isaiah, and Malachi all derive from different factions within the post-exilic community, some of them more central and elite groups and some, Third Isaiah's faction in particular, more marginal. These writings were composed at different points in the Persian period, but none of them ties community identity to empire as Ezra–Nehemiah does. Nor do any of them link this identity to descent from Babylonian migrants like the author of Ezra–Nehemiah. Haggai and Zechariah say nothing at all about marriage or a need to prohibit marital unions with individuals outside of the community, and Chronicles refers to non-Israelites marrying Judeans without suggesting that this violates any law, norm, or social boundary.[88] Third Isaiah, as

---

87. For helpful studies of the Chronicler's doctrine of immediate retribution, something the author applies consistently only to Judean kings, see Brian E. Kelly, "'Retribution' Revisited: Covenant, Grace and Restoration," in *The Chronicler as Theologian: Essays in Honor of Ralph W. Klein*, ed. M. Patrick Graham, Steven L. McKenzie, and Gary N. Knoppers, JSOTSup 371 (London: T&T Clark International, 2003), 206–27; Ehud Ben Zvi, *History, Literature and Theology in the Book of Chronicles*, BW (London: Equinox, 2006), 160–73; G. Galil, "'The secret things belong to the Lord our God' (*Deut* 29:29): Retribution in the Persian Period," *Transeu* 39 (2010): 91–6; Janzen, *Chronicles and the Politics of Davidic Restoration*, 87–94.

88. As the first section of this chapter points out, the Chronicler passes no judgment on Judeans who marry foreigners. In 2 Chron. 8:11, Solomon says that the daughter of Pharaoh, one of his wives, is not to live in David's house (according to the MT's version of the verse) because the ark has been there, and it is holy. (The MT more

the first section of the chapter discusses, is open to foreigners joining the assembly and even participating in the cult, and so Yahwism—the version of it preferred by Third Isaiah's faction, at any rate—and ethical behavior, not descent, define community boundaries for this group.[89] This too differs sharply from Ezra–Nehemiah's view of community identity, for the author of Ezra–Nehemiah does not use Yahwism as a way to distinguish the community from outsiders, and the first representatives of the people of the land, the community's foil, are Yahwists themselves, and are also described as the group's "adversaries" (Ezra 4:1-5). The only other Persian-period writing that opposes marriages to foreign women is Malachi (see Mal. 2:10-16),[90] but this is not because it is from the same

likely reflects the original text than the OG, which says that she is not to live in the City of David, since it is more likely that a copyist changed an original בית דויד to עיר דויד in order to correspond to the action in the first part of the verse, which takes place in עיר דויד.) It is not clear that this has anything to do with his wife being a foreigner, however, and may only reflect the idea that a woman is not to be in proximity to the holy (so, e.g., Sara Japhet, *I and II Chronicles: A Commentary*, OTL [Louisville: Westminster/John Knox, 1993], 625–6). And while 2 Chron. 21:6 and 22:3, which suggest Athaliah bears some responsibility for the cultic sins of her husband and son, could be read as a warning of the pernicious influence of foreign women upon Judean families, the Chronicler is in general quite positive about Israelites from the Northern tribes; see, e.g., Williamson, *Israel in the Books of Chronicles*; Sara Japhet, *The Ideology of the Book of Chronicles and its Place in Biblical Thought*, BEATAJ 9 (Frankfurt am Main: Peter Lang, 1989), 318–24; Knoppers, *Jews and Samaritans*, 75–99. The problem the Chronicler identifies in the story of Athaliah has nothing to do with women from the North, but with the leadership of that region, which he or she consistently portrays as sinful; see Janzen, *Chronicles and the Politics of Davidic Restoration*, 132–5.

89. Third Isaiah remains as general as possible as to what constitutes ethical behavior, notes Jill Middlemas, so as to make the prerequisites for joining the assembly as minimal as possible; see her "Trito-Isaiah's Intra- and Internationalization: Identity Markers in the Second Temple Period," in Lipschits, Knoppers, and Oeming, eds, *Judah and the Judeans in the Achaemenid Period*, 105–25 (118–19).

90. Because Mal. 2:10-16 condemns marriage to "a daughter of a foreign god" (so MT rather than the freer translation of the OG—see the following note), some have seen the problem the verses appear to be addressing as worship of foreign gods. The passage, however, condemns Judah of being faithless to and abandoning "the wife of your youth," and if 2:10-16 attacks apostasy then it metaphorically portrays the community as husband and Yhwh as wife, a metaphor found nowhere else in the Hebrew Bible. The verses indict those within the community who marry women from outside of it in part because these women worship other gods; see, e.g., Herbert Donner, "Ein Vorschlag zum Verständnis von Maleachi 2,10-16," in *Von*

assembly faction as the author of Ezra–Nehemiah; the former emerges from a Levitical group and the latter from a group of elites associated in some fashion with the governor's office. Referring to the authors of both documents as belonging to an exclusivist group would be misleading, since those who accepted the messages broadcast by Ezra–Nehemiah may have had little in common with those who largely accepted the messages of Malachi. Malachi links marriages with outsiders to the problem of foreign worship (2:11),[91] while Ezra–Nehemiah does not,[92] and in Malachi it is problematic that such marriages have resulted in the divorce of

Gott reden: Beiträge zur Theologie und Exegese des Alten Testaments, ed. Dieter Vieweger and Ernst-Joachim Waschke (Neukirchen-Vluyn: Neukirchener, 1995), 97–103 (98); Markus Zehnder, "A Fresh Look at Malachi ii 13-16," *VT* 53 (2003): 224–59; Schaper, "The Priests of the Book of Malachi," 178–9; Tiemeyer, *Priestly Rites*, 193–5; Snyman, *Malachi*, 99–119.

91. Malachi 2:11 refers to the specific problem of marriage to "a daughter of a foreign god," which points to a concern with bringing non-Yahwists into the community; see the citations in the previous note. The LXX here has ἐπετήδευσεν εἰς θεοὺς ἀλλοτρίους "he invented other gods," which is likely an attempt to exegete, rather than indicative of a different Hebrew text; see Ming Him Ko, "Be Faithful to the Covenant: A Technical Translation of and Commentary on Malachi 2.10-16," *BT* 65 (2014): 34–48 (37). We see a similar choice on the part of the Syriac translator (*wrḥm wplḥ l'lh' nwkry'*), but this too is an exegetical choice rather than a reflection of a different text than the MT.

92. Neither Ezra 9–10, Neh. 10, nor Neh. 13 ever explicitly mentions apostasy as a factor that demands the expulsion of foreign spouses from the community. Nehemiah 13:23-27 comes closest to this, since here Nehemiah refers to foreign wives causing Solomon to sin, assumedly a reference to the story of 1 Kgs 11, where Solomon builds places for his foreign wives to worship their gods. But even 1 Kgs 11 does not say that other Israelites worshiped at those places, and Nehemiah does not make that claim, either. Some read the use of words such as מעל and תועבה in Ezra 9 as alluding to apostasy as at the root of the desire to expel the foreign wives (e.g., Becking, *Ezra, Nehemiah*, 38), but not only are both words used for many different kinds of sin, which would suggest they are poor choices for an author who wanted to specify foreign worship as a problem, but in Ezra 9–10 it is the very presence of the foreigners themselves, not their actions, that is the "abomination"; see Karrer, *Ringen um die Verfassung Judas*, 270–1. As Hannah Harrington argues, Ezra–Nehemiah was influenced by a movement that began in exile to associate holiness and purity with the people (*The Purity and Sanctuary of the Body*, 97; see 71–95 for a discussion of the development of such thought during the exile), and as the people are understood to be a metaphorical holy sanctuary, there is no place for foreigners, who are impure, that which does not belong in the sanctuary (106–8).

women within the community (2:15-16),[93] apparently done in order to facilitate intercommunal marriages. Malachi refers to these divorces as חמס "violence," and however Persian-period readers might have understood this specific condemnation, concern surrounding such divorces and the harm they cause the community and women in it does not motivate the objections to foreign marriages we read about in Ezra–Nehemiah. Since Malachi is concerned that marriages to outsiders will introduce non-Yahwistic worship into the community, then like Third Isaiah it uses Yahwism and not descent from Babylonian families to define community boundaries, which is a different definition of community identity than that of Ezra–Nehemiah.

It is likely not possible to identify every faction within the post-exilic temple community, but the preceding discussion shows we cannot simply see Ezra–Nehemiah's portrayal of group identity and empire as one accepted by everyone in the assembly; indeed, as far as we can tell, the views of the book in this regard reflected the opinion of only one very elite group. Because it is not clear if Ezekiel 40–48 is from the exilic or post-exilic period, this section of the chapter did not discuss this pro-Zadokite material that does not refer to empire at all; group identity in these chapters is defined by communal life that centers around a renewed temple cult. Ezekiel 44:6-9, like Ezra 9:6-15, uses language of holiness and impurity to refer pejoratively to foreigners, although in Ezekiel 44 this is specifically directed against the presence of foreigners in the sanctuary rather than in the community in general.[94] Ezekiel 40–48 allows

---

93. The first line of MT 2:16 reads כי שנא שלח "for he hates divorce," where Yhwh is assumedly the subject of the verb. On the other hand, 4QXII[a] reads כי אם שנתה שלח "if you hate [your wife], divorce [her]," a tradition reflected by the Targum (ארי אם סנית לה פטרה). The MT is almost certainly original, however; later copyists saw it as a difficult reading, since God permits divorce according to the law of Deut. 24:1-4, and altered the original text so that it did not conflict with Torah. The OG does not entirely reflect the wording of the MT, but like the MT it censures those who divorce; see David Clyde Jones, "A Note on the LXX of Malachi 2:16," *JBL* 109 (1990): 683–5.

94. Isaiah 56:1-8, which welcomes foreigners into the sanctuary, is often read as a reaction against Ezek. 44:6-9; see, e.g., Joachim Schaper, "Rereading the Law: Inner-Biblical Exegesis of Divine Oracles in Ezekiel 44 and Isaiah 56," in *Recht und Ethik im Alten Testament: Beiträge des Symposiums "Das Alte Testament und die Kultur der Moderne" anlässlich des 100. Geburtstags Gerhard von Rads*, ed. Bernard M. Levinson and Eckart Otto, ATM 13 (Münster: LIT Verlag, 2004), 125–44; Steven Shawn Tuell, "The Priesthood of the 'Foreigner': Evidence of Competing Politics in Ezekiel 44:1-14 and Isaiah 56:1-8," in *Constituting the Community: Studies on the Polity of Ancient Israel in Honor of S. Dean McBride, Jr.*, ed. John T. Strong and

that foreigners may live among Israel (47:21-23), even though they are not part of the community, and so unlike Ezra–Nehemiah it does not demand that they be physically separated and sent away from the temple assembly,[95] and it certainly does not justify their exclusion on the basis of a law sponsored by the empire as Ezra–Nehemiah does. It is also not clear how much if any of the pro-Aaronide Priestly material is exilic or post-exilic, but it was part of the post-exilic Pentateuch, and in P the only real empire is Egypt, an entity that oppresses Israel. In P's story, and that of the Pentateuch as a whole, Egypt and Pharaoh are God's antagonist and entirely at God's mercy, and God even controls Pharaoh's thoughts, leading to Egypt's ruin and the destruction of its army (e.g., Exod. 7:1-6; 12:12; 14:1-4, 26-27a, 28-29). This clearly is not the picture of empire, nor of the relationships between empire, God, and community, that we see in Ezra–Nehemiah. And, as the first section of this chapter notes, P portrays a series of divine covenants that include peoples not descended from Israel, and so P and the Holiness material in the Pentateuch depict foreigners as living within Israel and following the same law (e.g., Exod. 12:19, 49; Lev. 17:8; 22:18). Based on the material at our disposal, Ezra–Nehemiah's portrayal of a community as defined by its descent from Babylonian migrants who act (or should act) as loyal subjects to the foreign dynasty God has installed to carry out the divine will was not one shared by the majority of the assembly's groups. Ezra–Nehemiah's portrayals of empire and identity may have been amenable to some of those who associated themselves with the governor and his office, but we should not believe that they were widely accepted.

3. Post-exilic Prophetic Critiques of Empire

Ezra–Nehemiah's suspicion of prophecy is one that fits a writing representing an elite worldview. Prophecy certainly can be used to promote an elite agenda; that is the case of the Neo-Assyrian collections of prophecy, which always speak favorably of and to the king (see SAA 9), and this

---

Steven S. Tuell (Winona Lake, IN: Eisenbrauns, 2005), 183–204; Nihan, "Ethnicity and Identity," 77–8. However, it is also possible to see these verses in Ezekiel as a reaction against Third Isaiah's openness to foreigners in the sanctuary (so MacDonald, *Priestly Rule*, 146–8). The contrast between the two pericopes, however, points to a disagreement in the temple community about the place of foreigners in the temple.

95. Besides the use of the verb בדל "to separate" in regard to a physical separation of the community from foreigners in Ezra–Nehemiah (Ezra 6:21; 9:1; 10:8, 11, 16; Neh. 9:2; 10:29 [28]; 13:3), note also the appearance of the verb יצא in the Hiphil in this regard in Ezra 10:3, 19.

is also the case of the prophets Haggai and Zechariah, who promoted the goals and leadership of elite groups in the temple assembly. But the phenomenon of prophecy could also endanger the agendas of the ruling classes, since it could claim a divine origin for a challenge to the current status quo, and the first-person divine speech in Third Isaiah, for example, sharply critiques the ruling elite among the temple personnel. We can see, then, why the author of Ezra–Nehemiah wanted to avoid quoting divine speech and included a story that says prophets can be bribed to lie (Neh. 6:10-14). Yet prophets in Persian-period Judah did speak against empire, since we know that Haggai refers to its imminent overthrow and Zechariah alludes to its punishment, while Third Isaiah warns that any kingdom that does not serve the temple community and rebuild Judah will be destroyed (Isa. 60:12). In this section of the chapter we see that anti-imperial prophetic speech continued in Judah beyond the early Persian period, and even if some in the temple assembly preferred to see prophecy as a literary phenomenon—this generally seems to be the Chronicler's preference, for example—there is some evidence that prophets challenged the authority of empire throughout this era. While the author of Ezra–Nehemiah and the governor's office in general would have understood such oracles to be false prophecy, which is how Nehemiah the governor presents all prophetic speech directed against him, given the view of empire in the Persian-period community the previous section of the chapter surveyed, that would not have been the conclusion of everyone in the temple assembly.

In the middle of the fifth century Nehemiah refers to prophetic activity, and this tells us that prophecy was still a living cultural phenomenon at that time, as does the prophecy of Second Zechariah. It is not clear if Zechariah 9–14 is from the Persian or early Hellenistic period,[96] but even if it is from the later of those two eras it demonstrates that a tradition of prophets rejecting the claims of empire continued through the Persian period. Zechariah 9:1-8 refers to a divine defeat of Aramean and

---

96. For some scholars, the reference to יָוָן "Ionia, Greece" in 9:13 puts Second Zechariah in the time of Alexander or later; see, e.g., Floyd, *Minor Prophets*, 2:315–16; Ina Willi-Plein, *Haggai, Sacharja, Maleachi*, ZBKAT 24/4 (Zurich: Theologischer Verlag, 2007), 152. Others argue that Greeks were present in Palestine in the Persian period, that Persia's wars with Greek cities in Ionia and the mainland were well known, and that there is nothing that indicates a Hellenistic setting for these chapters; see, e.g., Bryan G. Curtis, "The *Mas'ot* Triptych and the Date of Zechariah 9–14: Issues in the Latter Formation of the Book of the Twelve," in Albertz, Nogalski, and Wöhrle, eds, *Perspectives on the Formulation of the Book of the Twelve*, 191–206; Boda, *The Book of Zechariah*, 34–6.

Phoenician cities, and while Second Zechariah as a whole says nothing about Persia, 9:13-15 refers to God using the people of Zion to defeat יון "Ionia," the Hebrew term for Greece, which, if Second Zechariah is Hellenistic, would point to a divine overthrow of the ruling empire. Zechariah 12:1-6 sounds much like this, referring to a "day" of divine action on which God will use אלפי יהודה "the clans/leaders[97] of Judah" to "devour" the peoples, and 14:1-9 discusses a divine victory over the nations at Jerusalem, at the conclusion of which "Yhwh will be king over all the earth."[98] The nations that survive will be forced to come to Jerusalem every year to celebrate Sukkoth (14:16-19),[99] a festival that, by the Persian period, the community had connected to the wilderness

---

97. The term אָלֻף, which derives from the root that means "thousand," can refer to clans, as it does in Zech. 9:7, where it appears in the context of a discussion of different groups of peoples, but it can also refer to leaders. So in Exod. 15:15, אלפים is in parallel with both אילים "leaders" and ישבים "inhabitants." Here in Zech. 12:6, the LXX translates the word with χιλίαρχοι, the Targum with רברבין, the Syriac with *rwrby'*, and the Vulgate with *duces*, all of which understand the word as referring to the leaders of Judah.

98. Zechariah 14 is sometimes seen as a later addition and described as part of a redactional summary of the Book of the Twelve; e.g., Odil Hannes Steck, *Der Abschluss der Prophetie im Alten Testament: Ein Versuch zur Frage der Vorgeschichte des Kanons*, BTS 17 (Neukirchen-Vluyn: Neukirchener, 1991), 43–60; Judith Gärtner, *Jesaja 66 und Sacharja 14 als Summe der Prophetie: Eine traditions- und redaktionsgeschichtliche Untersuchung zum Abschluss des Jesaja- und des Zwölfprophetenbuches*, WMANT 114 (Neukirchen-Vluyn: Neukirchener Verlag, 2006), 93–101. It is not really clear, however, that Zech. 14 truly does summarize the Book of the Twelve, or even the earlier parts of Zechariah. It breaks new ground, as Tiemeyer points out ("Death or Conversion," 4), but it also has enough in common with the rest of Second Zechariah—it focuses on a divine victory over the nations on "that day"—that we can understand it as coming from the writer responsible for the earlier chapters.

99. Jakob Wöhrle argues that 14:16-19 is from a pro-Gentile redactor, and so from a different hand than the one responsible for 14:1-15 with its much more negative view of the nations' future (*Der Abschluss des Zwölfprophetenbuches: Buchübergreifende Redaktionsprozesse in den späten Sammlungen*, BZAW 389 [Berlin: W. de Gruyter, 2008], 138). Seeing strands of redaction throughout the Book of the Twelve based on different views of the nations, as Wöhrle does, is unlikely to help us isolate additions to the various parts of Zechariah. Second Zechariah as a whole, just like the other parts of the Book of the Twelve, is insistent that Yhwh is sovereign over the nations, and so is able to both punish and have mercy on them. Given that ideological context, there is no contradiction between the divine defeat of the nations in 14:1-15 and the command that the survivors of the nations participate in Sukkoth in 14:16-19, a command that comes with a dire warning of punishment for the recalcitrant.

wandering (Lev. 23:42-43). The nations that survive destruction, then, are required to participate in a festival that in Ezra–Nehemiah is celebrated by the temple community alone (Ezra 3:4; Neh. 8:14-17) and that connects them with a period in Israel's history. So we see in Second Zechariah a continuation through the Persian period of an insistence that God will destroy empires and will welcome foreigners into at least some aspect of the temple assembly's cultic celebrations, views that are antithetical to those of Ezra–Nehemiah.

Elite groups who were worried about prophetic voices that refused to support their agendas had reason to sow suspicion of the institution, but they could also harness prophecy for their own benefit. The Chronicler, speaking for a pro-Davidic group within the assembly, does this when he or she asserts that the Levites were responsible for prophecy (1 Chron. 25:1), likely as part of the group's attempt to win Levitical support for a Davidic restoration by demonstrating the important roles the Davidides had bestowed on the Levites in the past, which, Chronicles implies, would be restored to them once the Davidides returned to power.[100] As a result, the Chronicler refers to the ancestors of some Levitical houses as "seers" (e.g., 2 Chron. 29:30; 35:15), but in Chronicles the ability to directly communicate with the divine is something that can be done by many figures, including Davidic kings (e.g., 1 Chron. 22:8; 28:3, 19; 2 Chron. 1:7-12), individual Israelites who are given no prophetic title (e.g., 1 Chron. 12:19 [18]; 2 Chron. 15:1), priests (2 Chron. 24:20), and even foreign suzerains (2 Chron. 35:20-21; 36:22-23). The picture of prophecy in Chronicles differs from that in Samuel–Kings, for not only does the Chronicler avoid biographical information about prophets and stories of their miraculous acts,[101] but these omissions appear related to his or her tendency to present most prophets as inspired only to speak to one particular situation, rather than as figures who spend their careers conveying divine messages.[102] Since the Chronicler believes the divine

---

100. See Harry V. Rooy, "Prophet and Society in the Persian Period According to Chronicles," in Eskenazi and Richards, eds, *Second Temple Studies 2*, 163–79 (179); Janzen, *Chronicles and the Politics of Davidic Restoration*, 95–117.

101. E.g., Pancratius C. Beentjes, *Tradition in Transformation in the Book of Chronicles*, SSN 52 (Leiden: Brill, 2008), 129–30; Gary N. Knoppers, "Democratizing Revelation? Prophets, Seers and Visionaries in Chronicles," in *Prophecy and Prophets in Ancient Israel: Proceedings of the Oxford Old Testament Seminar*, ed. John Day (New York: T&T Clark International, 2010), 391–409 (399–401).

102. Yairah Amit, "The Role of Prophecy and Prophets in the Chronicler's World," in Floyd and Haak, eds, *Prophets, Prophecy, and Prophetic Texts*, 80–101 (85–6).

spirit can empower anyone to speak on God's behalf, he or she appears to admit that prophecy is a widespread social phenomenon, but, as scholars frequently point out, prophetic voices in Chronicles largely function to interpret past events in accordance with the main emphases of the author's theology,[103] particularly his or her concept of immediate retribution (e.g., 2 Chron. 12:5, 7-9; 15:1-7; 21:12-15), the need for fidelity to the law and cult (e.g., 2 Chron. 21:11-15; 24:20), the importance of repentance (e.g., 2 Chron. 25:15-16; 28:9-11; 33:10), and the necessity to avoid foreign alliances (e.g., 2 Chron. 16:7-9; 19:1-3; 20:14-17, 35-37; 25:7-9). For the Chronicler, one can recognize a prophetic word as true if it corresponds to true theological ideas, which one can find in Chronicles. The Chronicler believes that God can lie to prophets (2 Chron. 18:18-22) and that prophets can lie to protect God's lies (18:12-14), but if a prophetic message corresponds to Chronistic theology then one can trust it absolutely.[104] It is no wonder, then, that the Chronicler claims that much of the information he or she has used to compose the work comes from prophetic writings (e.g., 1 Chron. 29:29-30; 2 Chron. 9:29; 13:22; 20:34), for he or she sees no difference between the kinds of things about which true prophets speak (and write) and the theological emphases of his or her book.

So while the Chronicler might seem to broaden the power of prophecy by claiming that God could inspire anyone, he or she actually works to limit it by presenting it as something that will not disagree with his or her own worldview.[105] For Chronicles, prophecy is a written as well as

103. E.g., Japhet, *The Ideology of the Book of Chronicles*, 176–9; William M. Schniedewind, "Prophets and Prophecy in the Books of Chronicles," in *The Chronicler as Historian*, ed. M. Patrick Graham, Kenneth G. Hoglund, and Steven L. McKenzie, JSOTSup 238 (Sheffield: Sheffield Academic Press, 1997), 204–24 (212–13, 219–21); Amit, "The Role of Prophecy," 87–8.

104. In the case of 2 Chron. 18, part of Jehoshaphat's story, the Chronicler saw no need for him to consult a prophet in order to determine whether or not he and Ahab should go into battle. An important aspect of Chronistic theology is the condemnation of foreign alliances, which is what Jehoshaphat was making with Ahab (18:3), and, in fact, prophets in Chronicles often condemn such alliances. As far as the Chronicler is concerned, God always provides victory for Davidic kings who are faithful to the law and defeat for those who are wicked, and so Jehoshaphat needed no prophet to tell him that he would face defeat in a battle he entered as Ahab's ally, something made clear in a prophetic message he receives immediately afterward (2 Chron. 19:1-3).

105. So the case is not quite that the Chronicler was presenting his or her own work as having prophetic status (contra Steven J. Schweitzer, "Exile, Empire, and Prophecy: Reframing Utopian Concerns in Chronicles," in *Worlds that Could Not Be: Utopia in Chronicles, Ezra and Nehemiah*, ed. Steven J. Schweitzer and Frauke

a spoken phenomenon, and although we have no good evidence that the written prophetic sources to which the book refers actually existed, the Chronicler did know of biblical prophetic writings in some form. In 2 Chron. 15:2-7, for example, Azariah speaks with divine inspiration, and for this otherwise unknown figure the Chronicler created a monologue that draws from Jer. 31:16; Amos 3:9; Hos. 3:4; Zeph. 3:16; and Zech. 8:10,[106] and there are other examples like this in the book.[107] Such a selective use of the developing prophetic corpus allowed the Chronicler to ignore aspects of those works that disagreed in any way with his or her own view of things;[108] there is a "domestication" of prophecy in Chronicles,[109] one that reflects a written collection of prophecy, and the process of creating this collection was already underway in the early Persian period, as we see when Zechariah draws on the concept of a seventy-year exile (1:12; 7:5) from Jer. 25:11, or when he uses language from Isa. 11:1 and/or Jer. 23:5 about a figure called "the Branch" (3:8; 6:12).[110] A written collection of prophecy could be seen as a supplement to and complement of a written Torah,[111] and for elite groups concerned that other community factions

---

Uhlenbruch, LHBOTS 620 [London: Bloomsbury, 2016], 81–104 [97–8]), but that one can judge the validity of prophetic utterances or writings based on their correspondence to the Chronistic worldview.

106. Beentjes, *Tradition in Transformation*, 137–9; Ehud Ben Zvi, "Chronicles and its Reshaping of Memories of Monarchic Period Prophets: Some Observations," in Boda and Beal, eds, *Prophets, Prophecy, and Ancient Israelite Historiography*, 167–88 (185 n. 39).

107. See Amber K. Warhurst, "The Chronicler's Use of the Prophets," in *What Was Authoritative for Chronicles?*, ed. Ehud Ben Zvi and Diana Edelman (Winona Lake, IN: Eisenbrauns, 2011), 165–81.

108. Christopher Begg argues that the Chronicler largely avoids referring to individual prophets that he or she would have known from written sources available in the Persian period because he or she would have disagreed with many aspects of their theologies ("The Classical Prophets in the Chronistic History," *BZ* 32 [1988]: 100–107).

109. So Raymond Kuntzmann, "La fonction prophétique en 1–2 Chroniques: Du ministère de la Parole au service de l'institution Communautaire," in *Ich bewirke das Heil und erschaffe das Unheil (Jesaja 45,7): Studien zur Botschaft der Propheten*, ed. Friedrich Diedrich and Bernd Willmes, FzB 88 (Würzburg: Echter Verlag, 1998), 245–58 (252).

110. L. Stephen Cook, *On the Question of the "Cessation of Prophecy" in Ancient Judaism*, TSAJ 145 (Tübingen: Mohr Siebeck, 2011), 51–2.

111. E.g., Joseph Blenkinsopp, "'We pay no heed to heavenly voices': The 'End of Prophecy' and the Formation of the Canon," in *Biblical and Humane: A Festschrift for John F. Priest*, ed. Linda Bennett Elder, David L. Barr, and Elizabeth Struthers Malbon (Atlanta: Scholars Press, 1996), 19–31 (24–8); Erhard S. Gerstenberger,

could summon the cultural power of prophecy to challenge the status quo, this creation of prophecy as something written comes with the added benefits that it limits prophecy to the past and to documents that exist within a literary culture controlled by the elite.[112] In the Persian period, prophecy becomes, at least in part, a written phenomenon that provides readers with information about the past, as is the case when the Chronicler invents prophetic sources that the book says provide information about the Davidides, as well as something that fourth-century authors could carve up and reassemble into entirely new messages, as the Chronicler does in creating an oracle for Azariah in 2 Chronicles 15.

Yet the prophecy we see in Second Zechariah from the later Persian or early Hellenistic period tells us that, despite the attempts of some factions in the assembly to domesticate it, the institution continued to exist and to challenge the claims of empire and of local community leadership, and, as Jason Silverman notes, we should not assume that everyone in the Persian period encountered prophecy as a written rather than an oral phenomenon.[113] Zechariah 11:4-17 condemns the shepherding or leadership of the people, and regardless of how one identifies the three shepherds or leaders whom 11:8 says have already been removed,[114] 11:16-17 refers to a contemporary

"Prophetie in den Chronikbüchern: Jahwes Wort in zweierlei Gestalt?," in *Schriftprophetie: Festschrift für Jörg Jeremias zum 65. Geburtstag*, ed. Friedhelm Hartenstein, Jutta Krispenz, and Aaron Schart (Neukirchen-Vluyn: Neukirchener Verlag, 2004), 351–67.

112. See, e.g., Blenkinsopp, "'We pay no heed,'" 23–4; Diana Edelman, "From Prophets to Prophetic Books: The Fixing of the Divine Word," in *The Production of Prophecy: Constructing Prophecy and Prophets in Yehud*, ed. Diana V. Edelman and Ehud Ben Zvi, BW (London: Equinox, 2009), 29–54 (29); Martti Nissinen, "Prophecy and Omen Divination: Two Sides of the Same Coin," in *Divination and Interpretation of Signs in the Ancient World*, ed. Amar Annus, OIS 6 (Chicago: The Oriental Institute of the University of Chicago, 2010), 341–51 (344–5).

113. Silverman, *Persian Royal–Judaean Elite Engagements*, 22.

114. A partial list of attempts to identify them includes Persian officials in Judah (Robert L. Foster, "Shepherds, Sticks, and Social Destabilization: A Fresh Look at Zechariah 11:4-17," *JBL* 126 [2007]: 735–53 [740–3]), leaders in the local civil leadership (Curtis, *Up the Steep and Stony Road*, 200–201), three Persian kings (Sweeney, *The Twelve Prophets*, 2:677–8), the final three kings of Judah (Petterson, "The Shape of the Davidic Hope," 233–5), or the three offices of king, priest, and prophet (Michael R. Stead, "The Three Shepherds: Reading Zechariah 11 in the Light of Jeremiah," in *A God of Faithfulness: Essays in Honour of J. Gordon McConville on his 60th Birthday*, ed. Jamie A. Grant, Alison Lo, and Gordon J. Wenham, LHBOTS 538 [New York: T&T Clark International, 2011], 149–65). Regardless of who these individuals might have been, the pericope is clearly critiquing some level of the leadership of the community.

or imminent shepherd of the people who is אליל "worthless," and this may be an allusion to the imperial king or to a figure in the local leadership of the assembly such as the high priest. The creation of a prophetic corpus in the Persian period did not bring an end to prophecy that challenged the elite, and we cannot conclude that a push to limit prophecy to something written was the work of figures who held the same pro-imperial ideology as the author of Ezra–Nehemiah. No work among the prophetic writings ever refers to Persia, but those books do insist that God controls and can punish and overthrow empires and peoples (e.g., Isa. 13–23; Jer. 46–51; Ezek. 25–32; Amos 1; Obadiah; Nah. 2–3; Zeph. 2), just as Persian-period prophets proclaim, and it would not have been difficult for members of the temple assembly, if they were so inclined, to understand such passages as communicating a very different picture of the empire and the assembly's place as a colonized people than Ezra–Nehemiah does. Merely claiming that prophecy was a matter of the past and something confined to written documents would not, in and of itself, prevent community members from accessing those writings to challenge a pro-imperial ideology, and factions in the assembly not disposed to adopt Ezra–Nehemiah's picture of community identity as defined through its place as a group that needed Achaemenid leadership could appeal to prophetic voices like the one that speaks in Second Zechariah, or to the oracles against the nations in the developing prophetic corpus. Even Nehemiah the governor understood prophecy to be a contemporary, albeit dangerous, phenomenon, and so both he and the author of Ezra–Nehemiah had a need to disparage it, but Judeans from other assembly factions, as we have seen, continued to embrace it as something that could challenge imperial claims like the ones Ezra–Nehemiah so fervently promotes.

4. Conclusion: The End of History and the Last King, Part 2

If modern readers find key aspects of Ezra–Nehemiah's worldview unpalatable, it would appear that the same could be said for many of the author's contemporaries in the Judean temple community. It is unlikely that any other Persian-period biblical writing came from a group quite as elevated in the political hierarchy as the one that produced Ezra–Nehemiah, a work that derives from the governor's office, or perhaps from a group of elite figures closely associated with and dependent upon its links to the governor's power and resources, and it does not seem that the book's presentation of the Achaemenids as the necessary form of leadership appointed by God was broadly shared in the assembly. This is not because there was some sort of divide in the community between groups inspired by prophetic visionaries and an entrenched political status quo, since the chapter has shown that some prophets spoke for elite groups in the assembly, but because the different social locations of other factions of the assembly, elite or otherwise, had somewhat different worldviews than that of Ezra–Nehemiah's author. Even the Chronicler, who was willing to acknowledge the legitimacy of the Achaemenids, is unwilling to define community identity through the dynasty's ideology and to make the community's status as a colonized people the basis of the assembly's sense of self. Other factions in the temple community appear far more dismissive of imperial claims, and the groups that produced Haggai and First Zechariah looked to a divine punishment and even overthrow of empire, while the more marginalized one from which Third Isaiah emerged understood the purpose of empire as a power that would serve the community under threat of divine punishment. As far as we can tell, Malachi's Levitical group ignored empire altogether when they thought about community identity, since for Malachi the assembly should be defined by Yahwism and righteousness, especially proper attention to the cult. The Chronicler's Davidic group may have wanted to avoid offending the Achaemenids, but it tied community identity to Judah's Davidic past, not their colonized present, and its ideal picture of the community's future was of a restoration of righteous Davidides promoting proper Yahwistic cult and ruling with the assistance of priests, Levites, and the assembly.

The Chronicler's Davidic faction may have agreed with Ezra–Nehemiah's group that Achaemenid rule was not negotiable, but that has a very different meaning in Chronicles, where it is unimportant, than it does in Ezra–Nehemiah, where it is the key to the community's survival. The Chronicler does not seem to believe that Persian rule would last forever, whereas in Ezra–Nehemiah this is of utmost necessity, for in that author's worldview the community is too unrighteous to survive without them. The Achaemenids are history's last kings in that book, all loyal to God, just as they themselves claimed, but in Chronicles Neco the Egyptian was Judah's suzerain at one point (2 Chron. 36:1-4), and he was succeeded by Nebuchadnezzar the Babylonian (36:6, 10, 13), who was followed in that role by Cyrus the Persian (36:22-23). The larger empire or dynasty did not matter to the Chronicler, any more than it does to the author of Second Zechariah, who also had pro-Davidic leanings.[115] The most important king

---

115. In Zech. 12:1–13:1, the prophet says that, after a divine victory against the nations, "the house of David will be like God, like the angel of Yhwh" as it leads the inhabitants of Jerusalem (12:8). The same section of the writing, however, indicts "the house of David" along with the inhabitants of Jerusalem in the case of "the one

in Second Zechariah, however, is not from the house of David or from any empire, for, the prophet says, after God defeats all the nations, "Yhwh will be king over all the earth" (Zech. 14:9). In a very different way than Achaemenid ideology, Zechariah 14 also refers to an end of history, in which night will be turned into day and waters will flow from Jerusalem (14:6-10) and those among the nations who have survived defeat at Yhwh's hands will be forced to worship the king of the cosmos at Sukkoth every year (14:16). It is possible that Second Zechariah was written in the early Hellenistic period, but even if so it reflects ideas present within the Judean community from the beginning of the Persian period, the kind of thing we can see in Haggai when God refers to an imminent overthrow of "the kingdoms of the nations," and in Third Isaiah when the prophet refers to the creation of a new heavens and earth and the replacement of the sun and moon by the light of Yhwh, which would suggest that these sorts of beliefs were held by different assembly factions throughout the Persian period.

The divine culmination of history in Second Zechariah—history as its readers experienced it, at any rate, history before God's cosmic alteration of it—involves God's overwhelming victory over the nations at Jerusalem (14:1-4) and a divine torture of the nations' survivors after that victory (14:12-15). The massive levels of violence inherent in such divine actions makes Second Zechariah an unlikely candidate to serve as a replacement for Ezra–Nehemiah's pro-imperial worldview for modern readers concerned with the way Ezra–Nehemiah has God, divine law, people, and community identity serve the interests of empire and Judah's elite, for Second Zechariah simply replaces legitimate imperial violence with legitimate divine violence.[116] We would imagine, however, that long before Ezra–Nehemiah was composed, different groups in the assembly found advantages to working closely with the governor and adopting aspects of Achaemenid ideology, just as Ezra–Nehemiah's group did. The depictions of divine violence in the writings this chapter discusses,

---

whom they stabbed" (12:10), a crime that will demand purification (13:1). Second Zechariah, then, is unlikely to have been produced by the group known as "the house of David," but its faction maintained some sort of place for future Davidic rule.

116. Tat-siong Benny Liew makes the same point in regard to the Gospel of Mark which, he argues, transfers the Roman understanding of legitimate imperial violence to that which Mark's author associates with the eschatological Kingdom of God (*What Is Asian American Biblical Hermeneutics? Reading the New Testament*, Intersections [Honolulu: University of Hawai'i Press, 2008], 23–5), and Carol Newsom comes to a similar conclusion in regard to the language of imperial power in Daniel 7 ("'Resistance is futile!': The Ironies of Danielic Resistance to Empire," *Int* 71 [2017]: 167–77).

then, reflect reactions of different assembly factions against such groups that accepted the empire's ideology, or at least the versions of it the Achaemenid administration in Judah would have insisted on, the sort of thing we see in Ezra–Nehemiah. They reflect the refusal of some, probably most, community members to be defined as a sinful colonized people with a failed local governance who were unable to survive without Achaemenid leadership, at the mercy of imperial violence should they disobey the law of God and the law of the king, and as far as they understood things this meant they had to appeal to an entity more powerful than Persia who could overthrow the empire. The conclusions at which Second Zechariah arrives in regard to the end of history and the last king are diametrically opposed to those of Ezra–Nehemiah, but echo the sort of worldview we see in Haggai and First Zechariah, where God controls and even overthrows kingdoms. Malachi, on the other hand, avoids discussing empire altogether, as Chronicles and Third Isaiah largely do. The Chronicler's faction saw the Davidides as the only dynasty with which God had made an eternal covenant, and so empire is no more than a footnote to its story. The Chronicler looks to no vast cosmic change such as other Persian-period groups did, but if one could talk about the concept of a last king in the context of Chronicles it would be the righteous Davidides that the author believed would return to the throne, having learned the important lessons from the past Chronicles narrates so that they could all enact proper leadership in regard to cult and law in the same faithful manner. Third Isaiah also relegates empire to a footnote of history, and Malachi can avoid mentioning it altogether, because these two writings are focused on what they identify as injustices propagated by community factions more powerful than their own. Both of these works appeal to a coming divine judgment of the community, but not because the whole assembly is inherently sinful, which is Ezra–Nehemiah's view of things, but because parts of it are, and judgment does not mean the community's annihilation, as it does in Ezra–Nehemiah, but rather the vindication of the righteous. The end of history in Ezra–Nehemiah is a concept drawn from Achaemenid ideology, and unrelated to the notion of divine judgment; Achaemenid rule of an inherently unrighteous colonized people who cannot, left to their own devices, act in the way God and king want them to act, is what keeps this judgment from destroying the community. But the sort of end of history we see in Third Isaiah, Malachi, and Second Zechariah derives from earlier Yahwistic concepts of God's utter control of the cosmos, and could not seem less like the end of history in eternal imperial rule that is the inevitable result of Ezra–Nehemiah's worldview, since the factions behind those writings refused to use imperial ideology to define their community.

Chapter 6

CONCLUSION:
THE STRUGGLE OVER COMMUNITY IDENTITY
IN THE PERSIAN PERIOD

The previous chapter has shown that there was no single definition of community that all factions of the post-exilic assembly would have agreed upon, although the available evidence leads us to the conclusion that most assembly members would not have accepted Ezra–Nehemiah's. For one thing, Ezra–Nehemiah's portrayal of the temple community is a relentlessly negative one, with the exception of the generation of Ezra 1–6, the group of Persia's loyal Yahwists who had lived at the center of empire and been commissioned by the king, defined in important part by their loyalty to the king and their unique access to the cult, which corresponds to Cyrus's command that they alone must restore it. The picture of the later generation as an inherently sinful people takes up much more space in Ezra–Nehemiah, however, and this picture served imperial interests, since it provided a justification for the necessity of Achaemenid rule, and so community identity in Ezra–Nehemiah has much in common with the Achaemenid understanding of the nature of the colonized. The notion that all of Israel is inherently disobedient was not the invention of Ezra–Nehemiah's author, and to encounter this idea he or she could have looked to a Yahwistic writing such as the Deuteronomistic History, for example, which portrays the people as a whole as "rebellious" and "stiff-necked" or stubborn, turning to idolatry from the moment God saved them from Egypt (Deut. 9:4–10:5, and see also 10:16 and 31:27) and unable to learn any lesson from the divine punishment that always followed upon their sin after entering the land (Judg. 3:7–13:1). That is, in fact, just how the prayer of Neh. 9:6-37 describes the community, but the author of Ezra–Nehemiah fused this particular portrayal of the people from earlier Yahwistic traditions with Achaemenid ideology. It is the kings of Persia, whom Yhwh appointed, who are ultimately responsible for keeping this wayward people in adherence to the law, for they send the law to Judah and take responsibility for establishing judges who will enforce it, and they send good leaders from the center of the empire to help the Judeans at the world's margins survive, despite their tendency to sin.

The notion that obedience to Yahwistic law is the basis upon which God will judge the people was no innovation on the part of Ezra–Nehemiah's author, either, but Ezra–Nehemiah is the only biblical writing that makes a foreign king responsible for promoting and enforcing the law, and by claiming that it is part of an imperial apparatus in which the same judges oversee "the law of your God and the law of the king," Yahwistic law works hand-in-hand with royal law and command to govern the community. This is why two key aspects that define the ideal community of Ezra–Nehemiah are loyalty to the king and obedience to the law, for they amount to the same thing, something that reflects the correspondence of royal and divine law in Achaemenid ideology, which allows the king to claim divine support for his violent punishments of those who oppose his will. In Ezra–Nehemiah, Yhwh is the God who gives all the kingdoms of the earth to Persia and who speaks and acts through the Persian kings, who are the ones who take responsibility for building Yhwh's temple and authorizing Yhwh's law. There is no sense in Ezra–Nehemiah that Yhwh would ever command rebellion against Persia, nor any sense that Yhwh's law threatens Persian interests in any way. In Ezra 7–Nehemiah 13, however, there are places where the book points to the fear of destruction for disobedience, implicitly validating any violence the Achaemenids might enact against the community that repetitively returns to its sin. Whatever violent measures the Achaemenids may choose to visit upon Judah, whether for violations of divine or royal law—there being no real difference between them—will be richly deserved by a people who have always been unfaithful. Were it not for the leaders whom the Achaemenids had sent, in fact, this destruction might already have taken place.

So the assembly that readers see in Ezra 7–Nehemiah 13 is simply one more of the Persians' colonized peoples, inherently evil and in need of both the Achaemenids' imperial leadership and the fear inspired by the dynasty's punishments of peoples disloyal to them to stave off destruction. It is a portrayal not merely inspired by Achaemenid ideology, but one that serves Achaemenid interests, since it makes the dynasty's rule seem necessary, rebellion appear the equivalent of sacrilege, royal command correspond to divine law, and imperial violence of any sort the result of divine order. No other faction of the post-exilic temple assembly was, as far as we know, willing to present the community and its relationship to empire in this way, which is why divine judgment is something that, among the Persian-period biblical writings, only Ezra–Nehemiah claims must be avoided at all costs. All of the other texts that can be dated with some certainty to the Persian period report failures on the part of some within the community—even Chronicles, which looks to Judah's past, refers to Davidic sin—but for all of the factions from which these other writings emerged divine intervention is part of their future hope. This is the case because, in the views of those groups, the community in its entirety is not inherently sinful, as it is in Ezra–Nehemiah where it must be so in order to justify continued Achaemenid rule. Third Isaiah and Malachi criticize the existing leadership in the temple, but because of their respective factions' beliefs in upcoming divine intervention, they hold out hope for change. Haggai looks forward to a divine cosmic shaking that will overthrow kingdoms, and First Zechariah to a punishment of empire. Third Isaiah foresees a new heavens and earth that will result in the vindication of God's true servants, a group on the assembly's margins, and Malachi points to such a vindication (although with a different group in mind) on a day of divine judgment when a purification of the Levites allows them to replace a failed Aaronide priesthood, while Second Zechariah's faction awaited a divine defeat and torture of the nations that would conclude with Yhwh's kingship over the world. Chronicles avoids any overt predictions of divine intervention in the future, yet the work refers to so many acts on Yhwh's part in support of the Davidides (e.g., 1 Chron. 10:13-14; 2 Chron. 13:13-20; 14:8-14 [9-15]; 17:3-6, 10-11; 20:1-20) that we cannot rule out the possibility that there were some in his or her pro-Davidic community who believed God would intervene in history yet again to fulfill the eternal covenant with David. For Ezra–Nehemiah, however, any sort of massive divine intervention could only mean the community's inherently sinful nature had caused God to punish them. The community's future in the book lies precisely in a lack of major change and the continuation of Achaemenid rule that would ensure the assembly's fidelity to God, something that corresponds to fidelity to the king who speaks and acts on God's behalf.

Another way in which Ezra–Nehemiah's view of community identity differs from those of the other Persian-period biblical writings is in regard to its social boundaries. We can use the terms "temple community" or "temple assembly" to refer to the group of lay and clerical ancestral houses who supported and governed the temple in Jerusalem and exercised some power in the local administration of Persian-period

Judah, but even in this post-exilic context the term "community" can be used in a broader sense as referring to an in-group which need not be understood to be coterminous with the assembly. Ezra–Nehemiah does not use Yahwism to distinguish the community from outsiders, and so in the book Sanballat and Tobiah are foreigners. The narrative of Ezra–Nehemiah itself shows us, however, that not all within the assembly—not even the high priest, in fact—agreed with that construction of community. Sanballat may not have been a member of the Jerusalem temple assembly, for he was the governor of a different province which by the mid-fifth century had already built, or was about to build, its own Yahwistic sanctuary at Gerizim, but the high priest in Jerusalem saw nothing untoward in forging a bond of marriage between their two families (Neh. 13:28), just as other community members did with Tobiah's family (6:17-19). In their eyes, Sanballat and Tobiah were Yahwists and still part of their community writ large, even if they were not part of the temple assembly. From the point of view of the governor's office and those tied closely to it, however, the difficulty with allowing this broader concept of community to include Yahwists outside of Judah and its assembly as part of their community rather than as adversaries is that such figures could then exercise influence within the group with whom the governor had to negotiate in matters of local concern. Nehemiah complains about this directly (Neh. 6:17-19), but the first time Ezra–Nehemiah raises the issue of intermarriage as a problem, the author couches it in the language of holiness and impurity (Ezra 9), portraying outsiders as figures who must be expelled from the community because foreign impurity and community holiness are antithetical. Nehemiah too understands foreigners to be ritually impure (Neh. 13:9, 28-29), a status that he believes prohibits them from marrying into priestly families or entering the sanctuary, even if they are Yahwists. It is notable, then, that Malachi and his Levitical group oppose intermarriage not on the basis of the impurity of those outside of the assembly, but because of the potential of non-Yahwistic worship that accompanies it and because it has led to the divorce of women within the temple assembly, something that Malachi sees as damaging. For Malachi, Yahwists are part of the community in its larger sense, even those Yahwists who are not members of the temple assembly in Jerusalem.

To some degree, one could say that the Chronicler's faction held a view like that of Malachi's. Chronicles portrays pre-exilic Northerners as participating in an illegitimate cult that promotes idolatry and does not employ the Levites and priests God chose to lead worship (e.g., 2 Chron. 11:14-15; 13:8-9), but because the Chronicler considers Northerners to be as much a part of Israel as Judeans are[1]—as much a part of the true community, in other words—they should come to Jerusalem where proper Yahwistic worship takes place (2 Chron. 11:16-17; 30:4-11).[2] The Chronicler's negative portrayal of the Northern cult likely reflects his or her view of Gerizim as an illegitimate shrine, a position that he or she may have adopted to gain support from groups in the Jerusalem assembly who saw Gerizim as a rival, but one that also allowed the author to attack the Northern leadership as illegitimate because of its support and promotion of this temple (e.g., 2 Chron. 11:14-15; 13:8-9; 19:2; 21:12-13; 28:1-4), since characterizing the leadership there as illegitimate potentially opens the future of the North to Davidic rule. But in suggesting that Northerners should recognize the sole validity of the cult in Jerusalem, the Chronicler not only accepts them as part of the true community, but potentially also believes that membership in the temple assembly should be open to them as well, and so his or her faction's understanding of community is far more expansive than that of Ezra–Nehemiah, since it includes Samarian Yahwists and could even be understood to imply that they should have some role in Jerusalem's governing assembly once they abandon Gerizim. Third Isaiah's group had an even broader understanding of community, since they believed בני נכר "foreigners" could join the temple assembly (Isa. 56:6-8), a concept that extended beyond Yahwists who were currently outside of the assembly, such as ones in Samaria, but also included peoples whose ancestors had not traditionally worshiped Yhwh (66:18-19).

Ezra–Nehemiah, however, creates a genealogical boundary around the concept of community that claims everyone in the temple assembly was descended from Babylonian migrants, and its understanding of community extends no further than this. This genealogical boundary thus corresponds to a cultic one, limiting the community to those with a right to participate in rituals at the Jerusalem temple, something confined to the assembly

---

1. See, e.g., Williamson, *Israel in the Books of Chronicles*; Japhet, *The Ideology of the Book of Chronicles*, 318–24; Yigal Levin, "Who Was the Chronicler's Audience? A Hint from his Genealogies," *JBL* 122 (2003): 229–45 (238); Louis Jonker, "Who Constitutes Society? Yehud's Self-understanding in the Late Persian Era as Reflected in the Books of Chronicles," *JBL* 127 (2008): 703–24 (715); Knoppers, *Jews and Samaritans*, 75–99.

2. So, e.g., Gary N. Knoppers, "Mt. Gerizim and Mt. Zion: A Study in the Early History of Samaritans and Jews," *SR* 34 (2005): 309–38 (315–16, 323–4); Ben Zvi, *History, Literature and Theology in the Book of Chronicles*, 198–9; Louis Jonker, "Textual Identities in the Books of Chronicles: The Case of Jehoram's History," in Knoppers and Ristau, eds, *Community Identity in Judean Historiography*, 197–217.

alone. This is a view that suited the governor of Judah and the elite of the community who wanted to be seen as his allies, since it denied elites from outside of the province an important means of exercising political influence in Judah, but it is possible that, in the fourth century, Ezra–Nehemiah's faction may have been the only one with that particular understanding of the assembly's origins and that narrow of a definition of community. Dalit Rom-Shiloni rightly points out that Ezekiel already distinguishes in the exilic period between the Judeans in Babylonia, whom Ezekiel recognizes as the true community, and Judean families who remained in the land, whom Ezekiel identifies as the people God rejected, and Rom-Shiloni sees a reflection of this exclusive understanding of community identity in Ezra–Nehemiah.[3] Ezra–Nehemiah, like Ezekiel, does limit the picture of the true Israel to the exiles and their descendants; they alone are the sole heirs to Israel's history, existing in a covenant relationship with God, who has punished them less than they deserve (compare, e.g., Ezek. 20:1-44 and Ezra 9:6-15; Neh. 9:6-37). The author of Ezra–Nehemiah, however, ensured that this view of community corresponded to imperial ideology. Restoration to the land has not made the community righteous, and had God not ordered the construction of the temple, they would have been better off remaining in Babylonia, at the imperial center. After the first generation of colonizers sent by Cyrus, the community in Ezra–Nehemiah is as unrighteous as their pre-exilic ancestors, and so depends upon the Achaemenids not only for their happiness but for their very existence. The book may have an exclusive view of community, but the post-exilic temple assembly that has spent generations in the land is not inherently better than the peoples around them, Yahwistic or otherwise, and they are law-abiding only because God has appointed the Achaemenids to enforce the law, to send leaders to curb their sinful impulses, and to threaten them with destruction. Ezra–Nehemiah's genealogical boundary that defines community allows its faction to link the assembly to the center of empire, the origin of the ideal generation of Ezra 1–6, and to see it as the גולה, the group that is still in exile in some sense, still guilty of the same crimes as its ancestors, a claim the book makes at numerous points (Ezra 9:6-15; Neh. 9:33; 13:17-18).

It is tempting to believe that Ezra–Nehemiah largely represents post-exilic beliefs in regard to community identity because it is the only history-like work from the Persian period that claims to report what went on at that time. However, its author has constructed an identity for the temple community that suits imperial interests and those of Judah's

---

3. Rom-Shiloni, *Exclusive Inclusivity*, 34–41, 144–96.

governor and the community elite who depended upon him for their positions. Ezra–Nehemiah emphasizes the community's need for royal rule and the presence of the king's representative, the need to keep royal and divine law, the implicit threat of imperial retaliation for failures in that regard, and the danger of entering into marriage alliances that would give groups outside of the governor's jurisdiction political leverage in the province. It is certainly possible that an event like that narrated in Ezra 9–10 truly did happen, and the temple assembly largely agreed that outsiders, defined as people not descended from Babylonian immigrants, truly are impure and must be expelled from the community. On the other hand, there is nothing else in Persian-period biblical writings that suggests the temple assembly broadly agreed with Ezra–Nehemiah's definition of community, and the story may be more of a reflection of what some associated with the governor's office would have liked to see happen than an event that actually took place. In the same way, the book's insistence that it was the Achaemenids who authorized Torah, making it an official part of imperial law so that there was no distinction between loyalty to Yhwh and loyalty to the king, sounds much more like the wish of an elite who benefitted from their connection to empire than a widely accepted truth in Persian-period Judah. For anyone interested in the history and beliefs of the larger post-exilic assembly, or troubled by Ezra–Nehemiah's insistent validation of imperial rule, ideology, and violence, it is important to understand the imperial ideology and the interests of the local elite that shaped the construction of Ezra–Nehemiah. When we contrast its portrayals of empire and community with those of other Persian-period biblical writings, it becomes clear that the depictions of these things in Ezra–Nehemiah reflect only the view of a small but locally powerful minority.

Bibliography

Abadie, P. "Le fonctionnement symbolique de la figure de David dans l'œuvre du Chroniste." *Transeu* 7 (1994): 143–51.
Achenbach, Reinhard. *Die Vollendung der Tora: Studien zur Redaktionsgeschichte des Numeribuches im Kontext von Hexateuch und Pentateuch*. BZABR 3. Wiesbaden: Harrassowitz, 2003.
Adams, Douglas Q. "Ask." Page 33 in *Encyclopedia of Indo-European Culture*. Edited by Douglas Q. Adams and J. P. Mallory. London: Fitzroy Dearborn, 1997.
Adams, Douglas Q., and J. P. Mallory. "Speak." Pages 534–36 in *Encyclopedia of Indo-European Culture*. Edited by J. P. Mallory and Douglas Q. Adams. London: Fitzroy Dearborn, 1997.
Ahmadi, Amir. "Avestan *xratu-*." *IrSt* 47, no. 6 (2014): 1–11.
Albertz, Rainer. "The Controversy about Judean versus Israelite Identity and the Persian Government: A New Interpretation of the Bagoses Story (*Jewish Antiquities* XI.297-301)." Pages 483–504 in *Judah and the Judeans in the Achaemenid Period: Negotiating Identity in an International Context*. Edited by Oded Lipschits, Gary N. Knoppers, and Manfred Oeming. Winona Lake, IN: Eisenbrauns, 2011.
Albertz, Rainer. "More and Less than a Myth: Reality and Significance of Exile for the Political, Social, and Religious History of Judah." Pages 20–33 in *By the Irrigation Canals of Babylon: Approaches to the Study of Exile*. Edited by John J. Ahn and Jill Middlemas. LHBOTS 526. New York: T&T Clark International, 2012.
Albertz, Rainer. "The Thwarted Restoration." Pages 1–17 in *Yahwism after the Exile: Perspectives on Israelite Religion in the Persian Era*. Edited by Rainer Albertz and Bob Becking. STAR 5. Assen: Royal Van Gorcum, 2003.
Altmann, Peter. *Economics in Persian-Period Biblical Texts: Their Interactions with Economic Developments in the Persian Period and Earlier Biblical Traditions*. FAT 109. Tübingen: Mohr Siebeck, 2016.
Amit, Yairah. "The Role of Prophecy and Prophets in the Chronicler's World." Pages 80–101 in *Prophets, Prophecy, and Prophetic Texts in Second Temple Judaism*. Edited by Michael H. Floyd and Robert D. Haak. LHBOTS 427. New York: T&T Clark International, 2006.
Anderson, Cheryl B. "Reflections in an Interethnic/Racial Era on Interethnic/Racial Marriages in Ezra." Pages 47–64 in *They Were All Together in One Place? Toward Minority Biblical Criticism*. Edited by Randall C. Bailey, Tat-siong Benny Liew, and Fernando F. Segovia. SemeiaSt 57. Atlanta: Society of Biblical Literature, 2009.
Andrés-Toledo, Miguel Ángel. "Primary Sources: Avestan and Pahlavi." Pages 519–28 in *The Wiley Blackwell Companion to Zoroastrianism*. Edited by Michael Stausberg and Yuhan Sohrab-Dinshaw Vevaina. Chichester: John Wiley & Sons, 2015.

Assis, Elie. "To Build or Not to Build: A Dispute between Haggai and his People (Hag 1)." *ZAW* 119 (2007): 514–27.

Baden, Joel S. "Why Is the Pentateuch Unreadable? Or, Why Are We Doing This Anyway?" Pages 243–51 in *The Formation of the Pentateuch: Bridging the Academic Cultures of Europe, Israel, and North America*. Edited by Jan C. Gertz et al. FAT 111. Tübingen: Mohr Siebeck, 2016.

Badghbidi, Hassan Rezai. "Darius and the Bisotun Inscription: A New Interpretation of the Last Paragraph of Column IV." *JPerSt* 2 (2009): 44–61.

Balcer, Jack. "Ancient Epic Conventions in the Bisitun Text." Pages 257–64 in *Achaemenid History VIII: Continuity and Change*. Edited by Heleen Sancisi-Weerdenburg, Amélie Kuhrt, and Margaret Cool Root. Leiden: Instituut voor het Nabije Oosten, 1994.

Barag, Dan. "Silver Coin of Yohanan the High Priest and the Coinage of Judea in the Fourth Century B.C." *INJ* 9 (1986–87): 4–14.

Bar-Kochva, Bezalel. *Pseudo-Hecataeus,* On the Jews: *Legitimizing the Diaspora*. HCS 21. Berkeley, CA: University of California Press, 1996.

Bautch, Richard J. *Developments in Genre between Post-Exilic Penitential Prayers and the Psalms of Communal Lament*. SBLAB 7. Atlanta: Society of Biblical Literature, 2003.

Beaulieu, Paul-Alain. "Uruk before and after Xerxes: The Onomastic and Institutional Rise of the God Anu." Pages 189–206 in *Xerxes and Babylonia: The Cuneiform Evidence*. Edited by Caroline Waerzeggers and Maarja Seire. OLA 277. Leuven: Peeters, 2018.

Becking, Bob. *Ezra, Nehemiah, and the Construction of Early Jewish Identity*. FAT 80. Tübingen: Mohr Siebeck, 2011.

———. "'We All Returned as One!' Critical Notes on the Myth of a Mass Return." Pages 3–18 in *Judah and the Judeans in the Persian Period*. Edited by Oded Lipschits and Manfred Oeming. Winona Lake, IN: Eisenbrauns, 2006.

Bedford, Peter Ross. "Diaspora: Homeland Relations in Ezra–Nehemiah." *VT* 52 (2002): 147–65.

Bedford, Peter Ross. "Discerning the Time: Haggai, Zechariah, and the 'Delay' in the Rebuilding of the Temple." Pages 71–94 in *The Pitcher Is Broken: Memorial Essays for Gösta W. Ahlström*. Edited by Steven W. Holloway and Lowell K. Handy. JSOTSup 190. Sheffield: Sheffield Academic Press, 1995.

Bedford, Peter Ross. *Temple Restoration in Early Achaemenid Judah*. JSJSup 65. Leiden: Brill, 2001.

Beentjes, Pancratius C. *Tradition in Transformation in the Book of Chronicles*. SSN 52. Leiden: Brill, 2008.

Begg, Christopher. "The Classical Prophets in the Chronistic History." *BZ* 32 (1988): 100–107.

Benveniste, E. *Titres et noms propres en iranien ancien*. TIEIUP 1. Paris: C. Klincksieck, 1966.

Ben Zvi, Ehud. "Chronicles and its Reshaping of Memories of Monarchic Period Prophets: Some Observations." Pages 167–88 in *Prophets, Prophecy, and Ancient Israelite Historiography*. Edited by Mark J. Boda and Lissa M. Wray Beal. Winona Lake, IN: Eisenbrauns, 2013.

Ben Zvi, Ehud. *History, Literature and Theology in the Book of Chronicles*. BW. London: Equinox, 2006.

Ben Zvi, Ehud. "Memory and Political Thought in the Late Persian/Early Hellenistic Yehud/Judah: Some Observations." Pages 9–26 in *Leadership, Social Memory and Judean Discourse in the Fifth-Second Centuries BCE*. Edited by Diana V. Edelman and Ehud Ben Zvi. WANEM. Sheffield: Equinox Publishing, 2016.

Berges, Ulrich. "Trito-Isaiah and the Reforms of Ezra/Nehemiah: Consent or Conflict?" *Bib* 98 (2019): 173–90.

Berquist, Jon L. *Judaism in Persia's Shadow: A Social and Historical Approach*. Minneapolis: Fortress Press, 1995.

Betlyon, John. "The Provincial Government of Persian Period Judea and the Yehud Coins." *JBL* 105 (1986): 633–42.

Beuken, Wim. "Isaiah Chapters lxv-lxvi: Trito-Isaiah and the Close of the Book of Isaiah." Pages 204–21 in *Congress Volume: Leuven, 1989*. Edited by J. A. Emerton. VTSup 43. Leiden: E. J. Brill, 1991.

Bianchi, F. "Le rôle de Zorobabel et de le dynastie davidique en Judée du VIe siècle au IIe siècle av. J.-C." *Transeu* 7 (1994): 153–65.

Blenkinsopp, Joseph. "Bethel in the Neo-Babylonian Period." Pages 93–107 in *Judah and the Judeans in the Neo-Babylonian Period*. Edited by Oded Lipschitz and Joseph Blenkinsopp. Winona Lake, IN: Eisenbrauns, 2003.

Blenkinsopp, Joseph. *David Remembered: Kingship and National Identity in Ancient Israel*. Grand Rapids, MI: Eerdmans, 2013.

Blenkinsopp, Joseph. "Did the Second Jerusalemite Temple Possess Land?" *Transeu* 21 (2001): 61–68.

Blenkinsopp, Joseph. *Ezra–Nehemiah: A Commentary*. OTL. London: SCM, 1989.

Blenkinsopp, Joseph. *Isaiah 56–66: A New Translation with Introduction and Commentary*. AB 19B. New York: Doubleday, 2003.

Blenkinsopp, Joseph. *Judaism: The First Phase. The Place of Ezra and Nehemiah in the Origins of Judaism*. Grand Rapids, MI: Eerdmans, 2009.

Blenkinsopp, Joseph. "The Mission of Udjahorresnet and Those of Ezra and Nehemiah." *JBL* 106 (1987): 409–21.

Blenkinsopp, Joseph. "The Mystery of the Missing 'Sons of Aaron.'" Pages 65–77 in *Exile and Restoration: Essays on the Babylonian and Persian Periods in Memory of Peter R. Ackroyd*. Edited by Gary N. Knoppers and Lester L. Grabbe. LSTS 73. London: T&T Clark, 2009.

Blenkinsopp, Joseph. *Sage Priest Prophet: Religious and Intellectual Leadership in Ancient Israel*. LAI. Louisville: Westminster John Knox Press, 1995.

Blenkinsopp, Joseph. "The Social Roles of Prophets in Early Achaemenid Judah." *JSOT* 93 (2001): 39–58.

Blenkinsopp, Joseph. "Trito-Isaiah (Isaiah 56–66) and the Gôlāh Group of Ezra, Shecaniah, and Nehemiah (Ezra 7–Nehemiah 13): Is There a Connection?" *JSOT* 43 (2019): 661–77.

Blenkinsopp, Joseph. "'We pay no heed to heavenly voices': The 'End of Prophecy' and the Formation of the Canon." Pages 19–31 in *Biblical and Humane: A Festschrift for John F. Priest*. Edited by Linda Bennett Elder, David L. Barr, and Elizabeth Struthers Malbon. Atlanta: Scholars Press, 1996.

Boccaccini, Gabriele. *Roots of Rabbinic Judaism: An Intellectual History from Ezekiel to Daniel*. Grand Rapids, MI: Eerdmans, 2002.

Boda, Mark J. *The Book of Zechariah*. NICOT. Grand Rapids, MI: Eerdmans, 2016.

Boda, Mark J. *Praying the Tradition: The Origin and Use of Tradition in Nehemiah 9*. BZAW 277. Berlin: W. de Gruyter, 1999.

Boda, Mark J. "Redaction in the Book of Nehemiah: A Fresh Proposal." Pages 25–54 in *Unity and Diversity in Ezra–Nehemiah: Redaction, Rhetoric, and Reader*. Edited by Mark J. Boda and Paul L. Redditt. HBM 17. Sheffield: Sheffield Phoenix Press, 2008.

Boda, Mark J. "Terrifying the Horns: Persia and Babylon in Zechariah 1:7–6:15." *CBQ* 67 (2005): 22–41.

Bodi, D. "La clémence des Perses envers Néhémie et ses compatriotes: Faveur ou opportunisme politique?" *Transeu* 21 (2001): 69–86.

Bodi, D. "*Néhémie* ch. 3 et la charte des bâtisseurs d'une tablette néo-babylonienne de l'époque perse." *Transeu* 35 (2008): 55–70.

Boorer, Suzanne. *The Vision of the Priestly Narrative: Its Genre and Hermeneutics of Time*. SBLAIL 27. Atlanta: SBL Press, 2016.

Borger, Rykle. *Die Chronologie des Darius-Denkmals am Behistun-Felsen*. Göttingen: Vandenhoeck & Ruprecht, 1982.

Boswick, James. "Characters in Stone: Royal Ideology and Yehudite Identity in the Behistun Inscription and the Book of Haggai." Pages 87–117 in *Community Identity in Judean Historiography: Biblical and Comparative Perspectives*. Edited by Gary N. Knoppers and Kenneth A. Ristau. Winona Lake, IN: Eisenbrauns, 2009.

Boucharlat, Rémy. "Gardens and Parks at Pasargadae: Two 'Paradises'?" Pages 557–74 in *Herodot und das Persische Weltreich/Herodotus and the Persian Empire*. Edited by Robert Rollinger, Brigitte Truschnegg, and Reinhold Bichler. CeO 3. Wiesbaden: Harrassowitz, 2011.

Boucharlat, Rémy. "Susa under Achaemenid Rule." Pages 54–67 in *Mesopotamia and Iran in the Persian Period: Conquest and Imperialism 539–331 BC*. Edited by John Curtis. London: British Museum Press, 1997.

Boyce, Mary. *A History of Zoroastrianism. Volume One: The Early Period*. HOS 8/1. 3rd ed. Leiden: E. J. Brill, 1996.

Boyce, Mary. "The Religion of Cyrus the Great." Pages 15–31 in *Achaemenid History III: Method and Theory*. Edited by Heleen Sancisi-Weerdenburg. Leiden: Nederlands Instituut voor het Nabije Oosten, 1988.

Brett, Mark. "National Identity as Commentary and as Metacommentary." Pages 29–40 in *Historiography and Identity (Re)formulation in Second Temple Historiographical Literature*. Edited by Louis C. Jonker. LHBOTS 534. New York: T&T Clark International, 2010.

Briant, Pierre. *From Cyrus to Alexander: A History of the Persian Empire*. Translated by Peter T. Daniels. Winona Lake, IN: Eisenbrauns, 2002.

Briant, Pierre. *Kings, Countries, Peoples: Selected Studies on the Achaemenid Empire*. Translated by Amélie Kuhrt. OeO 26. Stuttgart: Franz Steiner, 2017.

Brosius, Maria. "New out of Old? Court and Court Ceremonies in Achaemenid Persia." Pages 17–57 in *The Court and Court Society in Ancient Monarchies*. Edited by A. J. S. Spawforth. Cambridge: Cambridge University Press, 2007.

Burt, Sean. *The Courtier and the Governor: Transformations of Genre in the Nehemiah Memoir*. JAJSup 17. Göttingen: Vandenhoeck & Ruprecht, 2014.

Byun, Paul. "Diminishing the Effectiveness of the Wall in Nehemiah: A Narratological Analysis of the Nehemiah Memoir and Third-person Narration." *JHS* 18 (2018): art. 5.

Calmeyer, Peter. "Textual Sources for the Interpretation of Achaemenian Palace Decorations." *Iran* 18 (1980): 55–63.

Carr, David M. "Criteria and Periodization in Dating Biblical Texts to Parts of the Persian Period." Pages 11–18 in *On Dating Biblical Texts to the Persian Period: Discerning Criteria and Establishing Epochs*. Edited by Richard J. Bautch and Mark Lackowski. FAT 2/101. Tübingen: Mohr Siebeck, 2019.

Carr, David M. *The Formation of the Hebrew Bible: A New Reconstruction*. Oxford: Oxford University Press, 2011.

Carr, David M. "The Rise of Torah." Pages 39–56 in *The Pentateuch as Torah: New Models for Understanding its Promulgation and Acceptance*. Edited by Gary N. Knoppers and Bernard M. Levinson. Winona Lake, IN: Eisenbrauns, 2007.

Carter, Charles E. *The Emergence of Yehud in the Persian Period: A Social and Demographic Study*. JSOTSup 294. Sheffield: Sheffield Academic Press, 1999.

Cataldo, Jeremiah W. *Breaking Monotheism: Yehud and the Material Formation of Monotheistic Identity*. LHBOTS 565. New York: Bloomsbury, 2012.

Cataldo, Jeremiah W. *A Theocratic Yehud? Issues of Government in a Persian Period*. LHBOTS 498. New York: T&T Clark International, 2009.

Chaumont, M.-L. "Un nouveau gouvernour de Sardes à l'époque achéménide d'après une inscription récemment découverte." *Syria* 67 (1990): 579–608.

Chrostowski, Waldemar. "An Examination of Conscience by God's People as Exemplified in Neh 9,6–37." *BZ* 34 (1990): 253–61.

Clauss, Jan. "Understanding the Mixed Marriages of Ezra–Nehemiah in the Light of Temple-Building and the Book's Concept of Jerusalem." Pages 109–31 in *Mixed Marriages: Intermarriage and Group Identity in the Second Temple Period*. Edited by Christian Frevel. LHBOTS 547. New York: Bloomsbury T&T Clark, 2011.

Clines, David J. A. *Ezra, Nehemiah, Esther*. NCBC. Grand Rapids, MI: Eerdmans, 1984.

Clines, David J. A. "The Nehemiah Memoir: The Perils of Autobiography." Pages 124–64 in *What Does Eve Do to Help? and Other Readerly Questions*. JSOTSup 94. Sheffield: Sheffield Academic Press, 1990.

Cohen, Mark E. *Cultic Calendars of the Ancient Near East*. Bethesda, MD: CDL Press, 1993.

Colburn, Henry. "Art of the Achaemenid Empire, and Art in the Achaemenid Empire." Pages 773–800 in *Critical Approaches to Ancient Near Eastern Art*. Edited by Brian A. Brown and Marian H. Feldman. Boston: W. de Gruyter, 2014.

Conklin, Blake W. "[Review of] Dirk Schwiderski, *Handbuch des nordwestsemitischen Breifformulars*." *JSS* 48 (2003): 137–40.

Cook, L. Stephen. *On the Question of the "Cessation of Prophecy" in Ancient Judaism*. TSAJ 145. Tübingen: Mohr Siebeck, 2011.

Cornelius, Izak. "'A Tale of Two Cities': The Visual Imagery of Yehud and Samaria, and Identity/Self-Understanding in Persian-period Palestine." Pages 213–37 in *Texts, Contexts and Readings in Postexilic Literature: Explorations into Historiography and Identity Negotiation in Hebrew Bible and Related Texts*. Edited by Louis Jonker. FAT 2/53. Tübingen: Mohr Siebeck, 2011.

Crüseman, Frank. *Torah: Theology and Social History of Old Testament Law*. Translated by Allan W. Mahnke. Minneapolis: Fortress Press, 1995.

Curtis, Byron G. "The *Mas'ot* Triptych and the Date of Zechariah 9–14: Issues in the Latter Formation of the Book of the Twelve." Pages 191–206 in *Perspectives on the Formulation of the Book of the Twelve: Methodological Formulations—Redactional Processes—Historical Insights*. Edited by Rainer Albertz, James Nogalski, and Jakob Wöhrle. BZAW 433. Berlin: W. de Gruyter, 2012.

Curtis, Byron G. *Up the Steep and Stony Road: The Book of Zechariah in Social Location Trajectory Analysis*. SBLAB 25. Leiden: Brill, 2006.
Curtis, John. "The Archaeology of the Achaemenid Period." Pages 30–49 in *Forgotten Empire: The World of Ancient Persia*. Edited by John Curtis and Nigel Tallis. Berkeley: University of California Press, 2005.
Curtis, John, and Shahrokh Razmjou. "The Palace." Pages 50–55 in *Forgotten Empire: The World of Ancient Persia*. Edited by John Curtis and Nigel Tallis. Berkeley: University of California Press, 2005.
Dandamaev, M. A. "Babylonian Popular Assemblies in the First Millennium B.C." *BCSMS* 30 (1995): 23–29.
Dandamaev, M. A. "Neo-Babylonian and Achaemenid State Administration in Mesopotamia." Pages 373–98 in *Judah and the Judeans in the Persian Period*. Edited by Oded Lipschits and Manfred Oeming. Winona Lake, IN: Eisenbrauns, 2006.
Dandamaev, M. A. "The Neo-Babylonian Elders." Pages 38–41 in *Societies and Languages of the Ancient Near East: Studies in Honour of I. M. Diakonoff*. Edited by M. A. Dandamaev et al. Westminster: Aris & Phillips, 1982.
Dandamaev, M. A. "The Neo-Babylonian Popular Assembly." Pages 63–71 in *Šulmu: Papers on the Ancient Near East Presented at International Conference of Socialist Countries*. Edited by Petr Vavroušek and Vladimír Souček. Prague: Charles University, 1988.
Della Volpe, Angela. "Wall." Pages 628–29 in *Encyclopedia of Indo-European Culture*. Edited by J. P. Mallory and Douglas Q. Adams. London: Fitzroy Dearborn, 1997.
Donner, Herbert. "Ein Vorschlag zum Verständnis von Maleachi 2,10–16." Pages 97–103 in *Von Gott reden: Beiträge zur Theologie und Exegese des Alten Testaments*. Edited by Dieter Vieweger und Ernst-Joachim Waschke. Neukirchen-Vluyn: Neukirchener, 1995.
Dor, Yonina. "The Composition of the Episode of the Foreign Women in Ezra ix-x." *VT* 53 (2003): 26–47.
Dozeman, Thomas B. "Geography and History in Herodotus and Ezra–Nehemiah." *JBL* 122 (2003): 449–66.
Duggan, Michael W. *The Covenant Renewal in Ezra–Nehemiah (Neh 7:72B–10:40): An Exegetical, Literary, and Theological Study*. SBLDS 164. Atlanta: Society of Biblical Literature, 2001.
Duggan, Michael W. "Ezra 9:6–15: A Penitential Prayer within its Literary Setting." Pages 1:165–80 in *Seeking the Favor of God*. 3 volumes. Edited by Mark J. Boda, Daniel K. Falk, and Rodney A. Werline. SBLEJL 21–23. Atlanta: Society of Biblical Literature, 2006–2008.
Dusinberre, Elspeth R. M. "Anatolian Crossroads: Achaemenid Seals from Sardis and Gordion." Pages 323–35 in *The World of Achaemenid Persia: History, Art and Society in Iran and the Ancient Near East*. Edited by John Curtis and St John Simpson. London: I. B. Tauris, 2010.
Dusinberre, Elspeth R. M. *Aspects of Empire in Achaemenid Sardis*. Cambridge: Cambridge University Press, 2003.
Dusinberre, Elspeth R. M. *Empire, Authority, and Autonomy in Achaemenid Anatolia*. Cambridge: Cambridge University Press, 2013.
Dusinberre, Elspeth R. M. "King or God? Imperial Iconography and the 'Tiarate Head' Coins of Achaemenid Anatolia." Pages 157–71 in *Across the Anatolian Plateau: Readings in the Archaeology of Ancient Turkey*. AASOR 57. Boston: ASOR, 2002.

Dyck, Jonathan E. "Ezra 2 in Ideological Critical Perspective." Pages 129–45 in *Rethinking Contexts, Rereading Texts: Contributions from the Social Sciences to Biblical Interpretation*. Edited by M. Daniel Carroll R. JSOTSup 299. Sheffield: Sheffield Academic Press, 2000.

Edelman, Diana. "Ezra 1–6 as Idealized Past." Pages 47–59 in *A Palimpsest: Rhetoric, Ideology, Stylistics, and Language Relating to Persian Israel*. Edited by Ehud Ben Zvi, Diana V. Edelman, and Frank Polak. PHSC 5. Piscataway, NJ: Gorgias Press, 2009.

Edelman, Diana. "From Prophets to Prophetic Books: The Fixing of the Divine Word." Pages 29–54 in *The Production of Prophecy: Constructing Prophecy and Prophets in Yehud*. Edited by Diana Vikander Edelman and Ehud Ben Zvi. BW. London: Equinox, 2009.

Edelman, Diana. "Identities within a Central and Peripheral Perspective: The Use of Aramaic in the Hebrew Bible." Pages 109–31 in *Centres and Peripheries in the Early Second Temple Period*. Edited by Ehud Ben Zvi and Christoph Levin. FAT 108. Tübingen: Mohr Siebeck, 2016.

Edelman, Diana. *The Origins of the "Second" Temple: Persian Imperial Policy and the Rebuilding of Jerusalem*. BW. London: Equinox, 2005.

Edelman, Diana. "Seeing Double: Tobiah the Ammonite as an Encrypted Character." *RB* 113 (2006): 570–84.

Eidsvåg, Gunnar Magnus. *The Old Greek Translation of Zechariah*. VTSup 170. Leiden: Brill, 2016.

Eph'al, Israel. "Changes in Palestine during the Persian Period in Light of Epigraphic Sources." *IEJ* 48 (1998): 106–19.

Eph'al, Israel. "The Western Minorities in Babylonia in the 6th–5th Centuries B.C.: Maintenance and Cohesion." *Or* 47 (1978): 74–90.

Eskenazi, Tamara Cohn. *In an Age of Prose: A Literary Approach to Ezra–Nehemiah*. SBLMS 36. Atlanta: Scholars Press, 1988.

Eskenazi, Tamara Cohn. "The Missions of Ezra and Nehemiah." Pages 509–29 in *Judah and the Judeans in the Persian Period*. Edited by Oded Lipschits and Manfred Oeming. Winona Lake, IN: Eisenbrauns, 2006.

Eskenazi, Tamara Cohn. "Nehemiah 9–10: Structure and Significance." *JHS* 3 (2001): art. 9.

Eskenazi, Tamara Cohn, and Eleanore P. Judd. "Marriage to a Stranger in Ezra 9–10." Pages 266–85 in *Second Temple Studies 2: Temple Community in the Persian Period*. Edited by Tamara C. Eskenazi and Kent H. Richards. JSOTSup 175. Sheffield: JSOT, 1994.

Esler, Philip F. "Ezra–Nehemiah as a Narrative of (Re-Invented) Identity." *BibInt* 11 (2003): 413–26.

Fantalkin, Alexander, and Oren Tal. "Judah and its Neighbors in the Fourth Century BCE: A Time of Major Transformations." Pages 133–96 in *From Judah to Judaea: Socio-economic Structures and Processes in the Persian Period*. Edited by Johannes Unsok Ro. HBM 43. Sheffield: Sheffield Phoenix Press, 2012.

Fantalkin, Alexander, and Oren Tal. "Redating Lachish Level I: Identifying Achaemenid Imperial Policy at the Southern Frontier of the Fifth Satrapy." Pages 167–97 in *Judah and the Judeans in the Persian Period*. Edited by Oded Lipschits and Manfred Oeming. Winona Lake, IN: Eisenbrauns, 2006.

Faust, Avraham. "Forts or Agricultural Estates? Persian Period Settlement in the Territories of the Former Kingdom of Judah." *PEQ* 150 (2018): 34–59.

Finitsis, Antonios. *Visions and Eschatology: A Socio-Historical Analysis of Zechariah 1–6*. LSTS 79. New York: T&T Clark International, 2011.
Finkelstein, Israel. *Hasmonean Realities behind Ezra, Nehemiah, and Chronicles*. SBLAIL 34. Atlanta: SBL Press, 2018.
Finn, Jennifer. "Gods, Kings, Men: Trilingual Inscriptions and Symbolic Visualizations in the Achaemenid Empire." *ArsOr* 41 (2011): 219–75.
Fitzpatrick-McKinley, Anne. *Empire, Power and Indigenous Elites: A Case Study of the Nehemiah Memoir*. JSJSup 169. Leiden: Brill, 2015.
Floyd, Michael H. *Minor Prophets*. 2 vols. FOTL 22. Grand Rapids, MI: Eerdmans, 2000.
Foster, Robert L. "Shepherds, Sticks, and Social Destabilization: A Fresh Look at Zechariah 11:4-17." *JBL* 126 (2007): 735–53.
Frei, Peter. "Persian Imperial Authorization: A Summary." Pages 5–40 in *Persia and Torah: The Theory of Imperial Authorization of the Pentateuch*. Edited by James W. Watts. SBLSymS 17. Atlanta: Society of Biblical Literature, 2001.
Frevel, Christian, and Benedikt J. Conczorowski. "Deepening the Water: First Steps to a Diachronic Approach to Intermarriage in the Hebrew Bible." Pages 15–45 in *Mixed Marriages: Intermarriage and Group Identity in the Second Temple Period*. Edited by Christian Frevel. LHBOTS 547. New York: Bloomsbury T&T Clark, 2011.
Fried, Lisbeth S. "150 Men at Nehemiah's Table? The Role of the Governor's Meals in the Achaemenid Provincial Economy." *JBL* 137 (2018): 821–31.
Fried, Lisbeth S. "The *'am hā'āreṣ* in Ezra 4:4 and Persian Imperial Administration." Pages 123–45 in *Judah and the Judeans in the Persian Period*. Edited by Oded Lipschits and Manfred Oeming. Winona Lake, IN: Eisenbrauns, 2006.
Fried, Lisbeth S. "The Concept of 'Impure Birth' in 5th Century Athens and Judea." Pages 121–41 in *In the Wake of Tikva Frymer-Kensky*. Edited by Steven Holloway, Jo Ann Scurlock, and Richard Beal. GPP 4. Piscataway, NJ: Gorgias Press, 2009.
Fried, Lisbeth S. "*Deus ex Machina* and Plot Construction in Ezra 1–6." Pages 189–207 in *Prophets, Prophecy, and Ancient Israelite Historiography*. Edited by Mark J. Boda and Lissa M. Wray Beal. Winona Lake, IN: Eisenbrauns, 2013.
Fried, Lisbeth S. "Exploitation of Depopulated Land in Achaemenid Judah." Pages 151–64 in *The Economy of Ancient Judah in its Historical Context*. Edited by Marvin Lloyd Miller, Ehud Ben Zvi, and Gary N. Knoppers. Winona Lake, IN: Eisenbrauns, 2015.
Fried, Lisbeth S. *Ezra: A Commentary*. Sheffield: Sheffield Phoenix Press, 2015.
Fried, Lisbeth S. *Ezra and the Law in History and Tradition*. SPOT. Columbia, SC: University of South Carolina Press, 2014.
Fried, Lisbeth S. "Ezra's Use of Documents in the Context of Hellenistic Rules of Rhetoric." Pages 11–26 in *New Perspectives on Ezra–Nehemiah: History and Historiography, Text, Literature, and Interpretation*. Edited by Isaac Kalimi. Winona Lake, IN: Eisenbrauns, 2012.
Fried, Lisbeth S. "From Xeno-Philia to -Phobia—Jewish Encounters with the Other." Pages 179–204 in *A Time of Change: Judah and its Neighbours in the Persian and Early Hellenistic Periods*. Edited by Yigal Levin. LSTS 65. London: T&T Clark International, 2007.
Fried, Lisbeth S. *The Priest and the Great King: Temple-Palace Relations in the Persian Empire*. BJSUCSD 10. Winona Lake, IN: Eisenbrauns, 2004.
Fried, Lisbeth S. "A Silver Coin of Yoḥanan Hakkôhēn." *Transeu* 26 (2003): 65–85.

Fried, Lisbeth S. "'You shall appoint judges': Ezra's Mission and the Rescript of Artaxerxes." Pages 63–89 in *Persia and Torah: The Theory of Imperial Authorization of the Pentateuch*. Edited by James W. Watts. SBLSymS 17. Atlanta: Society of Biblical Literature, 2001.

Fröhlich, I. "*Mamzēr* in Qumran Texts—the Problem of Mixed Marriages from Ezra's Time: Law, Literature, and Practice." *Transeu* 29 (2005): 103–15.

Frolov, Serge. "The Prophecy of Jeremiah in Esr 1,1." *ZAW* 116 (2004): 595–601.

Fulton, Deirdre N. *Remembering Nehemiah's Judah: The Case of MT and LXX Nehemiah 11–12*. FAT 2/80. Tübingen: Mohr Siebeck, 2015.

Gafney, Wilda. "A Prophet-Terrorist(a) and an Imperial Sympathizer: An Empire-Critical, Postcolonial Reading of the Noʻadyah/Nechemyah Conflict." *BlTh* 9 (2011): 161–76.

Galil, G. "'The secret things belong to the Lord our God' (*Deut* 29:29): Retribution in the Persian Period." *Transeu* 39 (2010): 91–96.

Gamkrelidze, Thomas V., and Vjačeslav V. Ivanov. *Indo-European and the Indo-Europeans: A Reconstruction and Historical Analysis of a Proto-Language and a Proto-Culture*. 2 vols. Translated by Johanna Nichols. TLSM 80. Berlin: W. de Gruyter, 1995.

Garrison, Mark B. "Achaemenid Iconography as Evidenced by Glyptic Art: Subject Matter, Social Function, Audience and Diffusion." Pages 115–63 in *Images as Media: Sources for the Cultural Hero of the Near East and the Eastern Mediterranean (1st Millennium BCE)*. Edited by C. Uehlinger. OBO 175. Göttingen: Vandenhoeck & Ruprecht, 2000.

Garrison, Mark B. "*By the Favor of Auramazdā*: Kingship and the Divine in the Early Achaemenid Period." Pages 15–104 in *More than Men, Less than Gods: Studies on Royal Cult and Imperial Worship*. Edited by Panagiotis P. Iossif, Andrzej S. Chankowski, and Catherine C. Lorberf. StHel 11. Leuven: Peeters, 2011.

Garrison, Mark B. *The Ritual Landscape at Persepolis: Glyptic Imagery from the Persepolis Fortification and Treasury Archives*. SAOC 72. Chicago: The Oriental Institute of the University of Chicago, 2017.

Garrison, Mark B. "Seals and the Elite at Persepolis: Some Observations on Early Achaemenid Art." *ArsOr* 21 (1991): 1–29.

Garrison, Mark B., and Margaret Cool Root. *Seals on the Persepolis Fortification Tablets. Volume I: Images of Heroic Encounter*. UCOIP 117. Chicago: The Oriental Institute of the University of Chicago, 2001.

Gärtner, Judith. *Jesaja 66 und Sacharja 14 als Summe der Prophetie: Eine traditions- und redaktionsgeschichtliche Untersuchung zum Abschluss des Jesaja- und des Zwölfprophetenbuches*. WMANT 114. Neukirchen-Vluyn: Neukirchener Verlag, 2006.

Gerson, Stephen N. "Fractional Coins of Judea and Samaria in the Fourth Century BCE," *NEA* 64 (2001): 106–21.

Gerstenberger, Erhard. *Israel in the Persian Period: The Fifth and Fourth Centuries B.C.E.* Translated by Siegfried S. Schatzmann. SBLBE 8. Leiden: Brill, 2012.

Gerstenberger, Erhard. "Prophetie in den Chronikbüchern: Jahwes Wort in zweierlei Gestalt?" Pages 351–67 in *Schriftprophetie: Festschrift für Jörg Jeremias zum 65. Geburtstag*. Edited by Friedhelm Hartenstein, Jutta Krispen, and Aaron Schart. Neukirchen-Vluyn: Neukirchener Verlag, 2004.

Gitler, Haim. "The Earliest Coin of Judah." *INR* 6 (2011): 21–33.

Gitler, Haim. "Identities of the Indigenous Coinages of Palestine under Achaemenid Rule: The Dissemination of the Image of the Great King." Pages 105–19 in *More than Men, Less than Gods: Studies on Royal Cult and Imperial Worship*. Edited by Panagiotis P. Iossif, Andrzej S. Chankowski, and Catherine C. Lorberf. StHel 11. Leuven: Peeters, 2011.

Gmirkin, Russell E. *Berossus and Genesis, Manetho and Exodus: Hellenistic Histories and the Date of the Pentateuch*. LHBOTS 433. New York: T&T Clark International, 2006.

Goldingay, John. *A Critical and Exegetical Commentary on Isaiah 56–66*. ICC. London: Bloomsbury, 2014.

Goswell, Greg. "The Fate and Future of Zerubbabel in the Prophecy of Haggai." *Bib* 91 (2010): 77–90.

Grabbe, Lester L. *Ezra–Nehemiah*. London: Routledge, 1998.

Grabbe, Lester L. "Hecataeus of Abdera and the Jewish Law: The Question of Authenticity." Pages 613–26 in *Berührungspunkte: Studien zur Sozial- und Religionsgeschichte Israels und seiner Umwelt*. Edited by Ingo Kottsieper, Rüdiger Schmidt, and Jakob Wöhrle. AOAT 350. Münster: Ugarit-Verlag, 2008.

Grabbe, Lester L. "Hyparchs, *Oikonomoi* and Mafiosi: The Governance of Judah in the Ptolemaic Period." Pages 70–90 in *Judah between East and West: The Transition from Persian to Greek Rule (ca. 400–200 BCE)*. Edited by Lester L. Grabbe and Oded Lipschits. LSTS 75. London: T&T Clark, 2011.

Grabbe, Lester L. "Josephus and the Reconstruction of the Judean Restoration." *JBL* 106 (1987): 231–46.

Grabbe, Lester L. *Judaism from Cyrus to Hadrian*. 2 vols. Minneapolis: Fortress Press, 1992.

Grabbe, Lester L. "The Last Days of Judah and the Roots of the Pentateuch: What Does History Tell Us?" Pages 19–45 in *The Fall of Jerusalem and the Rise of the Torah*. Edited by Peter Dubovsky, Dominik Martl, and Jean-Pierre Sonnet. FAT 107. Tübingen: Mohr Siebeck, 2016.

Grabbe, Lester L. "The Law of Moses in the Ezra Tradition: More Virtual than Real?" Pages 91–113 in *Persia and Torah: The Theory of Imperial Authorization of the Pentateuch*. Edited by James W. Watts. SBLSymS 17. Atlanta; Society of Biblical Literature, 2001.

Grabbe, Lester L. "The 'Persian Documents' in the Book of Ezra: Are They Authentic?" Pages 531–70 in *Judah and the Judeans in the Persian Period*. Edited by Oded Lipschits and Manfred Oeming. Winona Lake, IN: Eisenbrauns, 2006.

Grabbe, Lester L. "The Terminology of Government in the Septuagint—in Comparison with Hebrew, Aramaic, and Other Languages." Pages 225–37 in *Jewish Perspectives on Hellenistic Rulers*. Edited by Tessa Rajak et al. HCS 50. Berkeley, CA: University of California Press, 2007.

Granerød, Gard. "'By the favour of Ahuramazda I am king': On the Promulgation of a Persian Propaganda Text among Babylonians and Judaeans." *JSJ* 44 (2013): 455–80.

Grätz, Sebastian. "The Adversaries in Ezra/Nehemiah—Fictitious or Real? A Case Study in Creating Identity in Late Persian and Hellenistic Times." Pages 73–88 in *Between Cooperation and Hostility: Multiple Identities in Ancient Judaism and the Interaction of Foreign Powers*. Edited by Rainer Albertz and Jakob Wöhrle. JAJSup 11. Göttingen: Vandenhoeck & Ruprecht, 2012.

Grätz, Sebastian. "Die Aramäische Chronik des Esrabuches und die Rolle der Ältesten in Esr 5–6. *ZAW* 118 (2006): 405–22.

Grätz, Sebastian. *Das Edikt des Artaxerxes: Eine Untersuchung zum religionspolitischen und historischen Umfeld von Esra 7,12–26*. BZAW 337. Berlin: W. de Gruyter, 2004.
Green, Stefan. "The Temple of God and Crises in Isaiah 56–66 and *1 Enoch*." Pages 47–66 in *Studies in Isaiah: History, Theology and Reception*. Edited by Tommy Wasserman, Greger Andersson, and David Willgren. LHBOTS 654. London: T&T Clark, 2017.
Greenfield, Jonas C., and Bezalel Porten. *The Bisitun Inscription of Darius the Great: Aramaic Version*. CII 1/5/1. London: Lund Humphries, 1982.
Gregory, Bradley C. "The Postexilic Third Isaiah: Isaiah 61:1-3 in Light of Second Temple Hermeneutics." *JBL* 126 (2007): 475–96.
Grenet, Franz. "Where Are the Sogdian Magi?" *BAI* 21 (2007): 159–77.
Grol, Harm van. "'Indeed, servants we are': Ezra 9, Nehemiah 9 and 2 Chronicles 12 Compared." Pages 209–27 in *The Crisis of Israelite Religion: Transformation of Religious Tradition in Exilic and Post-Exilic Times*. Edited by Bob Becking and Marjo C. A. Korpel. OTS 42. Leiden: Brill, 1999.
Guillaume, Philippe. *Land and Calendar: The Priestly Document from Genesis 1 to Joshua 18*. LHBOTS 391. New York: T&T Clark, 2009.
Gunneweg, Antonius H. J. *Esra*. KAT 19/1. Gütersloh: Gerd Mohn, 1985.
Gunneweg, Antonius H. J. *Nehemia*. KAT 19/2. Gütersloh: Gütersloher Verlagshaus, 1987.
Hallaschka, Martin. "From Cores to Corpus: Considering the Formation of Haggai and Zechariah 1–8." Pages 171–90 in *Perspectives on the Formation of the Book of the Twelve: Methodological Foundations, Redactional Processes, Historical Insights*. Edited by Rainer Albertz, James D. Nogalski, and Jakob Wöhrle. BZAW 433. Berlin: W. de Gruyter, 2012.
Hallaschka, Martin. *Haggai und Sacharja 1–8: Eine redaktionsgeschichtliche Untersuchung*. BZAW 411. Berlin: W. de Gruyter, 2011.
Hallaschka, Martin. "Zechariah's Angels: Their Role in the Night Visions and in the Redaction History of Zech 1,7–6,8." *SJOT* 24 (2010): 13–27.
Hanson, Paul D. *The People Called: The Growth of Community in the Bible*. San Francisco: Harper & Row, 1986.
Harrington, Hannah K. "Holiness and Purity in Ezra–Nehemiah." Pages 98–116 in *Unity and Diversity in Ezra–Nehemiah: Redaction, Rhetoric, and Reader*. Edited by Mark J. Boda and Paul L. Redditt. HBM 17. Sheffield: Sheffield Phoenix Press, 2008.
Harrington, Hannah K. *The Purity and Sanctuary of the Body in Second Temple Judaism*. JAJSup 33. Göttingen: Vandenhoeck & Ruprecht, 2019.
Harrington, Hannah K. "The Use of Leviticus in Ezra–Nehemiah." *JHS* 13 (2012): art. 3.
Harrison, Thomas. *Writing Ancient Persia*. CIE. London: Bristol Classical Press, 2011.
Häusl, Maria. "'So I prayed to the God of heaven' (Neh 2:4): Praying and Prayers in the Books of Ezra and Nehemiah." Pages 53–82 in *Prayers and the Construction of Israelite Identity*. Edited by Susanne Gillmayr-Bucher and Maria Häusl. SBLAIL 35. Atlanta: SBL Press, 2019.
Hayes, Christine E. *Gentile Impurities and Jewish Identities: Intermarriage and Conversion from the Bible to the Talmud*. Oxford: Oxford University Press, 2002.
Heckl, Raik. *Neuanfang und Kontinuität in Jerusalem: Studien zu den hermeneutischen Strategien im Esra-Nehemia-Buch*. FAT 104. Tübingen: Mohr Siebeck, 2016.
Hempel, Charlotte. "Do the Scrolls Suggest Rivalry between the Sons of Aaron and the Sons of Zadok and if so Was It Mutual?" *RevQ* 24 (2009): 135–53.
Henkelman, Wouter F. M. "The Achaemenid Heartland: An Archaeological-Historical Perspective." Pages 931–62 in *A Companion to the Archaeology of the Ancient Near East*. Edited by D. T. Potts. Chichester: Blackwell, 2012.

Henkelman, Wouter F. M. "'Consumed before the king': The Table of Darius, that of Irdabama and Irtaštuna, and that of his Satrap Karkiš." Pages 667–775 in *Der Achämenidenhof/The Achaemenid Court*. Edited by Bruno Jacobs and Robert Rollinger. CeO 2. Wiesbaden: Harrassowitz, 2010.

Henkelman, Wouter F. M. "An Elamite Memorial: The *šumar* of Cambyses and Hystapes." Pages 101–72 in *A Persian Perspective: Essays in Memory of Heleen Sancisi-Weerdenburg*. Edited by Wouter Henkelman and Amélie Kuhrt. AchHist 13. Leiden: Nederlands Instituut voor het Nabije Oosten, 2003.

Henkelman, Wouter F. M. "Humban and Auramazdā: Royal Gods in a Persian Landscape." Pages 273–346 in *Persian Religion in the Achaemenid Period/La religion perse à l'époque achéménide*. Edited by Wouter F. M. Henkelman and Céline Richard. CeO 16. Wiesbaden: Harrassowitz, 2017.

Henkelman, Wouter F. M. *The Other Gods Who Are: Studies in Elamite–Iranian Acculturation Based on the Persepolis Fortification Texts*. AchHist 14. Leiden: Nederlands Instituut voor het Nabije Oosten, 2008.

Henkelman, Wouter F. M. "Parnakka's Feast: *šip* in Pārsa and Elam." Pages 89–116 in *Elam and Persia*. Edited by Javier Álvarez-Mon and Mark B. Garrison. Winona Lake, IN: Eisenbrauns, 2011.

Hensel, Benedikt. "Ethnic Fiction and Identity-Formation: A New Explanation for the Background of the Question of Intermarriage in Ezra–Nehemiah." Pages 133–48 in *The Bible, Qumran, and the Samaritans*. Edited by Magnar Kartveit and Gary N. Knoppers. StJud 104. StSam 10. Berlin: W. de Gruyter, 2018.

Herrenschmidt, Clarisse. "Désignation de l'empire et concepts politiques de Darius Ier d'après ses inscriptions en vieux-perse." *StIr* 5 (1976): 33–65.

Herrenschmidt, Clarisse. "Vieux-perse *šiyāti-*." Pages 13–21 in *La religion iranienne à l'époque achéménide*. Edited by Jeans Kellens. IrAntSup 5. Leuven: Iranica Antiqua, 1990.

Herrenschmidt, Clarisse. "Writing between Visible and Invisible Worlds in Iran, Israel, and Greece." Pages 69–146 in *Ancestor of the West: Writing, Reasoning, and Religion in Mesopotamia, Elam, and Greece*. Edited by Jean Bottéro, Clarisse Herrenschmidt, and Jean-Pierre Vernant. Translated by Teresa Lavender Fagan. Chicago: The University of Chicago Press, 2000.

Hill, Andrew E. *Malachi: A New Translation with Introduction and Commentary*. AB 25D. New York: Doubleday, 1998.

Himbaza, Innocent. "Les themes théologiques de Malachie et le concept du livre des XII Prophètes." Pages 82–96 in *The Book of the Twelve—One or Many?* Edited by Eleana Di Pede and Donatella Sciaola. FAT 2/91. Tübingen: Mohr Siebeck, 2016.

Himmelfarb, Martha. *A Kingdom of Priests: Ancestry and Merit in Ancient Judaism*. JCC. Philadelphia: University of Pennsylvania Press, 2006.

Höffken, Peter. "Einige Beobachtungen zum Juda der Perserzeit in der Darstellung des Josephus, *Antiquitates* Buch 11." *JSJ* 39 (2008): 151–69.

Hoglund, Kenneth G. *Achaemenid Imperial Administration in Syria-Palestine and the Missions of Ezra and Nehemiah*. SBLDS 125. Atlanta: Scholars Press, 1992.

Hogue, Timothy. "Return from Exile: Diglossia and Literary Code-Switching in Ezra 1–7." *ZAW* 130 (2018): 54–68.

Humbach, Helmut. "Gathas I: Texts," *EIr*, www.iranicaonline.org/articles/gathas-i-texts; accessed 13 January 2020.

Hunt, Alice. *Missing Priests: The Zadokites in History and Tradition*. LHBOTS 452. New York: T&T Clark International, 2006.

Hyland, John O. "The Casualty Figures in Darius' Bisitun Inscription." *JANEH* 1 (2014): 173–99.
Jacobs, Bruno. "Berossos and Persian Religion." Pages 123–35 in *The World of Berossos: Proceedings of the 4th International Colloquium on "The Ancient Near East between Classical and Ancient Oriental Traditions*. Edited by Johannes Haubold et al. Wiesbaden: Harrassowitz, 2013.
Jacobs, Bruno. "From Gabled Hut to Rock-Cut Tomb: A Religious and Cultural Break between Cyrus and Darius?" Pages 91–101 in *The World of Achaemenid Persia: History, Art and Society in Iran and the Ancient Near East*. Edited by John Curtis and St John Simpson. London: I. B. Tauris, 2010.
Janzen, David. *Chronicles and the Politics of Davidic Restoration: A Quiet Revolution*. LHBOTS 655. London: Bloomsbury T&T Clark, 2017.
Janzen, David. "A Colonized People: Persian Hegemony, Hybridity, and Community Identity in Ezra–Nehemiah." *BibInt* 24 (2016): 27–47.
Janzen, David. "The Cries of Jerusalem: Ethnic, Cultic, Legal, and Geographic Boundaries in Ezra–Nehemiah." Pages 117–35 in *Unity and Diversity in Ezra–Nehemiah: Redaction, Rhetoric, and Reader*. Edited by Mark J. Boda and Paul L. Redditt. HBM 17. Sheffield: Sheffield Phoenix Press, 2008.
Janzen, David. "The 'Mission' of Ezra and the Persian-Period Temple Community." *JBL* 119 (2000): 619–43.
Janzen, David. "Politics, Settlement, and Temple Community in Persian-Period Yehud." *CBQ* 64 (2002): 490–510.
Janzen, David. *Witch-hunts, Purity and Social Boundaries: The Expulsion of the Foreign Women in Ezra 9–10*. JSOTSup 350. Sheffield: Sheffield Academic Press, 2002.
Janzen, David. "Yahwistic Appropriation of Achaemenid Ideology and the Function of Nehemiah 9 in Ezra–Nehemiah." *JBL* 136 (2017): 839–56.
Japhet, Sara. *I and II Chronicles: A Commentary*. OTL. Louisville: Westminster/John Knox, 1993.
Japhet, Sara. *From the Rivers of Babylon to the Highlands of Judah: Collected Studies on the Restoration Period*. Winona Lake, IN: Eisenbrauns, 2006.
Japhet, Sara. *The Ideology of the Book of Chronicles and its Place in Biblical Thought*. BEATAJ 9. Frankfurt am Main: Peter Lang, 1989.
Japhet, Sara. "What May Be Learned from Ezra–Nehemiah about the Composition of the Pentateuch?" Pages 543–60 in *The Formation of the Pentateuch: Bridging the Academic Cultures of Europe, Israel, and North America*. Edited by Jan C. Gertz et al. FAT 111. Tübingen: Mohr Siebeck, 2016.
Jigoulov, Vadim S. *The Social History of Achaemenid Phoenicia: Being a Phoenician, Negotiating Empires*. BW. London: Routledge, 2010.
Johnson, Willa M. *The Holy Seed Has Been Defiled: The Interethnic Marriage Dilemma in Ezra 9–10*. HBM 33. Sheffield: Sheffield Phoenix Press, 2011.
Jones, Christopher M. "Embedded Written Documents as Colonial Mimicry in Ezra–Nehemiah," *BibInt* 26 (2018): 158–81.
Jones, Christopher M. "Seeking the Divine, Divining the Seekers: The Status of Outsiders Who Seek Yahweh in Ezra 6:21." *JHS* 15 (2015): art. 5.
Jones, David Clyde. "A Note on the LXX of Malachi 2:16." *JBL* 109 (1990): 683–85.
Jong, Albert de. "Ahura Mazdā the Creator." Pages 85–89 in *The World of Achaemenid Persia: History, Art and Society in Iran and the Ancient Near East*. Edited by John Curtis and St John Simpson. London: I. B. Tauris, 2010.

Jong, Albert de. "Religion at the Achaemenid Court." Pages 533–58 in *Der Achämenidenhof/The Achaemenid Court*. Edited by Bruno Jacobs and Robert Rollinger. CeO 2. Wiesbaden: Harrassowitz, 2010.

Jonker, Louis C. *Defining All-Israel in Chronicles: Multi-levelled Identity Negotiation in Late Persian-Period Yehud*. FAT 106. Tübingen: Mohr Siebeck, 2016.

Jonker, Louis C. "Textual Identities in the Books of Chronicles: The Case of Jehoram's History." Pages 197–217 in *Community Identity in Judean Historiography: Biblical and Comparative Perspectives*. Edited by Gary N. Knoppers and Kenneth A. Ristau. Winona Lake, IN: Eisenbrauns, 2009.

Jonker, Louis C. "Who Constitutes Society? Yehud's Self-understanding in the Late Persian Era as Reflected in the Books of Chronicles." *JBL* 127 (2008): 703–24.

Jonker, Louis C. "Who's Speaking? On Whose Behalf? The Book of Haggai from the Perspective of Identity Formation in the Persian Period." Pages 197–214 in *History, Memory, Hebrew Scriptures: A Festschrift for Ehud Ben Zvi*. Edited by Ian Douglas Wilson and Diana V. Edelman. Winona Lake, IN: Eisenbrauns, 2015.

Joyce, Paul M. *Ezekiel: A Commentary*. LHBOTS 482. New York: T&T Clark International, 2007.

Jursa, Michael. *Aspects of the Economic History of Babylonia in the First Millennium BC*. AOAT 377. Münster: Ugarit-Verlag, 2010.

Jursa, Michael. "Taxation and Service Obligations in Babylonia from Nebuchadnezzar to Darius and the Evidence for Darius' Tax Reform." Pages 431–48 in *Herodot und das Persische Weltreich/Herodotus and the Persian Empire*. Edited by Robert Rollinger, Brigitte Truschnegg, and Reinhold Bichler. CeO 3. Wiesbaden: Harrassowitz, 2011.

Jursa, Michael, J. Paszkowiak, and C. Waerzeggers. "Three Court Records." *AfO* 50 (2003/2004): 255–68.

Kanetsyan, Aminia. "Urartian and Early Achaemenid Palaces in Armenia." Pages 145–53 in *The Royal Palace Institution in the First Millennium BC: Regional Development and Cultural Interchange between East and West*. Edited by Inge Nielsen. MDIA 4. Athens: The Danish Institute of Athens, 2001.

Kaptan, Deniz. *The Daskyleion Bullae: Seal Images from the Western Achaemenid Empire*. 2 vols. AchHist 12. Leiden: Nederlands Instituut voor het Nabije Oosten, 2002.

Karrer, Christiane. *Ringen um die Verfassung Judas: Eine Studie zu den theologisch-politischen Vorstellungen im Esra-Nehemiah-Buch*. BZAW 308. Berlin: W. de Gruyter, 2001.

Karrer-Grube, Christiane. "Scrutinizing the Conceptual Unity of Ezra and Nehemiah." Pages 136–59 in *Unity and Disunity in Ezra–Nehemiah: Redaction, Rhetoric, and Reader*. Edited by Mark J. Boda and Paul L. Redditt. HBM 17. Sheffield: Sheffield Phoenix Press, 2008.

Kellens, Jean. "L'âme entre le cadavre et le paradis." *JA* 283 (1996): 19–56.

Kellens, Jean. "Yima et la mort." Pages 329–34 in *Languages and Cultures: Studies in Honor of Edgar C. Polomé*. Edited by Mohammed Ali Jazayery and Werner Winter. Berlin: Mouton de Gruyter, 1988.

Kelly, Brian E. "'Retribution' Revisited: Covenant, Grace and Restoration." Pages 206–27 in *The Chronicler as Theologian: Essays in Honor of Ralph W. Klein*. Edited by M. Patrick Graham, Steven L. McKenzie, and Gary N. Knoppers. JSOTSup 371. London: T&T Clark International, 2003.

Kent, Roland. *Old Persian: Grammar, Texts, Lexicon*. AOS 33. 2nd ed. New Haven, CT: American Oriental Society, 1953.

Kessler, John. *The Book of Haggai: Prophecy and Society in Early Persian Yehud*. VTSup 91. Leiden: Brill, 2002.

Kessler, John. "Diaspora and Homeland in the Early Achaemenid Period: Community, Geography and Demography in Zechariah 1–8." Pages 137–66 in *Approaching Yehud: New Approaches to the Study of the Persian Period*. Edited by Jon L. Berquist. SemeiaSt 50. Atlanta: Society of Biblical Literature, 2007.

Kessler, John. "The Diaspora of Zechariah 1–8 and Ezra–Nehemiah: The Role of History, Social Location, and Tradition in the Formulation of Identity." Pages 119–45 in *Community Identity in Judean Historiography: Biblical and Comparative Perspectives*. Edited by Gary N. Knoppers and Kenneth A. Ristau. Winona Lake, IN: Eisenbrauns, 2009.

Kessler, John. "Haggai, Zechariah, and the Political Status of Yehud: The Signet Ring in Haggai 2:23." Pages 102–19 in *Prophets, Prophecy, and Prophetic Texts in Second Temple Judaism*. Edited by Michael H. Floyd and Robert D. Haak. LHBOTS 427. New York: T&T Clark International, 2007.

Kessler, John. "Images of Exile: Representations of the 'Exile' and 'Empty Land' in the Sixth to Fourth Century BCE Yehudite Literature." Pages 309–51 in *The Concept of Exile in Ancient Israel and its Historical Contexts*. Edited by Ehud Ben Zvi and Christoph Levin. BZAW 404. Berlin: W. de Gruyter, 2010.

Kessler, John. "'Is Haggai among the Exclusivists?' A Response to Dalit Rom-Shiloni's *Exclusive Inclusivity*." *JHS* 18 (2018): art. 1, 13–35.

Kessler, John. "Persia's Loyal Yahwists: Power, Identity and Ethnicity in Achaemenid Judah." Pages 91–121 in *Judah and the Judeans in the Persian Period*. Edited by Oded Lipschits and Manfred Oeming. Winona Lake, IN: Eisenbrauns, 2006.

Kessler, Karlheinz. "Urukäische Familien versus babylonische Familien: Die Namengebung in Uruk, die Degradierung der Kulte von Eanna und der Aufstieg des Gottes Anu." *AoF* 31 (2004): 237–62.

Kessler, Rainer. "The Unity of Malachi and its Relation to the Book of the Twelve." Pages 223–36 in *Perspectives on the Formulation of the Book of the Twelve: Methodological Formulations—Redactional Processes—Historical Insights*. Edited by Rainer Albertz, James Nogalski, and Jakob Wöhrle. BZAW 433. Berlin: W. de Gruyter, 2012.

Khatchadourian, Lori. *Imperial Matter: Ancient Persia and the Archaeology of Empire*. Oakland, CA: University of California Press, 2016.

Klawans, Jonathan. *Impurity and Sin in Ancient Judaism*. Oxford: Oxford University Press, 2000.

Klein, Ralph W. *1 Chronicles: A Commentary*. Herm. Minneapolis: Fortress Press, 2006.

Klein, Ralph W. "Were Joshua, Zerubbabel, and Nehemiah Contemporaries? A Response to Diana Edelman's Proposed Late Date for the Second Temple." *JBL* 127 (2008): 697–701.

Knauf, Ernst Axel. *Ismael: Untersuchungen zur Geschichte Palästinas und Nordarabiens im 1. Jahrtausend v. Chr.* ADPV. Wiesbaden: O. Harrassowitz, 1985.

Knoppers, Gary N. *1 Chronicles 1–9: A New Translation with Introduction and Commentary*. AB 12. New York: Doubleday, 2004.

Knoppers, Gary N. "An Achaemenid Imperial Authorization of Torah in Yehud?" Pages 115–34 in *Persia and Torah: The Theory of Imperial Authorization of the Pentateuch*. Edited by James W. Watts. SBLSymS 17. Atlanta: Society of Biblical Literature, 2001.

Knoppers, Gary N. "Aspects of Samaria's Religious Culture during the Early Hellenistic Period." Pages 159–74 in *The Historian and the Bible: Essays in Honour of Lester L. Grabbe*. Edited by Philip R. Davies and Diana V. Edelman. LHBOTS 530. New York: T. & T. Clark International, 2010.

Knoppers, Gary N. "Beyond Jerusalem and Judah: The Mission of Ezra in the Province of Transeuphrates." *EI* 29 (2009): 78*–87*.

Knoppers, Gary N. "The Construction of Judean Diasporic Identity in Ezra–Nehemiah." *JHS* 15 (2015): art. 3.

Knoppers, Gary N. "Democratizing Revelation? Prophets, Seers and Visionaries in Chronicles." Pages 391–409 in *Prophecy and Prophets in Ancient Israel: Proceedings of the Oxford Old Testament Seminar*. Edited by John Day. New York: T&T Clark International, 2010.

Knoppers, Gary N. "Ethnicity, Genealogy, Geography, and Change: The Judean Communities of Babylon and Jerusalem in the Story of Ezra." Pages 141–71 in *Community Identity in Judea's Historiography: Biblical and Comparative Perspectives*. Edited by Gary N. Knoppers and Kenneth A. Ristau. Winona Lake, IN: Eisenbrauns, 2009.

Knoppers, Gary N. "Exile, Return and Diaspora: Expatriates and Repatriates in Late Biblical Literature." Pages 29–61 in *Texts, Contexts and Readings in Postexilic Literature: Explorations into Historiography and Identity Negotiation in Hebrew Bible and Related Texts*. Edited by Louis Jonker. FAT 2/53. Tübingen: Mohr Siebeck, 2011.

Knoppers, Gary N. "Intermarriage, Social Complexity, and Ethnic Diversity in the Genealogy of Judah." *JBL* 120 (2001): 15–30.

Knoppers, Gary N. *Jews and Samaritans: The Origins and History of their Early Relations*. Oxford: Oxford University Press, 2013.

Knoppers, Gary N. "Mt. Gerizim and Mt. Zion: A Study in the Early History of Samaritans and Jews." *SR* 34 (2005): 309–38.

Knoppers, Gary N. "Nehemiah and Sanballat: The Enemy without or within?" Pages 305–31 in *Judah and the Judeans in the Fourth Century B.C.E.* Edited by Oded Lipschits, Gary N. Knoppers, and Rainer Albertz. Winona Lake, IN: Eisenbrauns, 2007.

Knoppers, Gary N. "The Samaritan Schism or the Judaization of Samaria? Reassessing Josephus's Account of the Mount Gerizim Temple." Pages 163–78 in *Making a Difference: Essays on the Bible and Judaism in Honor of Tamara Cohn Eskenazi*. Edited by David J. A. Clines, Kent Harold Richards, and Jacob L. Wright. HBM 99. Sheffield: Sheffield Academic Press, 2012.

Knoppers, Gary N., and Paul B. Harvey, Jr. "The Pentateuch in Ancient Mediterranean Context: The Publication of Local Lawcodes." Pages 105–41 in *The Pentateuch as Torah: New Models for Understanding its Promulgation and Acceptance*. Edited by Gary N. Knoppers and Bernard M. Levinson. Winona Lake, IN: Eisenbrauns, 2007.

Ko, Ming Him. "Be Faithful to the Covenant: A Technical Translation of and Commentary on Malachi 2.10-16." *BT* 65 (2014): 34–48.

Kraemer, David. "On the Relationship of the Books of Ezra and Nehemiah." *JSOT* 59 (1993): 73–92.

Kratz, Reinhard G. *The Composition of the Narrative Books of the Old Testament*. Translated by John Bowden. London: T&T Clark International, 2005.

Kratz, Reinhard G. "Temple and Torah: Reflections on the Legal Status of the Pentateuch between Elephantine and Qumran." Pages 77–103 in *The Pentateuch as Torah: New Models for Understanding its Promulgation and Acceptance*. Edited by Gary N. Knoppers and Bernard M. Levinson. Winona Lake, IN: Eisenbrauns, 2007.

Kugler, Gili. "Present Affliction Affects the Representation of the Past: An Alternative Dating of the Levitical Prayer of Nehemiah 9." *VT* 63 (2013): 605–26.

Kuhrt, Amélie. "Achaemenid Images of Royalty and Empire." Pages 87–105 in *Concepts of Kingship in Antiquity: Proceedings of the European Science Foundation Exploratory Workshop*. Edited by Giovanni B. Lanfranchi and Robert Rollinger. HANEM 11. Padua: S.A.R.G.O.N., 2010.

Kuhrt, Amélie. "Can We Understand how the Persians Perceived 'Other' Gods/'the Gods of Others'?" *AfR* 15 (2013): 149–65.

Kuhrt, Amélie. "Nabonidus and the Babylonian Priesthood." Pages 119–55 in *Pagan Priests: Religion and Power in the Ancient World*. Edited by Mary Beard and John North. Ithaca, NY: Cornell University Press, 1990.

Kuhrt, Amélie. "The Palace(s) of Babylon." Pages 77–93 in *The Royal Palace Institution in the First Millennium BC: Regional Development and Cultural Interchange between East and West*. Edited by Inge Nielsen. MDIA 4. Athens: The Danish Institute of Athens, 2001.

Kuntzmann, Raymond. "La fonction prophétique en 1–2 Chroniques: Du ministère de la Parole au service de l'institution Communautaire." Pages 245–58 in *Ich bewirke das Heil und erschaffe das Unheil (Jesaja 45,7): Studien zur Botschaft der Propheten*. Edited by Friedrich Diedrich and Bernd Willmes. FzB 88. Würzburg: Echter Verlag, 1998.

Laato, Antti. *A Star Is Rising: The Historical Development of the Old Testament Royal Ideology and the Rise of Jewish Messianic Expectations*. ISFCJ 5. Atlanta: Scholars Press, 1997.

Labahn, Antje. "Antitheocratic Tendencies in Chronicles." Pages 115–35 in *Yahwism after the Exile: Perspectives on Israelite Religion in the Persian Era*. Edited by Rainer Albertz and Bob Becking. STAR 5. Assen: Royal Van Gorcum, 2003.

Labouvie, Sandra. *Gottesknecht und neuer David: Der Heilsmittler für Zion und seine Frohbotschaft nach Jesaja 60–62*. FzB 129. Würzburg: Echter Verlag, 2013.

Laird, Donna. *Negotiating Power in Ezra–Nehemiah*. SBLAIL 26. Atlanta: SBL Press, 2016.

Lau, Peter H. W. "Gentile Incorporation into Israel in Ezra–Nehemiah?" *Bib* 90 (2009): 356–73.

Lee, Kyong-Jin. *The Authority and Authorization of Torah in the Persian Period*. CBET. Leuven: Peeters, 2011.

Lemaire, André. "Fifth- and Fourth-Century Issues: Governorship and Priesthood in Jerusalem." Pages 406–25 in *Ancient Israel's History: An Introduction to Issues and Sources*. Edited by Bill T. Arnold and Richard S. Hess. Grand Rapids, MI: Baker Academic, 2014.

Lemaire, André. "Zorobabel et la Judée à lumière de l'épigraphie (fin du VIᵉ s. av. J.-C.)." *RB* 103 (1996): 48–57.

Leuchter, Mark. "Inter-Levitical Polemics in the Late 6th Century BCE: The Evidence from Nehemiah 9." *Bib* 95 (2014): 269–79.

Levin, Yigal. "Judea, Samaria and Idumaea: Three Models of Ethnicity and Administration in the Persia Period." Pages 4–53 in *From Judah to Judaea: Socio-economic Structures and Processes in the Persian Period*. Edited by Johannes Unsok Ro. HBM 43. Sheffield: Sheffield Phoenix Press, 2012.

Levin, Yigal. "Who Was the Chronicler's Audience? A Hint from his Genealogies." *JBL* 122 (2003): 229–45.

Liew, Tat-siong Benny. *What Is Asian American Biblical Hermeneutics? Reading the New Testament*. Intersections. Honolulu: University of Hawai'i Press, 2008.
Lincoln, Bruce. *"Happiness for Mankind": Achaemenian Religion and the Imperial Project*. ActIr 53. Leuven: Peeters, 2012.
Lincoln, Bruce. "Religion, Empire, and the Spectre of Orientalism: A Recent Controversy in Achaemenid Studies." *JNES* 72 (2013): 253–65.
Lincoln, Bruce. *Religion, Empire, and Torture: The Case of Achaemenian Persia with a Postscript on Abu Ghraib*. Chicago: University of Chicago Press, 2007.
Lipschits, Oded. "Ammon in Transition from Vassal Kingdom to Babylonian Province." *BASOR* 335 (2004): 37–52.
Lipschits, Oded. "Between Archaeology and Text: A Reevaluation of the Development Process of Jerusalem in the Persian Period." Pages 145–65 in *Congress Volume Helsinki 2010*. Edited by Martti Nissinen. VTSup 148. Leiden: Brill, 2012.
Lipschits, Oded. *The Fall and Rise of Jerusalem: Judah under Babylonian Rule*. Winona Lake, IN: Eisenbrauns, 2005.
Lipschits, Oded. "'Here is a man whose name is Ṣemaḥ' (Zechariah 6:12)." Pages 124–36 in *The Historian and the Bible: Essays in Honour of Lester L. Grabbe*. Edited by Philip R. Davies and Diana V. Edelman. LHBOTS 530. New York: T&T Clark International, 2010.
Lipschits, Oded. "Literary and Ideological Aspects of Nehemiah 11." *JBL* 121 (2002): 423–40.
Lipschits, Oded. "Persian Period Finds from Jerusalem: Facts and Interpretations." *JHS* 9 (2009): art. 20.
Lipschits, Oded. "Shedding New Light on the Dark Years of the 'Exilic Period': New Studies, Further Elucidation, and Some Questions Regarding the Archaeology of Judah as an 'Empty Land.'" Pages 57–90 in *Interpreting Exile: Displacement and Deportation in Biblical and Modern Contexts*. Edited by Brad E. Kelle, Frank Ritchel Ames, and Jacob L. Wright. SBLAIL 10. Atlanta: Society of Biblical Literature, 2011.
Lipschits, Oded, et al. "Palace and Village, Paradise and Oblivion: Unraveling the Riddles of Ramat Raḥel." *NEA* 74 (2011): 2–49.
Lipschits, Oded, et al. *What Are the Stones Whispering? Ramat Raḥel: 3000 Years of Forgotten History*. Winona Lake, IN: Eisenbrauns, 2017.
Lipschits, Oded, Y. Gadot, and D. Langgut. "The Riddle of Ramat Raḥel: The Archaeology of a Royal Persian Period Edifice." *Transeu* 41 (2012): 57–79.
Llewellyn-Jones, Lloyd. "The Great Kings of the Fourth Century and the Greek Memory of the Persian Past." Pages 317–46 in *Greek Notions of the Past in the Archaic and Classical Eras: History without Historians*. Edited by John Marincola, Lloyd Llewellyn-Jones, and Calum Maciver. ELS 6. Edinburgh: Edinburgh University Press, 2012.
Llewellyn-Jones, Lloyd. *King and Court in Ancient Persia 559 to 331 BCE*. DDAH. Edinburgh: Edinburgh University Press, 2013.
Lloyd, Alan. "Darius I in Egypt: Suez and Hibis." Pages 99–115 in *Persian Responses: Political and Cultural Interaction with(in) the Achaemenid Empire*. Edited by Christopher Tuplin. Swansea: The Classical Press of Wales, 2007.
Lortie, Christopher R. "These Are the Days of the Prophets: A Literary Analysis of Ezra 1–6." *TynBul* 64 (2013): 161–9.
Maachi, J.-D., and C. Nihan. "Le prétendu conflit entre exilés et non-exilés dans la province de Yehud à l'époque achéménide: Plaidoyer pour une approche différenciée." *Transeu* 42 (2012): 19–47.

MacDonald, Nathan. *Priestly Rule: Polemic and Biblical Interpretation in Ezekiel 44*. BZAW 476. Berlin: W. de Gruyter, 2015.

Machinist, Peter. "The First Coins of Judah and Samaria: Numismatics and History in the Achaemenid and Early Hellenistic Periods." Pages 365–79 in *Continuity and Change: Proceedings of the Last Achaemenid History Workshop*. Edited by Heleen Sancisi-Weerdenburg, Amélie Kuhrt, and Margaret Cool Root. AchHist 8. Leiden: Nederlands Instituut voor het Nabije Oosten, 1994.

Magen, Yitzhak, and Haggai Misgav, and Levana Tsfania. *Mount Gerizim Excavations Volume I: The Aramaic, Hebrew and Samaritan Inscriptions*. JSP 2. Jerusalem: Israel Antiquities Authority, 2004.

Marbury, Herbert R. "Reading Persian Dominion in Nehemiah: Multivalent Language, Co-option, Resistance, and Cultural Survival." Pages 158–76 in *Focusing Biblical Studies: The Crucial Nature of the Persian and Hellenistic Periods*. Edited by Jon L. Berquist and Alice Hunt. LHBOTS 544. New York: T&T Clark International, 2012.

Mein, Andrew. *Ezekiel and the Ethics of Exile*. OTM. Oxford: Oxford University Press, 2001.

Ménant, J. "La stele de Chalouf." *RTRPA* 9 (1897): 131–57.

Meshorer, Ya'akov. *A Treasury of Jewish Coins: From the Persian Period to Bar Kokhba*. Jerusalem: Yad Ben-Zvi Press, 2001.

Metso, Sarianna. *The Textual Development of the Qumran Community Rule*. STDJ 21. Leiden: Brill, 1997.

Meyers, Carol L., and Eric M. Meyers. *Haggai, Zechariah 1–8: A New Translation with Introduction and Commentary*. AB 25B. Garden City, NY: Doubleday, 1987.

Middlemas, Jill A. "The Future of the 'Exile.'" Pages 63–81 in *By the Irrigation Canals of Babylon: Approaches to the Study of Exile*. Edited by John J. Ahn and Jill Middlemas. LHBOTS 526. New York: T&T Clark International, 2012.

Middlemas, Jill A. "Going beyond the Myth of the Empty Land: A Reassessment of the Early Persian Period." Pages 174–94 in *Exile and Restoration Revisited: Essays on the Babylonian and Persian Periods in Memory of Peter R. Ackroyd*. Edited by Gary N. Knoppers and Lester L. Grabbe. LSTS 73. London: T&T Clark, 2009.

Middlemas, Jill A. "Trito-Isaiah's Intra- and Internationalization: Identity Markers in the Second Temple Period." Pages 105–25 in *Judah and the Judeans in the Achaemenid Period: Negotiating Identity in an International Context*. Edited by Oded Lipschits, Gary N. Knoppers, and Manfred Oeming. Winona Lake, IN: Eisenbrauns, 2011.

Milevski, I. "Palestine's Economic Formation and the Crisis of Judah (Yehud) during the Persian Period." *Transeu* 40 (2011): 135–66.

Milgrom, Jacob. *Leviticus 17–22: A New Translation with Introduction and Commentary*. AB 3A. New York: Doubleday, 2000.

Miller, Margaret C. "Luxury Toreutic in the Western Satrapies: Court-Inspired Gift-Exchange Diffusion." Pages 853–97 in *Der Achämenidenhof/The Achaemenid Court*. Edited by Bruno Jacobs and Robert Rollinger. CeO 2. Wiesbaden: Harrassowitz, 2010.

Min, Kyung-Jin. *The Levitical Authorship of Ezra–Nehemiah*. JSOTSup 409. London: T&T Clark International, 2004.

Mitchell, Christine. "Achaemenid Persian Concepts Pertaining to Covenant and Haggai, Zechariah, and Malachi." Pages 291–306 in *Covenant in the Persian Period: From Genesis to Chronicles*. Edited by Richard J. Bautch and Gary N. Knoppers. Winona Lake, IN: Eisenbrauns, 2015.

Mitchell, Christine. "A Paradise at Ramat Rahel and the Setting of Zechariah." *Transeu* 48 (2016): 81–95.

Moffat, Donald P. *Ezra's Social Drama: Identity Formation, Marriage and Social Conflict in Ezra 9 and 10*. LHBOTS 579. New York: Bloomsbury, 2013.
Moffat, Donald P. "The Metaphor at Stake in Ezra 9:8." *VT* 63 (2013): 290–8.
Mowinckel, Sigmund. "Die vorderasiatischen Königs- und Fürsteninschriften." Pages 278–322 in *Eucharistérion: Studien zur Religion und Literatur des Alten und Neuen Testaments. Hermann Gunkel zum 60. Geburtstage, dem 23. Mai 1922*. Edited by Hans Schmidt. FRLANT 36. Göttingen: Vandenhoeck & Ruprecht, 1923.
Na'aman, N. "In Search of Reality behind the Account of the Philistine Assault on Ahaz in the Book of *Chronicles*." *Transeu* 26 (2003): 47–63.
Newsom, Carol. "'Resistance is futile!': The Ironies of Danielic Resistance to Empire." *Int* 71 (2017): 167–77.
Nichols, Andrew G. "The Iranian Concept of *aša* and Greek Views of the Persians." *SCO* 62 (2016): 61–86.
Niehr, Herbert. "Religio-Historical Aspects of the 'Early Post-Exilic' Period." Pages 228–40 in *The Crisis of Israelite Religion: Transformation of Religious Tradition in Exilic and Post-Exilic Times*. Edited by Bob Becking and Marjo C. A. Korpel. OTS 42. Leiden: Brill, 1999.
Nielsen, John P. "'I overwhelmed the king of Elam': Remembering Nebuchadnezzar I in Persian Babylonia." Pages 53–73 in *Political Memory in and after the Persian Empire*. Edited by Jason M. Silverman and Caroline Waerzeggars. ANEM 13. Atlanta: SBL Press, 2015.
Nihan, Christophe. "Ethnicity and Identity in Isaiah 56–66." Pages 67–104 in *Judah and the Judeans in the Achaemenid Period: Negotiating Identity in an International Context*. Edited by Oded Lipschits, Gary N. Knoppers, and Manfred Oeming. Winona Lake, IN: Eisenbrauns, 2011.
Nihan, Christophe. *From Priestly Torah to Pentateuch: A Study in the Composition of the Book of Leviticus*. FAT 2/25. Tübingen: Mohr Siebeck, 2007.
Nihan, Christophe. "Remarques sur la question de l''unité' des XII." Pages 145–65 in *The Book of the Twelve—One or Many?* Edited by Eleana Di Pede and Donatella Sciaola. FAT 2/91. Tübingen: Mohr Siebeck, 2016.
Nimchuk, Cindy L. "The 'Archers' of Darius: Coinage or Tokens of Royal Esteem?" *ArsOr* 32 (2002): 55–79.
Nissinen, Martti. "Falsche Prophetie in neuassyrischer und deuteronomistische Darstellung." Pages 172–95 in *Das Deuteronomium und seine Querbeziehungen*. Edited by Timo Veijola. SEFJ 62. Göttingen: Vandenhoeck & Ruprecht, 1996.
Nissinen, Martti. "Prophecy and Omen Divination: Two Sides of the Same Coin." Pages 341–51 in *Divination and Interpretation of Signs in the Ancient World*. Edited by Amar Annus. OIS 6. Chicago: The Oriental Institute of the University of Chicago, 2010.
Nogalski, James D. *The Book of the Twelve*. 2 volumes. SHBC. Macon, GA: Smyth & Helwys, 2011.
Nogalski, James D. *Literary Precursors to the Book of the Twelve*. BZAW 217. Berlin: W. de Gruyter, 1993.
Nogalski, James D. *Redactional Processes in the Book of the Twelve*. BZAW 218. Berlin: W. de Gruyter, 1993.
Nurmela, Risto. *The Levites: Their Emergence as a Second-Class Priesthood*. SFSHJ 193. Atlanta: Scholars Press, 1998.

Nykolaishen, Douglas J. E. "The Restoration of Israel by God's Word in Three Episodes from Ezra–Nehemiah." Pages 176–99 in *Unity and Diversity in Ezra–Nehemiah: Redaction, Rhetoric, and Reader*. Edited by Mark J. Boda and Paul L. Redditt. HBM 17. Sheffield: Sheffield Phoenix Press, 2008.

Nzimande, Makhosazana K. "*Imbokodo* Explorations of the Prevalence of Historical Memory and Identity Contestations in the Expulsion of the *Nāšîm Nokriyyōt* in Ezra 9–10." Pages 269–94 in *Texts, Contexts and Readings in Postexilic Literature: Explorations into Historiography and Identity in Hebrew Bible and Related Texts*. Edited by Louis Jonker. FAT 2/53. Tübingen: Mohr Siebeck, 2011.

Oded, Bustenay. "Exile-Homeland Relations during the Exilic Period and Restoration." Pages 153*–60* in *Tᵉshûrôt LaAvishur: Studies in the Bible and the Ancient Near East, in Hebrew and Semitic Languages*. Edited by Michael Heltzer and Meir Maul. Tel Aviv-Jaffa: Archaeological Center Publications, 2004.

Oeming, Manfred. "The Real History: The Theological Ideas behind Nehemiah's Wall." Pages 131–49 in *New Perspectives on Ezra–Nehemiah: History and Historiography, Text, Literature, and Interpretation*. Isaac Kalimi. Winona Lake, IN: Eisenbrauns, 2012.

Oeming, Manfred. "'See, we are serving today' (Nehemiah 9:36): Nehemiah 9 as a Theological Interpretation of the Persian Period." Pages 571–88 in *Judah and the Judeans in the Persian Period*. Edited by Oded Lipschits and Manfred Oeming. Winona Lake, IN: Eisenbrauns, 2006.

Oeming, Manfred. *Das wahre* Israel: Die *"genealogische Vorhalle"1 Chronik 1–9*. BWANT 128. Stuttgart: W. Kohlhammer, 1990.

Olyan, Saul M. "Purity Ideology in Ezra–Nehemiah as a Tool to Reconstitute the Community." *JSJ* 35 (2004): 1–16.

Oswald, Wolfgang. "Foreign Marriages and Citizenship in Persian-Period Judah." *JHS* 12 (2012): art. 6.

Pakkala, Juha. "Centers and Peripheries in the Ezra Story." Pages 295–314 in *Centres and Peripheries in the Early Second Temple Period*. Edited by Ehud Ben Zvi and Christoph Levin. FAT 108. Tübingen: Mohr Siebeck, 2016.

Pakkala, Juha. *Ezra the Scribe: The Development of Ezra 7–10 and Nehemiah 8*. BZAW 347. Berlin: W. de Gruyter, 2004.

Pakkala, Juha. "Intermarriage and Group Identity in the Ezra Tradition (Ezra 7–10 and Nehemiah 8)." Pages 78–88 in *Mixed Marriages: Intermarriage and Group Identity in the Second Temple Period*. Edited by Christian Frevel. LHBOTS 547. New York: Bloomsbury T&T Clark, 2011.

Pakkala, Juha. "Why 1 Esdras is Probably Not an Early Version of the Ezra–Nehemiah Tradition." Pages 93–107 in *Was 1 Esdras First? An Investigation into the Priority and Nature of 1 Esdras*. Edited by Lisbeth S. Fried. SBLAIL 7. Atlanta: Society of Biblical Literature, 2011.

Pearce, Laurie E. "Identifying Judeans and Judean Identity in the Babylonian Evidence." Pages 7–32 in *Exile and Return: The Babylonian Context*. Edited by Jonathan Stökl and Caroline Waerzeggers. BZAW 478. Berlin: W. de Gruyter, 2015.

Pearce, Laurie E. "'Judean': A Special Status in Neo-Babylonian and Achaemenid Babylonia?" Pages 267–77 in *Judah and the Judeans in the Achaemenid Period: Negotiating Identity in an International Context*. Edited by Oded Lipschits, Gary N. Knoppers, and Manfred Oeming. Winona Lake, IN: Eisenbrauns, 2011.

Pearce, Laurie E. "New Evidence for Judeans in Babylonia." Pages 399–410 in *Judah and the Judeans in the Persian Period*. Edited by Oded Lipschits and Manfred Oeming. Winona Lake, IN: Eisenbrauns, 2006.

Peltonen, Kai. "A Jigsaw without a Model? The Date of Chronicles." Pages 225–71 in *Did Moses Speak Attic? Jewish Historiography in the Hellenistic Period*. Edited by Lester L. Grabbe. JSOTSup 317. ESHM 3. Sheffield: Sheffield Academic Press, 2001.

Petersen, David. *Zechariah 9–14 and Malachi: A Commentary*. OTL. Louisville: Westminster John Knox Press, 1995.

Petit, Thierry. "L'évolution sémantique des termes hébreux et araméens *phh* et *sgn* et accadiens *pāḫatu* et *šaknu*." *JBL* 107 (1988): 53–67.

Petterson, Anthony R. *Behold your King: The Hope for the House of David in the Book of Zechariah*. LHBOTS 513. New York: T&T Clark International, 2009.

Petterson, Anthony R. "A New Form-Critical Approach to Zechariah's Crowning of the High Priest Joshua and the Identity of the 'Shoot' (Zechariah 6:9-15)." Pages 285–304 in *The Book of the Twelve and the New Form Criticism*. Edited by Mark J. Boda, Michael H. Floyd, and Colin M. Toffelmire. ANEM 10. Atlanta: SBL Press, 2015.

Petterson, Anthony R. "The Shape of the Davidic Hope across the Book of the Twelve." *JSOT* 35 (2010): 225–46.

Pirart, É. "Le mazdéisme politique de Darius Ier." *IIJ* 45 (2002): 121–51.

Pokorny, Julius. *Indogermanisches etymologisches Wörterbuch*. 2 vols. Bern: Francke, 1959–1969.

Polak, Frank H. "Sociolinguistics and the Judean Speech Community in the Achaemenid Empire." Pages 589–628 in *Judah and the Judeans in the Persian Period*. Edited by Oded Lipschits and Manfred Oeming. Winona Lake, IN: Eisenbrauns, 2006.

Polaski, Don. "Nehemiah: Subject of the Empire, Subject of Writing." Pages 37–59 in *New Perspectives on Ezra–Nehemiah: History and Historiography, Text, Literature, and Interpretation*. Edited by Isaac Kalimi. Winona Lake, IN: Eisenbrauns, 2012.

Portier-Young, Anathea E. "Languages of Identity and Obligation: Daniel as a Bilingual Book." *VT* 60 (2010): 98–115.

Potts, D. T. "Cyrus the Great and the Kingdom of Anshan." Pages 7–28 in *Birth of the Persian Empire, Volume I*. Edited by Vesta Sarkhosh Curtis and Sarah Stewart. London: I. B. Tauris, 2005.

Powell, Marvin A. "Weights and Measures." *ABD* 6:897–908.

Pröbstl, Volker. *Nehemia 9, Psalm 106 und Psalm 136 und die Rezeption des Pentateuchs*. Göttingen: Cuvillier Verlag, 1997.

Quintana, Enrique. "Elamitas Frente a Persas: El Reino Independiente de Anšan." Pages 167–86 in *Elam and Persia*. Edited by Javier Álvarez-Mon and Mark B. Garrison. Winona Lake, IN: Eisenbrauns, 2011.

Raban, Avner. "A Group of Objects from a Wreckage Site at Athlit." *Michmanim* 6 (1992): 31–53 [Hebrew].

Rad, Gerhad von. *Das Geschichtsbild des Chronistischen Werkes*. BWANT 54. Stuttgart: Kohlhammer, 1930.

Razmjou, Shahrokh. "Assessing the Damage: Notes on the Life and Demise of the Statue of Darius from Susa." *ArsOr* 32 (2002): 81–104.

Razmjou, Shahrokh. "Religion and Burial Customs." Pages 150–80 in *Forgotten Empire: The World of Ancient Persia*. Edited by John Curtis and Nigel Tallis. Berkeley: University of California Press, 2005.

Redditt, Paul L. *Haggai, Zechariah, and Malachi*. NCBC. Grand Rapids, MI: Eerdmans, 1995.

Redditt, Paul L. "The King in Haggai-Zechariah 1–8 and the Book of the Twelve." Pages 56–82 in *Tradition in Transition: Haggai and Zechariah 1–8 in the Trajectory of Hebrew Theology*. Edited by Mark J. Boda and Michael H. Floyd. LHBOTS 475. New York: T&T Clark, 2008.

Redditt, Paul L. "King, Priest, and Temple in Haggai-Zechariah-Malachi and Ezra–Nehemiah." Pages 157–72 in *Priests and Cults in the Book of the Twelve*. Edited by Lena-Sofia Tiemeyer. ANEM 14. Atlanta: SBL Press, 2016.

Reinmuth, Titus. *Der Bericht Nehemias: Zur literarischen Eigenart, traditionsgeschichtlichen Prägung und innerbiblischen Rezeption des Ich-Berichts Nehemias*. OBO 183. Göttingen: Vandenhoeck & Ruprecht, 2002.

Rendtorff, Rolf. "Noch einmal: Esra und das 'Gesetz.'" *ZAW* 111 (1999): 89–91.

Rollinger, Robert. "Herrscherkult bei Teispiden und Achaimeniden: Realität oder Fiktion?" Pages 11–54 in *Studien zum vorhellenistischen und hellenistischen Herrscherkult*. Edited by Linda-Marie Günther and Sonja Plischke. Oik 9. Berlin: Verlag Antike, 2011.

Rollinger, Robert. "Royal Strategies of Representation and the Language(s) of Power: Some Considerations on the Audience and the Dissemination of the Achaemenid Royal Inscriptions." Pages 117–30 in *Official Epistolography and the Language(s) of Power: Proceedings of the First International Conference of the Research Network Imperium and Officium*. Edited by Stephan Procházka, Lucian Reinfandt, and Sven Tost. PapVin 8. Vienna: Österreichischen Akademie der Wissenschaften, 2015.

Rollinger, Robert. "Thinking and Writing about History in Teispid and Achaemenid Persia." Pages 185–212 in *Thinking, Recording, and Writing History in the Ancient World*. Edited by Kurt A. Raaflaub. AWCH. Malden, MA: John Wiley & Sons, 2014.

Rollinger, Robert. "Xerxes und Babylon." NABU 1999-8, www.achemenet.com/pdf/nabu/nabu1999-008.pdf; accessed 13 January 2020.

Römer, Thomas. "Conflicting Models of Identity and the Publication of the Torah in the Persian Period." Pages 33–51 in *Between Cooperation and Hostility: Multiple Identities in Ancient Judaism and the Interaction with Foreign Powers*. Edited by Rainer Albertz and Jakob Wöhrle. JAJSup 11. Göttingen: Vandenhoeck & Ruprecht, 2013.

Römer, Thomas. "The Exodus Narrative According to the Priestly Document." Pages 157–74 in *The Strata of the Priestly Writings: Contemporary Debate and Future Directions*. Edited by Sarah Shectman and Joel S. Baden. ATANT 95. Zurich: Theologischer Verlag Zürich, 2009.

Rom-Shiloni, Dalit. *Exclusive Inclusivity: Identity Conflicts between the Exiles and the People Who Remained (6th–5th Centuries BCE)*. LHBOTS 543. New York: Bloomsbury, 2013.

Rom-Shiloni, Dalit. "From Ezekiel to Ezra–Nehemiah: Shifts of Group Identities within Babylonian Exilic Ideology." Pages 127–51 in *Judah and the Judeans in the Achaemenid Period: Negotiating Identity in an International Context*. Edited by Oded Lipschits, Gary N. Knoppers, and Manfred Oeming. Winona Lake, IN: Eisenbrauns, 2011.

Rooke, Deborah. *Zadok's Heirs: The Role and Development of the High Priesthood in Ancient Israel*. OTM. Oxford: Oxford University Press, 2000.

Root, Margaret Cool. "Achaemenid Imperial Architecture: Performative Porticoes of Persepolis." Pages 1–63 in *Persian Kingship and Architecture: Strategies of Power in Iran from the Achaemenids to the Pahlavis*. Edited by Susan Babaie and Talinn Grigor. London: I. B. Tauris, 2015.

Root, Margaret Cool. "Defining the Divine in Achaemenid Persian Kingship: The View from Bisitun." Pages 23–65 in *Every Inch a King: Comparative Studies on Kings and Kingship in the Ancient and Medieval Worlds*. Edited by Lynette Mitchell and Charles Melville. RE 2. Leiden: Brill, 2013.

Root, Margaret Cool. "Imperial Ideology in Achaemenid Persian Art: Transforming the Mesopotamian Legacy." *BCSMS* 35 (2000): 19–27.

Root, Margaret Cool. *The King and Kingship in Achaemenid Art: Essays on the Creation of an Iconography of Empire*. ActIr 19. Leiden: E. J. Brill, 1979.

Root, Margaret Cool. "The Legible Image: How Did Seals and Sealing Matter in Persepolis?" Pages 87–148 in *L'Archive des Fortifications de Persépolis: État des questions et perspectives de recherches*. Edited by Pierre Briant, Wouter F. M. Henkelman, and Matthew W. Stolper. Pers 12. Paris: De Boccard, 2008.

Root, Margaret Cool. "The Lioness of Elam: Politics and Dynastic Fecundity at Persepolis." Pages 9–32 in *A Persian Perspective: Essays in Memory of Heleen Sancisi-Weerdenburg*. Edited by Wouter Henkelman and Amélie Kuhrt. AchHist 13. Leiden: Nederlands Instituut voor het Nabije Oosten, 2003.

Root, Margaret Cool. "Reading Persepolis in Greek: Gifts of the Yauna." Pages 177–224 in *Persian Responses: Political and Cultural Interaction with(in) the Achaemenid Empire*. Edited by Christopher Tuplin. Swansea: The Classical Press of Wales, 2007.

Rooy, Harry V. "Prophet and Society in the Persian Period According to Chronicles." Pages 163–79 in *Second Temple Studies 2: Temple Community in the Persian Period*. Edited by Tamara C. Eskenazi and Kent H. Richards. JSOTSup 175. Sheffield: JSOT, 1994.

Rose, Wolter H. *Zemah and Zerubbabel: Messianic Expectations in the Early Postexilic Period*. JSOTSup 304. Sheffield: Sheffield Academic Press, 2000.

Rosenthal, Franz. *A Grammar of Biblical Aramaic*. 7th ed. PLO 5. Wiesbaden: Harrassowitz, 2006.

Rothenbusch, Ralf. *"...Abgesondert zur Tora Gottes hin": Ethnisch-religiöse Identitäten im Esra/Nehemiabuch*. HBS 70. Freiburg: Koch Neff & Volkmar, 2012.

Rothenbusch, Ralf. "Die Auseinandersetzung um die Identität Israels im Esra- und Nehemiabuch." Pages 111–44 in *Die Identität Israels: Entwicklungen und Kontroversen in alttestamentlicher Zeit*. Edited by Hubert Irsigler. HBS 56. Freiburg: Herder, 2009.

Rothenbusch, Ralf. "The Question of Mixed Marriages between the Poles of Diaspora and Homeland: Observations in Ezra–Nehemiah." Pages 60–77 in *Mixed Marriages: Intermarriage and Group Identity in the Second Temple Period*. Edited by Christian Frevel. LHBOTS 547. New York: Bloomsbury T&T Clark, 2011.

Rudolph, Wilhelm. *Esra und Nehemiah samt 3. Esra*. HAT 1/20. Tübingen: Mohr, 1949.

Ruiz, Jean-Pierre. *Readings from the Edges: The Bible and People on the Move*. SLC. Maryknoll, NY: Orbis Books, 2011.

Russell, Stephen C. "Enemies, Lands, and Borders in Biblical Crossing Traditions." *JANEH* 4 (2017): 163–76.

Sancisi-Weerdenburg, Heleen. "The Persian Kings and History." Pages 91–112 in *The Limits of Historiography: Genre and Narrative in Ancient Historical Texts*. Edited by Christina Shuttleworth Kraus. Mnemosyne. Leiden: Brill, 1999.

Schaper, Joachim. *Priester und Leviten im achämenidischen Juda: Studien zur Kult- und Sozialgeschichte Israels in persischer Zeit*. FAT 31. Tübingen: Mohr Siebeck, 2000.

Schaper, Joachim. "The Priests of the Book of Malachi and their Opponents." Pages 177–88 in *The Priests in the Prophets: The Portrayal of Priests, Prophets and Other Religious Specialists in the Latter Prophets*. Edited by Lester L. Grabbe and Alice Ogden Bellis. JSOTSup 408. London: T&T Clark International, 2004.

Schaper, Joachim. "Rereading the Law: Inner-Biblical Exegesis of Divine Oracles in Ezekiel 44 and Isaiah 56." Pages 125–44 in *Recht und Ethik im Alten Testament: Beiträge des Symposiums "Das Alte Testament und die Kultur der Moderne" anlässlich des 100. Geburtstags Gerhard von Rads*. Edited by Bernard M. Levinson and Eckart Otto. ATM 13. Münster: LIT, 2004.

Schaudig, Hanspeter. "The Magnanimous Heart of Cyrus: The Cyrus Cylinder and its Literary Models." Pages 67–91 in *Cyrus the Great: Life and Lore*. Edited by M. Rahim Shayegan. Boston: Ilex Foundation, 2019.

Schmid, Konrad. "How to Identify a Persian Period Text in the Pentateuch." Pages 101–18 in *On Dating Biblical Texts to the Persian Period: Discerning Criteria and Establishing Epochs*. Edited by Richard J. Bautch and Mark Lackowski. FAT 2/101. Tübingen: Mohr Siebeck, 2019.

Schmid, Konrad. "Judean Identity and Ecumenicity: The Political Theology of the Priestly Document." Pages 3–26 in *Judah and the Judeans in the Achaemenid Period: Negotiating Identity in an International Context*. Edited by Oded Lipschits, Gary N. Knoppers, and Manfred Oeming. Winona Lake, IN: Eisenbrauns, 2011.

Schmitt, Rüdiger. *The Old Persian Inscriptions of Naqsh-i Rustam and Persepolis*. CII 1/1/2. London: School of African and Oriental Studies, 2000.

Schmitt, Rüdiger. "Rites of Family and Household Religion." Pages 429–73 in *Family and Household Religion in Ancient Israel and the Levant*. Edited by Rainer Albertz and Rüdiger Schmitt. Winona Lake, IN: Eisenbrauns, 2012.

Schniedewind, William M. "Prophets and Prophecy in the Books of Chronicles." Pages 204–24 in *The Chronicler as Historian*. Edited by M. Patrick Graham, Kenneth G. Hoglund, and Steven L. McKenzie. JSOTSup 238. Sheffield: Sheffield Academic Press, 1997.

Schöttler, Günther. *Gott inmitten seines Volkes: Die Neuordnung des Gottesvolkes nach Sacharja 1–6*. TTS 43. Trier: Paulinus-Verlag, 1987.

Schramm, Brooks. *The Opponents of Third Isaiah: Reconstructing the Cultic History of the Restoration*. JSOTSup 193. Sheffield: Sheffield Academic Press, 1995.

Schuele, Andreas. "Who Is the True Israel? Community, Identity, and Religious Commitment in Third Isaiah." *Int* 73 (2019): 174–84.

Schulte, Lucas L. *My Shepherd, though You Do Not Know Me: The Persian Royal Propaganda Model in the Nehemiah Memoir*. CBET 78. Leuven: Peeters, 2016.

Schunck, Klaus-Dietrich. *Nehemia*. BKAT 23. Neukirchen-Vluyn: Neukirchener Verlag, 2008.

Schweitzer, Steven J. "Exile, Empire, and Prophecy: Reframing Utopian Concerns in Chronicles." Pages 81–104 in *Worlds that Could Not Be: Utopia in Chronicles, Ezra and Nehemiah*. Edited by Steven J. Schweitzer and Frauke Uhlenbruch. LHBOTS 620. London: Bloomsbury, 2016.

Schwiderski, Dirk. *Handbuch des nordwestsemitischen Briefformulars: Ein Beitrag zur Echtheitsfrage der aramäischen Briefe des Esrabuches*. BZAW 295. Berlin: W. de Gruyter, 2000.

Scolnic, Benjamin. *Chronology and Papponymy: A List of the Judean High Priests of the Persian Period*. SFSHJ 206. Atlanta: Scholars Press, 1999.

Seidl, Ursula. Ein Monument Darius' I. aus Babylon." *ZA* 89 (1999): 101–14.
Shahbazi, Alireza S. "An Achaemenid Symbol II: Farnah '(God-Given) Fortune' Symbolized." *AMI* 9 (1980): 119–47.
Siedlicki, Armin. "Contextualizations of Ezra–Nehemiah." Pages 263–76 in *Unity and Diversity in Ezra–Nehemiah: Redaction, Rhetoric, and Reader*. Edited by Mark J. Boda and Paul L. Redditt. HBM 17. Sheffield: Sheffield Phoenix Press, 2008.
Silverman, Jason M. "Iranian-Judaean Interaction in the Achaemenid Period." Pages 133–68 in *Text, Theology, and Trowel: New Investigations in the Biblical World*. Edited by Lidia D. Matassa and Jason M. Silverman. Eugene, OR: Pickwick Publications, 2011.
Silverman, Jason M. *Persian Royal–Judaean Elite Engagements in the Early Teispid and Achaemenid Empire: The King's Acolytes*. LHBOTS 690. London: T&T Clark, 2020.
Skjævrø, Prods Oktor. "The Achaemenids and the *Avesta*." Pages 52–84 in *Birth of the Persian Empire, Volume I*. Edited by Vesta Sarkhosh Curtis and Sarah Stewart. London: I. B. Tauris, 2005.
Skjævrø, Prods Oktor. "Achaemenid **Vispašiyātiš*, Sasanian *Wipšād*." *StIr* 23 (1994): 79–80.
Skjævrø, Prods Oktor. "Zarathustra: A Revolutionary Monotheist?" Pages 317–50 in *Reconsidering the Concept of Revolutionary Monotheism*. Edited by Beate Pongratz-Leisten. Winona Lake, IN: Eisenbrauns, 2011.
Smelik, Klaas A. D. "Nehemiah as a 'Court Jew.'" Pages 61–72 in *New Perspectives on Ezra–Nehemiah: History and Historiography, Text, Literature, and Interpretation*. Edited by Isaac Kalimi. Winona Lake, IN: Eisenbrauns, 2012.
Snyman, Gerrie. "Why Asa Was Not Deemed Good Enough: A Decolonial Reading of 2 Chronicles 14–16." Pages 241–68 in *Texts, Contexts and Readings in Postexilic Literature: Explorations into Historiography and Identity Negotiation in Hebrew Bible and Related Texts*. Edited by Louis Jonker. FAT 2/53. Tübingen: Mohr Siebeck, 2011.
Snyman, S. D. *Malachi*. HCOT. Leuven: Peeters, 2015.
Sommer, Benjamin D. "Dating Pentateuchal Texts and the Perils of Pseudo-Historicism." Pages 85–108 in *The Pentateuch: International Reflections on Current Research*. Edited by Thomas B. Dozeman, Konrad Schmid, and Baruch J. Schwartz. FAT 78. Tübingen: Mohr Siebeck, 2011.
Soudavar, Abolala. *The Aura of Kings: Legitimacy and Divine Sanction in Iranian Kingship*. BibIr 10. Costa Mesa, CA: Mazda Publishers, 2003.
Soudavar, Abolala. "The Formation of Achaemenid Ideology and its Impact on the *Avesta*." Pages 111–38 in *The World of Achaemenid Persia: History, Art and Society in Iran and the Ancient Near East*. Edited by John Curtis and St John Simpson. London: I. B. Tauris, 2010.
Southwood, Katherine. "'But now…do not let all this hardship seem insignificant before you': Ethnic History and Nehemiah 9." *SEÅ* 79 (2014): 1–23.
Southwood, Katherine. *Ethnicity and the Mixed Marriage Crisis in Ezra 9–10: An Anthropological Approach*. OTM. Oxford: Oxford University Press, 2012.
Southwood, Katherine. "The Holy Seed: The Significance of Endogamous Boundaries and their Transgression in Ezra 9–10." Pages 189–224 in *Judah and the Judeans in the Achaemenid Period: Negotiating Identity in an International Context*. Edited by Oded Lipschits, Gary N. Knoppers, and Manfred Oeming. Winona Lake, IN: Eisenbrauns, 2011.
Sparks, James T. *The Chronicler's Genealogies: Towards an Understanding of 1 Chronicles 1–9*. SBLAB 28. Leiden: Brill, 2008.

Spek, R. J. van der. "Cyrus the Great, Exiles, and Foreign Gods: A Comparison of Daskyleion and Persian Policies on Subject Nations." Pages 233–64 in *Extraction and Control: Studies in Honor of Matthew W. Stolper*. Edited by Michael Kozuh et al. SAOC 68. Chicago: The Oriental Institute of the University of Chicago, 2014.

Stausberg, Michael. "Hell in Zoroastrian History." *Numen* 56 (2009): 217–53.

Stead, Michael R. *The Intertextuality of Zechariah 1–8*. LHBOTS 506. New York: T&T Clark International, 2009.

Stead, Michael R. "The Three Shepherds: Reading Zechariah 11 in the Light of Jeremiah." Pages 149–65 in *A God of Faithfulness: Essays in Honour of J. Gordon McConville on his 60th Birthday*. Edited by Jamie A. Grant, Alison Lo, and Gordon J. Wenham. LHBOTS 538. New York: T&T Clark International, 2011.

Steck, Odil Hannes. *Der Abschluss der Prophetie im Alten Testament: Ein Versuch zur Frage der Vorgeschichte des Kanons*. BTS 17. Neukirchen-Vluyn: Neukirchener, 1991.

Steiner, Margaret. "The Persian Period City Wall of Jerusalem." Pages 307–15 in *The Fire Signals of Lachish: Studies in the Archaeology and History of Israel in the Late Bronze Age, Iron Age, and Persian Period in Honor of David Ussishkin*. Edited by Israel Finkelstein and Nadav Na'aman. Winona Lake, IN: Eisenbrauns, 2011.

Steiner, Richard C. "Bishlam's Archival Search Report in Nehemiah's Archive: Multiple Introductions and Reverse Chronological Order as Clues to the Origin of the Aramaic Letters in Ezra 4–6." *JBL* 125 (2006): 641–85.

Stern, Ephraim. *Archaeology of the Land of the Bible, Volume II: The Assyrian, Babylonian, and Persian Periods 732–332 BCE*. ABRL. New York: Doubleday, 2001.

Stern, Sacha. *Calendars in Antiquity: Empires, States, and Societies*. Oxford: Oxford University Press, 2012.

Stolper, Matthew W. *Entrepreneurs and Empire: The Murašû Archive, the Murašû Firm, and Persian Rule in Babylonia*. UNHAII 54. Leiden: Nederlands Instituut voor het Nabije Oosten, 1985.

Stolper, Matthew W. "The šaknu of Nippur." *JCS* 40 (1988): 127–55.

Stromberg, Jacob. *Isaiah after Exile: The Author of Third Isaiah as Reader and Redactor of the Book*. OTM. Oxford: Oxford University Press, 2011.

Stronach, David. "Description and Comment." *JA* 260 (1972): 241–6.

Stronach, David. "From Cyrus to Darius: Notes on Art and Architecture in Early Achaemenid Palaces." Pages 95–111 in *The Royal Palace Institution in the First Millennium BC: Regional Development and Cultural Interchange between East and West*. Edited by Inge Nielsen. MDIA 4. Athens: The Danish Institute of Athens, 2001.

Strübind, Kim. *Tradition als Interpretation in der Chronik: König Josaphat als Paradigma chronistischer Hermeneutik und Theologie*. BZAW 201. Berlin: W. de Gruyter, 1991.

Summerer, Lâtife. "Picturing Persian Victory: The Painted Battle Scene on the Munich Wood." Pages 3–30 in *Achaemenid Culture and Local Traditions in Anatolia, Southern Caucasus and Iran*. ACSS 13. Leiden: Brill, 2007.

Sweeney, Marvin A. *Isaiah 40–66*. FOTL 19. Grand Rapids, MI: Eerdmans, 2016.

Sweeney, Marvin A. *The Twelve Prophets*. 2 vols. BerO. Collegeville, MN: Liturgical Press, 2000.

Tadmor, Hayim. "'The appointed time has not yet arrived': The Historical Background of Haggai 1:2." Pages 401–8 in *Ki Baruch Hu: Ancient Near Eastern, Biblical, and Judaic Studies in Honor of Baruch A. Levine*. Edited by Robert Chazan, William W. Hallo, and Lawrence H. Schiffman. Winona Lake, IN: Eisenbrauns, 1999.

Tadmor, Miriam. "Fragments of an Achaemenid Throne from Samaria." *IEJ* 24 (1974): 37–43.

Tammuz, Oded. "Will the Real Sanballat Please Stand up?" Pages 51–8 in *Samaritans: Past and Present*. Edited by Menahem Mor and Friedrich V. Reiterer. StJud 53. StSam 5. Berlin: W. de Gruyter, 2010.

Thames, John Tracy Jr. "A New Discussion of the Meaning of the Phrase *'am hā'āreṣ* in the Hebrew Bible." *JBL* 130 (2011): 109–25.

Thiessen, Matthew. "The Function of a Conjunction: Inclusivist or Exclusivist Strategies in Ezra 6.21 and Nehemiah 10.29–30?" *JSOT* 34 (2009): 63–79.

Tiemeyer, Lena-Sofia. "Abraham—A Judahite Perspective." *ZAW* 120 (2008): 49–66.

Tiemeyer, Lena-Sofia. "Death or Conversion: The Gentiles in the Concluding Chapters of the Book of Isaiah and the Book of the Twelve." *JTS* 68 (2017): 1–22.

Tiemeyer, Lena-Sofia. *Ezra–Nehemiah: Israel's Quest for Identity*. TTCSGOT. London: Bloomsbury T&T Clark, 2017.

Tiemeyer, Lena-Sofia. "'The Haughtiness of the Priesthood' (Isa 65,5)." *Bib* 85 (2004): 237–44.

Tiemeyer, Lena-Sofia. *Priestly Rites and Prophetic Rage: Post-Exilic Prophetic Critique of the Priesthood*. FAT 2/19. Tübingen: Mohr Siebeck, 2006.

Tiemeyer, Lena-Sofia. *Zechariah's Vision Report and its Earliest Interpreters: A Redaction-Critical Study of Zechariah 1–8*. LHBOTS 626. London: T&T Clark, 2016.

Tigay, Jeffrey. *The Evolution of the Gilgamesh Epic*. Philadelphia: The University of Pennsylvania Press, 1982.

Tiňo, Jozef. *King and Temple in Chronicles: A Contextual Approach to their Relation*. FRLANT 234. Göttingen: Vandenhoeck & Ruprecht, 2010.

Trichet, Jean and Pierre Poupet. "Étude pétrographique de la roche constituant la statue de Darius découverte à Suse en décembre 1972." *CDAFI* 4 (1974): 47–59.

Trimm, Charlie. *Fighting for the King and the Gods: A Survey of Warfare in the Ancient Near East*. RBS 88. Atlanta: SBL Press, 2017.

Tuell, Steven Shawn. "The Priesthood of the 'Foreigner': Evidence of Competing Politics in Ezekiel 44:1-14 and Isaiah 56:1-8." Pages 183–204 in *Constituting the Community: Studies on the Polity of Ancient Israel in Honor of S. Dean McBride, Jr.* Edited by John T. Strong and Steven S. Tuell. Winona Lake, IN: Eisenbrauns, 2005.

Tuplin, Christopher. *Achaemenid Studies*. Hist 99. Stuttgart: Franz Steiner, 1996.

Tuplin, Christopher. "The Changing Pattern of Achaemenid Persian Royal Coinage." Pages 127–68 in *Explaining Monetary and Financial Innovation: A Historical Analysis*. Edited by Peter Berhnholz and Roland Vaubel. FMPS 39. Cham: Springer, 2014.

Tuplin, Christopher. "The Justice of Darius: Reflections on the Achaemenid Empire as a Rule-Bound Environment." Pages 73–126 in *Assessing Biblical and Classical Sources for the Reconstruction of Persian Influence, History and Culture*. Edited by Anne Fitzpatrick-McKinley. CeO 10. Wiesbaden: Harrassowitz, 2015.

Tuplin, Christopher. "Managing the World: Herodotus on Achaemenid Imperial Organization." Pages 39–63 in *Herodot und das Persische Weltreich/Herodotus and the Persian Empire*. Edited by Robert Rollinger, Brigitte Truschnegg, and Reinhold Bichler. CeO 3. Wiesbaden: Harrassowitz, 2011.

Tuplin, Christopher. "War and Peace in Achaemenid Imperial Ideology." *Electrum* 14 (2017): 31–54.

Uehlinger, Christoph. "'Powerful Persianisms' in Gyltpic Iconography of Persian Period Palestine." Pages 134–82 in *The Crisis of Israelite Religion: Transformation of Religious Tradition in Exilic and Post-Exilic Times*. Edited by Bob Becking and Marjo C. A. Korpel. OTS 42. Leiden: Brill, 1999.

Ussishkin, David. "On Nehemiah's City Wall and the Size of Jerusalem during the Persian Period: An Archaeologist's View." Pages 101–30 in *New Perspectives on Ezra–Nehemiah: History and Historiography, Text, Literature, and Interpretation*. Edited by Isaac Kalimi. Winona Lake, IN: Eisenbrauns, 2012.

Vaka'uta, Nāsili. *Reading Ezra 9–10 Tu'a-Wise: Rethinking Biblical Interpretation in Oceania*. SBLIVBS 3. Atlanta: Society of Biblical Literature, 2011.

Van De Mieroop, Marc. *The Ancient Mesopotamian City*. Oxford: Clarendon Press, 1997.

VanderKam, James. "Ezra–Nehemiah or Ezra and Nehemiah?" Pages 55–75 in *Priests, Prophets and Scribes: Essays on the Formation and Heritage of Second Temple Judaism in Honour of Joseph Blenkinsopp*. Edited by Eugene Ulrich et al. JSOTSup 149. Sheffield: Sheffield Academic Press, 1992.

VanderKam, James. *From Joshua to Caiaphas: High Priests after the Exile*. Minneapolis: Fortress, Press, 2004.

Vermeylen, Jacques. "The Gracious God, Sinners and Foreigners: How Nehemiah 9 Interprets the History of Israel." Pages 77–114 in *History and Identity: How Israel's Later Authors Viewed its Earlier History*. Edited by Núria Calduch-Benages and Jan Liesen. DCLY 2006. Berlin: W. de Gruyter, 2006.

Viberg, Åke. "An Elusive Crown: An Analysis of the Performance of a Prophetic Symbolic Act (Zech 6:9–15)." *SEÅ* 65 (2000): 161–69.

Waerzeggers, Caroline. *The Ezida Temple of Borsippa: Priesthood, Cult, Archives*. AchHist 15. Leiden: Nederlands Instituut voor het Nabije Oosten, 2010.

Waerzeggers, Caroline. "The Pious King: Patronage of Temples." Pages 725–51 in *The Oxford Handbook of Cuneiform Culture*. Edited by Karen Radner and Eleanor Robson. Oxford University Press, 2011.

Waerzeggers, Caroline. "A Statue of Darius in the Temple at Sippar." Pages 323–39 in *Extraction and Control: Studies in Honor of Matthew W. Stolper*. Edited by Michael Kozuh et al. SAOC 68. Chicago: The Oriental Institute of the University of Chicago, 2014.

Warhurst, Amber K. "The Chronicler's Use of the Prophets." Pages 165–81 in *What Was Authoritative for Chronicles?* Edited by Ehud Ben Zvi and Diana Edelman. Winona Lake, IN: Eisenbrauns, 2011.

Washington, Harold C. "Israel's Holy Seed and the Foreign Women of Ezra–Nehemiah: A Kristevan Reading." *BibInt* 11 (2003): 427–37.

Wasmuth, Melanie. "Political Memory in the Achaemenid Empire: The Integration of Egyptian Kingship into Persian Royal Display." Pages 203–37 in *Political Memory in and after the Persian Empire*. Edited by Jason M. Silverman and Caroline Waerzeggars. ANEM 13 Atlanta: SBL Press, 2015.

Waters, Matt. "Cyrus and the Achaemenids." *Iran* 42 (2004): 91–102.

Weinberg, Joel. *The Citizen-Temple Community*. Translated by D. L. Smith-Christopher. JSOTSup 151. Sheffield: JSOT, 1992.

Weingart, Kristin. "What Makes an Israelite an Israelite? Judean Perspectives on the Samarians in the Persian Period." *JSOT* 42 (2017): 155–75.

Werline, Rodney Alan. *Penitential Prayer in Second Temple Judaism: The Development of a Religious Institution*. SBLEJL 13. Atlanta: Scholars Press, 1998.

Weyde, Karl William. "'For I am about to create new heavens and a new earth': Prophecy and Torah in Isaiah 65:17-25." Pages 206–29 in *New Studies in the Book of Isaiah: Essays in Honor of Hallvard Hagelia*. Edited by Markus Zehnder. PHSC 21. Piscataway, NJ: Gorgias Press, 2014.

Wiesehöfer, Joseph. "The Achaemenid Empire in the Fourth Century B.C.E.: A Period of Decline?" Pages 11–30 in *Judah and the Judeans in the Fourth Century B.C.E.* Edited by Oded Lipschits, Gary N. Knoppers, and Rainer Albertz. Winona Lake, IN: Eisenbrauns, 2007.

Wiesehöfer, Joseph. "Achaemenid Rule and its Impact on Yehud." Pages 171–85 in *Texts, Contexts and Readings in Postexilic Literature: Explorations into Historiography and Identity Negotiation in Hebrew Bible and Related Texts*. Edited by Louis Jonker. FAT 2/53. Tübingen: Mohr Siebeck, 2011.

Wiesehöfer, Joseph. *Ancient Persia from 550 BC to 650 AD*. Translated by Azizeh Azodi. London: I. B. Tauris, 2001.

Wiesehöfer, Joseph. "'Denn ihr huldigt nicht einem Menshen als eurem Herrscher, sondern nur den Göttern': Bemerkungen zur Proskynese in Iran." Pages 447–52 in *Religious Themes and Texts of Pre-Islamic Iran and Central Asia: Studies in Honour of Professor Gherardo Gnoli on the Occasion of his 65th birthday on 6th December 2002*. Edited by Carlo G. Cereti, Mauro Maggi, and Elio Provasi. BzI 24. Wiesbaden: Reichert, 2003.

Willi, Thomas. *Juda—Jehud—Israel: Studien zum Selbstverständnis des Judentums in persischer Zeit*. FAT 12. Tübingen: J.C.B. Mohr, 1995.

Willi, Thomas. "Leviten, Priester und Kult in vorhellenistischer Zeit: Die chronistische Optik in ihrem geschichtlichen Kontext." Pages 75–98 in *Gemeinde ohne Tempel: Zur Substitutierung und Transformation des Jerusalemer Tempels und seines Kults im Alten Testament, antiken Judentum und frühen Christentum*. Edited by Beate Ego et al. WUNT 118. Tübingen: Mohr, 1999.

Williamson, H. G. M. *1 and 2 Chronicles*. NCBC. Grand Rapids, MI: Wm. B. Eerdmans, 1982.

Williamson, H. G. M. "The Aramaic Documents in Ezra Revisited." *JTS* 59 (2008): 41–62.

Williamson, H. G. M. *Ezra, Nehemiah*. WBC 16. Waco, TX: Word Books, 1985.

Williamson, H. G. M. "The Family in Persian Period Judah: Some Textual Reflections." Pages 469–85 in *Symbiosis, Symbolism, and the Power of the Past: Ancient Israel and their Neighbors from the Late Bronze Age through Roman Palaestina*. Edited by William G. Dever and Seymour Gitin. Winona Lake, IN: Eisenbrauns, 2003.

Williamson, H. G. M. *Israel in the Books of Chronicles*. Cambridge: Cambridge University Press, 1977.

Williamson, H. G. M. *Studies in Persian Period History and Historiography*. FAT 28. Tübingen: Mohr Siebeck, 2004.

Williamson, H. G. M. "The Temple and History in Presentations of Restoration in Ezra–Nehemiah." Pages 156–70 in *Reading the Law: Studies in Honour of Gordon J. Wenham*. Edited by J. G. McConville and Karl Möller. LHBOTS 461. New York: T&T Clark International, 2007.

Williamson, H. G. M. "Welcome Home." Pages 113–23 in *The Historian and the Bible: Essays in Honour of Lester L. Grabbe*. Edited by Philip R. Davies and Diana V. Edelman. LHBOTS 530. New York: T&T Clark International, 2010.

Willi-Plein, Ina. *Haggai, Sacharja, Maleachi*. ZBKAT 24/4. Zurich: Theologischer Verlag, 2007.

Windfuhr, Gernot. "Dialectology and Topics." Pages 5–42 in *The Iranian Languages*. Edited by Gernot Windfuhr. London: Routledge, 2009.

Winter, Irene. "'Seat of Kingship'/'A Wonder to Behold': The Palace as Construct in the Ancient Near East." *ArsOr* 23 (1993): 27–55.

Wöhrle, Jakob. *Der Abschluss des Zwölfprophetenbuches: Buchübergreifende Redaktionsprozesse in den späten Sammlungen*. BZAW 389. Berlin: W. de Gruyter, 2008.
Wöhrle, Jakob. *Die frühen Sammlungen des Zwölfprophetenbuches: Entstehung und Komposition*. BZAW 360. Berlin: W. de Gruyter, 2006.
Wöhrle, Jakob. "On the Way to Hierocracy: Secular and Priestly Rule in the Books of Haggai and Zechariah." Pages 173–89 in *Priests and Cult in the Book of the Twelve*. Edited by Lena-Sofia Tiemeyer. ANEM 14. Atlanta: SBL Press, 2016.
Wright, Jacob L. *Rebuilding Identity: The Nehemiah-Memoir and its Earliest Readers*. BZAW 348. Berlin: W. de Gruyter, 2004.
Wu, Xin. "'O young man…make known of what kind you are': Warfare, History, and Elite Ideology of the Achaemenid Persian Empire." *IrAnt* 49 (2014): 209–99.
Wyssman, Patrick. "The Coinage Imagery of Samaria and Judah in the Late Persian Period." Pages 221–66 in *A "Religious Revolution" in Yehûd? The Material Culture of the Persian Period as a Test Case*. Edited by Christian Frevel, Katharina Pyschny, and Izak Cornelius. OBO 267. Fribourg: Academic Press, 2014.
Yoo, Philip Y. *Ezra and the Second Wilderness*. OTRM. Oxford: Oxford University Press, 2017.
Yoyotte, Jean. "Les inscriptions hiéroglyphiques: Darius et l'Égypte." *JA* 260 (1972): 253–66.
Zadok, Ran. "Some Issues in Ezra–Nehemiah." Pages 151–81 in *New Perspectives on Ezra–Nehemiah: History and Historiography, Text, Literature, and Interpretation*. Edited by Isaac Kalimi. Winona Lake, IN: Eisenbrauns, 2012.
Zehnder, Markus. "A Fresh Look at Malachi ii 13–16." *VT* 53 (2003): 224–59.
Zevit, Ziony. "Is There an Archaeological Case for Phantom Settlements in the Persian Period?" *PEQ* 141 (2009): 124–37.
Zlotnick-Sivan, H. "The Silent Women of Yehud: Notes on Ezra 9–10." *JJS* 51 (2000): 3–18.

Index of References

Hebrew Bible/Old Testament

Genesis
9.1-17	184
17.1-27	184
17.26	184
25.12-18	184
45.10	74

Exodus
6.25	174
7.1-6	205
12.4	74
12.12	205
12.19	184, 205
12.49	184, 205
14.1-4	205
14.26-27	205
14.28-29	205
15.15	207
23.5	65
28.42	176
29.1	176
29.9	178
29.14	178
32.27	74
34.11-16	58, 59
40.15	178

Leviticus
1.5-9	176
2.1-3	176
3.1-5	176
4.11	178
4.16-21	176
8.12	176
8.17	178
8.30	176
10	59
10.3	59
10.19	59
13	59
13.45-46	59
14.1-9	59
14.33-53	75
15.19-33	59
16.27	178
17.8	205
18.24-30	59
21.1-5	59
21.2	74
21.3	74
22.2-3	59
22.18	205
23.42-43	208
25.25	74

Numbers
3.5-10	176
4.15	176
4.20	176
18.1-7	176
18.3	176
19.5	178
19.18	75
22.24	36
27.11	74

Deuteronomy
7	59
7.1-4	58, 59
9.4–10.5	216
10.16	216
13.7 Eng.	74
13.8	74
17.9	172
18.18	172
21.5	172
24.1-4	204
31.27	216
32.36	65

Joshua
3.3	172
8.3	172
11.20	57
15	30

Judges
3.7–13.1	216

Ruth
2.20	74

2 Samuel
7.5	187
8–10	157

1 Kings
4.2	173
4.7-18	157
8.28	57
8.30	57
8.38	57
8.45	57
11	203
11.32	187
11.36	187

12.31	172	15.3	201	18.12-14	209
14.10	65	16.39	174	18.18-22	209
21.8	188	17.10-14	200	19.1-3	209
		18-119	157	19.2	220
2 Kings		18.16	174	19.8-11	176, 201
11.2	32	22.6-16	200	20.1-20	218
12.1 Eng.	32	22.8	208	20.14-17	209
12.2	32	22.10	200	20.34	209
12.2 Eng.	32	23.2-5	172	20.35-37	209
12.3	32	23.24	33	21.6	202
12.19 Eng.	32	23.27	33	21.11-15	209
12.20 Eng.	32	25.1	208	21.12-15	209
17.24-41	49	28.3	208	21.12-13	220
21-125	157	28.6-7	200	21.18-19	200
24.1	157	28.19	208	22.3	202
24.6	32	29.23	200	22.8-9	200
24.8	32	29.29-30	209	23.3	201
				23.6	176
1 Chronicles		*2 Chronicles*		24.20	208, 209
1.13-16	45	1.3	201	24.25	200
2.3	184	1.7-12	208	25.7-9	209
2.17	184	5.2-6	201	25.15-16	209
2.35	184	7.17-18	200	26.1	201
2.51	45	8.11	201	26.19-21	200
2.54	45	9.29	209	28	200
3	198	11.14-15	219, 220	28.1-4	220
3.2	184	11.16-17	220	28.5	200
3.19-24	198	12.1-12	200	28.9-11	209
3.19	187	12.5	209	29.11	176
3.21	198	13.8-9	219, 220	29.30	208
3.24	198	13.13-20	218	29.33	176
4.4	45	13.22	209	29.34	176
4.18	184	14.8-14	218	30.4-11	220
5.29-30	174	14.9-15 Eng.	218	30.15	176
5.34	174	15	211	30.16-17	176
6.3-4 Eng.	174	15.1-7	209	31.10	174
6.8 Eng.	174	15.1	208	31.17	33
9.2-17	68	15.2-7	210	33.10-11	200
9.33	172	15.9	201	33.10	209
15.2	176	16	157	33.13	57
15.11	174	16.7-9	209	34.29-33	201
15.16-23	172	17.3-6	218	35.3	176
10.13-14	218	17.7-9	176, 201	35.6	176
12.18 Eng.	208	17.10-11	218	35.15	208
12.19	208	18	209	35.20-22	198
13.1-5	201	18.3	209	35.20-21	208

2 Chronicles (cont.)		1.6	114	2.70	41		
36.1-4	198, 213	1.7-11	43, 114	3–4	52		
36.1	32	1.8-11	116	3	48, 69,		
36.2	32	1.11	41, 114		116		
36.4	32	2–3	26	3.2-6	48		
36.6	201, 213	2	1, 2, 7, 9,	3.2-3	179		
36.10	201, 213		29, 41,	3.2	32, 48,		
36.11-21	200		44, 46,		49, 54,		
36.13	157, 198,		52, 53,		58, 124,		
	213		61, 68,		146, 147		
36.22-23	200, 208,		72, 171	3.3	48, 49		
	213	2.1–3.1	25, 68	3.4-5	69		
		2.1-2	169	3.4	48, 58,		
Ezra		2.1	41, 45,		147, 208		
1–10	13, 14, 62		55, 152	3.6	116		
1–6	7–9, 28,	2.2-35	41	3.7	42, 48		
	29, 40,	2.2	32, 54	3.8-13	116		
	41, 43,	2.3-39	61	3.8-9	54		
	44, 52–8,	2.3-35	69	3.8	32, 41,		
	64, 65,	2.3-20	44, 45		124, 171		
	69, 76,	2.3-19	46	3.9	64		
	77, 114,	2.3-15	55	3.10	116		
	116, 118,	2.3	44	3.12	64, 116,		
	121, 122,	2.4	44		169		
	124, 125,	2.10	69	3.14	64		
	128, 129,	2.18	69	3.16	64		
	152, 164,	2.21-35	44, 45	3.18	64		
	183, 221	2.21	44	4–6	6, 27		
1–3	116	2.22	45	4	49, 50,		
1–2	55	2.23	45		63–6,		
1	42, 46,	2.27	45		115, 125,		
	51, 55,	2.28	45		156–8		
	114, 116,	2.30	69	4.1-24	144, 158		
	119, 146	2.34	45	4.1-5	65, 202		
1.1-3	200	2.35	44	4.1-3	42, 53,		
1.1	42, 51,	2.36-58	41		156		
	113, 144	2.36-57	171	4.1	41, 49,		
1.2	42, 43,	2.59-63	52		115		
	113, 144,	2.59	42, 46, 68	4.2	49, 169		
	145	2.61-63	46	4.3	41, 49,		
1.3-11	145	2.62-63	19		54, 58,		
1.3	42, 49,	2.62	68		115, 124		
	113	2.64	41, 169	4.4-5	49, 50		
1.4	43, 114	2.68-69	68	4.4	49, 50,		
1.5	43, 113	2.68	169		115		
1.6-11	127	2.69	47, 114, 120	4.5	156		

4.6-24	37	6.5	127, 152	7.7	34, 42, 54
4.6-7	50	6.7	169	7.10	56, 146
4.8–6.18	50, 117	6.8-9	127	7.11	18–20
4.8-23	14, 50	6.8	116	7.12-29	120
4.8-10	49	6.9-10	116	7.12-26	5, 37, 55,
4.8-9	50, 157	6.9	51		56, 119
4.11-22	50, 116,	6.14	42, 51,	7.13	42
	118, 130,		56, 117,	7.14	151
	156, 158		118, 144,	7.15-24	55, 127
4.11-16	50, 115,		185	7.15-22	19
	157	6.15	52	7.15	119
4.11	50	6.16	41, 117,	7.21-23	120
4.13	115, 157		127, 171	7.25-26	56, 60,
4.15	115, 157	6.17	41		120, 148,
4.16	115	6.18	58, 146,		149
4.17-22	52, 71,		147	7.25	37, 56,
	116, 157	6.19-22	52		148, 151
4.17	157	6.19	41, 118	7.26	58, 148,
4.19-20	157	6.20	41, 178		149, 151
4.19	157	6.21	41, 52,	7.27–9.15	17
4.20	157		53, 56,	7.27–9.5	16
4.23	50, 63		58, 205	7.27–8.36	15, 16
4.24	50, 117,	7–10	8, 19, 54,	7.27	120, 145
	144, 158		62, 65	7.28	42
5–6	27, 50,	7–8	55, 64,	8	15, 22, 64
	51, 118,		119, 121	8.1-14	21, 55, 61
	158	7	6-9, 14,	8.1	20
5	116, 153		18, 23,	8.2	174, 198
5.1–6.18	51		40, 41,	8.3-14	55
5.1	42, 49,		54–6, 60,	8.4	20
	51, 117,		77, 110,	8.5	20
	144, 185		120, 125,	8.9	20
5.5	169		129, 147,	8.13	20
5.9	169		152, 153,	8.15-20	21, 22
5.11-17	51		217	8.18-19	55
5.12-16	116	7.1-11	16	8.21	21, 22
5.12	115, 152,	7.1-10	55	8.25-27	55, 120,
	153, 157	7.1-6	19		127
5.14	64, 152	7.1-5	18, 19	8.26-27	120
5.16	116	7.1	18, 20	8.26	120
6	54, 64	7.5	174	8.29	178
6.1-12	118, 146	7.6	18-21, 49,	8.30	178
6.1-5	51		55, 56,	8.33	55, 174
6.1-4	116		64, 120,	8.35-36	15
6.3	116		145, 146	8.35	41, 55
6.4	51	7.6 LXX	145	8.36	56

Ezra (cont.)		9.10	146, 153	10.23	179
9–10	2, 14,	9.11	59	10.34-43	61
	15, 17,	9.13-15	121	10.38	61
	20, 25,	9.13	57		
	26, 28,	9.14	57	Nehemiah	
	53, 56,	9.15	57	1–13	8, 14, 24,
	58–60,	10	14-18, 61,		66
	62, 64,		64, 146	1–7	8
	66, 67,	10.1-44	16	1–6	14, 25,
	76, 77,	10.1-18	17		125, 158
	120, 153,	10.1-5	15, 16	1	23, 62
	165, 168,	10.1	15, 17,	1.1–13.3	62
	222		41, 60	1.1-11	22
9	14–17,	10.2-6	15, 16	1.1	22, 23, 62
	35, 63,	10.2	41, 60,	1.2	41, 62
	70, 71,		61, 76	1.3	41, 62, 63
	120, 122,	10.3	61, 195,	1.4	22, 63
	219		205	1.5-11	22, 63,
9.1	205	10.4	15		74, 115,
9.1-5	15, 16	10.6-8	15		145
9.1-2	56	10.6	32, 34,	1.5	22
9.1	41, 60		35, 41, 54	1.6-7	63
9.2	59, 76,	10.7-44	15, 16	1.7-8	153
	77, 122,	10.7	41, 61,	1.8-10	63
	182		169	1.11	22, 63,
9.3	57	10.8	41, 42,		123
9.4	41, 49,		61, 169,	1.11 LXX[a]	123
	56, 60,		194, 205	2	62, 63
	76, 195	10.9-44	16	2.1	22, 30, 62
9.6-15	15, 16,	10.9-15	16	2.2	63
	57, 60,	10.9	169	2.3-5	63, 66
	70, 76,	10.10	19, 60,	2.5	63, 145
	115, 146,		61, 76,	2.8	63, 125,
	149, 156,		123		127, 145,
	158, 204,	10.11	61, 205		146
	221	10.12	169	2.10	41, 74,
9.6-9	121	10.14	41, 60,		158
9.6-7	57		61, 169	2.16	122, 182
9.7	41, 57,	10.16	19, 41,	2.19	30, 31,
	121, 153		123, 205		65, 125
9.8-9	121	10.17	61	3–4	66
9.8	36, 57,	10.18-44	61, 73	3	29, 30, 72
	121, 155	10.18-43	17, 171	3.1	32
9.9	35, 36,	10.18-22	123	3.20	32
	57, 121	10.18	61, 76,	3.33–4.17	180
9.10-15	57, 66,		179	3.34	65, 125
	121	10.19	61, 205	3.35	30, 74

4	66		168, 180,	8.9	20, 34–6,
4.1-23 Eng.	180		219		69, 76,
4.1-17	65	6.17	77, 122		123, 127
4.1	65	7–8	26	8.13-18	147
4.2 Eng.	65, 125	7	1, 2, 7,	8.13	124, 169
4.3 Eng.	30, 74		53, 68,	8.14-17	208
4.7-23 Eng.	65		69, 72	8.14	42, 69, 70
4.7 Eng.	65	7.1-4	25	8.17	41, 42,
4.8	122, 182	7.5	68, 122		69, 127,
4.13	122	7.6-73	25, 68		169
4.14 Eng.	122, 182	7.6-72	68	8.18	69, 146
4.15	65	7.6	41, 68,	9–10	24, 26
4.19 Eng.	122		152	9	24, 70–2,
5	68, 155	7.8-38	69		153
5.1	67	7.15	69	9.1-3	124
5.2-3	67	7.24	69	9.1	41
5.4	115, 125,	7.33	69	9.2	70, 205
	155	7.61	46, 68	9.3	146
5.5	67	7.63-65	46	9.4-5	73
5.6-13	126	7.64	68	9.5	70
5.6-11	155	7.69-71	68	9.6 LXX	70
5.7-9	67	7.70-72 Eng.	68	9.6-37	69, 70,
5.7	67, 77,	7.70	127, 169		74, 76,
	122, 123,	7.73 Eng.	68		78, 115,
	182	8–13	8, 36, 78,		126, 146,
5.10-11	67		155, 159,		153, 155,
5.10	67, 68,		167, 181		167, 216,
	156	8–12	37		221
5.11	67, 68,	8–10	68, 69,	9.7-8	70
	156		70, 74, 76	9.8	72
5.13	41, 169	8–9	124	9.13-14	70
5.14-18	126, 181	8	14, 16,	9.13	146, 153
5.17-18	127		21, 35,	9.14	146
6	66, 128		36, 70,	9.16-30	153
6.1-19	180		76, 127,	9.16-17	152, 153
6.5-7	158		179	9.17	72
6.6-7	66, 125	8.1	42, 69,	9.19-21	153
6.6	30, 65		146, 169	9.22-25	126, 153
6.10-14	66, 125,	8.2-6	124	9.26-32	146
	128, 144,	8.2	20, 41,	9.26-31	70, 71
	206		69, 76,	9.26-30	126, 152,
6.10	42		123, 169		155
6.12	42	8.3	69	9.26	146, 154
6.15	30	8.7-8	124	9.27	154
6.17-19	66, 68,	8.7	69	9.28	154
	122, 158,	8.8	69, 146	9.29	154
		8.9-12	127	9.31	71, 155

Nehemiah (cont.)

9.32	126	10.32	72, 75, 76, 147	13	8, 9, 14, 40, 41, 54, 55, 65, 66, 73, 76, 77, 110, 125-27, 129, 152–4, 203, 217
9.33	154, 221	10.33-40	72, 74, 147, 194, 197		
9.35	70				
9.36	70, 126				
9.37	126, 155, 167	10.34-35 Eng.	75		
		10.34 Eng.	72		
9.38–10.27 Eng.	172	10.35-36	75		
9.38 Eng.	72	10.35	72		
10	14, 24, 70, 73, 74, 76, 154, 203	10.35 Eng.	72		
		10.36	72	13.1-3	53, 74
		10.37 Eng.	72	13.1	73
		10.38	72	13.3	73, 74, 205
10.1	72	10.38 Eng.	72, 174, 178		
10.1 Eng.	36			13.4-34	74
10.1-28	171	10.39	72, 174, 178	13.4-14	123
10.1-27 Eng.	72			13.4-12	158
10.1-8 Eng.	72	10.39 Eng.	41, 72	13.4-9	179
10.2-28	72	10.40	41, 72	13.4-6	32
10.2-9	72	11–12	66	13.4-5	74, 77
10.2	34, 36	11	21, 25, 127	13.4	32, 54, 74
10.9-13 Eng.	72			13.6-7	74
10.14-19 Eng.	72	11.1-24	73	13.6	27, 74, 114
10.15-20	72	11.1-2	25		
10.20-27 Eng.	72	11.1	73	13.8-9	74
10.21-28	72	11.3-19	68	13.9	219
10.28-39 Eng.	74	11.3	41	13.10-13	197
10.28 Eng.	72, 205	11.20	41	13.10	194
10.29	72, 205	11.25-36	30	13.11	74, 75, 77
10.29 Eng.	72, 146	12	21, 33	13.13	75
10.29-40	74	12.1-7	72	13.15-18	147
10.30-39 Eng.	24	12.1	178	13.16	75
10.30-31 Eng.	53	12.10-14	72	13.17-18	115, 147, 221
10.30	72, 146	12.10-11	32, 35, 54		
10.30 Eng.	72, 75, 146	12.12-21	72	13.17	77, 122, 123
		12.22	32, 33, 35		
10.31-40	24	12.26	34	13.18	75, 76, 146, 153
10.31-32	53	12.27-43	127		
10.31	72, 75, 146	12.27	25	13.19-22	75
		12.30	73, 178	13.23-29	25
10.31 Eng.	72, 75, 76, 147	12.36	34	13.23-28	53, 168
		12.43	127	13.23-27	203
10.32-39 Eng.	72, 74, 147, 194, 197	12.44	73, 178	13.23	75
		12.47	41, 73, 174, 179	13.24	65, 75
				13.26	153

13.27	76	60.19-20	189	*Ezekiel*	
13.28-29	179, 219	61.5-6	188	1.2	32
13.28	54, 75,	63.7–64.11	193	8.1	28, 169
	77, 123,	63.8	193	13.5	36
	158, 180,	63.10	193	14.1	28, 169
	219	63.16	193	20.1-44	221
13.29	178	63.17	193	20.1	28, 169
13.30-31	75	63.18	193	20.3	28
13.30	178	64.6-7	192	22.30	36
		64.7	193	25–32	212
Job		64.11	192	40–48	172, 173,
10.1	65	65.1–66.24	194		204
19.14	74	65.1–66.17	194	40.46	172
31.36	190	65.1-16	193	42.7	36
		65.1-7	193	42.10	36
Psalms		65.5	193	43.19	172
6.10	57	65.11	192	44	204
38.11 Eng.	74	65.17-25	193	44.6-9	204
38.12	74	65.17	192	44.10-16	172
55.1 Eng.	57	66.1-9	193	47.21-23	205
55.2	57	66.1-4	192, 193	48.11	172
80.12 Eng.	36	66.2	195		
80.13	36	66.5	195	*Daniel*	
119.170	57	66.18-24	194	1–6	23
		66.18-21	185	7	118
Ecclesiastes		66.18-19	220		
10.16-17	122			*Hosea*	
		Jeremiah		3.4	210
Isaiah		22.24-30	187		
11.1	210	23.5	210	*Amos*	
13–23	212	25.11	113, 196,	1	212
56–66	194		210	3.9	210
56.1-8	185, 194,	25.20	73		
	204	25.24	73	*Nahum*	
56.6-8	220	27	157	2–3	212
56.7	192	29.1	169		
57.3-13	193	29.10-14	113	*Haggai*	
57.3	193	29.10	196	1–2	185
58.1-14	192	30–33	113	1.1-2	196
59.9-15	192	31.16	210	1.1	185, 188,
60-162	188, 189	33.21-22	178		195
60.7	192	36.7	57	1.5-6	196, 197
60.10	189	37.20	57	1.9-11	196, 197
60.12	189, 206	46–51	212	1.12-15	195
60.13	192	50.37	73	1.14	188

Haggai		6.9-15	191	2.4	177
2.1-9	186	6.9-14	190, 195,	2.8	177
2.1	185		196	2.10-16	198, 202
2.2	188, 195	6.9	192	2.11	203
2.4	195	6.11	190	2.15-16	204
2.10	185, 187	6.12	190, 191,	2.16	204
2.15-19	196, 197		210	3.1-4	198
2.20-23	144, 186,	6.13	190, 191	3.3	178
	187, 195	6.14	190, 192	3.5	198
2.20	187	7.5	210	3.8-12	198
2.21-22	187	8.10	210	3.13-21	198
2.21	187, 188	9–14	206	3.16-21	198
2.23	187	9.1-8	206	4.3 Eng.	198
		9.13-15	207		
Zechariah		9.13	206	APOCRYPHA	
1–8	183, 185,	11.4-17	211	*1 Esdras*	
	186	11.8	211	2.18	37
1.7-11	189	11.16-17	211	2.20	115
1.7	185	12.1–13.1	213	5.5	188
1.8-11	189	12.1-6	207	5.53	43
1.12	210	12.6	207	6.8-9	37
1.18-21 Eng.	144, 189	12.8	198, 213	8.7	56
1.18-19 Eng.	189	12.10	198, 214	8.23	37
1.20-21 Eng.	189	12.12	198	9.6	70
1.20 Eng.	189	13.1	214	9.34	61
1.21 Eng.	189	14	207, 214	9.37-55	37
2.1-4	144, 189	14.1-15	207	9.39	37
2.1-2	189	14.1-9	207	9.40	37
2.3-4	189	14.1-4	214	9.49	37
2.3	189	14.6-10	214		
2.4	189	14.9	214	*2 Esdras*	
2.6-9 Eng.	144, 189	14.12-15	214	4.16	115
2.6-7 Eng.	189	14.16-19	207	7.10	56
2.10-13	189	14.16	214		
2.10-13	144			*Ecclesiasticus*	
2.10-11	189	*Zephaniah*		49.13	37
3–4	192	2	212		
3.1-10	195	3.16	210	*1 Maccabees*	
3.7	192			12.6	171
3.8	190, 195,	*Malachi*		13.36	171
	210	1.3-4	197	14.20	171
Zechariah (cont.)		1.6-14	198	14.27-49	171
4.1-14	195	1.6	177		
4.9	190, 191	2.1	177		
4.14	195	2.3	178		
6.1-8	189	2.4-9	177, 198		

Index of References

Josephus
Antiquities
7.363-382	172
11	33
11.73	188
11.120-158	37
11.159-183	37
11.297	33
11.302-325	34
11.302-324	175
11.306-308	171
11.317	171
11.329-39	171
11.347	33
12.138-144	171
12.154-236	30, 171
12.156-159	171
12.163	171
15.50	33
20.216-217	172

MISHNAH
Bava Qamma
1.3	122

Gittin
4.4	122
4.5	122

Middot
2.5-6	172

Sukkah
5.4	172

TARGUMIC TEXTS
Targ 2 Chron.
20.10	42

Targ. Neof. Exod.
12.23	42

Targ. Onq. Exod.
21.8	42

Peshitta
3 Ezra 1.7	42

CLASSICAL AND ANCIENT
CHRISTIAN LITERATURE
Aelian
Varia historia
1.33	101
12.43	124

Aeschines
Against Ctesiphon
132	54

Aeschylus
Persians
651	106
654-655	106
711	106

Arrian
Anabasis
4.11.8	106

Clement of Alexandria
Exhortation to the Heathen
5	141, 143

Diodorus
1.46.4	139
14.80.2	102
16.41.5	102
16.45.1-2	139
17.6.1-2	135
17.69.2	139
40.3.1-8	170

Diogenes Laertius
1.8	105

Herodotus
1.132	105
1.134.2	99
1.136	135
1.140.3	105
3.34.1	123
3.61-88	136
3.68	136
3.70	136
3.91.1	47, 120
3.95.2	47
4.202	139
4.204	139
5.15	139
6.19	139
6.20	139
6.101	139
6.119	139
7.136.1	106
8.85.3	100
8.90.4	100

Isocrates
Panathenaicus
157-158	54

Lysias
Funeral Oration
30	54

Plato
Alcibiades major
121e-122a	105

Pliny
Natural History
6.29	139

Plutarch
Alexander
18.7	124

Artaxerxes
14.5	138
25.1-2	102

Themistocles
27.4	106
29.4	98

Index of References

Pseudo-Aristotle		22–24	163	*DB*		
Economics		22–23	97, 143	1–4	159–61	
1348a	140			1	136	
		A²Ha		1.3-6	90	
Strabo		5–6	87	1.6-7	90	
11.11.4	139	6–7	143	1.8	90	
11.14.9	143			1.11-12	94	
15.3.14	105	*A²Hc*		1.12-17	150	
15.3.8	135	1–2	143	1.13-14	94	
16.1.11	101			1.14-17	99	
		A²Sa		1.19-20	95	
Thucydides		3–4	163	1.19	97, 121	
1.138.2-3	98	4–5	87, 97, 143	1.22	138	
				1.23-24	95, 150	
Xenophon		5	138, 163	1.33-34	94	
Anabasis				1.36	105	
1.2.27	101	*A²Sd*		1.44	105	
1.2.7	101	3–4	97	1.46	105	
1.4.10	101			1.50	105	
1.7.6	99	*A³Pa*		1.62-63	96	
1.9.13	139	25	143	1.64-66	96	
4.5.34-35	143			1.66	96	
		ABC		1.68-69	96	
Cyropaedia		7.ii.15	90	1.81-83	93	
8.1.23	105	9.1-8	139	1.82-83	137	
8.2.10	101			1.83	93	
8.3.11	105	*AOAT 256*		2.4-5	93	
8.6.12	101	K2.1.12	90	2.13	93	
				2.19-20	97	
Hellenica		*CII 1/2/1*		2.24-26	93, 160	
4.1.15	101	44	97	2.29-30	97	
4.1.35	106	48	97	2.34-36	93, 160	
		53	97	2.39-41	93, 160	
Oeconomicus		62	97	2.45-46	93	
4.4-17	103	69	97	2.49-50	97	
4.8	101, 103	73	97	2.73-76	137	
4.12	103	79	97	2.75	137	
4.13	101, 103	86	97	2.76-78	137	
14.4-7	150	9	138	2.76	93, 137	
14.6-7	150	97	138	2.82	97	
		105	138	2.88-90	137	
INSCRIPTIONS				2.89-90	137	
A¹Pa		*CIS*		2.90-91	93	
1-108	163	2.161.i.2	122	2.91	137	
13–14	95	2.4000.3-4	122	3.21-75	93	
17–22	163	2.990.2	122	3.52	137	

Index of References

3.56	97	35–36	151	22–30	150
3.88	137	36–38	95, 151	27–41	151
4.2-36	93	43–44	135	31–34	92
4.8-9	93	46–47	98, 135	31–32	151, 162
4.8	93	48–51	95	32–34	151
4.9-10	93	52	138	35–37	151
4.10-11	93			50–51	97
4.12	93	*DNb*			
4.13	93	1–3	134	*DSf*	
4.14	93	1–2	100	1–5	92
4.15	93	3–4	134	8–9	92
4.16	93	5–27	135	11–12	95
4.25-56	81	5–8	94	19–22	95
4.27	93	12–13	94, 157	29–30	99
4.29-30	93	13–15	94	56–57	100
4.33-36	93, 160	16–19	95		
4.35-36	95	17–19	138	*DSi*	
4.60-61	96	27–32	135	4	162
4.61	108, 143	32–33	134		
4.62-63	96, 108,	32–45	135	*DSj*	
	143	58	150	6	100
4.63	157				
4.83-86	136	*DPd*		*DSm*	
4.88-92	162	1–2	143	3–4	95
4.91-92	81, 137	2–3	92		
5	93, 160	6–9	162	*DSo*	
5.2-4	160	12–24	92	2–3	162
5.10-14	142	13–15	143	4	100
5.15-16	142	21–22	96, 143		
5.16-17	142	23–24	96, 143	*DSs*	
5.25-30	142			1	100
5.26	137	*DPe*			
5.31-32	142	10	99	*DSt*	
5.32-33	142			7–8	143
		DSa			
DNa		5	100	*DZc*	
1–8	91, 135,			1–3	110
	150	*DSab*		3–4	95, 110
1–2	151	1	111	8–9	111
11–12	95	2–3	112	12	111
20–22	99, 150,	4	112		
	151			*Gerizim*	
22–30	99, 135	*DSe*		1	175
22	99	19–21	150	24	175
31–34	151	19–20	95	25	175
32	92	21	99	32	175

Gerizim (cont.)		27–29	97, 143	INDO-IRANIAN	
61	175			LITERATURE	
149	175	*XPc*		*AWN*	
384	175	6–9	160	17.10-11	137
389	175			18.3-10	137
390	175	*XPd*		55.1	99
		8–14	160		
PF				*DD*	
757-1759	105	*XPf*		27.2-3	137
769	105	38–40	162	32.12-15	89
1798	105	40–43	162	32.12-13	138
1951	105			72.10-12	137
		XPh			
SAA		1–6	150	*Dk*	
2.6.108-118	144	17–19	150	3.35	89
9	205	19–28	150	3.124	87
15.69.rev2-5	144	19	99	6.1	87, 88
10.179	144	28–35	160	7.11.4	89
		28–25	133		
SEG		32–35	160	*GBd*	
29-1205.4-5	149	35–41	141, 160	1.53	87
		41	108	1.54	86
TAD		43–46	95	3.23	87
A4.7	30, 32, 34	46–50	150	6	88
A4.7.17-19	32	48	108	22–23	87
A4.7.29	30, 65	49–50	98, 120,	34	89
A4.9	31, 180		149	34.16-19	138
A6.3.6	149	50–51	108		
C2.1.19	97	51–53	98	*HN*	
C2.1.66-69	162	53–54	108	2.16	108
		55	108	2.25	99, 137
TSSI		57–58	138		
2.25	31			*IBd*	
		XPl		2.11	88
XE		1–3	134	28.1-2	88
2	143	1–2	100	28.47	137
		3–4	134	30	89
XPa		5–31	135	30.17-20	138
1–6	160, 161	5–8	94	30.29-32	138
9	95	13–14	94, 157	30.33	89
11–13	161	14–17	94		
13–15	161	17–21	95	*MX*	
15–17	161	19–21	138	7.27-28	99
16–28	99	31–36	135	31–32	88
		36–50	135	32.5-6	106
XPb		36–37	134	43	87
1–11	160				

Index of References

RV		27	86	44.12	88
5.63.7	87	28–34	86	45.4	88
		30.5	87	45.7	89
Vd		30.6	88	46.10-11	88
1	99	30.7	87	46.10	88
1.2-3	87	30.9	100	46.11	89
1.4	87	30.10	88	46.15	88, 98, 149
1.5	87	31.1	88		
2.5-19	87	31.4	87	47.2	87
3.23-24	88	31.7	86	50.11	100
19.1	99	31.8	87	51.13-14	88
19.5	89	31.11	86	51.13	88
19.30-31	108	31.13	88	51.15	88
		31.18	88		
Y		32.6	88	*Yt*	
9.4-5	87	34.3	87	10	87
10.7	87	35–41	86	19.89	89
19.2	86	43–51	86	19.92-93	89
19.6	88	43.5	88		
19.17	105	44.3-5	86		
21.1	88, 98, 149	44.3	87		

Index of Authors

Abadie, P. 177
Achenbach, R. 173
Adams, D. Q. 109, 138
Ahmadi, A. 134
Albertz, R. 34, 38, 122, 169
Altmann, P. 67
Amit, Y. 208, 209
Anderson, C. B. 4, 165
Andrès-Toledo, M. A. 86
Assis, E. 196

Baden, J. S. 21
Badghbidi, H. R. 162
Balcer, J. 96
Bar-Kochva, B. 170
Barag, D. 170
Bautch, R. J. 72
Beaulieu, P.-A. 142
Becking, B. 5, 7, 14, 59, 203
Bedford, P. R. 77, 183, 196
Beentjes, P. C. 208, 210
Begg, C. 210
Ben Zvi, E. 128, 166, 201, 210, 220
Benveniste, E. 108
Berges, U. 185
Berquist, J. L. 4
Betlyon, J. 170
Beuken, W. A. M. 194
Bianchi, F. 199
Blenkinsopp, J. 12, 15, 16, 18, 22–4, 35, 46, 68, 71, 147, 169, 172–4, 187, 193, 194, 210, 211
Boccaccini, G. 199
Boda, M. J. 24, 153, 168, 186, 189–91
Bodi, D. 5, 64
Boorer, S. 173, 174
Borger, R. 91, 159
Boswick, J. 187
Boucharlat, R. 84, 100, 101
Boyce, M. 85, 87, 94

Brett, M. 181
Briant, P. 38, 83, 85, 103, 111, 141, 143, 149
Brosius, M. 123
Burt, S. 12, 23, 25
Byun, P. 66

Calmeyer, P. 161
Carr, D. M. 5, 147, 173, 174, 197
Carter, C. E. 7
Cataldo, J. W. 38, 188, 195
Chaumont, M.-L. 149
Chrostowski, W. 71
Clauss, J. 44, 53, 59
Clines, D. J. A. 24, 50, 68
Cohen, M. E. 62
Colburn, H. 83
Conczorowski, B. J. 2, 25
Conklin, B. W. 27
Cook, S. L. 210
Cornelius, I. 47
Crüsemann, F. 147
Curtis, B. G. 186, 190, 206, 211
Curtis, J. 82, 84

Dandamaev, M. A. 122, 169, 182
Della Volpe, A. 101
Donner, H. 202, 203
Dor, Y. 15, 17
Dozeman, T. B. 120
Duggan, M. W. 8, 71, 124
Dusinberre, E. R. M. 80, 83, 107, 134
Dyck, J. E. 2

Edelman, D. 6, 8, 31, 118, 211
Eidsvåg, G. M. 192
Eph'al, I. 28, 169, 182
Eskenazi, T. C. 2–4, 8, 13, 58, 70, 72, 83, 155
Esler, P. F. 1, 53, 75

Fantalkin, A. 37, 197
Faust, A. 182
Finitsis, A. 190, 191
Finkelstein, I. 29, 31
Finn, J. 91, 104
Fitzpatrick-McKinley, A. 38, 124
Floyd, M. H. 177, 191, 206
Foster, R. L. 211
Frei, P. 5
Frevel, C. 2, 25
Fried, L. S. 2, 4, 33, 34, 38, 43, 50, 56, 61, 67, 98, 113, 118, 126, 148, 150, 170, 181, 182, 184
Fröhlich, I. 4, 166
Frolov, S. 113
Fulton, D. 21, 73

Gadot, Y. 82, 102
Gafney, W. 164, 165
Galil, G. 201
Gamkrelidze, T. V. 87, 108
Garrison, M. B. 84, 86, 89, 97, 103, 104, 133
Gärtner, J. 207
Gerson, S. N. 81
Gerstenberger, E. 119, 210, 211
Gitler, H. 47, 81, 107
Gmirkin, R. E. 171
Goldingay, J. 188, 194
Goswell, G. 188
Grabbe, L. L. 6, 24, 25, 30, 34, 35, 45, 83, 124, 170, 174
Granerod, G. 81
Grätz, S. 5, 27, 30, 157
Green, S. 193
Greenfield, J. C. 81, 136, 162
Gregory, B. C. 152, 188, 195
Grenet, F. 105
Grol, H. van 71, 72
Guillaume, P. 173
Gunneweg, A. H. J. 24, 33, 50, 113, 149

Hallaschka, M. 186, 187, 189
Hanson, P. D. 191, 194
Harrington, H. K. 59, 60, 75, 133, 142, 203
Harrison, T. 90
Harvey, P. B., Jr. 5
Häusl, M. 145
Hayes, C. E. 59, 60

Heckl, R. 1, 20, 28, 29
Hempel, C. 175
Henkelman, W. F. M. 89, 90, 107, 123, 142–4
Hensel, B. 2
Herrenschmidt, C. 93, 95, 106
Hill, A. E. 177
Himbaza, I. 198
Himmelfarb, M. 175
Höffken, P. 34
Hoglund, K. G. 4, 147, 166
Hogue, T. 117
Humbach, H. 86
Hunt, A. 173
Hyland, J. O. 136

Ivanov, V. V. 87, 108

Jonker, L. C. 176, 186, 220
Jacobs, B. 89, 143
Janzen, D. 5, 28, 38, 55, 60, 61, 67, 75, 78, 115, 137, 176, 177, 199–202, 208
Japhet, S. 8, 13, 45, 50, 59, 77, 123, 124, 147, 202, 209
Jigoulov, V. S. 47
Johnson, W. M. 2, 58, 166
Jones, C. M. 38, 53
Jones, D. C. 204
Jong, A. de 86, 92
Joyce, P. M. 172
Judd, E. P. 2, 58
Jursa, M. 48, 150

Kanetsyan, A. 84
Kaptan, D. 80, 104, 133
Karrer, C. 18, 60, 62, 203
Karrer-Grube, C. 14, 113, 127
Kellens, J. 88, 93
Kelly, B. E. 201
Kent, R. 91, 134, 138, 161
Kessler, J. 4, 43, 52, 77, 123, 142, 147, 148, 153, 166, 183, 184, 186, 188, 198
Khatchadourian, L. 84, 85, 97, 100, 103
Klawans, J. 59
Klein, R. W. 174, 186, 199
Knauf, E. A. 184
Knoppers, G. N. 5, 19, 34, 43, 56, 65, 77, 78, 120, 148, 168, 174, 175, 180, 184, 202, 208, 220
Ko, M. H. 203

Kraemer, D. 14
Kratz, R. G. 5, 8, 26
Kugler, G. 167
Kuhrt, A. 83, 84, 141, 163, 194
Kuntzmann, R. 210

Laato, A. 172
Labahn, A. 177
Labouvie, S. 189
Laird, D. 1, 44, 73, 113
Langgut, D. 82, 102
Lau, P. H. W. 52
Lee, K.-J. 5
Lemaire, A. 35, 37, 190, 191, 199
Leuchter, M. 168
Levin, Y. 183, 220
Liew, T.-s. B. 214
Lincoln, B. 85, 91–4, 99–101, 109, 133, 135, 137, 138
Lipschits, O. 5, 7, 29–31, 65, 82, 102, 190
Llewellyn-Jones, L. 54, 102, 107, 163
Lloyd, A. 111
Lortie, C. R. 51

Maachi, J.-D. 183
MacDonald, N. 175, 205
Machinist, P. 170
Magen, Y. 28
Mallory, J. P. 109
Marbury, H. R. 4
Mein, A. 172
Ménant, J. 111
Meshorer, Y. 33, 81, 170
Metso, S. 175
Meyers, C. L. 186
Meyers, E. M. 186
Middlemas, J. A. 153, 183, 202
Milevski, I. 64
Milgrom, J. 174
Miller, M. C. 80, 83
Min, K.-J. 35, 173, 179
Misgav, H. 28
Mitchell, C. 121, 190
Moffat, D. P. 2, 36
Mowinckel, S. 23

Na'aman, N. 38
Newsom, C. 214

Nichols, A. G. 85, 108
Niehr, H. 199
Nielsen, J. P. 112
Nihan, C. 174, 183, 193, 197, 205
Nimchuk, C. L. 104
Nissinen, M. 144, 211
Nogalski, J. D. 177, 187, 197
Nurmela, R. 172, 173, 178
Nykolaishen, D. J. E. 43
Nzimande, M. K. 165

Oded, B. 77
Oeming, M. 63, 71, 121, 125, 126, 155, 168, 176
Olyan, S. M. 59
Oswald, W. 4, 180

Pakkala, J. 12, 15, 16, 18, 21, 25, 37, 114
Paszkowiak, J. 150
Pearce, L. E. 170
Peltonen, K. 199
Petersen, D. 178
Petit, T. 122
Petterson, A. R. 186, 190, 191, 211
Pirart, É. 109
Pokorny, J. 87, 92, 94, 108, 109, 138
Polak, F. H. 117
Polaski, D. 51
Porten, B. 81, 136, 162
Portier-Young, A. E. 118
Potts, D. T. 90
Poupet, P. 111
Powell, M. A. 47
Pröbstl, V. 72, 168

Quintana, E. 90

Raban, A. 82
Rad, G. von 30, 176
Razmjou, S. 82, 108, 111, 112
Redditt, P. L. 178, 187, 190, 191
Reinmuth, T. 24, 25
Rendtorff, R. 70
Rollinger, R. 81, 107, 114, 159, 160, 162
Rom-Shiloni, D. 54, 152, 183, 184, 187, 221
Römer, T. 173, 185
Rooke, D. 170, 195

Root, M. C. 84, 90, 91, 98, 100, 102–4, 106, 107, 112, 133
Rooy, H. V. 208
Rose, W. H. 188, 190, 191
Rosenthal, F. 149
Rothenbusch, R. 1, 16, 25, 35, 45, 58
Rudolph, W. 33, 149
Ruiz, J.-P. 166
Russell, S. C. 30

Sancisi-Weerdenburg, H. 159, 160
Schaper, J. 173, 178, 203, 204
Schaudig, H. 90
Schmid, K. 174, 184, 185
Schmitt, R. 57, 124
Schniedewind, W. M. 209
Schöttler, G. 189
Schramm, B. 192, 193
Schuele, A. 185
Schulte, L. L. 143, 145
Schunck, K.-D. 33, 65, 73
Schweitzer, S. J. 209, 210
Schwiderski, D. 6, 27
Scolnic, B. 33
Seidl, U. 97, 112
Shahbazi, A. S. 97
Siedlicki, A. 71
Silverman, J. M. 83, 186, 190, 191, 211
Skjævro, P. O. 85, 92, 100, 102, 106, 145
Smelik, K. A. D. 71, 155
Snyman, G. 177, 200, 203
Sommer, B. D. 28
Soudavar, A. 86, 97
Southwood, K. 54, 58, 59, 61, 72, 78, 152
Sparks, J. T. 69
Spek, R. J. van der 139
Stausberg, M. 88, 99
Stead, M. R. 190, 211
Steck, O. H. 207
Steiner, M. 29, 50
Steiner, R. C. 7
Stern, E. 31, 47
Stern, S. 62
Stolper, M. W. 182
Stromberg, J. 188, 193, 194
Stronach, D. 84, 111, 112, 133
Strübind, K. 176
Summerer, L. 134
Sweeney, M. A. 191, 195, 211

Tadmor, H. 196
Tadmor, M. 82
Tal, O. 37, 197
Tammuz, O. 31
Thames, J. T., Jr. 49, 50
Thiessen, M. 53
Tiemeyer, L.-S. 1, 168, 178, 187, 189, 193, 194, 203, 207
Tigay, J. 13
Tiño, J. 177
Trichet, J. 111
Trimm, C. 133
Tsfania, L. 28
Tuell, S. S. 204, 205
Tuplin, C. 48, 98, 101, 135, 136, 151

Uehlinger, C. 81
Ussishkin, D. 29

Vaka'uta, N. 166
Van De Mieroop, M. 169
VanderKam, J. 14, 26, 33, 116, 171
Vermeylen, J. 167, 168
Viberg, Å. 190

Waerzeggers, C. 107, 150, 172, 176, 194
Warhurst, A. K. 210
Washington, H. C. 2
Wasmuth, M. 112
Waters, M. 89, 90
Weinberg, J. 27, 169
Weingart, K. 51
Werline, R. A. 155
Weyde, K. W. 195
Wiesehöfer, J. 91, 98, 107, 142
Willi, T. 5, 176, 177
Willi-Plein, I. 206
Williamson, H. G. M. 2, 7, 13, 18, 24, 25, 27, 28, 30, 31, 34, 35, 45, 56, 61–3, 65, 68–70, 72, 117, 147, 148, 169, 183, 202, 220
Windfuhr, G. 85
Winter, I. 84
Wöhrle, J. 185, 187, 191, 192, 207
Wright, J. L. 12, 22, 62
Wu, X. 134, 163
Wyssman, P. 81

Yoo, P. Y. 15, 25, 147
Yoyotte, J. 111

Zadok, R. 64
Zehnder, M. 203
Zevit, Z. 29
Zlotnick-Sivan, H. 1

www.ingramcontent.com/pod-product-compliance
Lightning Source LLC
Chambersburg PA
CBHW072129290426

44111CB00012B/1830